THE
COMPLETE
COARSE
FISHERMAN

THE
COMPLETE
COARSE
FISHERMAN

John Wilson

BⵑXTREE

Published in the UK in 1996
by Boxtree Limited

First produced in 1992
exclusively for WH Smith

1 3 5 7 9 10 8 6 4 2

© (text and photographs) John Wilson 1992
© (illustrations) Boxtree Ltd 1992

Illustrations by David Batten

Typeset by Cambrian Typesetters, Frimley
Colour origination by Fotographics, Hong Kong
Printed and bound in Italy by New Interlitho Spa
for
Boxtree Limited
Broadwall House
21 Broadwall
London SE1 9PL

A catalogue record for this book is available from
the British Library

ISBN 0 7522 1024 6

CONTENTS

INTRODUCTION

The complexity of our sport is such that no one, even after a full and varied lifetime spent fishing, can ever say they know or have done it all. There will always be new techniques to master, new tackle innovations to enjoy, new horizons to discover, and still bigger fish to catch.

Fishing epitomizes that element of optimism within the human race, and it should always be fun. The art of fishing is also, to a degree, based on luck. However, in my opinion luck plays a very small part – far less than non-anglers, especially, assume. It is possible, for instance, to be 'lucky' (and skilful) in landing a big fish against ridiculous odds on super-light tackle or from among an entanglement of tree roots, or 'unlucky' in losing it, should the hook inexplicably fall out. In either case, however, you must have the skill to hook into that fish in the first place, thereby creating your own 'luck'.

As with other aspects of life, when fishing you only get out of it as much as you are prepared to put in. Anglers who, every outing, simply wait for Lady Luck to shine on them could wait a very long time indeed. Those, however, who really get to know and understand their quarry by making a study of natural history, learning to identify individual habitats that are preferred by particular species, and who practise being stealthy and observant wherever they fish, will always catch more.

For this reason, I have structured this book in the same progressive order in which I think about my own fishing. Chapter One looks at the physical characteristics of each species, how its feeds and reproduces, the places it prefers to live in, and its distribution. After all, if the fish is not there, you cannot catch it. Chapter Two describes many types of habitat, both natural and man-made, in still and running water. The following chapters on tackle and bait then prime the reader for the last hurdle – selecting a suitable technique and rig.

I have tried to be as comprehensive as possible, but there has to be a cut-off point. Fishing for gudgeon, for instance, is not included, the dace being the smallest freshwater species that holds my attention. By the same token, there are certain facts omitted because they play no part in my own fishing. Presenting bloodworms on super-fine match tackle is one such example, and I see no point in trying to advise the reader on a method of which I have only limited experience.

This book is about the tackle, baits and methods that, over the years, I have found to be productive; not only in the British Isles, I might add, but in many other countries too. Most of the bait chapter, therefore, is not crammed with complicated recipes for making yet another different flavoured boilie, but offers a whole galaxy of ideas on bait selection and preparation, both natural and man-made, in the hope that wherever the reader finds himself beside freshwater, even having forgotten the bait, he will still be equipped to catch.

To many fishing is indeed a way of life. Long may it continue to be so. Good fishing and tight lines.

John Wilson
Great Witchingham, 1992

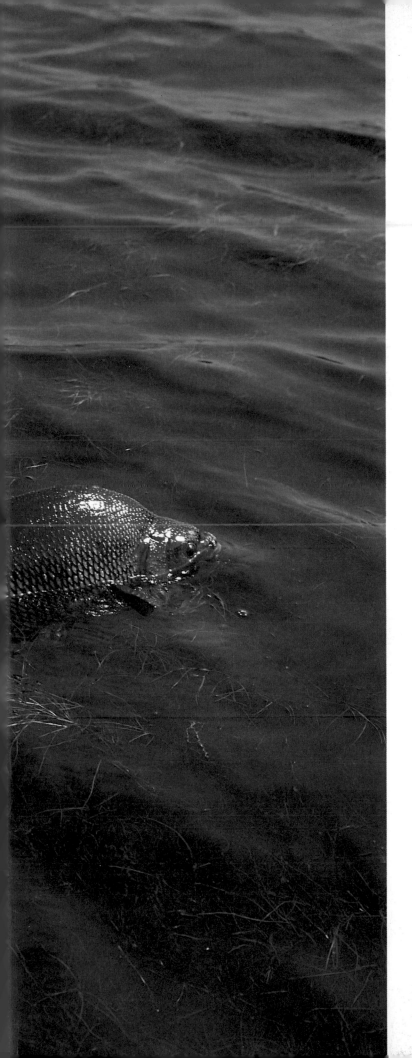

CHAPTER ONE

THE SPECIES

BARBEL
(Barbus barbus)

With its unique physical shape producing exhilarating speed and strength, the barbel is the most exciting adversary in British freshwater fishing in the opinion of many fishermen.

It is a member of the cyprinidae, or carp family of freshwater fish, by far the largest single group in Europe. Indeed, it is no coincidence that its powerful, elongated shape – round in cross-section except for its flat stomach – resembles that of a long drawn-out carp. It also shares many of the carp's physical characteristics and habits. As well as having four sensory barbels or barbules – one pair at the very point of the snout, the other situated way back at the rear of the top lip – and a protrusible, hoover-like mouth, the barbel also possesses a strong serrated spine at the start of its dorsal fin, exactly like the carp. Care must be taken when netting and retaining barbel, for this spine all too easily becomes entangled, and can be broken in all types of netting larger than micromes.

Like the grayling, the barbel is a lover of well-oxygenated river water, and if it has the choice, it prefers to occupy the fastest runs over a gravel or clean sandy bottom. However, it also thrives in slow-moving river systems, and, also like the grayling, it can even exist in clear, pure stillwaters with a high level of dissolved oxygen.

In overall colouration few fish, except perhaps the grayling, blend in against the bottom so efficiently as the barbel. Even when looking through polaroid glasses into crystal-clear fast water where the river-bed consists of clean gravel, it is often possible to see barbel hugging the bottom only by training your eyes to search for the subtle orange hue of their pectoral and pelvic fins.

The barbel's front end when viewed from above is triangular and skate-like, and it has similar powers of adhesion as the skate. Such is the power of even small barbel during the initial stages of a fight, that the line feels as if it is being 'ironed' to the river-bed.

When chub and barbel of more or less similar size are mixed together in runs between beds of streamer weed and their front ends are not immediately visible, the barbel are easily distinguished by their large, forked tails. The top lobe is sharply pointed while the lower is rounded.

Out of the water, the barbel's body seems quite warm in colour. The back can vary from an even olive-brown to brown-grey, which blends into flanks of pale brass and a matt white belly. Its scales are small, firmly embedded, and lie very flat to the body, with only the finest covering of protective mucus. However, even small barbel are difficult to hold, being wiry and extremely powerful. An adult, specimen barbel in the 9–12 lb range measures somewhere between 28 and 36 in, and in terms of its length to weight ratio it is one of the lightest freshwater species after the eel. Only the pike shares a similar weight to length ratio.

In many rivers barbel tend to shoal according to size. Most are in the 3–6 lb class, and anything exceeding 8 lb is a fine specimen. This is not to say, however, that a lone huge barbel will not be seen among a group of 2–3 pounders. They are a very gregarious species, and fight to the last with unbelievable power, whatever their size.

This powerful 12 lb plus barbel with large fins and sleek body is typical of the species, and well equipped for holding station in the strongest currents. Note the four long sensory barbels designed for rooting among gravel for food.

FEEDING

By nature barbel feed with greater confidence from dusk onwards and during the hours of darkness. Barbel fishermen soon become aware of this when fish that have been seen to refuse the hook bait during daylight suddenly produce slamming bites as the sun starts to go down and light values rapidly decrease.

This is not to say that they will not feed avidly even during bright sunshine, because they do, especially when sheltered beneath sanctuary or habitat swims where they can constantly nip in and out – gravel runs beneath overhead canopies of cut weed or flotsam, narrow sandy runs between scattered beds of tall bullrushes, or clear runs beneath low, overhanging willow or alder branches, where the sun's rays cannot directly reach to stimulate weed growth in otherwise heavily weeded parts of the river. Through regular introductions of loose feed such as hempseed, tares, maggots, corn and the like, barbel in these ideal swims can be tempted into feeding all day long during the summer, and especially the autumn.

Once winter frosts start to reduce weed cover, barbel become far less spread out. As they shoal in much tighter groups, pinpoint accuracy in assessing their position, and in your casting, becomes all important and can make the difference between bites and no bites (see Location).

Various conditions can trigger the barbel into feeding aggressively: a rising river, times when clear water starts to colour up; when the flow suddenly starts increasing due to a weir or hatch opening upstream; and during periods of consistently high air temperatures in what is generally considered to be the coldest part of the winter. Any prolonged mild spell brought about by warm winds calls out for barbel fishing.

The last few weeks of the season are invariably the best time for seeking winter barbel and finding them in a feeding mood. Though they will bite even in extremely cold water, once pinpointed, winter barbel fishing can prove to be a slow pastime, especially in rivers where they are not prolific, and at that time are certainly no match for the inexperienced.

This powerful, rather enigmatic fish is exceptionally well equipped for grubbing about along the river-bed, where the majority of its food exists. Although barbel do occasionally take food close to the surface among dense beds of rooted weeds such as the water crowfoot (the distinct carp-like sucking noises they make can sometimes be heard at night), they are in fact bottom-feeders *par excellence*.

Situated immediately above its thick, fleshy lips (so tough that few hooks ever pull out) the barbel's long whiskers, conveniently equipped with super-sensitive taste pads at the tips, probe between the particles of sand and gravel in search of its daily diet, which consists of shrimps, snails, crayfish and aquatic insect larvae. Barbel also eat small fish like minnows, loach, bullheads, gudgeon, lampreys and even their own kind, all of which are snuffed up and quickly minced by the powerful pharyngeal (throat) teeth into pulp for swallowing. A small, freshly killed fish makes a fine offering for barbel (see Baits, page 130), especially during the early season when they have easy access to fry shoals in the warm shallows.

A lone barbel competes with a shoal of chub for the fisherman's loose-fed hempseed and maggots on the well-scoured sandy bottom of a clear-flowing river. Barbel-spotting is easier if you look for its orange pelvic and pectoral fins.

Barbel are renowned for leaving the sanctuary of weed-beds or deep daytime retreats beneath undercuts and tree roots under the cloak of darkness in order to forage along the bottom of ridiculously shallow water for crustaceans and small fish – areas so shallow you would not believe they are frequented by barbel at night.

When barbel are feeding really aggressively, they can be seen with their noses tilted downwards, rooting along the bottom, overturning stones and regularly twisting over, conveniently showing a long brassy flash of their flank – this provides a most heartening visual pointer for those who are searching the fast, deep runs through polaroid glasses.

Born with a long conical nose, the barbel loses sight of its food long before it hoovers it up, and so characteristically moves its head from side to side in an agitated manner in order to centre the food immediately prior to swallowing. This explains why those who hold the line between thumb and forefinger and 'touch ledger' when barbel fishing can feel a sandpapery sensation on the line a moment or two before the rod arches over in that typical slamming bite for which barbel are famous. The barbel's long whiskers hit against the line as the barbel centres the bait before sucking it in.

Barbel tend to fluctuate in weight at various times of the year, and even from one year to the next – facts that have emerged from my studies of the Wensum's stock of double-figure barbel for over 15 years. Several of these large fish, again just like carp from popular fisheries, are caught with surprising regularity. This tends to give the impression that the whole of the upper Wensum is one long barbel river, but this is simply not the case. The same, easily recognizable old barbel are being caught time and time again.

REPRODUCTION

To observe numbers of barbel gathered on the vast, gravelly shallows during the late spring in readiness for the reproduction cycle is one of the most pleasurable highlights of the closed season. Most fish work their way upriver from their respective habitats to the weedy, gravel shallows and bubbly water, where spawning takes place en masse. And in a prolific barbel river, there could be hundreds of fish crammed together into the tiniest area during this time. Not only is this an exciting spectacle; close observation often confirms whether a particular stretch contains any monsters or not.

The shallows immediately downstream of mill and weir-pools are usually prime spawning areas because of the well-oxygenated water running speedily over the gravel beds. And these are the first spots to visit if you wish to

The only two species that a baby barbel might be confused with are gudgeon and stone loach. However, gudgeon sport two barbules and loach six, to the barbel's four.

witness the barbel's spawning ritual. Confluences are well used for spawning, too.

This annual event usually happens during the latter part of April or early May, with the males becoming distinct from the females through the white tubercles that appear over their heads and back. It is in fact the only time of the year when there appears to be any physical difference between the sexes. The female – whose belly is now heavily swollen with eggs, is attended by groups of smaller male fish that quickly gather around when she is ready to spawn, bumping into her flanks with their rough (tubercle-covered) noses and shoulders to stimulate her to release the eggs. Even large females are sometimes heaved with such force by the eager males that the upper part of their bodies can be seen above the surface. Fertilization is almost instant. Milt from the energetic males is distributed in a cloud over the small yellow eggs as they tumble downstream, sticking to the stones and rooted weeds. Incubation takes up to 14 days depending upon the water temperature, following which the young barbel emerge into an extremely hostile world.

During their early life, most fall prey to other fish, chub in particular, while the barbel itself is renowned, like all cypinids, for consuming much of its own spawn and fry. This is a natural and very efficient inbuilt safety mechanism and insurance policy to prevent over-population of a water by the species.

LOCATION

Barbel show an affinity with both chub and carp for choosing homes where they feel safe, with cover over their heads or at least close by. And if there is adjacent quiet water where they can rest away from the full force of the current, so much the better. They invariably prefer a clean bottom of well-scoured silt, sand or gravel, where the flow brings along a regular supply of natural food particles in addition to those found within the bottom strata and among the roots of nearby weeds, reeds and rushes.

Jungle-type swims among dense beds of flowering weeds or beneath lines of trees whose lower limbs are part sunken are especially suited to barbel, and for a reason that is not always immediately apparent to the fish-spotter above the surface. It is the increased current velocity caused by the river being channelled through narrow runs between dense vegetation, through gaps in an uneven bottom contour, between bridge arches and so on, that attracts the barbel.

Fortunately, in all but the deepest and widest rivers, barbel can be located visually in clear water during the summer months. And even if they are not given immediate attention, close studies of the depth and characteristics of each swim should be made, and the features mentally noted for later consideration (fig. 1.1).

There is a catch to all this observation, however, so be warned. Barbel-watching can become a fascinating but contagious disease for which there is no cure. You spend far more time stuck uncomfortably up a tree feeding and studying them than you do fishing for them. However, a useful spin-off is that you also learn to recognize the very definite features of barbel swims and habitats in other rivers where, through either excessive depth or water colour, the fish themselves cannot be seen. Remember, if you cannot find them, you certainly won't catch them.

Working tools of the trade for barbel location, in order of priority, start off with a good pair of scratch-resistant polaroid sunglasses, the importance of which cannot be over-stressed. A large proportion of anglers do not bother to buy the correct glasses for their particular requirements. They will happily pay over the top for designer rods and fancy reels, tackle gimmicks and the very latest in bait additives, but baulk at the suggestion that they purchase two pairs of good-quality polaroids with different coloured lenses. Nevertheless, that is what you should do.

For close observation of the river-bed in low light conditions, at dusk, dawn and during heavily overcast weather, I find the increased brightness provided by yellow lenses a real boon, with standard grey or amber lenses for use during bright, middle-of-the-day sessions.

For general observation of the river's contours and flow patterns, and for distant swims, it goes without saying that a pair of lightweight binoculars are also indispensible.

Lightweight, thigh-length waders are also indispensible for reaching swims that can only be fished effectively by wading, and for climbing in to extract a heavily weeded fish every so often. Those with material-type uppers are preferable as they do not become uncomfortable when walking long distances. I also consider money on a pair of supple, lightweight chest-waders equally well spent. They enable you to reach those inaccessible spots in the middle of the river, and to use float tackle to explore tempting runs between long, flowing weed-beds. In addition, they let you reach impenetrable or snaggy swims on the opposite bank, where thick weedbeds between you and the barbel rule out bank fishing. After all, there is no point in hooking a barbel from a swim where you have no chance of extracting it. And during the summer months, when aquatic vegetation in some rivers is at its most rampant, a good half of the potentially productive barbel swims might instantly be out of bounds.

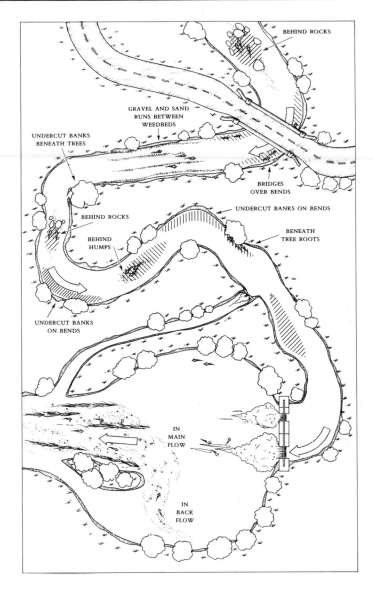

FIGURE 1.1 *Small to medium river, showing barbel swims in autumn*

DISTRIBUTION

During the last 30 years, barbel have been successfully introduced into several English river systems where they were not previously found, and in most cases they now provide exciting action in addition to the indigenous species of that river. They are absent from Ireland and Scotland, Yorkshire being the most northerly county where they are found. The Ouse and its tributaries are well populated. Many of the Irish and Scottish game rivers, being clear, fast and gravelly, would be perfectly suited to the species, which has thrived extremely well since being introduced into Wales and the upper reaches of the River Wye.

Barbel are also common to river systems throughout Europe. One of the most prolific barbel rivers I have ever fished is the River Ebro in Spain, which contains tremendous stocks of both carp and barbel. Ebro barbel look very similar to British barbel and bite with equal boldness, but their snouts appear less conical and their colouration is much drabber. I would hazard a guess that they are a sub-species of the barbel caught in Britain.

BREAM
(Abramis brama)

In coloured stillwaters the bream is a slow-moving, ponderous, bottom-feeding fish – an easy target for all the blood-sucking nasties, such as the transparent, flat-bodied argulus and the double-sucker leeches inhabiting the bottom detritus. Were it not for the protective mucus layer, the bream would live a most uncomfortable life. In clear water, whether running or still, the bream appear to be more adept at out-running or evading potential parasites, and are covered with a noticeably thinner layer of slime.

Bream living in clear waters are also much darker in general coloration, especially in high water-temperature conditions, but they lose this stark contrast during the winter months. Adults are a distinct and beautiful slate grey or dark bronze along the back, blending into shades of burnished bronze along their deep flanks. The large, deeply forked tail and the dorsal fin are dark blue-grey and there is often a warm, mauve hue to the long anal fin. The pelvic and pectoral fins are less coloured, and the belly is a very pale creamy bronze.

The mature bream inhabiting heavily coloured fisheries is far less attractively coloured, having geared its camouflage to the density of the water in which it lives, so shades along the back can vary from pale grey or bronze to pale pewter on the flanks, blending into creamy off-white on the belly. The fins appear noticeably more translucent, tinted with hues of light grey. Whenever prolonged river flooding occurs, turning the water to the colour of milky tea, the bream pales even further to an overall wishy-washy, parchment colour.

Whether living in clear or coloured, still or moving water, the bream is distinctly 'silvery' along the flanks during infancy, and exceptionally thin. Once adult, however, the bream is one of our longest cyprinids, with a potential length of up to 30 in, though most fully grown fish measure somewhere between 15 and 25 in.

As they mature, and depending on the richness and quantity of natural food at their disposal, individual specimens grow to varying 'thicknesses' or 'widths'. This accounts for the enormous weight differential that often occurs between two bream that appear identical in length and depth. Owing to their immense body area, bream always look much heavier than they are and fishermen are caught out in their estimation of a bream's weight more often than with any other species.

With its characteristically deep body and pronounced hump, which rises from immediately behind the head to the leading ray of the dorsal fin, the bream is by far the deepest of our freshwater fish. The species has been so designed to enable large shoals to pack tightly together while feeding in close proximity, with just an inch or two between each fish and its neighbour.

The top weight in Europe, where it is a commercially produced food fish, is close on 20 lb, and while the bream record in British waters remained for many years at 13½ lb, this past decade has seen an unusual advance in the species' weight potential to a current record of 16 lb 6 oz.

Many fisheries contain a larger head of adult bream than they do of any other year-class except fry and fingerlings. The reason for this phenomenon is certainly *not* all down to match fishing. In the richest, most mature lakeland and gravel-pit environments, which are rarely fished, entire populations of all year-classes between fry and adult bream are conspicuous by their absence. Farming chemicals, sewage effluent, winter run off (rivers), acid rain, habitat destruction by drainage departments, consecutive summers of poor fry recruitment due to unstable weather, and so on, all take their toll on young bream, which are extremely delicate fish.

All these factors added together probably explain why adult bream in so many fisheries now seem to attain far heavier weights than they once did. With far less competition for food from younger bream, or, in some cases (these waters produce the largest bream) a complete lack of intermediate-year classes, the adult bream enjoy a super-rich diet and consequently grow particularly thick in cross-section, increasing their expected weight potential by as much as one-third.

FEEDING

Like all cyprinids, the bream is equipped in the back of its throat with a pair of strong pharyngeal teeth, which it uses to chew its food into a pulp for swallowing. These teeth are responsible for the fisherman's maggots being returned as mere 'skins' on the hook, and for casters being crushed, because these teeth squeeze out the juices very efficiently.

While the bream is most adept at sucking in baits suspended well above bottom, and even on the drop, it obtains most of its natural food through the protrusible mouth, which extends like a giant vacuum-hose to siphon up goodies, such as bloodworms and other insect larvae, annelid worms, molluscs and shrimps, from the bottom.

Wherever the bottom sediment is soft and easily disturbed, the change in water colour caused by shoals, especially large ones, feeding in earnest is very noticeable, and provides a wonderful visual pointer for their location. Bubbles, emitted through the bream's gills as a direct result of chewing, will rise to the surface, and be seen in the clouded water. Not the long fizzes of carp, nor in the quantity emitted by tench; just small groups containing several quite small bubbles. If you view them through binoculars, you can even track the exceedingly slow route of an individual bream as it moves through the detritus, its body angled at half-tilt while it browses on the bottom.

Whether the bream feels safer from predators at night, or whether its food is easier to gather in low light values, I am not entirely sure, but bream start to feed heavily during darkness, and with considerably more confidence than they show during the hours of daylight. Strangely, this is true of coloured and clear-water fisheries alike.

During the daylight hours of summer, stillwater bream love to browse the warm, weedy shallows and follow available food sources that drift with the wind, such as Daphnia, the largest of the freshwater zooplanktons. They porpoise on the surface when feeding at dawn and dusk, particularly during humid conditions – another useful aid to location that the angler should be well aware of (see p. 16).

Terry Smith from Sheffield carefully unhooks a Danish Lakeland bream. Shoals of fish in the 2–3 lb bracket are so enormous that as long as the feed keeps going in, they continue to bite, even in bright sunshine.

REPRODUCTION

Bream propagate their species sometime between the end of May and early July. The shoals of adult fish gather in the warm, weedy shallows, the males being quite distinct from the females by the white, knobbly spawning tubercles that are clearly visible on their heads, shoulders and pectoral fins. Old males feel rather rough over their entire body, and their tubercles never entirely fade away after spawning. Though far less pronounced than in summer, the white dots can still be seen on the fish's nose and head even during the winter months.

Spawning usually takes place throughout the night and ceases when the sun rises, although beneath dense patches of surface weeds where the light is diffused, odd groups could continue in fits and starts throughout much of the day. The males usually far outnumber the females, and as they mingle among the soft weedbeds, the males continually bump into the soft flanks of the females in order to stimulate the females to release the eggs. The small, pale yellow, sticky eggs adhere to the soft weeds and are fertilized by sprays of milky white milt from the males.

It is easy to distinguish between male and female bream during the spawning season. Adult males grow knobbly white tubercles over their heads, shoulders and gill plates that stimulate the females into releasing the eggs when the males bump into them.

Depending on the water temperature, the eggs hatch within 6 to 10 days. The fry stay in their protective habitat, feeding on minute plankton in the warm shallows, until they are large enough to commence a diet of aquatic insect larvae and other bottom foods.

Silver bream

Once said to be common all over East Anglia, this species, also said to reach little more than 1½ lb in weight, is so elusive that for quite some time now I have wondered whether it ever existed, or was it not all along a roach/bream hybrid (see p. 52). After all, it is possible to catch a whole netful of hybrids from the same spawning that, although similar to each other, look as if they could be a different species of bream. As it stands, after close on 40 years of serious freshwater fishing, I cannot ever recall seeing a worthwhile colour photograph of what purported to be a silver bream in any reference book or magazine.

LOCATION

Stillwaters

It has long been believed that bream always prefer the slowest, deepest water – during the summer at least – but nothing could be further from the truth. Even stillwater bream with a varied choice of shallow and deep areas sometimes select the warm, weedy shallows in which to spend their days. There are at least two good reasons for this. Shallow water warms up quickly and provides the bream with a protective habitat of aquatic vegetation, lilies, ribbon-weed and the like. Secondly, the amount of natural food per square foot of water is far greater in warm, shallow areas than in deeper, colder areas, and the food multiplies more rapidly.

In most really deep parts of reservoirs and gravel pits – in depths of 20 ft or more – the amount of natural food on the bottom is minimal by comparison with shallow water. Unless the water is crystal clear below depths of 15 ft, insufficient sunlight penetrates to stimulate bottom-rooted plant growth. The only readily available food source in excessive depths is the bloodworm (the larvae of the midge) which 'layer' in the thick deposits of accumulated silts, even where the level of dissolved oxygen is at its very lowest. This lack of oxygen becomes more pronounced during the summer months, once the water temperature starts to increase. In fact, baits presented for any length of time on the bottom in deep water often come back smelling putrid, proving the lack of dissolved oxygen in that bottom band of water. This is the reason why large shoals of bream can sometimes be seen 'layering' above the very deep water during the daylight hours, anywhere from a few feet off bottom to within inches of the surface.

However, as the bottom starts to shelve upwards from 12 to 10 to 8 ft, and then to 6 ft of water, the character of the water changes dramatically from that at the bottom. It is within this depth band – at about 6 to 12 feet – that I would expect to find most bream shoals throughout most of the season. Fig. 1.2 illustrates a typical gravel-pit bream habitat, and shows where the shoals are most likely to be – in areas with beds of soft weeds and lilies full of food items, colonies of freshwater mussels, a veritable mountain of aquatic insects at various stages of their life cycles, plus shrimps, asellus, snails, leeches, water-boatmen, annelid worms and many more. They are all eeking a living from the bottom detritus – that rich layer of broken-down plant cells and leaves derived from both aquatic vegetation and overhanging grasses and trees. It is small wonder that fish prefer water shallower than 15 ft whenever they have the option.

Although in the majority of stillwaters bream will keep off the bottom in very deep areas (there are, of course, always exceptions), the one generalization I would make is that, taken on a calendar basis, the deeper areas are more likely to attract bream – because it is a large-bodied shoal fish – than the extreme shallows. However, depth by itself does not guarantee a good bream swim.

Bream in even-depthed stillwaters, such as meres, estate lakes, and to a large extent the Norfolk Broads (which are rather short of obvious holding-areas), can usually be located by visual signs during the months of summer and autumn. Again, dusk and dawn are the prime times to be present with binoculars at the ready, looking for patches of bubbles or the backs of bream as they porpoise. Sometimes the shoals frequent lily-beds, sometimes they are alongside dense reed-beds, so keep the binoculars handy at all times for spotting those tell-tale signs.

When the wind and sub-surface tow push vast clouds of natural food like daphnia and other zooplanktons into a particular bay, or up against a certain shoreline, the bream will feed in that area until the wind changes. At night they can be attracted to almost any spot by regular pre-baiting (see 'Pre-baiting', p. 125), with the most consistent results coming from areas on the shoal's natural feeding route. Pre-baiting holds the fish, and usually keeps a proportion feeding earnestly until the dawn chorus. However, bream bites cease instantly as the first cruiser of the day chugs

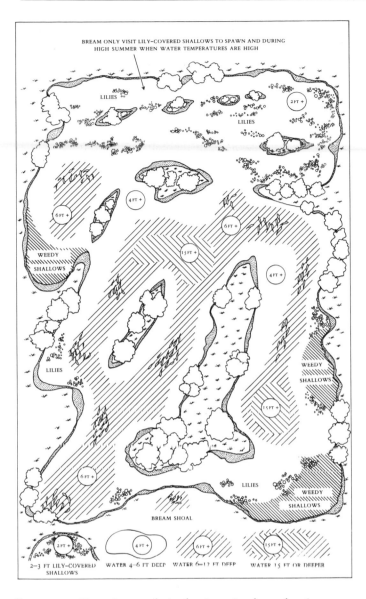

FIGURE 1.2 *Extensive gravel pit, showing prime bream locations*

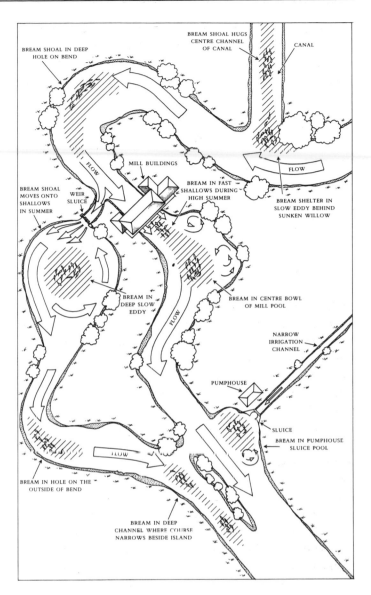

FIGURE 1.3 *River bream locations*

through. Many an unsuspecting holiday fisherman can be seen fishing on well into the day, completely mystified by the lack of action, and completely oblivious to the fact that the shoal his bait lay among only an hour earlier is now more than half a mile away.

Rivers

In rivers, where the water is continually on the move, thus oxygenating the bottom strata, bream can be expected in the deepest areas, where they will be feeding on shrimps, snails and aquatic insect larvae, at all times of the year except the spring, when they vacate the deeps for shallow spawning areas (fig. 1.3). There are always a few that pop up to the surface at dusk and dawn (and throughout the night), rolling tantalizingly and giving away the shoal's

exact position. These rolling bream are either responding to the joy of life or sucking in aquatic flies as they are about to hatch. They can even be seen lunging into concentrations of young fry massed in the warmer, upper water layers.

When bream appear at the surface on a deep river, it could be that the shoal is layered throughout 20 ft of water, with the occasional fish at the top of the shoal sticking its head out and porpoising; or it could be that the shoal is hugging the bottom, with the occasional fish suddenly deciding to swim upwards 20 ft to break surface. I would suggest that in most cases it is the former rather than the latter, having witnessed this layering and porpoising on numerous occasions when bream fishing the gin-clear waters of my local Norfolk rivers, the Wensum and the Upper Waveney, during the summer months. In such

Bream are often a two-tone colour. This superb specimen of over 10 lb was caught by Charlie Clay from the clear, rich environment of a Norfolk gravel pit on ledgered bread flake.

them to get their heads down, those occupying the upper layers quickly follow suit. This results in instant bites, sometimes within only a few seconds of the bait settling on the bottom.

This seemingly wonderful state of affairs, however, with every member of the shoal feeding with gay abandon, is not necessarily desirable, because false bites can result. Being exceptionally deep-bodied with large fins, and feeding in close proximity to each other, feeding fish cannot always avoid your line; and although the indicator registers a genuine bite, the line has simply caught around the bream's fins.

Weir-pools

As mentioned earlier, bream are attracted to the fast, swirling waters of weir-pools, both deep and shallow. During the hottest part of the year, when the water table is low and levels of dissolved oxygen throughout the entire river are correspondingly low, bream congregate in weir-pools, and even occupy the fastest runs. Being of slim profile when viewed head-on, they can in fact happily hold station against considerably faster currents than you would expect. Once winter sets in, they will be down on the bottom in a deep area where the flow is slowest.

Canals and the Fens

In narrow, slow-moving rivers that are similar throughout their length bream will predictably choose to occupy the area down the middle. During the summer months, the shoals are nomadic and browse like cattle. They often travel great distances in the course of a day, feeding from the thick, rich layer of organic silt that accumulates on the bottom of the central bowl.

waters, the antics of the entire shoal can be observed. Initially the shoal has been layered, with those on top most likely to break surface and roll. Once loose feed or groundbait are located by the lower fish, encouraging

DISTRIBUTION

Bream are found in every type of water throughout the British Isles, except in the north of Scotland. They are also found throughout the whole of Europe and much of Asia. Several species similar to the bream, including the Zope and the Danubian bream, also occur in European waters.

Although past angling literature suggested that the bream is more suited to slow-running rivers and stillwaters, it has been my experience that bream fare very well indeed

in fast-flowing rivers and even in quite shallow streams. They certainly exist in far greater numbers in stillwaters, lakes, pits, meres, broads, reservoirs and in slow-moving rivers, probably due to a higher fry survival-rate, but bream nevertheless grow to a good average size in fast water. Indeed, to catch them from deep, swirling waters provides the most thrilling of scraps, particularly when they turn their deep flanks side-on to the flow.

WILD CARP
(Cyprinus carpio)

Pound for pound there are few fish living in stillwaters to match the speed and the power of the true wild carp. They originated from Eastern Europe and Asia, where the Chinese were the first to cultivate them for food several hundred years before Christ. It was the European monks, however, who brought the species to Britain to rear them in stew ponds for their table. And it is that same race of carp which we today lovingly call 'wildies' or wild carp.

Although there are slight genetic differences between 'wild' and common, scaled 'king' carp there are no apparent visual differences other than shape. A particularly thin king common, for instance, might just be mistaken for a true wildie (in waters where both exist) while an over-fed wildie can look remarkably like an under-nourished king common. If you are confused you have every right to be, because unless a particular fishery is known to contain only an ancient stock of wild carp to which no other strains have been added, the exact definition of the inhabitants becomes arguable.

Generally the sleek, barbel-shaped wild carp averages between 2 and 5 lb as an adult in prolific waters, though fisheries with a lower stock density will produce fish of a higher average size if the food source is sufficient.

The very reason why wild carp were chosen as an important food source in the first place was that even in overcrowded shallow waters they made the very best of the available food supply and produced per acre far more pounds of edible flesh than any other species.

THE KING CARPS
(Cyprinus carpio)

From the original wild carp, different strains of carp have been produced by selective breeding throughout Europe during the past three centuries. This durable carp, due to its fast-growing qualities, massive ultimate weight and attractive scale patterns, forms the basis of British carp fishing. For this we owe Germany, Poland, Yugoslavia and Hungary much gratitude. In recent years the Belgians, Israelies, Italians and French have added still more variants within the king carp range.

Ultimate weight for a king carp is still uncertain. Monsters of 80 lb plus have been recorded so there is every reason to expect that in the right growing conditions a king carp in excess of 100 lb will one day be taken on rod and line from European waters. In Britain our summers do not get hot enough and are too short for such monsters to be produced, and it is doubtful whether the present ceiling weight of 50 lb will ever be substantially increased. But then with global warming imminent, who really knows for sure.

One of the nicest by-products to come from the selective breeding of king carp strains is the amount of varying scale patterns that occur between the fully-scaled king common carp and the completely scaleless leather carp.

THE KING COMMON CARP is the fully-scaled modern equivalent of the original wild carp, selectively bred to be thicker across the body, deeper and much faster growing with a far greater weight potential.

THE FULLY-SCALED MIRROR, being completely covered in scales of different sizes, is by far the prettiest and possibly the most desirable to catch of all the variants.

THE SCATTER-SCALE MIRROR generally has a continuous line of scales on both sides of the dorsal fin from head to tail, with single or odd groups appearing almost anywhere, particularly close to the tail root or head, or both. By far the most common form of mirror carp.

THE LINEAR MIRROR is known for its straight row of uniform scales along the lateral line, plus odd groups near the tail and on both sides of the dorsal fin.

THE STARBURST MIRROR is really a scatter-scale mirror with a preponderance of tiny, bright scales shot all over the lower half of its body. Italian goldfish and shubunkins have very similar scaleage, reminiscent of a burst of stars – hence this particular carp's nickname.

THE PLATED MIRROR again is really a scatter-scale fish with anything from one to several enormous plate-like scales set in an irregular-shaped group on one or both sides of its body. Not a fish that wears well in a busy fishery, because during the fight the line can catch behind these big scales and force them out.

THE LEATHER CARP is completely free of scales over the body with perhaps the odd line of small scales either side of the dorsal fin.

King carp provide the specialist fisherman with a galaxy of weights, shapes and scale patterns. This monster leather of over 30 lb has barely a scale on its entire body.

The true wild carp has slowly been losing its identity as fisheries are stocked with deep-bodied, fast-growing strains of king carp. This long, lean, fully-scaled carp, however, epitomizes the barbel-like shape of the true 'wildie'.

In addition to scaleage the king carp varies considerably in body shape, but usually has a distinct and characteristic hump between its head and dorsal fin. Those without a hump probably have some wild carp in their ancestry. Certain strains may be long and incredibly thick across the body without having much of an obvious belly, while others come short and deep with enormous pot bellies. In truth, there is so much cross-breeding now taking place in the wild as carp propagate all over the country that it would take an experienced carp culturist to be dogmatic about which is which. The fun of carp fishing lies in fishing waters where you never know what will come along next.

Colour

Genetic differences apart, colour variation is to some extent governed by the colour of water in which carp live. In sandy or green-pea coloured fisheries, for instance, body coloration often fades to an overall pale, pasty cast in either beige, grey or dull brass with a distinct warm tinge to the tail, pelvic and anal fins. This applies to both wild and king carp, whereas carp inhabiting lush, weedy, clear-watered fisheries can vary along the back from bronze to slate blue, with scales of burnished pewter, gold or silver. The fins will still contain a certain warmth together with hues of grey, purple and beige.

Coloured variants
(Metallic carp)

To catch a valuable, highly-coloured koi carp on hook and line would have been unthinkable prior to the mid-1980s. But now, stillwater horizons have broadened due to the general deterioration of river systems caused by abstraction, farming chemicals and increased amounts of sewage effluent. Anglers are ready to accept that king carp/ koi crosses or even true koi carp (koi simply means coloured) can provide exciting sport with beautiful, hard-fighting fish in selected waters. After all, the coloured carps are genetically no different from the wild carp.

This stunning breed of 'metallic' carp, so called because most colours suitable for stocking fisheries come in muted shades of metallic pewter, silver, pale gold and burnished beige, are indeed an exciting and extremely durable addition to specialist carp waters.

GRASS CARP
(Ctenopharyngoden idella)

This Asian import, which originates from China, adds another exciting chapter to modern stillwater carp fishing, though in appearance the grass carp resembles the chub very closely indeed. Unless its eyes and mouth can be clearly seen, only the fact that it loves to hover just beneath the surface with its head tilted upwards visually distinguishes this sleek battler from chub. Beneath the surface, its tail may also appear to be both darker and slightly larger than that of the chub, but in scaleage they look exactly the same.

The big give-away occurs when it turns head on and opens its noticeably smaller mouth. The eyes look distinctly odd too. They are in fact set much lower down the head, on a line only just above the jaw hinge.

In Germany, where the grass carp was introduced years ahead of the UK, 40 lb grass carp are not uncommon. As they tend to scrap very well indeed, making long runs close to the surface, who would not fancy the chances of contacting one. Grass carp are the perfect controllable carp for stocking the fisheries of today, because they cannot reproduce in our climate and over-populate a water. As yet, they have not been stocked on a widespread basis, but once fishery owners learn to appreciate their real worth anglers will enjoy them.

CRUCIAN CARP
(Carassius carassius)

The crucian carp has established itself, particularly among young anglers, as a popular summer pond fish. It is by far the smallest member of the 'angling carps', rarely exceeding 5 lb. Even this, however, is exceptional. Crucian carp of over 2 lb are considered large specimens because, due to over-breeding, the species becomes stunted and in many waters rarely grows above 12 oz and 10 in in length. This cheeky little carp is noticeably short and deep with distinctly 'rounded' fins. The dorsal is also rounded and convex, in complete contrast to the dorsal fin of other carps, which is concave.

The crucian has a small, neat mouth and barbules are absent – one sure way of differentiating between it and either wild or king carp. Coloration tends to vary from one water to another, just like other carp. But they are coloured very evenly in an overall hue of bronze, dull gold or buttery bronze. The fins are also very evenly coloured.

The curious thing about crucians is that they like to shoal in definite age or year groups. So if you catch one weighing, say, 1¼ lb followed by a dozen more, there is an excellent chance that they will all be a similar size.

Rounded, golden, gentle and friendly, crucian carp provide superb float fishing close in among lily-pads and other surface plants. John took this net of dogged fighters from a Swedish lake during the filming of his Go Fishing *television programmes.*

FEEDING

Carp are by far the most aggressive feeders in freshwater. During a five-month period throughout the winter I reared on in a large, heated aquarium 11 wels catfish and one mirror carp. I was concerned that the cats would dominate the food introduced, which initially consisted of high protein salmon-fry crumbs, followed by a completely live-fish diet, small gudgeon in fact, netted from the lake into which the cats and carp eventually went. Invariably it was the lone carp and not the cats which got to the food first – both granulated and live. In the wild, wherever both carp and catfish exist together, it is always carp which dominate the available food source and reach your bait first. The balance swings slightly more towards catfish only during darkness, when they naturally become more active, and during high water temperatures – say 70°F and above.

Having said all this, the non-angler may well ask the question, 'Why at times do they become so difficult to catch?' The answer is, that they learn. While carp are not the most intelligent of fish, as has been suggested by many specialist fishermen, they quickly learn through association (as all fish do) exactly what to be suspicious about. Baits they have recently been caught on and thus fooled by, over-thick line, insensitive terminal rigs, shadows on the water, unnatural sounds picked up through bank vibrations

The smile on Steve Williams' face says it all. Not only is this gravel-pit carp over the magical 20 lb mark, it is a fully-scaled mirror carp – to many carp fanatics the most desirable of all the variants.

and so on; these and many other factors, once the carp learns to associate each with danger, are enough to deter it from feeding naturally in its piggy, aggressive way.

While the carp is capable of obtaining nourishment from almost any food form we offer it, even large baits, its natural diet mostly consists of minute life forms. With its two pairs of barbules – one long pair at the corner of the mouth, which is protusible, and the other, short ones on the upper lip – the carp is a past master at seeking out midge larvae (blood worms) and annelid worms from the deepest silt concentrations. Deep craters 3 to 6 ft across can sometimes be observed through the clear water of shallow, silty lakes, where concentrations of midge larvae are richest. The carp have simply excavated them while feeding, their head and shoulders almost buried while the barbules, which have sensitive taste pads at the tips, 'feel' for the worms. Occasionally a carp may come up to the surface to take floaters, covered in fine mud all over its head; proof that shortly before, it was merrily rooting about in the silt with its head buried, feeding on midge larvae and sending those tell-tale feeding bubbles up to the surface.

These bubbles are caused by two things: gases which escape from the detritus (the rotting layer of vegetation on the bottom); and those created by the carp itself as it crushes up its food with its pharyngeal teeth (throat teeth), emitting the bubbles through its gills. Observing the bubbles of feeding carp is one of the most accurate ways of locating them and arranging subsequent bait presentation (see p. 24).

The carp also uses its flat, immensely powerful pharyngeal teeth for crushing the shells of molluscs upon which it feeds – the tiny pea mussel, snails and even the considerably larger swan mussel. Shells of 2 to 3 in long are light work for the carp's throat teeth, releasing the succulent meat inside. Small dead and live fish up to 6 in long are also easily minced, as anglers offering them after dark with the intention of luring catfish or eels have discovered.

In prolifically stocked waters, especially where competition for the natural aquatic food is high, carp consume far more fish than most anglers could imagine. During the spawning season it is natural for them to munch away on both the spawn and newly-hatched fry. And this does not stop them from enjoying larger 'small fish' either dead or alive at any time of the year.

Other favourite natural foods are all aquatic insects and beetles, shrimps, assellus and a certain amount of algae from silt and mud on the bottom. They will also gorge on the largest of the zooplanktons, the daphnia, when they are present in thick clouds. As a food converter the carp surpasses even the gluttony of the trout.

Crucians

By comparison with both wild and king carp, the crucian is very timid and deliberate in its feeding. Its diet is not dissimilar to the larger carp at the smaller end of the food chain, and it manages to eke out a living and even to compete with them in densely populated fisheries. I know of many so called 'fast' carp waters which are densely populated with either wildies, king carp or both, but where only crucian carp appear to maintain their existence in quite baggable numbers, whereas either tench or bream as a second species would simply be eaten out of house and home by the larger carp. Perhaps the crucians are simply better at exploiting the smaller food chains than all the other species.

Owing to the crucian carp's slightly upturned mouth structure, they need to stand on their heads (just like the tench) when sucking up food from the bottom. And on chewing it with their pharyngeal teeth they emit distinctive 'crucian bubbles', which rise to the surface in small groups. Ardent crucian fishermen could not mistake these bubbles for any other fish. The bubbles probably fall halfway between those of tench and the larger carps in size.

REPRODUCTION

In the British Isles carp have the capacity to spawn at any time between early May and the end of July, depending on water temperature. In sheltered, shallow lakes not affected by cold winds, for instance, where the water warms quickly, carp are most likely to spawn early. Whereas in large, open and very deep-watered gravel pits which take a long time to warm up, spawning may not occur until even the end of July.

When spawning occurs, the spectator can have little doubt it is happening. It is a very noisy event, particularly when every fish in the lake seems bent on propagation at the same time. Propagation usually starts in the early hours and continues until the sun gets high; it may resume again during the evening. The activity continues every morning for several days, unless the weather changes drastically with a sharp fall in temperature. Then spawning ceases, sometimes for many weeks, until carp feel the urge again, stimulated by a steady rise in water temperature.

During poor summers and continually long cold spells some females never get to shed their eggs, resulting in hideous pot-bellied fish which can eventually die from their spawn-bound condition unless they manage to re-absorb the eggs into their system. Each ripe female is usually accompanied by anywhere from two to several males, all eager to spray milt over the eggs as she sheds them among the fibrous sub-surface roots of marginal trees, through rushes, sedges, reeds, lilies, soft weeds and so on. This is accompanied by much audible shuddering and splashing as the entwining carp crash their way through marginal vegetation where the water is warmest. Such is the force of the males' attention that the female is often lifted bodily out of the water, while the odd over-zealous male can even find itself high and dry on the bank.

The sticky eggs are each about the size of a No. 8 split shot, and are a translucent pale colour unless they failed to receive milt from the male, in which case they remain unfertilized and quickly turn white. Eggs that are not quickly consumed by shoals of small roach, perch or rudd, which follow the spawning carp in anticipation, or by the carp themselves, hatch some six to ten days later. Again this depends on the amount of sunlight and subsequent water

Regardless of colour and scale pattern, there is no genetic difference between this orange hi-goi and all other carp. They share the same Latin name, Cyprinus carpio, *and interbreed freely, throwing up all sorts of exciting variations.*

temperature. The newly-hatched fry have yolk sacks to feed on for two to four days before coming to the surface and filling their swim bladders with air. They then become free swimming and commence feeding on microscopic life.

If a lake contains a varied stock of mixed carp, interbreeding occurs when they all get together at spawning time. Wildies spawn with kings, crucians with wildies, wildies with metallic king mirrors or leather or commons.

The wildie/crucian carp cross matures into an interesting fish which appears slightly too deep to be the true wildie everyone assumes it is, the give-away being its noticeably smaller barbules and an overall paler coloration.

The most attractive crosses of all come from the metallic carps with koi ancestry locked up in their genes. Most of the brightest ones never get beyond the fry stage. Being far more visible than the rest, they soon fall prey to the stealthy heron and predatory fish. But those that are only slightly tinted over the body and on the underside of the pectoral and pelvic fins in shades of muted silver and beige turn into breathtaking carp.

LOCATION

Tools of the trade, as important as the rod and reel, are polaroid glasses, binoculars, drab clothing and lightweight boots, whether waterproof or not, so that from the very start your approach is not at fault. The importance of being

quiet, stealthy and unseen against the skyline cannot be stressed enough if you wish to find and subsequently study your quarry before offering it a bait. When you can creep up (crawl if necessary) to within a few feet of carp, or

Chub-like in appearance, the enigmatic grass carp freely accept both bottom and surface baits. This 11-pounder was caught from a Norfolk lake by Adrian Morley on a small dog-biscuit floater presented on a weighted controller float and greased line.

watch them swim close by without their having the slightest inkling of your presence, you should then be qualified to catch them from any type of water.

Small stillwaters

Where carp cannot be bodily observed because the water is too coloured or temperatures too cold for them to be basking on the surface, there are many pointers to look for. Fortunately carp love features, gravel bars, sunken trees, lily pads, reedlines, etc., and are never far away. In diminutive waters, ponds, pits, meres, lakes – those for argument's sake of less than 3 acres (a football pitch is about 1 acre) – carp are not difficult to locate, and are fun to study. Nearly always they can be visually tracked down during the summer months. The most obvious indication

of fish is the characteristic way in which carp 'bubble' (see 'Feeding'). Their 'feeding bubbles', which could occur at any time of the day (especially during overcast, humid, thundery oppressive summer weather), are most likely to appear coinciding with dawn. They could well then continue until the sun's rays fall directly on the water. This post-dawn feeding period is by far the heaviest. More importantly, it pin-points areas which carp visit often, usually on a day-to-day basis, and most important of all where they feed 'naturally'.

Simply taking time for a stealthy stroll with a pair of binoculars at dawn can provide so much information, far more in fact than an entire week of midday sessions. What stands out when observing 'bubbles' is that many natural feeding areas are situated ridiculously close in. That's because shallow water warms up quickly and invariably contains per square foot a much richer larder of natural food, a fact of which carp quickly become aware. This is the reason margin fishing under quiet conditions can prove so effective.

Large stillwaters

Though seemingly more daunting because the action of strong winds rippling the surface destroys many of the easily recognizable points which aid location in small fisheries, there is in fact a similarity of approach to tackling the carp of large lakes and gravel pits. And the first step is to think of a large pit as nothing more than a collection of features, just like several small pits joined together (fig. 1.4). You isolate in your mind (with the help of a drawing if you prefer) all those previously mentioned features to which carp are attracted; the bars, routes between groups of islands, shorelines with dense reed beds, bays harbouring surface plants, overhanging and sunken trees, deep gullies with shallow water on either side and so on. Then spend

For the novice – young or old – and even for those who think they know it all, the spread of king carp fishing throughout the British Isles, in waters both huge and small, has created a wealth of fishing potential.

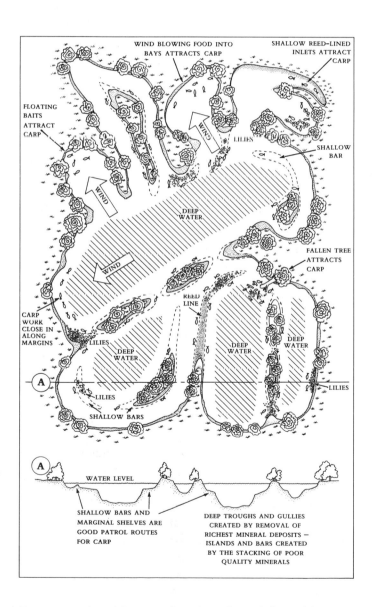

FIGURE 1.4 *A gravel pit seen from the surface and (bottom) in cross-section, showing the gullies and patrol routes of the carp*

time with the binoculars during reasonable weather conditions when there is a chance of locating fish visually, not during a raging gale.

A great way of locating carp at any time throughout the summer, especially when it is very warm and they are more liable to be close to the surface of generally deep waters, is to attract them up with floaters. From the furthest up-wind position on the bank catapult the surface with small floaters, chum mixers or cat biscuits, and allow the wind to drift this new food source down to the other end of the fishery. Don't be mean during these initial location sessions because they can provide great fun towards the end of the close season when you are itching to see carp. Carp may locate and start to feed on the floaters at any time during the drift, especially those which catch up among soft weedbeds touching the surface, lilies, or against marginal vegetation. On the other hand, they may not show the slightest interest until the floaters have completed the full length of the fishery and finally come to rest in a scum line hugging the windward shoreline – one very good reason why that old adage of 'fishing into the wind' can prove a winner.

Winter location

Many prime summer haunts will still hold carp through-out the winter months, particularly dense habitat areas where partly submerged trees and bushes overhang the margins into deepish water. Deep gullies or troughs in what are generally shallow lakes or pits are also certain to be holding fish.

The much deeper, 'dam' end of man-made estate-type lakes is the obvious choice in continually cold conditions. Even lily-beds (or what's left of them) maintain their attraction for carp despite the rotting stalks, and pads not being visible. Always keep a mental note (by lining up a particular tree or gate post on the opposite bank during the summer when the pads are up) as to exactly where the main structure of the plants are situated for winter attention. Carp will always be found among it.

River carp

These are really a law unto themselves. Although they are naturally attracted to all features associated with flowing water, like weir-pools, lock cuttings, junctions where side streams join the main flow, mill streams, deep holes on acute bends, beneath overhanging trees and so on, they are completely nomadic, travelling long distances in the course of just a few hours.

River carp respond wonderfully to regular pre-baiting and this is the most successful way of locating them. The ruse is to pick a few likely habitat-type swims where carp are occasionally seen, and then every other day introduce some loose feed. Stewed wheat, peanuts, maize (don't forget to pressure cook it), black-eyed beans and so on (see 'Baits') are all cheap enough to purchase in bulk for heavy and regular baitings. Taking into account the fact that water birds and unwanted species like chub will quickly try and mop up much of the bait, it is pointless putting in just the odd handful. We are talking about something like 3

to 6 pt a go, otherwise you are simply wasting your time and money, as you would be if you used baits such as maggots which every other fish gobbles up long before the carp arrive on the scene.

Locating crucians

This is a most pleasant exercise in the confines of small fisheries (and most crucian waters are small), due to the fact that they conveniently bubble away (see 'Feeding') from dawn onwards between June and September. They feed well into sunlight, even all day through on occasions, so long as the loose feed keeps going in.

They are so obliging and love to porpoise on the surface when in a feeding mood, particularly at dawn and dusk. They are also known for those spectacular jumps com-pletely clear of the surface.

Look for their distinctive bubbles in warm, shallow to medium-depth swims between beds of any floating-leaved plant, lilies especially (though broad-leaved pond weed, amphibious bistort and dwarf pond lily are also much loved by them) and you will have located the choicest of crucian habitats.

Where there are no lilies, explore just a few feet out from the reedline or close alongside partly submerged bushes (blackthorn, hawthorn, brambles, etc.) which grow out over the water and actually hang their foliage beneath the surface. Look for definite habitats, but above all from that 'pregnant dawn period' look for those groups of feeding bubbles.

Because crucians, unlike the larger carps, rarely roam to follow food lines, most fisheries have 'known' crucian carp swims or hot-spots where these obliging fish reside day in, day out regardless of angling pressure. Mind you, such fish learn to be incredibly crafty, and become the most delicately biting fish in freshwater. So the location of new and not so popular areas in which to fish for them is a worthwhile exercise.

DISTRIBUTION

Although there are still 'wildie only' waters in Wales, southern England and the Midlands, few exist in Scotland and Ireland. On the other hand, king carp and their variants are now being stocked into just about every new lake or gravel pit fishery through the North, the Midlands and southern England. Not that carp really need any help at this stage. They have steadily spread (and not always by

the design of water authorities) into numerous river systems all over the country.

The crucian does not spread so readily, and fares poorly in running water. It is, however, becoming increasingly popular among match and club fishermen because it is extremely durable, and it exists in prolific numbers even in diminutive stillwater fisheries.

CATFISH
(Silurus glanis)

This huge, rather enigmatic species originates from Eastern Europe where, in Russia, individual specimens have been commercially netted to 16 ft long and over 600 lb in weight, making the wels one of the world's largest freshwater species, along with the Nile perch and the Aripaima.

In countries such as Poland, Hungary, Russia, Germany and Romania, the wels is an important food source and extensively farmed for its delicate flesh. In Britain the wels offers the angler by far and away the best chance of his largest-ever catch. As yet, however, although massive wels are known to exist in a handful of southern fisheries, the 43½ lb wels caught from Tring Reservoirs in 1970 by Richard Bray remains the British record. There is no reason to doubt, however, that a potential weight of double this – maybe even over 100 lb is a possibility in the future now that wels are being extensively stocked throughout the country. The main factor against a monster British wels is the cold climate and inconstent summers, which result in an extremely short 'growing year' for a species that becomes most active once water temperatures reach and stay constantly above 70°F.

In outline, the wels has the strangest shape for such a powerful fish. It uses its long, tapered, scaleless body, which is not unlike that of a giant tadpole, in a sideways zigzag motion similar to that of the eel, setting up strong resistance on the end of the line. Its tail is stubby. Its head is huge and flattened, with a wide (ear-to-ear) smile. There are six sensitive feelers or barbules. A long one protrudes from each corner of the upper lip, characteristically pointing out in front when the fish is actively feeding, or folded neatly backwards when resting. Four short, soft barbules literally hang down from below the chin. The eye, which is really tiny and situated just above the jaw hinge, gives the distinct impression that this fish, more than most, hunts and catches its prey more through the senses of vibration, smell and touch, than it does by sight.

The cavernous mouth contains pads of tiny teeth

Catfish are nocturnal feeders, but in shallow, coloured lakes, action is likely at any time of the day. This nicely marked 7 lb catfish gobbled up a small whole squid.

situated just inside a pair of thick, rubbery lips. There are more bristle pads in the throat, against which the wels crushes its prey, employing the bony, sharp inside edges of the gill plate. There are no canine teeth – not that the wels needs them. It has such immense sucking power that a victim straying too close has merely to touch one of its long whiskers to be vacuumed up with incredible speed in one terrifying, convulsive gulp that usually lifts the wels completely off the bottom. Small fish go straight down into the gullet. A part of larger ones may hang out of its mouth, but after several minutes of strong clamping offer little resistance to being swallowed in a second enormous gulp.

The dorsal, pectoral and pelvic fins are small, but the anal fin is extremely long, occupying two-thirds of the fish's length. All are dark grey, brown or black, as is the upper body. The sides are most attractively mottled in a mosaic of purple, olive green and grey. There is a considerable difference in colour between individual fish.

FEEDING

The wels (just like the eel) is an avid night-feeder, preferring to hide in deep water or beneath sunken trees, huge weedbeds or undercut banks during daylight, and becoming extremely aggressive and active as dusk approaches. This is not to say that wels won't feed during daylight, however, because they do, especially in heavily

coloured lakes and during bouts of humid, thundery weather. Feeding is also influenced by water temperature, and wels are noticeably more active in hunting and feeding in temperatures above 65–70°F. Thus, in prolonged heat-wave conditions, even during daylight, the chances of contacting them are excellent. Otherwise, all-night fishing sessions are invariably more productive. The wels feeds on a diet of fish, both dead and alive, from a very early age. It also eats worms, crayfish, frogs, toads, newts and freshwater mussels, and can manage fish (including its own kind) of at least half its own body size. Although the wels does occasionally come to the surface in order to grab its prey, its primary feeding zone is along the bottom to 2 ft above it.

REPRODUCTION

Propagation of the species starts in the spring with the male fish excavating a shallow depression in the bottom, or constructing a nest from aquatic plants, fibrous roots, reedstems, etc., into which the female is attracted and where she lays her eggs. These are subsequently guarded by the male until they hatch 3 weeks later. Initially, the young feed heavily on zooplanktons, followed by crustacea, aquatic insect larvae and then a fish-dominated diet. When a rich food source is readily available, the wels is one of the fastest-growing of all freshwater species.

LOCATION

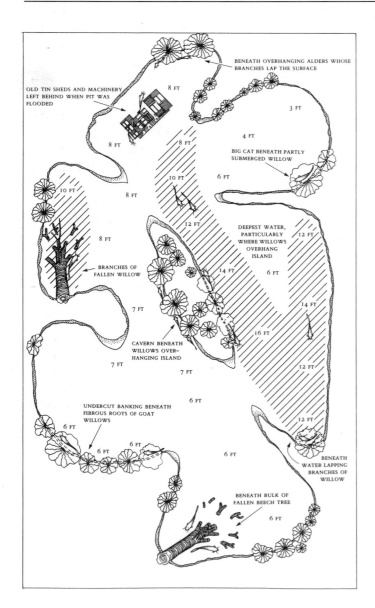

FIGURE 1.5 *Locating catfish in a mature gravel pit*

Though stocked into only a handful of stillwater fisheries, there is a future for the American channel catfish, which bites freely and grows to 50 lb. This 3-pounder was caught by Jonathan Todd on a cube of ledgered luncheon meat. Note its small dorsal and adipose fins. Unlike most catfish, it has a forked tail.

As only stillwaters in Britain contain wels, location is relatively easy. A small stock in even a large stillwater can, through perseverance and patience, eventually be tracked down. However, a small stock in a river system (and no doubt the wels will eventually find its way into British rivers) creates an almost impossible situation.

The fact that wels love deep, dark, cavernous spots in which to hide during daylight helps location. As can be seen from fig. 1.5 of an old gravel workings now well established and nicely matured, there are very definite hideaways to which the species is drawn naturally. Wherever majestic old willows preside along the margins of the pit, their branches hanging over deep water, a wels will not be far away. They find refuge among the massive sub-surface fibrous rootstock that grows down from branches floating on, or just below, the surface forming a dark, cavernous area beneath.

Any really deep water is attractive to wels – and even more so if situated close into the bank or running parallel with an island and heavily overhung by trees, willows and alders especially.

Old gravel workings have often been allowed to fill up from the water table before obsolete machinery and corrugated tin stores or sheds were removed. These habitats are tailor-made for the wels catfish, providing a large, dark home, as does any mature tree that topples over during gale-force conditions and even continues to grow (as willows do) forming a jungle of sub-surface hideouts and caverns beneath.

Where obvious habitat features do not exist in more featureless, open gravel-pit and lakeland fisheries, careful plummeting is imperative to locate the deepest areas such as holes, troughs and gullies. Any distinct area of considerably deeper water is worthy of attention, but remember that wels work and hunt very close to the bank during darkness, just like the carp. Incidentally, one of the problems when catfishing small, hungry waters that are prolifically stocked with carp in addition to wels, is that carp will suck up virtually any bait presented on the bottom – even small deadbaits, squid and exceptionally smelly pastes intended for wels. If you experience plenty of action every session, it is fair to assume that a large proportion of runs are from carp, which nearly always beat all but the largest catfish to your bait.

The most difficult waters on which to pinpoint areas where wels catfish could be lying are featureless, coloured, shallow, even-depth pits and lakes, which tend to be more productive. This is no doubt due to the fact that shallow, coloured water warms up quickly, so that throughout the summer months wels will be continually on the hunt, and action is a possibility at any time of day or night.

Coloured water also offers more protection to young wels from predators like the heron, pike, zander, eels, perch and, of course, their own kind. The fact remains, however, that until stimulated into scavenging along the bottom for its natural food or your bait, catfish could be lying in the mud virtually anywhere in an even-depthed, featureless fishery. Location then becomes an active, integral part of fishing, and during the course of several sessions using a two-rod set-up, you can experiment with varying baits in different parts of the lake until runs begin to occur.

DISTRIBUTION

The wels is widely distributed throughout Europe, even stretching north into southern Scandinavian countries. It has also been successfully stocked into Spanish waters, namely the River Ebro, which yearly produces numbers of wels in the 50–100 lb bracket.

The wels now is also becoming a popular angling species in Britain. Owing to the British catfish conservation group, who have been instrumental in the spread of the species during the 1980s, by the end of the 1990s almost every fisherman living in southern England should have the opportunity to match his skill against this powerful adversary.

CHUB
(Leuciscus cephalus)

Summer or winter, there are few occasions when the fisherman cannot interest chub. John took this plump 5 lb-plus river fish on stret-pegging tactics when the water was up and coloured.

Only occasionally is the chub mistaken for other indigenous freshwater species. Immature chub can be confused with and thus mistaken for large dace, although even the mouth of a small chub is unusually large, while both its dorsal and anal fins are convex (rounded), as opposed to those of the dace (and roach) which are concave and circle inwards along the outside edge.

The chub is renowned for its broad, blunt, almost bullet-shaped head and truly cavernous mouth rimmed by thick, white, rubbery lips, old rubber lips being just one of its numerous nicknames. At the rear of its throat, buried in soft tissue as with all cyprinids, the chub has a formidable pair of pharyngeal teeth, each with a double row of hooked crushers. These are incredibly powerful and are used by the chub for mincing up its food to pulp prior to swallowing. Hard-shelled crustaceans such as the crayfish, and the meaty flesh of other small fishes, are all gulped back and given the crushing treatment.

Body colouration often depends upon water colour and temperature. While the back is usually a dark grey, the flanks can vary from a distinct brassiness in the summer, to

pale silver in the colder water of winter. The dorsal fin and tail are painted a dark blueish grey. The pectoral fins appear translucent with little more than a light grey tint, and the flanks blend into a belly of creamy white.

Isaac Walton credited the chub with being the most fearful of fish, which of course is perfectly true. Learn to creep up upon a chub basking in a small clear-watered stream without its having an inkling of your presence, and you are almost there. Chub are nowhere near so difficult to tempt provided they have not been scared first. Clearwater chub, especially, seem to possess eyes in their tails and are particularly unforgiving of the slightest unnatural bankside vibrations or the sudden appearance of a silhouette against the skyline which should not be there.

The maximum length for the species is around 24 to 25 in, though most adult chub vary between 16 and 20 in, depending upon the richness of the environment in which they live. For instance, those competing in a shoal of 20 to 50 other chub, in a river that is densely populated with competition species as well as other chub shoals, may never exceed 2 to 3 lb in weight. Yet put that same chub (from an early age when growth potential is unlimited) into a rich environment low in fish stocks, and ultimately it may grow to exceed 5 lb in weight, perhaps even more. Even mature chub averaging 3 to 4 lb transferred from a fertile river to a stillwater where there is less competition will show a significant, even considerable, weight increase in individual fish, far surpassing the ultimate weight they would have attained in the river.

Because chub do not breed successfully in stillwater fisheries (unless a stream flows through it) perhaps, instead, they utilize all their energies in amassing a greater body size. Or is it that they simply expend less energy by not having to face and work against a strong flow. As a rule any species in a stillwater will ultimately grow to a far larger size than their running-water counterparts. And if ever a chub is caught topping that magical 10 lb barrier, I will wager that a stillwater fishery produces it. As it is, chub of between 7 and 8 lb are around the accepted optimum size likely to come from either still or running water.

FEEDING

Make no mistake about it, the chub is among the greediest of our freshwater fish. It may even be more of a glutton than the carp, which is the reason why, almost regardless

of water temperature and conditions, you can usually find a chub or two willing to suck in your bait. Its reputation for having a catholic taste towards food is an understatement. In fact, I cannot think of a single known freshwater bait that the chub will not eat or a technique by which it cannot be caught.

It feeds upon all available aquatic insect life, including the larger nasties such as the ditiscus beetle and dragonfly larvae, and the entire crustacean family from the lowly shrimps and snails to the freshwater crayfish, whose armour-plating is quickly smashed by the chub's powerful pharyngeal teeth. Chub will consume newts, frogs, toads and the tadpoles of each, and small fishes of every species including their own.

Although they thrive in stillwaters when stocked, chub are river fish first and foremost. They make full use of everything the river provides, from the mish-mash of titbits continually brought down by the current, to fry shoals hugging the shallows, and into which they can often be seen lungeing during the summer months.

Fish do at times make up a large part of the chub's daily diet, and from a very early age. Chub of just 4 to 5 in long, for instance, feed on tiny fry, and can pose a nuisance to trout fishermen, who regularly hook them on large, gaudy patterns representative of fish fry. Do not be fooled by the fact that chub in hard-fished, clear rivers can suck in a single caster and blow out the case without moving the float. A 3 lb chub can gobble up a 5 in roach, convert it to minced fish and swallow it in less time than it takes a pike

to do the same. And a really big chub, say 5 lb and more, easily has the capacity and equipment for dealing with round-bodied fish like dace of up to ½ lb.

Paradoxically, chub also eat a certain quantity of vegetation, blanket weed especially – perhaps for the shrimps, nymphs, or minute molluscs it contains, perhaps simply because they like it. Wild fruits are also popular with chub, blackberries, hawthorns and particularly elder berries which fall into the water during windy weather providing them with a juicy seasonal feast. There is no mystery in the fact that large, overhanging elder trees invariably produce the best sport of all on the river. Chub also rapidly discover a liking for particles intended for attracting barbel into the swim. Those pre-baited with stewed hempseed and hook baits, samples of mini boilies, luncheon-meat cubes, sweetcorn, casters, peanuts and so on (in fact, any particle and any boilie), invariably fill up with chub long before barbel.

During the winter months, like all cyprinids, the chub's metabolism drastically slows down and it requires a much smaller intake of food on a much less frequent basis. Quite simply, the colder the water becomes, fewer are the chances of chub becoming ravenous. In the most severe weather, when the river's surface is partly frozen over, it will neverless still continue to feed long after roach and bream have shut off.

REPRODUCTION

Chub are usually the next coarse species to spawn after pike, perch and dace, although a long, really chilly spring may still find the females pot-bellied at the end of June. I have in fact seen chub spawning as early as the middle of April and as late as the first week in July.

Always the shoals congregate in the fastest shallows, usually over a gravel and weedy bottom. Like the cyprinids, the males are distinguishable from the females by the white spawning tubercles which appear on their foreheads. These rough nodules are used for butting the females and to stimulate the release of the eggs, which are immediately sprayed with the white milt of the male as they fall to the bottom, adhering to stones and plants. If the water temperature remains constant, the fry will emerge within 10 days. They will feed initially on minute algae and planktons until they are large enough to manage aquatic insects and small, bottom-dwelling crustaceans.

As they need running water to stimulate the urge to reproduce, chub living in stillwaters do not usually even try to spawn. Only in lakes, reservoirs and pits into which water flows, therefore, can you expect to see chub gathering on the shallows during the spring.

Situated at the rear of the chub's throat is a pair of pharyngeal teeth, which it uses to crush and mince into a pulp any food item. Never put your finger down a chub's throat to remove the hook. Use forceps – it is less painful.

LOCATION

Summer

Find any sort of cover in freshwater, be the river a mere stream or a wide tidal channel, and you will have located a potential chub swim (fig. 1.6). Although chub do shoal up in open midstream swims in both deep and shallow rivers whether weed-beds are present or not, they much prefer, and are more likely to be found, wherever there is access to cover above their heads. Overhanging trees, undercut banks (fig. 1.7), rafts of weeds, fallen trees, marginal plant cover (fig. 1.8), bullrushes, weedheads and bridges all provide a refuge for the chub.

A word of advice for summer location, when most rivers run reasonably clear and when future sport relies upon visual proof, and your ability to spot the chub before it or they see you. Do not under any circumstances leave home without polaroid glasses. Forget the bait by all means, because natural baits can easily be gathered from beside the river, but make a point of including your polaroids above all else.

I much prefer those with bright yellow lenses, which not only eliminate reflective glare from the surface, but also provide increased visibility for the immediate surroundings both in and out of the water during low light values such as dusk and dawn. And these, of course, happen to be the best times for catching the chub off its guard, whether you are fishing or merely spotting. There is, however, a strong case for choosing polaroids with darker grey lenses for those rare occasions during bright sunshine in the middle of the day when chub are feeding ravenously.

SOME UNDERCUTS REACH SO FAR INTO THE BANKING (UP TO SEVERAL FEET) THAT IF YOU WERE TO STAND OR KNEEL ON THE VERY EDGE OF THE RIVER BENEATH A TREE AND PEER DOWNWARDS THE CHUB MIGHT BE COMPLETELY HIDDEN BEHIND YOU.

UNDERCUT CHUB HIDDEN FROM VIEW

FIGURE 1.7 *Undercut banks*

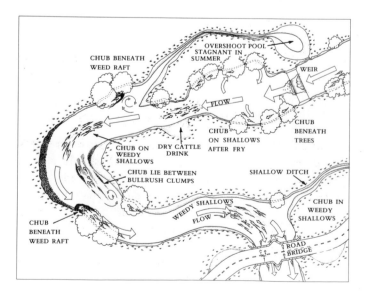

FIGURE 1.6 *Summer chub*

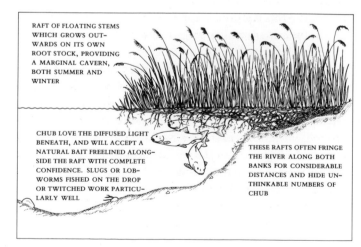

RAFT OF FLOATING STEMS WHICH GROWS OUTWARDS ON ITS OWN ROOT STOCK, PROVIDING A MARGINAL CAVERN, BOTH SUMMER AND WINTER

CHUB LOVE THE DIFFUSED LIGHT BENEATH, AND WILL ACCEPT A NATURAL BAIT FREELINED ALONGSIDE THE RAFT WITH COMPLETE CONFIDENCE. SLUGS OR LOBWORMS FISHED ON THE DROP OR TWITCHED WORK PARTICULARLY WELL

THESE RAFTS OFTEN FRINGE THE RIVER ALONG BOTH BANKS FOR CONSIDERABLE DISTANCES AND HIDE UNTHINKABLE NUMBERS OF CHUB

FIGURE 1.8 *Sweet reed grass*

Winter

Finding chub in winter with the rivers cold, running fast and often heavily coloured, is not so daunting as it would first appear. It is to a large extent merely a natural progression from summer chubbing. And it is just reward for the countless hours spent spotting and becoming familiar with the river's character when it was running clear, when the deeps and shallows, snags and clear runs, weed-beds and gravel bars were all plainly visible. Therefore those who have done their homework and studied the river exhaustively will know exactly where to look. They will find that most of the choice 'feature' swims which held chub during the summer will also produce throughout the the coldest months (fig. 1.9).

Swims beneath road bridges, mill and weir pools, trees overhanging acute bends, dense lines of trees, especially those whose trailing lower branches collect rafts of flotsam, rotting weed, reed stems and the like: these are the absolute certain winter chub haunts. Deep runs alongside thick beds of tall reeds or rushes, now brown and matted, or where the banking is almost vertical and reaches high above the water, are also much favoured by chub for winter quarters, particularly on the outside of wide or acute bends. Deep gullies in the middle of generally shallow stretches should also not be overlooked, particularly where more obvious features do not exist. After all, those chub haven't jumped out on the bank or swum to another river. Despite the water looking grey, cold and unwelcoming, they will be lying somewhere, and finding them is all part of the fun.

Flooded rivers

As anglers are only too aware, brooks, streams and even large rivers can become quite unrecognizable following weeks of heavy rain or snow. So again, prior knowledge of all the existing features helps enormously towards locating and subsequently extracting a few chub from situations which at first look to be hopeless (fig. 1.10).

Spots where ditches or side streams converge with the main flow, slacks behind large sunken willows, cow drinks, overshoot pools (stagnant during the summer), slacks immediately behind wide bridge supports, and so on: these are the natural hiding-places which chub seek out and quickly move into to avoid facing the full force and continual barrage of debris-laced flood waters.

In rivers absent of definite features, expect to find chub very close in – within inches of the bank immediately downstream of the bends, where current speed is noticeably that much slower. For example, swims which in the summer hold no more than a few inches of water or may

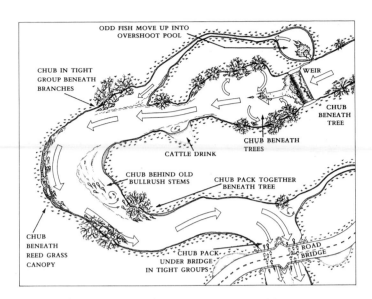

FIGURE 1.9 *Winter chub*

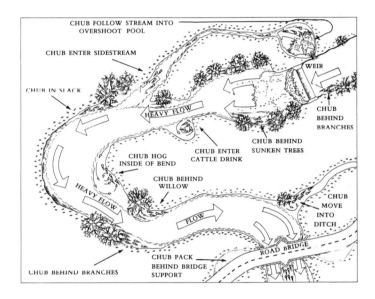

FIGURE 1.10 *Flooded river chub*

even be completely dry, such as the baked sides of cow drinks.

Locating chub in stillwaters

Finding chub in large stillwaters is one of the hardest tasks of all, especially when you consider that only a small percentage of gravel pits, even among those adjacent to river systems, actually contain any chub at all. And those which do, rarely hold more than the occasional small group or shoal. So ask around among other anglers and at your local specialist tackle shop, to find out exactly which pits, lakes or reservoirs are known for producing chub within the local area.

Armed with polaroid glasses and a pair of binoculars,

the best time for visual location is during the summer. At this time lakes and pits are warm and clear, and the chub are patrolling as they do in formation, forever on the move, and swimming noticeably faster than would seem appropriate for a fish seeking food.

Once stocked into stillwaters, chub definitely alter in character and become even more suspicious than carp. Gone is that instant, unthinking aggression seen in a river chub as it rushes from a standing start to suck in a freelined crust or slug in case one of its shoal buddies gets there first. Stillwater chub are renowned for taking their time and then refusing a bait. In small stillwaters full of character they certainly relate to the same kind of jungle swims which exist in rivers – such as over-hanging trees, sunken bushes and trees. However, in huge, featureless, wind-swept gravel pits lacking any obvious habitats, they become nomadic and possibly spend much of their time following the fry shoals. They do, however, respond to surface baits like floating crust and to surface-popping plugs. They also respond to regular pre-baiting along the margins with both bread and deadbaits (see pp. 122 and 130). The fact remains, however, that stillwater chub pose an exasperating proposition on the basis of their limited numbers alone. At best, you could well be trying to locate (with the possibility of catching just one or two of them) a group of just eight or nine fish in a lake or a gravel pit several acres in size. Nevertheless, they offer the ultimate freshwater challenge.

As I mentioned before, an enormous amount of recon-naissance work in pure location needs to be done before even considering making a few sessions after stillwater chub, particularly during the winter months when, on the temperature factor alone, all species are noticeably less active.

During the winter months, when the weeds have died off, chub group in larger shoals, so a bag is always on the cards, even from small rivers. Kevin Gardner took this sextet of 3–4 pounders on ledgered bread flake from a glide only 3 ft deep.

DISTRIBUTION

Chub are found throughout most of the large river systems of Europe, particularly in the middle and lower reaches, as indeed they are throughout most river systems in England except for Devon and Cornwall. They live only in the most southern of Scottish rivers and while rivers like the Anan breed chub of huge proportions, their presence is barely tolerated by salmon and seatrout anglers. They have only limited distribution in Wales, although the mighty River Wye is arguably the most prolific chub fishery within the British Isles.

Chub find their way into gravel pits, reservoirs and lakes adjacent to many rivers either by following the course of feeder streams and inlets or across flooded meadows during periods of high spate. Only in recent years has the chub's worth as an ideal, controllable stock fish for selected stillwaters been fully realized. It grows large, while at the same time helping to control shoals of stunted nuisance fish, without competing for the same food source as say tench, carp or bream. For this reason, more and more stillwater fisheries are now being stocked with chub.

DACE
(Leuciscus leuciscus)

What I like most of all about dace fishing is that many of the rivers that hold them, and where they grow largest, are pretty little rivers and beautiful chalkstreams meandering through picturesque farmlands where you can enjoy a peaceful day's sport roaming from swim to swim carrying the absolute minimum of tackle, whether wielding a float rod, a quivertip rod or a light fly rod.

Optimum weight for the dace is less than 1½ lb. The British record weighed 1 lb 4½ oz and was caught by J. L. Gasson from the Little Ouse near Thetford, Norfolk, in 1960. In reality, however, any dace of 10 oz upwards is a most worthy catch, and in larger rivers an average size of somewhere between 3 and 6 oz is more likely.

The dace has a slim, rounded, smooth body with small, flat-lying scales, small head and a neat mouth. Along the back, colouration is grey-olive blending into flanks of silver enamel, the belly being matt white. The forked tail and dorsal fin are both a translucent grey, while the pectorals, pelvics and the anal fin vary from dull yellow to pale pink.

The outer edge of both its dorsal and anal fins are concave, as opposed to those of the chub, which are convex. So there should never really be any confusion between small chub and dace. Length for length, the chub's mouth is, of course, twice the size, and its colouration brassy compared to the distinct silver of the dace. With the dace a vertical line can be drawn at the front edge of both its dorsal and its pelvic fins, whereas the chub's dorsal starts in a vertical line midway along the pelvic fins.

Though small, the silvery dace is a popular species with float fishermen – both match anglers and long-trotting enthusiasts alike. In all but the lowest temperatures, dace bite freely in the fast shallows, and in the warmer months can be taken on the dry fly.

FEEDING

The natural food eaten by dace consists of all forms of aquatic insect life, from nymphs that spend the best part of their yearly (or two-yearly) cycle crawling about on the river-bed, to the rising and hatching pupa, to the adult fly that dances on the surface. Their pharyngeal teeth are well developed, consisting of two rows of five large and two or three small respectively, on each plate. With such an armoury it is small wonder that adult dace can maul a large lobworm and send it back to you so chewed you would assume the culprit a chub.

Then again, in low water temperatures that coincide with clear water conditions, educated, well-fished dace can be exasperatingly choosey over a single caster in which a size 20 hook is hidden.

REPRODUCTION

The dace is not unlike the European ide or silver orfe, whose beautiful cousin, the golden orfe, is so loved by pond-keepers. In fact, the dace shares a peculiarity with orfe in that only prior to and during the spawning season, when the males develop hundreds of tiny tubercles over their heads and bodies and are decidedly 'rough' to the touch, is it possible to differentiate between the sexes.

Dace spawn earlier than most species of coarse fish, usually in April. There is actually a pre-spawning segregation of the sexes during February and March. The noticeably slimmer, wiry males, now sandpapery to the touch, gather in their hundreds in the turbulent runs while the deep-chested, spawn-laden females remain in deep, slower swims until the time is ready for them to amalgamate on the fast, gravel shallows where the pinky-orange coloured eggs are laid, usually under the cloak of darkness. When dace have deposited their eggs, gestation can take up to three weeks.

LOCATION

Diminutive rivers and streams that twist and wind through rich farmland are usually full of character and thus easy to read (see fig. 1.11). Where the water runs sparklingly clear through beds of lush vegetation and over a gravel or sandy bed, expect to find the dace. During the summer, search through polaroid sunglasses along the shallow straights between bends, at the tail ends of small weir-pools or hatches, in the fast junction runs where carriers merge with the main course, even in tiny side streams and ditches narrow enough to be jumped, in water from a mere 6 to 24 in deep.

During the coldest weeks of the winter the larger, female dace will retreat into the secluded holes on bends and into the deep back eddies of weir or overshoot pools. And when the little river is in full rip-roaring spate and the colour of strong tea, both male and female dace, together with roach, chub and even the odd trout, will all pack into slacks immediately downstream of acute bends where the flow is least forceful and the water carrying less debris.

To find dace in larger, deeper rivers, look for stretches or smaller areas within a long reach where the flow is noticeably faster. Such swims occur whenever the river narrows, thus forcing the flow along at a faster pace. Weir-pools always attract dace like bees to a honey pot, right at the end of each flush in the well-oxygenated, bubbly water, and invariably at the very tail end of the pool, where the bottom shelves up and the water glides over gravel runs separated by flowing weedbeds. Whenever the flow is increased by the extra water from sidestreams converging with the main river, dace will almost certainly be in residence.

It is fair to say, and this may seem contradictory, that large shoals of dace may also be found in the slow, deep stretches of certain rivers in the company of roach shoals.

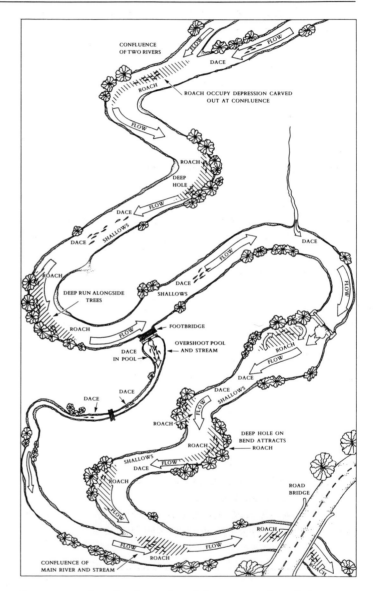

FIGURE 1.11 *Locating dace and roach in streams and small rivers*

DISTRIBUTION

The dace has a more easterly distribution than both roach and rudd, existing throughout much of Europe and even stretching into Asia. It is common throughout England in both slow and fast-flowing rivers, but absent from western Wales and Scotland. It has been introduced into a few rivers in southern Ireland.

EEL
(Anguilla anguilla)

It is thought that the eel, which migrates into and from European freshwater, is exactly the same species as the American eel (*Anguilla rostrata*), both of which reproduce in the Sargasso Sea in mid-Atlantic, but no one really knows for sure.

The eel is distinctly round in cross-section and snake-like in movement, possessing the ability to propel itself as quickly backwards, in that characteristic winding, zigzag movement, as it can move forwards. It is covered in a thick layer of protective mucus, below which its tiny scales, not visible to the eye, are deeply embedded in a tough skin.

The eel has a strange arrangement of fins. It has no pelvics, and one long combined anal and dorsal fin (starting immediately behind the vent), which merge into the tail. The only separate fins are the pectorals, which are rounded and situated immediately behind the gill opening.

The eel's head is pointed and slightly flattened. The teeth are small, numerous and bristle-like, set in a pair of strong jaws with the bottom one noticeably protruding. This latter feature is the easiest way of differentiating between the freshwater or common eel and the saltwater eel (the conger), whose jaws are level. The eye is relatively small throughout the eel's existence in fresh water, but becomes enlarged prior to its seaward migration, which occurs after a life of somewhere between 12 and 20 years in fresh water. During this time, eels find their way up river into the narrowest dykes and brooks and into the most inaccessible locations, such as tiny farm ponds miles from anywhere and any flowing water or connecting streams.

It is thought that a percentage of eels never acquire the urge to reproduce and so attain hugh proportions, with a potential maximum weight of 15 lb plus. The British record weighed 11 lb 2 oz and was caught by Mr S. Terry in 1978 from Kingfisher Lakes in Hampshire. However, we are talking only about real monsters here. Being long and thin (the lightest freshwater species on a weight for

When it comes to eels, freshwater fishermen are divided: there are those who love them, and those who do not. Either way, specimen eels provide a wonderful challenge to the enthusiast. Colin Dyson caught this eel from the Great Ouse Relief Channel on a dead gudgeon intended for zander.

length basis) even an eel of 3–4 lb looks absolutely enormous. Fish of this size measure between 30 and 36 in and are readily attainable to those who fish after dark in stillwaters containing only small numbers of eels.

When eels decide to migrate, their colour changes from yellow-brown (they are often called green or brown eels at this stage) to a striking metallic, silvery bronze, and simultaneously the snout becomes more pointed. In addition, the silver eel amasses a much higher fat content for its intended mammoth journey.

FEEDING

Eels eat virtually any kind of food that finds its way into fresh water and onto the bottom. They are voracious night-time feeders, and never (especially small eels) say no to an easy meal. They consume vast quantities of natural food such as aquatic insects, snails, worms, crayfish, newts, frogs, toads plus drowned mice, rats and birds.

During the daylight hours smelly animal baits, such as maggots, worms, cheese paste, luncheon meat or dead fish

are all pounced upon, and for most of the time, the majority of anglers spend more time trying *not* to catch eels, than the reverse.

Once a regular and easily attainable food source has been recognized, eels do not confine their interest to smelly baits alone. Offerings like sweetcorn and even boilies will, once introduced in sufficient quantities, eventually be accepted by eels. And most infuriating it is too.

REPRODUCTION

After the massive reproduction cycle that takes place on the bottom of the Sargasso Sea, the resulting larvae drift eastwards like planktons with the Gulf Stream towards Europe for a full 3 years. Once their destination is reached, more through luck that judgement, the Zeppelin-shaped larvae change in character and shrink to glass eels, and finally to elvers, which migrate from the sea into river systems by the million.

LOCATION

Small eels spend a large part of the day holed up in weedbeds, beneath large stones and buried in the bottom mud. The rich organic layers of silt that have accumulated over many decades contain both a huge eel population and a rich supply of food, namely insect larvae such as the bloodworm. By far the best way to obtain a good supply of smallish (8–14 in) eels to freeze down for later use as deadbaits with pike and zander in mind, is to wait beside a dredger working from the bank along a river or dyke, and grab the eels as they squirm from the silt.

Eels are particularly attracted to the bottom of deep mill-pools, weir-pools and pools by road bridges where accumulated debris lies on the bottom. In such locations, most eels do not have very far to run before threading the angler's line around an obstruction.

It is difficult to think of a part of a river system that does not attract eels. They are everywhere. However, spots such as pools, old lock cuttings and beneath the scoured-out supports and crumbling brickwork of bridges invariably contain a higher proportion of specimens.

Stillwaters, particularly those that contain neither inlet nor outlet streams (prison waters), and which are situated a fair distance from any dyke or river system, usually contain considerably smaller stocks of eels. However, they do contain individuals of a consistently high average size. So if you wish to get away from 'boot-laces' and catch quality eels, these are the waters to search. As can be seen from fig. 1.12, such eels seek out all the choice habitat features, like areas of really deep water, caverns beneath the fibrous, submerged roots of large overhanging trees, the rotten woodwork of old boat-houses, fallen trees and so on, where much of their daylight hours are spent resting. As dusk approaches, they scavenge the bottom well outside their lairs, often in really shallow water.

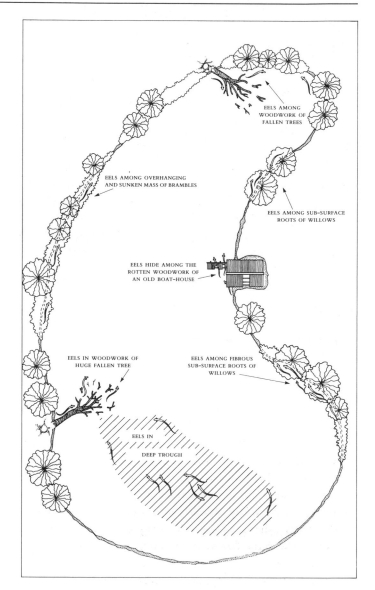

FIGURE 1.12 *Locating eels in stillwaters*

DISTRIBUTION

There can be very few waters in Europe, including the most remote hill lochs and mountain streams, which are not reached by at least a few eels. Their manoeuvrability is truly staggering. All major river systems north into Scandinavia and south into North Africa enjoy huge runs of eels, as do the rivers of America's eastern coastline.

GRAYLING
(*Thymallus thymallus*)

The grayling provides superlative sport for those long trotting with a centre-pin reel and chunky float working a bunch of maggots or redworms through the shallowest runs, as Trevor Housby knows only too well.

On a cold, bright winter's day, to wander the river with just a bait pouch and trotting outfit is surely one of the great delights that freshwater fishing has to offer.

'Lady of the stream' and 'Shadow of the river' – as the French say '*L'ombre de la rivière*' – are two lovely nicknames that wonderfully describe this unusual fish. Some anglers might even consider grayling the proverbial 'missing link' between the salmonoid game fish and coarse species, owing to the presence of an adipose fin and the fact that it, too, prefers cold, fast, well-oxygenated flowing water.

However, the grayling is a unique species. It is, for instance, the only British freshwater species possessing a distinct smell – one of thyme, as its Latin name of *Thymallus thymallus* suggests – a characteristic it shares with the smelt.

With its beautiful dorsal fin sporting several rows of blue spots, edged with a band of scarlet, the grayling can never be confused with any other species. In fact, the dorsal is the only sure way of differentiating between the sexes. The male has a long sail-like dorsal fin starting low in the front and high at the rear, which, when folded flat, almost touches the adipose fin. That of the female is much shorter

and almost square when extended by hand. The tail is pointed and light grey in colour, as is the tiny adipose fin. The pectorals and anal fin are also a translucent grey, but the pelvics sometimes show striking colouration like the dorsal.

The grayling has a thickish, elongated, wiry body with a narrow tail root, small head and a decidedly pointed snout. Its jaws are bony (which sometimes inhibits hook penetration) and its teeth are no longer or stronger than, for instance, the bristles inside the jaws of the perch. The jaw hinge itself is bevelled and not dissimilar to that of the herring.

The back is coloured in steel grey to mauve, fusing down the sides into dark silver with horizontal flashes of pewter and mauve, plus a liberal spotting of small, black flecks, unusually confined to the front half of the body. Its scales are small and embedded very flat to the body. Other characteristics and most distinctive markings include small, brownish/mauve flecks set either side immediately below the throat, and a thin line of similar colouration set horizontally along the lower body between pelvic root and the end of the pectoral.

Although the British record for the species weighed 4 lb

Male and female grayling are easy to sex. Just look at the huge, sail-like dorsal fin of the male on the left, compared to the box-like dorsal of the plumper hen fish on the right.

3 oz and came from the River Frome in 1989, any grayling becomes a specimen over the magical weight of 2 lb, which usually coincides with a length of between 15 and 17 in. In most rivers, however, fish over 1 lb are very worthy opponents. It is not so much the grayling's actual weight or size that attracts, it is rather that it suits the opportunist, wandering fisherman who enjoys long trotting and sport with the fly rod.

FEEDING

The grayling's natural food consists of all forms of aquatic insect life, from the nymph to the airborne fly, plus shrimps, snails and small fish. Grayling also eat the spawn of other species, especially trout, which is possibly why game fishermen hate them so. They also love maggots, especially small redworms offered by trotting enthusiasts, and bite really boldly, zooming the float under in the coldest, most severe winter weather when species like the

roach and chub have long stopped feeding. It is interesting to note that grayling can also be tempted by trotted bread flake and sweetcorn.

Grayling are usually very quick upon a profuse natural food source, but show a distinct lack of interest in feeding whenever the river colours up heavily in flood. I would not bother to fish for them during flooding, though I have caught them while ledgering for roach and dace.

REPRODUCTION

Grayling spawn between April and May on fast gravelly shallows, the eggs being deposited into a shallow redd cut by the female and simultaneously fertilized by a cloud of milt from the attendant male. The fry can take up to 25 days to hatch, and once 2 to 3 in long, sport distinctive parr blotches just like salmonoids.

LOCATION

There is no better barometer of water quality than the grayling, which will tolerate only pure, cold, swift-flowing rivers and, in certain circumstances, sweet, cold-water lakes. It is not difficult, therefore, even when viewing a river for the first time, to imagine where, if it holds any grayling at all, they will be lying (fig. 1.13).

Prime hot-spots and habitats are in the fast, bubbly water of weir-pools where grayling will hug the bottom in the 'filter lane', that narrow strip of fast, even-paced water between unfishable turbulence and much slower currents. They can, in fact, easily hold station in the fastest, most turbulent of currents almost regardless of depth. Certainly water just 1 ft deep is none too shallow, so expect to find a percentage of a river's grayling population in exactly the kind of swims you would not trot for dace, roach and chub. Hence the reason, when grayling trotting, for using short, chunky floats that carry a good shotting capacity and which cannot easily be pulled under by the swirling surface currents.

By the same token, grayling will also occupy some of the choicest, roachy-looking swims, such as confluences where a long sandy or gravel run is continually kept clean by the force of two currents converging with each other. Grayling also love clear, fast runs beneath narrow foot-bridges, and any long, fast runs between flowing beds of streamer weed so long as the bottom structure consists of clean sand or gravel. Slow water where beds of silt and debris collect, grayling do not like at all.

Grayling are also attracted to spots wherever the flow suddenly increases due to the presence of a small hatch or sluice diverting water from the main river into a carrier or side stream. And at the end of a pool created by such diversions there will be more grayling, attracted by the bubbly water and greater level of dissolved oxygen.

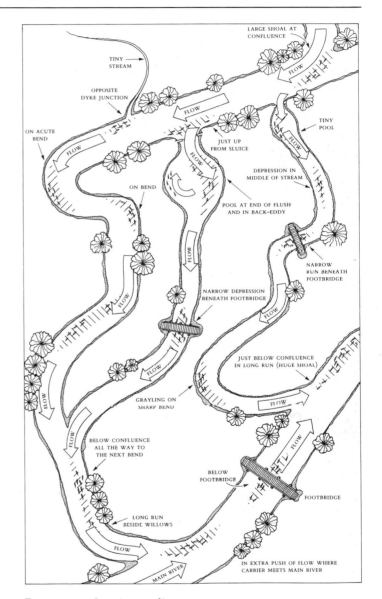

FIGURE 1.13 *Locating grayling*

DISTRIBUTION

The grayling is a fish of the northern hemisphere, being common throughout North America in both rivers and lakes, and throughout almost the entirety of northern Europe. It is absent from Ireland, but prolific in certain Scottish and English rivers. The crystal-clear chalkstreams of southern England, such as the Test, Itchen, Dever and Kennet produce a noticeably more intensely coloured grayling than the large river systems in Scotland.

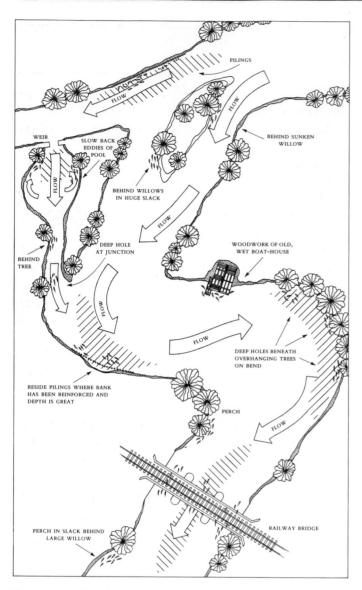

FIGURE 1.14 *Locating perch in running water*

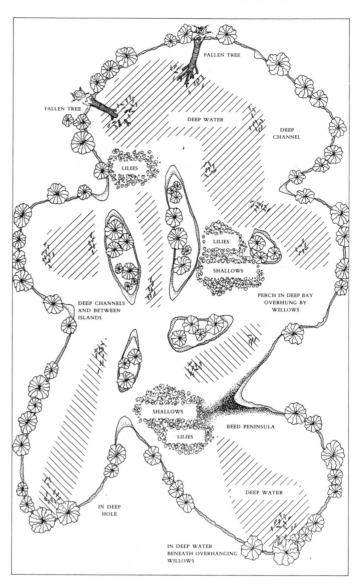

FIGURE 1.15 *Locating perch in gravel pits*

scuba-diver who rises faster than his bubbles, they instantly get 'the bends'. This is because, unlike the trout, which has a pneumatic duct connecting its air bladder to the alimentary canal, allowing it to release the pressure from rapidly expanding gasses by 'passing wind' as it is being played, the perch has a closed air bladder. Perch very often pay for this oversight on nature's part, when caught from deep water, with their life. Do not, therefore, attempt to retain perch taken from deep water in a keep-net. Return them immediately after unhooking in the hope they will go straight back down again to the pressure to which their bodies were acclimatized.

DISTRIBUTION

The perch enjoys an extremely wide distribution, being common throughout the British Isles, Europe and much of Asia. It thrives in parts of Australasia and South Africa, and in North America.

PIKE
(Esox lucius)

Not only is the pike the ultimate predator, one might also say it is the ultimate survivor. From fossil remains it would appear that the pike has been around longer than all other freshwater species in the British Isles.

Physically the pike is exceptionally well equipped. The pike lacks the top speed of trout, but its acceleration off the blocks is legendary. From a standing start the thrust from its large, powerful tail instantly propels the pike forwards (the dorsal fin is set far back to assist this) at incredible speed. Prey fish do escape, however, because sometimes the pike's timing is out and it misses, in spite of its monstrously large jaws. Nevertheless, it catches more often than not. The pike is also able to swallow almost anything – in fur, feather or scales – little smaller than itself.

Occasionally the pike takes on more than it can chew and chokes to death in the process. For example, on the Norfolk Broads, where eels are particularly plentiful in the thick layers of organic silt, it commonly happens that a pike is caught on a large deadbait and is found to have the tail end of a partly digested eel protruding from its jaws. It is understandable that, in a flash of aggression, a pike might make a reflex hit on a spinner or livebait that passes close by while it is digesting a reasonably-sized eel. But deliberately to locate and suck up a large static deadbait from the bottom when its jaws and throat are already full can surely only be attributed to greed.

Those odd occurrences when we catch a pike and return it, only to have the very same pike grab hold again an hour later, tend to make us believe that because it has teeth and is a predator, the pike is less sensitive than non-predators. Don't believe it. Pike are better equipped physically – in the hunting senses of sight, hearing and sonar – than all the fish they catch and eat, which includes every species of fish that swims in freshwater. Otherwise their prey would get away and the pike would starve.

The pike's wonderful colouration and its camouflage pattern, both of which change to blend in with its surroundings, are unequalled among freshwater species. In clear water the prominent grey-green colour, the zigzag markings across its back and the intricate pattern of blotches or spots along its flanks are accentuated, and help to camouflage it as it lies in wait between reed stalks or tree stumps. However, in heavily coloured water the pike changes colour accordingly. When rivers are in full flood and the colour of milky tea, or when the water of a broad, pit or lake turns peaty or brownish due to strong winds disturbing the bottom sediment, the pike takes on a low-key colour scheme. The intensity of the spots against the usually contrasting background colour of its flanks is greatly reduced, and the beige, brown and yellow in its body coloration are emphasized, so that its form blends into the bottom silt or decaying weed.

Pike tend to vary in colour from one clear water to another depending on the nature of the background, so it would be impossible for even the most brilliant artist to provide an exact colour guide.

Its ultimate weight potential in British waters is probably slightly better than 50 lb, although in most fisheries a 20-pounder is considered the specimen size to aim for. And in truth, pike of this calibre, which usually measure around 40 in, can turn up anywhere given a rich food source – from a gravel pit of little more than 1 acre to a narrow Lincolnshire drain you can almost jump across. That is the nice thing about the pike and pike fishing. It provides diverse, exciting sport with a fish that can be caught at any time from June through until March, almost regardless of weather conditions.

FEEDING

Pike catch their food by scavenging dead or dying fish from the bottom. They do this either by lying in wait between reed stems or the sub-surface woodwork of fallen trees or old stagings to ambush an unsuspecting fish, or by grouping together and herding a large shoal of fry and small fish into a small bay or boat dyke from which there is no escape other than running the gauntlet. Contrary to popular belief, pike also hunt their prey in open water by following shoals of roach, bream or perch.

A pike's open jaws, as would be seen by a small fish immediately before meeting its maker, are not the most welcoming sight. Embedded in the lower jaw is a series of large, piercing, crushing teeth with which the pike both grips and immobilizes its prey; set into the roof of its mouth are hundreds of much smaller teeth all pointing backwards towards the throat, so there is only one direction for its food to go. Only a small percentage of the fish gripped between these powerful jaws ever get away. Occasionally one catches a small roach or bream that was lucky, and still has the scars to prove it, but not often.

Irish pike are renowned for putting a healthy bend in your rod. A nice fish hooked at distance on a ledgered deadbait is netted for Terry Smith by Hugh Gough, Angling Officer of the Central Fisheries Board.

Small fish often disappear in one quick flash of the jaws and are gulped down immediately. Larger meals, on the other hand, are gripped sideways tightly between the jaws until almost dead, then turned with the help of the tongue (sandpapery to the touch) and swallowed head first.

As with all freshwater species, the pike's metabolic rate is greatly retarded in low temperatures, so in the most severe of winter weather it eats far less than during the summer months and is much slower about it. The implications of this for the fisherman are that in warm water the pike gulps its food down quickly, and in cold water it takes its time about turning and swallowing the same-sized meal.

This is a point well worth remembering if you are presenting large baits and are continually experiencing missed fish on the strike. In all probability, the bait will not have been turned by the pike when you attempt to put the hooks home. The pike feels undue pressure from the rod tip, and promptly opens its mouth and ejects the bait. This chain of events can sometimes actually be seen through clear water, even at the end of the fight just before you net the fish, when the head and tail of the bait are clearly visible either side of the pike's jaws. The fact is that at no time during the fight did the pike release its grip on the bait with a view to turning it so that the hooks could catch

hold. And of course at this late stage the pike swims off with a disgruntled look on its face and minus its meal, which it releases at the last moment.

The pike possesses exceptional eyesight, which enables it to capture its prey and evade enemies. In addition, it can determine the presence of other fish and other objects, even when it cannot see them, by way of a highly sensitive nervous system. This operates through tiny ducts connected by cords to the lateral line, which runs the entire length of the pike's body from gill plate to tail root. These ducts or sense organs detect vibrations, sound and even sudden pressure changes. On the head there are additional sensors, in the form of small holes around the eyes and beneath the chin running along the undersides of the lower jaw.

Esox has a highly developed sense of smell, too. When its other senses are effectively reduced through the lack of movement of its prey, or by poor visibility (in heavily coloured water, for instance), the aroma of a dead fish lying static on the bottom enables the pike to locate it easily, especially in flowing water when the pike simply follows the scent trail up to the food source.

So acute are these senses that even totally blind pike are able to lunge confidently at a live fish or an artificial lure, or sniff up a dead fish from the bottom.

In addition to consuming other fish including its own kind, plus rodents and water birds, the pike eats amphibians such as newts, frogs and toads and larger crustaceans like the crayfish. It will, if given the chance and in a hungry mood, have a go at virtually anything edible.

As with all species, pike relate their feeding to light values. On some days, when pike are coming out thick and fast to whatever is offered them, this would not appear to be so. But on other occasions, particularly during the winter months when the sky may be heavily overcast all day, it might need the sun's rays to break through the clouds for only an hour to trigger off a feeding spree. I have noticed this on so many occasions, and most particularly when presenting static deadbaits on the bottom of deep, heavily coloured pits and lakes. Fish which have been lying dormant for several hours are suddenly motivated into moving by the increased light values. And when pike are moving, they are willing to feed. So while sunlight penetrates the gloom, runs on static deadbaits can be expected, but when it disappears again the pike seem to lose interest.

REPRODUCTION

Pike spawn earlier than most other coarse fish species: usually during the month of April (possibly in the latter part of March following a mild winter). I am not totally

against the theory that Mother Nature has organized it this way purposefully, because old *Esox* is then ready for the inevitable banquet which occurs several weeks later when shoal fish like roach, rudd and bream gather by the thousands on the shallows for spawning, presenting week upon week of easy meals.

Accompanied by up to three or four eager and much smaller males, often referred to as 'jacks' (male pike are thought rarely to attain much heavier weights than 12–13 lb), the female, heavy with spawn, seeks out shallow weedy areas where the eggs can be shed. When soft weeds are absent any fibrous medium is used, such as the foliage of sunken bushes or trees, sedges, reed or rush stems. Pike have even been known to move on to flooded meadows or marshlands, laying the spawn among the long grass.

The commotion made by pike spawning in the shallows can be heard from a long way off on a still day. With jacks in attendance ready to spray milt over the eggs as she sheds them, the shuddering noise made by a large female in the act is quite distinct. A non-angler wandering along close by could easily believe that a couple of dogs were chasing each other through the water, the disturbance is that loud.

The eggs hatch within two weeks and the fry, which keep close to the weeds for safety, grow rapidly; initially they feed on a diet of plankton and minute crustacea, followed by aquatic insects and, at a very early age, the fry of other fish including their own kind. Really weedy lakes, full of Canadian pondweed, for instance, inevitably contain an unusually prolific head of small pike because the survival rate of the fry protected by dense vegetation is greater than in less weedy environments.

The proportion of eggs to bodyweight carried by a healthy female is quite considerable. A 20-pounder, for instance, might be carrying up to 3 or 4 lb, and the spawn in a 40-pounder could weigh as much as 6–7 lb. The monstrous 35–45 lb pike taken from trout fisheries in recent years have truly enormous roes. And with a rich diet of trout to gorge on, plus coarse species of all weights and size ranges from fry upwards, no wonder more huge pike are taken from trout reservoirs than anywhere else within the British Isles. Even the huge Irish and Scottish lochs that have produced so many of the biggest pike in years gone by now have to take second place behind the trout reservoirs.

LOCATION

As pike do not shoal as such, although they do group together at various times, location is not quite the same as with other species. You need to find the pike's preferred habitat rather than individual fish. For instance, with tench you look for their bubbles, which tell you exactly where they are. Bream can be seen rolling on the surface and they too send up bubbles, so their position can be pinpointed by looking through binoculars. Carp also bubble, so you know exactly where they are.

With many species, observation alone will tell you their exact position immediately, but this is not usually the case with pike. The odd occasion does present itself when pike can be seen through clear water and offered a bait, and it is then fun, and most enlightening, to watch their subsequent reactions. Generally speaking, however, and this applies to most methods of pike fishing, you need to select likely areas. You do this using a combination of imagination, watercraft, perseverance and a knowledge of the various ambush habitats preferred by pike, taking into account water and weather conditions, and the presence of prey fish.

Rivers

Consider the features of a typical, medium-paced river, for instance (see fig. 1.16). As pike never wish to be far from their next meal, they tend to occupy the obvious habitats where shoals of dace, roach, bream or chub live.

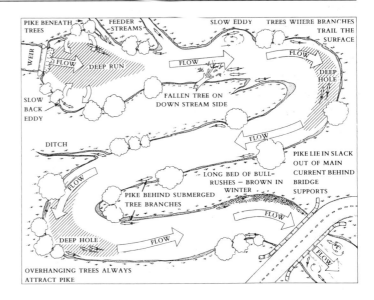

FIGURE 1.16 *River features where pike lie in ambush*

Only very rarely are pike found fighting the current in really fast, turbulent swims; the effort required expends too much energy. Besides, they are lazy and much prefer to lie in wait to ambush shoal fish as they pass by. So expect to find pike behind clumps of bullrushes, tall reeds, sunken trees, in slow back-eddies, deep channels, sudden depressions in the river-bed, in holes on the bends, at the confluence of a ditch or side stream and the main river, in

The pike's ferocity is legendary. They attack and swallow water-birds such as dab chicks, moorhens and cootes, with more regularity than anglers may realize.

weir and mill pools and so on. During the summer months pike love to lie in wait among the huge lettuce-type leaves (usually called cabbages) of the yellow water-lily which fringes the margins of slow-moving rivers and their backwaters (see 'Lure fishing' p. 212). Once the frosts of winter destroy the lily-beds, pike seek the sanctuary of deeper areas and alternative ambush points.

For much of the time, both summer and winter, the pike lives in close proximity to its prey, often lying mere feet away from, say, a shoal of roach. These tolerate its presence, knowing full well that until it is aroused they have little to fear. However, they soon become agitated and very alert when they sense a predator moving in for the kill, and they close ranks in mock security when the pike sets its fins and starts slowly to curl its tail in gentle waves – the classic pose from which it makes those sudden, explosive lunges.

Knowledge of the various depths in each swim along a river's course is the greatest short cut to catching pike and catching them quickly. If you fish the river regularly for other species, you will no doubt already have such details logged in your mind in readiness for pike fishing during the winter, when the water is substantially more coloured and the bottom contours cannot be seen.

If you know the depth of a swim, you can trot a livebait downstream at the most productive depth, which is from 1 to 2 ft off bottom (just above the pike), or retrieve a wobbled deadbait or an artificial lure immediately above the bottom contours in that same layer without snagging upon every other cast and continually having to pull for a break in the line. The latter is not exactly conducive to putting pike on the bank. And to leave multi-hook rigs or lures on the bottom is not only costly, it is extremely harmful to wildlife.

Try to visualize in your mind's eye how the pike will be lying in low water temperatures, with its lower fins almost touching bottom. Winter pike invariably carry numerous parasites like double-sucker leeches, which cling to their fins, proving their preference for the bottom strata of mud and silt. Obviously a moving bait needs to be presented in that 2 ft layer of water immediately above the bottom – a point that should always be considered.

In mild weather, pike will willingly leave the bottom and rush several feet upwards to intercept a bait near the surface, creating a glorious vicious swirl in the process. During the summer you can expect them to move double the distance because in warm water, when their metabolic rate is working overtime, pike are unbelievably aggressive and always willing to have a go. Sport during the warmer months can be wonderfully hectic, particularly with surface lures (see 'Summer plugging' p. 214). But in the cold depths of winter when increased water colour reduces visibility, your bait needs to be placed close by the fish, and sometimes right on their noses, or you won't catch many pike.

Stillwaters

In most stillwaters the deep-water habitats into which small shoal fish like perch, roach, bream and rudd move to spend the winter months, once vegetation cover has disappeared, and thus where pike may also be found, are not always obvious.

Indeed, compared to river systems, which are easy to read because most pike habitats stand out clearly, stillwaters require much preparatory work with a plummet to obtain an accurate plan of the bottom contours. After all, one sheet of water looks more or less like another once leaves have left the trees, the marginal rushes have died back, and the surface plants have rotted away. Compared to summer, the stillwater in winter takes on unfriendly proportions, which are exaggerated by cold weather, heavy rain, strong winds, or a mixture of these. But have faith; the fish have not jumped out onto dry land. They are all still there, they just have to be located.

If a boat is available plummeting is much easier, especially on large fisheries, but by far the quickest results are achieved by using an echo-sounder such as one of the portable Humminbird fish-finders, which not only provide a digital depth read-out, but actually indicate both shoals and even individual fish situated beneath the boat on the display screen (see p. 104).

However, only a small percentage of pike anglers at the moment use, or indeed can even afford, such modern technology. So let us assume that a plan of the bottom contours will be arrived at by old-fashioned means – the good old plummet used in conjunction with a sliding float that can be moved up and down the line to gauge the exact depth. For this job, a 2 oz bomb tied direct to the reel line is perfect for easy casting, and where long distances are necessary. Tie on a nylon sliding stop knot above the sliding float and you have the perfect plummeting rig.

If it helps, take along a clipboard and foolscap paper, and as you plumb each section fill in the respective depths on an outline of the fishery. It is not only fun and workmanlike; the results will stand you in good stead for many years to come. The pike fisherman who cannot tell you the approximate depth of the water into which his bait has been cast does not deserve to catch much – and invariably doesn't.

Consider the multitude of features in fig. 1.17, which is part of a typical gravel pit complex. The minerals have been removed in a series of clearly defined channels creating a network of deep gullies, holes and bays separated by tree-clad islands and shallow bars or plateaux. Old gravel workings such as this mature into beautiful environments completely over-grown along the margins, with thick beds of reeds fringing the shallows, and features like overhanging trees providing additional winter pike habitats wherever they shade the surface of deep water close in.

Small shoal fish always seek the sanctuary of deep water during low water temperatures, a fact of which pike are only too aware, so most of the shallow areas of this particular pit can be discounted. It is true that, whatever the conditions, a small proportion of the pit's pike population will be scattered around the margins, even in ridiculously shallow water beside reed-beds, old lily roots and the like. However, the bulk of the pike, especially the larger fish, spend most of their time working the gullies, holes or deep bays feeding from the heavy concentrations of small shoal fish that congregate there. During the autumn, before the water temperature drops drastically and before really chilly weather sets in, these same shoals

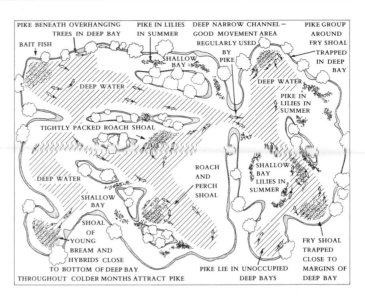

FIGURE 1.17 *Locating pike within a large gravel-pit complex*

of small fish will become more widely spread, roaming along the edges of drop-offs into deep water and in mid-depth plateaux or bays. The exact position of these shoals, and so to some extent the pike, is determined by the clouds of zooplankton upon which the small fish feed. So if, for instance, the wind blows hard in a particular direction for a couple of days and the sub-surface tow pushes mountains of zooplankton into a particular bay, the shoal fish will follow. And they in turn will be followed by the pike, which tend to pack or group around the perimeter of the shoal, lunging in for a meal whenever the fancy takes them.

The visible sign of this activity is dozens of fry scattering repeatedly on the surface as pike strike from beneath. But you need to make hay while the sun shines, because when the wind changes direction and moves the food that the shoal fish are feeding on, they and the pike will also move.

As I have already mentioned, there will always be pike scattered along the margins in and around reed-beds. And of course in shallow stillwaters that are nowhere deeper than about 4 ft – such as lakes, meres and broads – thick reed-beds are the only habitats left once winter frosts have removed lilies and soft weeds. So you have a good idea of where the pike will be lying. What is more, if the water remains clear, as it is likely to if the weather stays cold, still and frosty, the shoals of fish upon which the pike preys will also seek sanctuary in the reeds, thus creating fabulous hot-spots wherever the water is deep enough. However, not all thick reed-beds will contain pike, although when they are viewed from a boat or the bank their potential would look to be the same all the way around the perimeter of the water.

Tania Wilson is not afraid to play her pike hard, which encourages it to jump and tailwalk when water temperatures are still quite high.

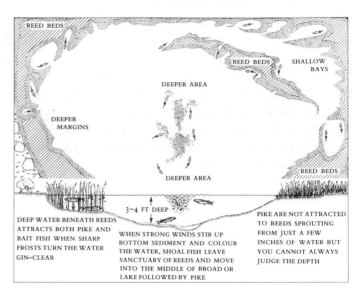

FIGURE 1.18 *A typical broad: in shallow stillwaters no deeper than 3 to 4 ft, reed-beds provide the only habitat for both pike and their prey*

Depth is the critical factor in these shallow stillwaters. Consider fig. 1.18, for instance, a shallow Norfolk Broad, although it could be a mere, a lake or even an Irish lough or a shallow gravel or sand pit. Along one shoreline the reeds are sparse and covered by only a few inches of water, a fact which is not always obvious in the dim light of dawn, or when fishing from a distance. But along the opposite shoreline not only is the reed-line thicker, it extends further back into the marshland. This potentially gives more space for both pike and compacted shoals of small fish, among reeds which have their roots in a good 3 ft of water.

DISTRIBUTION

Within the British Isles no other fish enjoys such wide distribution as the pike. Indeed, there cannot be many fisheries in either still or running water in which the pike does not help maintain the delicate balance between predator and prey. Only modern, man-made fisheries and carp-only waters, where the balancing presence of the pike is not required because only mature fish are introduced, are not purposefully stocked with pike. On a world-wide basis, the pike is exceptionally well represented. It is fished for across the entire northern hemisphere from North America and Canada all the way across Europe and even into Northern Asia.

ROACH
(Rutilus rutilus)

Although the friendly, silvery roach is among the smallest British freshwater species, in my eyes it remains the most worthy of all catches; deep-bodied specimen roach especially, because my early, formative years were all based on roach-fishing techniques.

Roach are blessed with the classical 'fish form'. A smooth, rounded body, distinctly oval in cross-section, with a short head and small mouth. The lips when open are level, compared with the lower lip of the rudd, which protrudes (see Hybrids, p. 52).

Colouration can vary tremendously from summer to winter, and especially from one environment to another. Clear-water roach, for instance, are far more brightly coloured, and have a minimal layer of protective mucus, whereas those inhabiting coloured waters produce a noticeably thicker layer of slime and are much paler in overall colouration. There is usually, however, a dark grey-greenish sheen along the back, fusing into silvery flanks, where the lateral line is most noticeable. The belly is always a creamy white. The scales are relatively large, certainly much larger than those of the dace or bream of equal size, and covered in bright reflective enamel, which is more intense in young roach.

During the winter months, when water temperatures are low, there is a distinct blue tinge to each scale along the upper sides and back, whereas in the summer the overall colouration is rather brassy. The pectoral fins have the least amount of colour, being a translucent warm grey-brown, while the pectoral and anal fins show more warmth in tones of muted orange or red. The dorsal and tail, which is deeply forked, are both more darkly coloured and tinged in crimson. Whenever a mystery fish porpoises momentarily on the surface and might be any one of four species – bream, roach, chub or barbel – it is the distinct, dark crimson of its tail that identifies and separates the roach from the others. A wonderful sight to the roach enthusiast. The body becomes noticeably deeper in roach that inhabit exceedingly rich stillwaters such as reservoirs, and also in clear flowing rivers lush in aquatic flora and fauna, where

World-champion match fisherman, Bob Nudd, catches roach from all over Europe. These beauties came from the lakes at Moycullen in the south of Ireland.

competition for food is low. As a very general rule of thumb, a healthy roach measuring around 8 in from the snout to the very tip of the tail will weigh approximately 4 oz. It is interesting to note that up to a length of 12 in, the roach is, on a weight-for-length basis, one of the heaviest of our freshwater fish. Ultimate potential weight for the roach must be getting close to the 5 lb mark. Specimens of this size have been reported from European waters. The current British record, however, is 4 lb 3 oz and was caught by Ray Clarke from the Dorset Stour in 1990.

Traditionally, once over the magical weight of 2 lb, a roach becomes a specimen.

FEEDING

What makes the roach so interesting and unpredictable is that while much of its natural food consists of minute particles, aquatic insects such as midge larvae, and freshwater shrimps, small molluscs and vegetable matter, once it is over ½ lb in weight, there are occasions, especially in the low light values of dawn and dusk, when it will happily gobble up a piece of bread flake the size of a 2 pence piece concealing a number 6 hook.

Size for size, compared to other cyprinid species, the throat or pharyngeal teeth of the roach are quite large and easily capable of crunching to pulp the shells of snails. Each of the two bony plates situated inwards of the gills contain a single row of up to five knobbly teeth, compared to the double row on each of the rudd's pharyngeals. Despite the power of its jaws (which explains why your maggots come back crushed to skins and devoid of inner juices) in the cold depths of winter when its metabolic rate has fallen drastically the roach will keep you waiting while it decides whether or not to suck in a single maggot or caster sensitively presented on a size 22 hook to a 1 lb bottom. When it so chooses, the roach can become the most frustrating of all freshwater species, particularly in clear water when alarmed. Remember that as a member of a living, forever-moving shoal, each fish is completely dependent on the others for general awareness – what affects one roach will usually affect the others almost instantly. Scare one by a clumsy or noisy approach or by casting your shadow unthinkingly upon crystal-clear water, and it could prove impossible to motivate that same shoal into feeding for some while. You are then obliged to wait until the shoal regains its confidence or until it becomes naturally less suspicious.

In coloured water, of course, shoal fish like roach are nowhere near so jittery, especially those living in small over-stocked ponds and pits lacking in predators. Generally speaking, however, having spent every day of its life from the fry stage upwards avoiding diving birds such as grebes, herons and cormorants, and predatory fish like eels, trout, zander, chub, perch and pike, it is small wonder that the roach is constantly on its guard. And this, of course, is why large, mature roach are so wily and so difficult to tempt. Until the day it stops breathing, the possibility of being mauled by a pike or stabbed by a heron is always present, even for a large roach.

REPRODUCTION AND HYBRIDS

Roach can be seen moving onto the weedy shallows for spawning as early as April and as late as June. It all depends on water temperature and whether spring occurs late or early. This applies to the roach of both rivers and stillwaters, but in each case the males are easily distinguished from the females by the white spawning tubercules that cover their heads and pectoral fins.

The noisy act of spawning, where numerous separate groups thrash and cavort on the surface simultaneously, may last several days, until the weeds or submerged tree roots are thick with pale yellowy eggs. These hatch in 10 to 12 days given consistent water temperature, and once the larvae are strong enough to shoal in the margins, they feed on minute plankton.

Given the right circumstances, roach will freely inter-breed with both bream and rudd when they arrive on the spawning grounds at the same time. Roach/bream hybrids are a fine-looking and most desirable fish to catch, combining the fast, dogged fight of a big roach with the slab-sided resistance and weight of the bream. However, hybridization does not always produce a fish that appears to be halfway between each species. The most prominent giveaway signs are the much paler body colouration and drab fins that are almost completely lacking in red pigment. The mouth is usually slightly protrusible. The best indication of all is the hybrid's longer, bream-like anal fin, often coloured along the outside edge with a band of black (see Roach/Rudd hybrids, p. 56).

LOCATION

Overgrown streams and small rivers

Locate a small shoal in a rich, overgrown environment lacking other roach and additional competition species, and each individual has the potential to reach specimen proportions, perhaps 2 lb and over. This is not the case, however, with the members of a shoal numbering hundreds, or in the case of big river shoals numbering several hundreds, or even thousands. Individual size is always governed by the available food source and, of course, the fish's age.

Roach generally prefer a good amount of water over their backs, and of a slowish pace. Through clear water, look for them hugging the bottom in all the deeper runs, especially in holes on the bends and those close into the bank where overhanging foliage shades the surface from strong sun-light. Confluences where the continual force of merging currents keep a long, deepish run free of debris and silt, bringing the shoal a regular supply of food particles, are at the very top of the list. Roach also feel happy in deep weir-pools and in lay-bys, which afford the shoal immediate rest from the full current force. And they love long, even-paced glides immediately downstream from an acute bend. They hate turbulence where the flow switches direction every few seconds, so when roach are not visible (as they are in the summer) learn to study

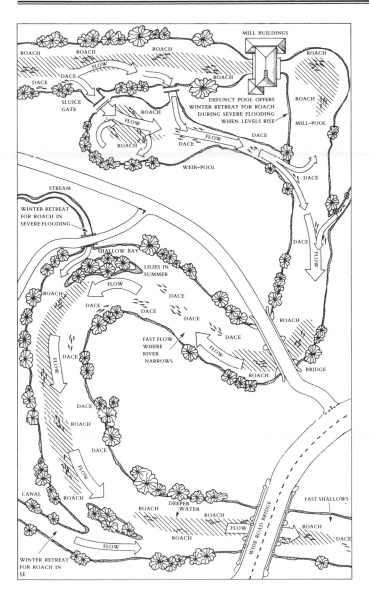

FIGURE 1.19 *Locating roach and dace in big rivers*

In many river systems during the latter part of the season, roach shoals pack into noticeably slower sections. John uses this phenomenon to good effect by regularly taking catches of quality roach from his local River Wensum during February and March.

surface currents, immediately ignoring swims where spirals of water continually spew up to the surface. Opt for steady water if you wish to catch small river roach with any degree of consistency, especially throughout the cold winter months, when their metabolic rate slows down, making them far less keen to chase their food.

Big rivers

During the summer in low water levels and slow currents, the roach shoals of larger rivers tend to spread out and might be found almost anywhere, from the cabbage patches along the marginal shelf, which provide a wealth of natural food and cover from predators, to the bubbly water of large weir-pools (see fig. 1.19).

Roach can often be seen porpoising on the surface at dawn and again at dusk, pinpointing their exact location to the enthusiast throughout the entire season except in sub-zero conditions. Once the summer weeds have rotted away, the shoals, feeling naked and vulnerable, tend to group together and move into the choicest swims. As they do in overgrown streams, the roach of larger rivers predictably select runs where the flow is steady. If there is the choice of protection overhead, such as a road or train bridge, or a line of overhanging willows or alders, then so much the better. The shoal may even happily exist in a relatively shallow swim. Generally, however, the pointers to look for are long runs, say from 5 to 10 ft deep, beyond the marginal shelf where the flow is steady.

All deep, slow eddies in weir-pools are potential roach hot-spots, as are those last few hundred yards of the river immediately above a weir or mill pool where the flow smooths down, particularly at the back-end of the season from mid-February until mid-March.

Never ignore shallow backwaters and sidestreams that join the river and which, during the clear water of summer, are full of weed and fry shoals. At flood time, especially when the main river is 3 or 4 ft up and heavily coloured, roach pack like sardines into these havens.

It is most important to become familiar with the river's character and its topography; something only hard work with the plummet and reconnaissance trips with polaroid glasses during the summer months will achieve.

Ponds

It is quite possible with two ponds of identical size and character, situated not far apart, that one will contain roach and the other rudd. A third in close proximity might contain a mixture of both species, and this is far more likely. In shallow and thus warm little ponds that turn pea green during the summer, both species breed so prolifically they become over-populated. With a limited food source the fish become stunted (unless a head of predators are present or introduced) and incredibly easy to catch, whether you present your bait just below the surface or on the bottom, in the edge under the rod-tip or bang in the middle.

Irrigation drains and canals

While drain and canal roach tend to be widespread during the warmer months and spread across from bank to bank, once cold weather really sets in they pack tightly together close to the bottom along the centre channel, where the depth is greatest. This results in long stretches of water being almost devoid of fish. Then, quite suddenly, several yards or more of the middle basin is crammed with roach.

Estate lakes and meres

While roach never really seem able to capitalize on the available natural food supply, they do breed most prolific-ally in estate lakes (fig. 1.20). During the winter months the shoals vacate the marginal shallows for the protection of deeper water, and pack together near the dam itself. Pick a mild spell and you could enjoy a netful.

Gravel pits

The best roach (and rudd) fishing exists in well-established and mature old gravel-workings, which, through the build-up of silt from leaves from surrounding trees and aquatic plant breakdown, have over the years developed an exceptionally rich and abundant food source.

Rudd, if present, are more prolific and grow to a good average size in pits where the gravel seams were shallow, resulting in irregular bottom contours and large areas of weedy, shallow water interspersed with tree-clad islands.

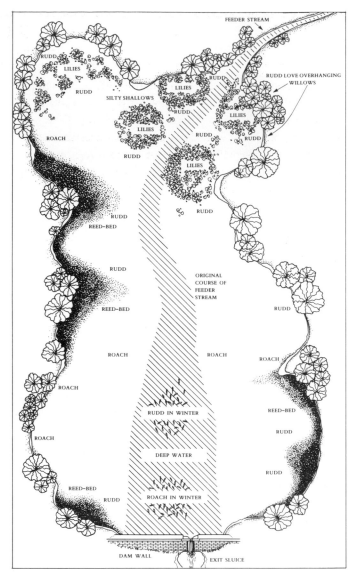

FIGURE 1.20 *Locating roach and rudd in estate lakes*

Roach much prefer the larger, more open pits, which provide a consistently good depth of 8 ft and more. Those that contained long, deep seams of gravel prior to excavation, result in deep holes and gullies capable of holding massive roach stocks.

DISTRIBUTION

The roach is common throughout the continent of Europe, from the brackish waters of the Caspian Sea in the east, to Yugoslavia in the south, Scandinavia in the north and Ireland in the west.

Once absent from Irish waters, the roach is now abundant throughout Ireland's major river systems, including the Blackwater, the Erne, the Shannon and the River Bann that feeds massive Lough Neagh, the largest lake in the British Isles. While roach are far from common in Devon, Cornwall and western Wales, in southern Scotland the species is well represented in Loch Lomond and in Perthshire's River Tay, where the tidal reaches are prolific in roach stocks. Elsewhere in England, almost without exception, the roach is the most common river fish.

RUDD
(Scardinius erythrophthalmus)

Despite having a fancier Latin name and being slightly slimmer than the roach in cross-section, the rudd is not totally dissimilar to the roach in body shape. The main difference, when viewed side on, is a characteristic angled 'keel' between its vent and tail root. In addition, the rudd's dorsal fin, which is set noticeably further back, overlaps the anal fin on a vertical line when folded, whereas that of the roach does not.

The real difference between the two species is the herring-like, up-turned mouth of the rudd. Its bottom jaw protrudes at an upwards angle, suggesting what most anglers quickly find out, that the rudd is built for surface feeding and intercepting falling food particles, although it also readily accepts baits presented on the bottom. And if these features are not sufficient to distinguish between the two species, in colouration the rudd wins hands down and is, without question, the most beautiful of all our freshwater fish.

Resplendent in the brightest livery, its fins are orange-scarlet, while the scales along the flank, if anything slightly larger than those of the roach, are lacquered in the most reflective, burnished, buttery gold enamel imaginable. So reflective are the rudd's scales that a tip for photographing them in bright sunshine is to always underexpose by one full stop. Otherwise your photo could easily be over-exposed. The back is brassy bronze, often with a distinct green hue in adolescent rudd.

There is a factor common to all waters where rudd flourish best, whether flowing or still; they are clean, weedy, chemical-free environments, unaffected by excessive eutrophication, where a healthy natural balance of aquatic insects and plants still exists.

Golden rudd

Though perhaps difficult to comprehend, this interesting variant is actually more intensely coloured than the common rudd. The salmon pink colouring along its back enables it to be seen easily from overhead in the clear, filtered water of garden ponds, and this is the sole reason for this variant being developed. The golden rudd is bred specifically for the pond-fish trade and is imported into the UK from North America and Germany. Nevertheless, it has found its way into isolated angling waters and freely interbreeds with indigenous rudd, adding a touch of mystery and an extra splash of colour. It grows to nowhere near such large proportions, and a golden rudd of 1 lb plus should be considered a fine specimen.

FEEDING

A strange feeding characteristic of the rudd is that invariably shoal members all tend to be more or less of the same size and of the same year or spawning class. You can catch stunted rudd from small farm ponds and irrigation reservoirs, all 4 or 5 in long, one after another, and from an estate lake or reed-fringed mere specimen rudd averaging just below and just above the 2 lb mark, with only 1–2 oz separating them. Crucian carp are known for a similar phenomenon.

Rudd being a shoal fish, much that I have already mentioned about roach also applies to it, especially the importance of light values, because rudd also commence feeding with real aggression and far less caution under the cloak of dusk when the surface is littered with hatching flies. They also sometimes respond in reverse to light values by becoming active at midday when the sun is at its highest point and the surface water layers that much warmer. Indeed, the rudd more than any other is the fish of summer, as anyone seeking to catch them in really cold winter weather soon appreciates. In winter often they only become active enough to accept your bait an hour or so either side of midday when light penetration through the cold water is at its highest.

Their dietary requirements demand a regular supply of hatching aquatic insects within the upper water layers,

The breathtaking golden buttery-yellow colour of the true rudd permits little confusion with other species. Note the protruding lower jaw and brilliant scarlet fins.

particularly midges and sedges, and zooplankton such as daphnia. Rudd also eat crustaceans and other bottom-dwellers, and an amount of vegetable matter. They seem particularly partial to the algae growing on reed stems.

Rudd have a slightly greater weight potential than roach, the British record being a 4 lb 8 oz specimen caught way back in 1933 by the late Rev. E. C. Alston from a mere near Thetford, Norfolk. For a short time this exceptionally old-established record was replaced on the list by a fish 2 oz heavier caught on a nymph from Pitsford Reservoir in Northamptonshire in 1986 by Mr D. Webb when fly-fishing for trout. However, at a later date his catch was judged to be a rudd/roach hybrid and deleted, and the Rev. Alston's Norfolk rudd was reinstated.

This chain of events highlights two points: firstly, how even experts have difficulty distinguishing between rudd/roach hybrids (the British Record Fish Committee no less), and secondly, how susceptible rudd are to artificial flies. Reservoirs like Pitsford, well known for its prolific stocks of rudd (and roach), offers wonderful specimen fish potential to those bent on catching monster rudd with the fly rod. While presenting a slow-sinking nymph in the upper water layers would seem the best technique, big Pitsford rudd are often caught on large, fry-imitating attractor flies of 2–3 in in length. Like most cyprinids, when massive fry shoals pack tightly together (a ready food source) adult rudd become cannibalistic and regularly chomp into their own offspring (see Fly-fishing, p. 217).

REPRODUCTION AND HYBRIDS

Rudd move onto the weedy shallows to spawn at some time during the very same April to June period in which roach and bream also endeavour to propagate their species. The tiny, pinkish, translucent eggs adhere to whatever medium is available at the time; soft weeds, rush and reed stems, submerged marginal grasses, fibrous tree roots, etc., and take from 10 to 12 days to hatch.

Although rudd sometimes spawn slightly later than the roach, inevitably where all three species are present in a river or stillwater, rudd/roach hybrids, rudd/bream and roach/bream are all a very real possibility. I have already described what to look for in a roach/bream hybrid (see p. 52), and owing to the obvious golden rudd-like sheen along its flanks, a rudd/bream hybrid is not difficult to identify.

The rudd/roach hybrid, as I have already suggested, really does cause the most confusion, and even arguments, between anglers. Many such hybrids look remarkably like a true rudd or a true roach. Some will have the extended bottom lip of the rudd, but a considerably paler body colour when compared to the rich, buttery gold of a true rudd, while others will be roach-like in colouration with a noticeable rudd-like angle or keel between the tail root and vent. The lips vary anywhere between level and the bottom one fully protruding.

The best way to approach the subject is firstly to enjoy the fight and physical being of such a lovely fish, especially if it is a specimen, and then if in any doubt whatsoever as to its parentage, simply call it a hybrid.

LOCATION

Big rivers

To the best of my knowledge, while the rudd is not prolific in any large river in England, it is common throughout most of the river systems in southern Ireland – even the larger, deep and often fast rivers like the mighty Shannon. Like roach, rudd, too, give away their position by porpoising at dawn and again at dusk during the summer, and may be taken at almost any depth from just beneath the surface to just above bottom in up to 20 ft of water.

Generally speaking, however, they are more commonly located immediately beyond the shallow marginal shelf, among the surface covering of yellow water-lilies or beside clumps of bullrushes.

Irrigation drains and canals

Rudd are most prolific in systems that remain clear for much of the season, and which contain extensive beds of bottom-rooted plants such as Canadian pond-weed, mill-foil and hornwort. The same can be said of defunct, over-grown canals, even those not particularly rich in aquatic plants. Find a lone patch of lilies or a strip of sweet reed grass, and if there are any rudd present, you will have located them.

Estate lakes and meres

Rudd fair best of all, and usually grow to specimen proportions, in meres and the kind of rich and weedy

Rudd love thick beds of bullrush and reeds, lily-pads and fertile, clean, clear water where they can be seen sucking in hatching flies and their nymphs from the surface during the summer months.

clear-water habitat created by damming streams meandering through prime farmland. Estate lakes all follow a similar similar format. They are shallow one end, where rich silt beds form due to sediment brought down by the feeder stream, and increase in depth gradually towards the dam wall at the other end.

In the summer, rudd feed among the shallows from the surface on hatching midges, whose larvae, the bloodworm, live by the million in the layers of rich organic silt. And in winter they tend to shoal up tightly in the deepest water by the dam itself. Rudd love the shade provided by overhanging willows and extensive beds of water-lilies,

whether fringing the margins or planted way out in the middle. Look through binoculars and you will observe the pads shake as rudd pick off snails and their eggs from the undersides. They also love to patrol and work along tall reedbeds, feeding on insects and algae clinging to the stems, which can be seen 'knocking' together on a perfectly still day.

Even estate lakes that contain few predators and are over-populated with rudd still produce a large enough larder of natural food for the adult rudd to average out at somewhere between 6 and 12 oz, plus the occasional one over 1 lb.

Reservoirs and huge lakes

In huge natural lakes pinpoint the largest beds of common reeds or lilies skirting shallow bays and you will have found rudd. Watch, too, for their splashy rises during that last hour of evening light, when they furrow the surface sucking in hatching flies, sedges and the like. As they are never slow to move with their food source, when huge clouds of daphnia, for instance, drift with the surface tow to a particular shoreline, rudd will be there. In this situation, small amounts of loose feed catapulted regularly around the float are the only attraction required.

One of the best means of location is attraction, and a ruse that works especially well when you are afloat on a large water (because you then have the means to follow the shoal) is to scatter a pint of floating casters over the surface and watch from afar through binoculars. Once rudd find the free meal and start feeding in earnest, row quietly up to within a long float cast, and keep the shoal interested by catapulting out extra casters every so often (see Flat peacock quill rig, p. 165).

In vast man-made reservoirs where great depths exist, particularly at the dam end, make a point of seeking out the shallowest, weediest bays and inlets if you want summer rudd. For roach, explore areas of medium depths during the summer months by keeping an eye on the surface for rolling fish, switching attention to the deepest swims when really cold weather sets in and there are few visual pointers.

DISTRIBUTION

Just like the roach, rudd are common throughout most of Europe, even in southern Scandinavia. Although it is quite rare in Scotland, Ireland, especially the south, offers superlative rudd fishing for both quality and quantity in just about every stillwater and river system. It is indeed far more widely distributed than the roach.

As I have hinted already, it is a sad fact that due to the species' intolerance of doctored waters (chemical and farming pollution) the rudd is nowhere near so widespread as it once was. It nevertheless still seems to flourish in reed-fringed meres and in man-made pits, lakes, reservoirs and especially in estate lakes.

TENCH
(Tinca tinca)

This 5 lb tench was attracted to a carpet of sweetcorn scattered just beyond the fringe of overhanging trees, and succumbed to three kernels on a size 10 hook presented with the lift method.

With its distinctive olive green livery, tiny red 'teddy bear eyes' and dark grey-brown fins, the tench is seldom confused, by fishermen, with any other species. Even those who never practise the gentle art will know of the tench by its odd name and be aware of its green body, for there is not another freshwater species so unusually coloured. Yet we take its unique, friendly form for granted.

Everything about the tench suggests strength and durability – its thick-set, oval body shape, incredibly large, rounded fins and particularly thick tail root. Small wonder they fight so doggedly. The males appear noticeably chunky and shorter than the females, and are easily distinguishable by their 'crinkly' spoon-shaped pelvic fins, the second ray of which is enlarged, and by the lumpy muscles or 'gonads' just above the pelvic fin. When gently compressed against the body the pelvics completely hide the male's vent, whereas the neater, almost pointed pelvic fins of the female do not. The mouth, which if anything is upward pointing (one reason why tench must stand on their heads when feeding from the bottom – see 'Feeding') with thick-rimmed rubber lips, has a tiny barbel at each corner and is semi-protrusible.

Situated in the back of its throat are the powerful pharyngeal teeth used for mincing larger food items into pulp for swallowing. Maggots, for instance, which re-appear as mere skins have obviously been crushed by the pharyngeal teeth, the soft insides sucked out and the unwanted parts (including your hook) spat out, even

though the bite was not identified at the time. Because these teeth are never seen (unless you cut them from a decaying fish) most anglers would perhaps not realize tench are so equipped. But like all cyprinids (even gudgeon and dace have them), tench could not masticate their food without these flatish plates of bone, which are not dissimilar to those of the crucian carp.

Tench are a decidedly lethargic, ponderous fish. They thrive best in stillwaters, slow-moving stretches of low-land rivers, canals, drains and so on, especially where vegetation is dense, because from soft weeds it obtains much of its natural diet – insect larvae, snails, shrimps, asellus, water boatmen, and so on. It also gorges on free-roaming zooplanktons such as daphnia, the largest of the water fleas, and is well equipped to siphon through the detritus, that first few inches of decaying bottom vegeta-tion, in search of annelid worms and midge larvae (see 'Feeding'). It never seems to be bothered by the lack of oxygen down amongst the silt, and is probably more tolerant of low levels of dissolved oxygen than any other freshwater species.

A curiosity that has occurred only during the last decade or so is the fact that in a fair proportion of fisheries tench are now attaining very much larger weights than ever before – the current British record being a monster of 14 lb 3 oz caught by Phil Gooriah from Wrasbury pits in 1987. For instance, for over 30 years up until 1963 the tench record had slowly increased from 7 lb to just over 9 lb. Yet as I write this, tench of 7 lb and 8 lb are everyday catches in certain southern fisheries, particularly the rich gravel pits in Kent, Hertfordshire and Oxfordshire. For a high-value specimen these days enthusiasts in the know are looking towards tench of 9 lb plus, a fish which, 30 years ago, would have broken the record.

Lots of theories have been put forward as to why this is happening, of course. The favourite is that the huge quantities of high-nutritional-value paste and boiled baits that have been introduced (initially to attract carp), and which the tench have subsequently learnt to accept as natural food, has resulted in their growing very much larger.

However, is it really all down to the high-nutritional-value (HNV) baits? I have my doubts about this. Certainly the fluctuating seasons and weather patterns we are now experiencing on a global scale surely have some bearing on the matter, although it's difficult to isolate a direct link other than because the summers on average start later, more tench are caught at the beginning of the season so grossly over-full with spawn they weigh considerably heavier than their natural weight, probably by 2–3 lb.

Golden tench

This beautiful, breathtaking creature is more an aquariast's fish than an angler's quarry, though it does exist in a handful of fisheries around the country, particularly those without large predators like pike, which is not difficult to understand. To a predator the golden tench right from the fry stage must stand out like the proverbial sore thumb, just like albino fish, so their survival rate with every creature trying to get in on the act, including the ever-watchful heron, must be miniscule.

Often nicknamed 'banana fish', the golden tench is indeed the colour of a ripe banana even down to the black spots irregularly flecked over its body, though I have seen a fair number of golden tench completely free of any dark markings. It also sports a black eye, pink, translucent, rather petite fins, and overall a much slimmer profile than the common green tench. It is thus by comparison a poor fighter, nowhere near so powerful, though dogged nonetheless. Optimum size rarely exceeds 3 lb and this is large for the golden tench.

As with green tench the males are distinguishable from the females by their spoon-shaped pelvic fins and the lumpy muscles or gonads positioned immediately above them.

Strangely the two types, green and golden, to the best of my knowledge do not inter-breed or throw up mutants. Occasionally one catches a green tench etched with purple markings or blotches all over its head and body. But these I have always taken to be colour disorders in the pigmentation rather like purplish birth marks. Such markings have nothing to do with inter-breeding between golden and green tench.

FEEDING

Compared to carp for example, especially when living alongside and therefore in direct competition with them, tench come a poor second in making full use of the natural food at their disposal. They are by nature nowhere near so aggressive, and in reality are probably the most deliberate feeders of all freshwater fish. For tench to grow large they require an exceptionally rich environment, and only in such circumstances are both tench and carp able to attain huge proportions living together. Even then tench still need to outnumber the carp. Switched the other way around, carp will eat them out of house and home.

On really heavily stocked carp fisheries with next to no weed from which the tench can eek a living, and where the water is kept in a continual state of turbidity from the sheer number of carp feeding from the bottom at various times of the day, tench may not even be able to exist beyond a weight of 1 lb or so. Miniature tench of a few ounces seem able to grow among densely stocked carp because their infant food requirements are different. But once they require larger food particles higher up the chain, carp rule the roost and the tench can never reach anywhere near their full growth potential. Even adult tench of fully 2 to 3 lb purchased from fish farmers by clubs and lake-owners for stocking into densely populated carp fisheries can never compete. Inevitably they become thinner and thinner, barely scratching a living and merely surviving at half their normal body weight (and it is surprising just how thin tench can become) before being reduced to starvation by the carp. Obviously, these are uncommon circumstances but events I have witnessed on a handful of club waters

In the male tench on the left, the crinkly pelvic fins cover the vent and almost touch the anal fin. The lumpy protruding muscles, or gonads, are immediately above it. The female on the right has smooth, classic lines.

where the members have thought a second species was needed without realizing the consequences.

The nice thing about tench when they are feeding in earnest is that they often (though not always) send bubbles up to the surface to tell you where they are. If you watch the surface very carefully (never forget the binoculars – even for close-range observation they are indispensible) the route of each individual fish can usually be followed simply by relating to the groups of bubbles as they appear. In heavily pre-baited swims full of numbers of fish all moving agitatedly about, when the surface looks to all intents and purposes like a witches' cauldron, this just isn't possible. But in swims occupied by just a handful of tench, following the bubbles of individuals can prove almost as fascinating as hooking into one of them. Wherever strong-limbed trees overhang the swim, endeavour to reach a position overhead where you can look directly into the area (providing the water is clear) and observe the stream of bubbles rising from the tench. It teaches you so much about the fish's behaviour. There are in fact various kinds of bubbles attributed to tench which rise to the surface and you must learn to identify them. The tiny 'needle' bubbles made by the tench itself, which escape through its gill filaments as a result of it masticating its food, are perhaps the easiest to identify. Large patches of frothy bubbles, on the other hand, gases released from rotten vegetation in silty waters by the tench in their search for blood-worms, (midge larvae) their favourite natural food, just might be the work of carp or eels. So beware, even experienced anglers come to grief with these gas bubbles on occasion, and view anything 'frothy' with an open mind.

Tench also send up small groups of bubbles in clusters of just two or three, five or six at a time when they are feeding over hard gravel. These are noticeably smaller than those produced by carp, and so there should be little confusion. They are made when the tench stands on its head to suck up baits one at a time and rights itself to chew them, thus emitting only a limited amount. It then moves on a foot or so to the next food item (a grain of corn, piece of flake, etc) and another small group of bubbles rise upwards.

The interpretation and identification of bubbles, and matching them to particular fish, is almost a separate hobby. So try whenever you are given the opportunity to observe tench feeding in crystal-clear water. As an experiment, take a landing-net pole or a bank stick and watch what happens on the surface when you rupture the detritus, that decaying top layer of bottom silt, just as a tench might do when it characteristically stands on its head and with a thrust of its tail runs its nose along the bottom to dislodge and throw up particles of natural food. This of course is why raking or dragging a silty swim proves so effective (p. 125) – the tench has its work done for it.

Tench are unquestionably at their most difficult to tempt when they are preoccupied on microscopic food items, in particular zooplankton such as daphnia. There is no mistaking this transparent water flea whose body is tinged a red-brown colour. When it is blown into the margins by wind drift or a strong underwater tow, the concentrations are so thick it's impossible to see the bottom even through gin-clear water. It appears to all intents and purposes as though the water is littered with brick dust. And during the warmer months when daphnia multiplies rapidly, it is to tench what krill is to whales.

REPRODUCTION

Courtship begins with groups of males, from two up to several at a time, following the females; four or five males all vying for the attentions of a single female is not out of the ordinary. Actual egg-laying sometimes continues throughout the entire day and night, but generally early mornings are chosen. The sudden change in air temperature at that time of day is enough to stimulate a response from the female. She spreads the sticky carpet of eggs through the weeds while the males disperse their milky white milt to fertilize them. As their quiet nature suggests, tench are nowhere near so noisy as carp when propagating their species. They prefer to lay their eggs (unlike carp) in the thickest clumps of soft weeds they can find, and even in the carpets of crunchy, bright green surface algae which clog the surface during summer when water levels are low and there are long periods of bright sunshine.

Each female carries an enormous amount of eggs – up to, and even over, one quarter of its body weight – which is why a 9½ lb female can easily tip the scales at over 12 lb when full of spawn. Once the tiny translucent eggs hatch, after 6–10 days, the alevins are initially reliant on yolk from the egg. They then feed on microscopic planktons amongst the weed in which they hide. Anglers may not come into contact with the small tench for at least several years.

In most fisheries the young stay in the weed, feeding on minute aquatic life, and rarely come into contact with an angler's bait. From about 1 lb upwards, the tench seems willing to leave the sanctity of the weed for long periods and to join its larger brethren in small groups in order to feed, by which time it is liable to suck in food containing a hook.

LOCATION

Tench give away their position by sending tiny feeding bubbles up to the surface, and a more exact, instant method of locating them does not exist. It is also true to say, however, that even with a fair-sized group of tench packed tightly into a relatively small area, they do not always bubble. It is imperative, therefore, that you know the type of habitats they prefer in various kinds of waters if you wish to catch tench with consistency. Make no mistake: there really is no substitute for learning the craft of observation at the waterside. There is invariably a visual pointer when tench are present, no matter what the conditions, although a situation such as continual really heavy rain can make it difficult to identify. Even on decidedly 'off days', however, when there is little feeling of activity and a complete lack of surface bubbles, there will be a sign or two of tench activity somewhere: reed stalks 'knocking', a sudden but distinctive calm patch amid a rippled surface, the rounded head and shoulders of a tench silently porpoising, patches of discoloured water, rocking lily pads, and so on

These are just a few of your pointers, so don't forget the binoculars. You will be able to observe things with them that it is not possible to see with the naked eye. Heavy, extremely powerful binoculars are more of a hindrance than a help, because after a while their weight around the neck becomes unbearable, and they spend the rest of the day back in their case. Ideally, you want a lightweight pair with a magnification of 8 × 30 or 10 × 40, which can be hung around the neck all day if required without discomfort. Then they are to hand at a moment's notice so that you can observe sudden surface disturbances in soft weed-beds or among lilies, locate sudden eruptions of bubbles beyond the swim being fished, and keep track of tench should they move on. Binoculars are very much a

working tool and should be used as such. No one should set off fishing for species like carp, bream and tench, which portray their presence by surface activity, without them.

It goes without saying that a pair of polaroid glasses are also indispensable.

Stillwater habitats

Many facets of watercraft are directly linked to location, and one of the most interesting (for some almost a hobby in itself) is the study of water plants. As tench are never far from vegetation when given the choice, locate their

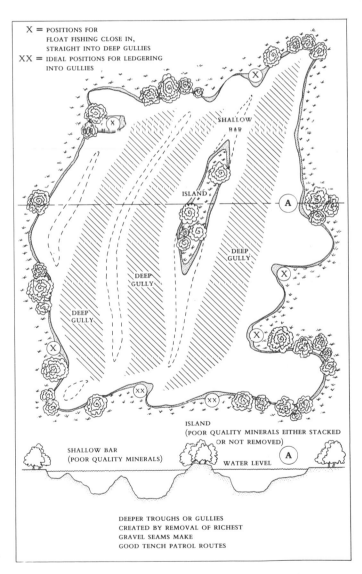

FIGURE 1.21 *A mature gravel pit seen from surface level, and (bottom) a cross-section of the same gravel pit, showing how gullies and deep holes – the tench patrol routes – are formed*

With distinct black eyes and irregular black flecks over a bright yellow body, the rare golden tench is nicknamed 'banana fish'.

favourite habitats and you have located tench. It's as simple as that. As small waters such as ponds and pits are a microcosm of much larger sheets of water, because each will in fact contain similar features, similar plants, and be overhung by similar trees, an understanding of the natural history of ponds and gravel pits will stand you in good stead for locating tench wherever you fish (fig. 1.21). For example, knowledge of the kind of bottom strata preferred by a particular plant will tell you the nature of the bottom in that area of water, be it soft or hard (see Habitats).

River tench

Though comparatively few anglers bother specifically with them, tench in slow, deepish lowland rivers offer an interesting and challenging proposition when they are most active throughout the summer months. The odd fish might even turn up in the winter, especially during and immediately after heavy flooding which has the tendency to wake them up. They are, however, considerably more active in moving water during the warmer months.

Like their stillwater counterparts, river tench love to browse through the soft, cabbage-like leaves of the common yellow water-lily. They might turn up anywhere, but are more liable to frequent choice habitats like beds of lilies. In addition, search deep and weedy mill pools, overshoot pools, confluences where ditches or sidestreams join the main flow creating a depression, deep holes on acute bends, beneath overhanging willows, and so on. These are the areas to concentrate on.

Curiously, I have also caught tench from the deepest

water beneath fast-flowing weir pools; however, it is very much quieter down on the bottom and obviously more to their liking. Built to face a fast flow continuously tench are certainly not; conversely, don't be surprised when large baits like a whole lobworm or lump of bread flake intended for bream or chub produces a tench.

Winter tench

In a typical British winter, with occasional falls of snow and stillwaters frozen over during much of the coldest weather, winter tench are not really a worthwhile proposition. Their metabolic rate seems to slow considerably more than that of carp, although where tench share carp fisheries, and so regularly feed on the boilies introduced to keep the carp interested, they are of course far more commonly caught. And during mild spells brought about by mild south-westerly or westerly winds, the odd tench can be expected at some time during the day.

In the right weather and water conditions combined, winter tench are certainly on the cards, especially from shallow lakes which warm quickly and get them moving about on the look out for food. Simply scale down a bit on summer strengths of line and hook sizes, and use smaller baits and far less groundbait or loose feed. And be rather more patient when waiting for bites. Otherwise, the techniques and baits do not really change.

Try swims close to habitats which offer some kind of protection, such as overhanging or partly submerged trees, or amongst the rotting roots where summer lily-beds once graced the surface. Tench will still be there even in winter.

DISTRIBUTION

Within the British Isles the tench is even more widely spread than carp. While they are not exactly common in Scotland, tench are distributed throughout England and Wales with tremendous concentrations all over Ireland. They have a natural preference for ponds, pits, lakes, meres, broads and reservoirs, but there are few rivers which do not harbour at least a few tench. They are so prolific in the slow-moving Lincolnshire drains and

throughout the Great Ouse system, for instance, that a good bag of river tench is very likely from any number of locations. Even well-known fast rivers like the Hampshire Avon contain tench, and periodically tench even choose to occupy fast-running areas. Weir pools in particular hold a special attraction during the summer months and whenever the river is in flood. The tench has also been stocked into North American waters and those of Australasia.

ZANDER
(Stizostedion lucioperca)

The zander is a predator and consumes large quantities of small fish including its own kind, just like the perch, the pike, the trout and the chub. Moreover, it does this successfully all over Europe in lakes and river systems, living in complete harmony and forming a natural balance with other predators and with all cyprinid species. And once British rivers are able to support cyprinid species in sufficient numbers again, through less damaging farming and drainage practices, I see no reason whatsoever why the zander cannot be a valuable part of the ecosystem. Indeed, proof of this lies in the fact that every stillwater (unaffected by water authorities and farmers) into which zander have been stocked in Britain has benefitted from an additional predator for anglers to catch, without a reduction in sport with cyprinid shoal fish.

The usual run of moderate-sized zander that pack together 10 or (on large waters) even 20 to a shoal, is between 2 and 5 lb. Anything topping 7 or 8 lb is a worthy catch, especially on reasonably light tackle (a 6 lb outfit). And, of course, the goal to aim for is one of over 10 lb – the proverbial 'double'. The largest ever caught in Britain came from a Cambridgeshire stillwater to the rod of R. Meadows in 1988 and weighed 18½ lb. In European waters, however, zander over 20 lb are far from uncommon.

Although the zander is a distinct species, and most certainly not a pike/perch hybrid, as non-anglers especially like to describe it, its second Latin name, *lucioperca*, does refer to its similarity to the pike and perch. Its elongated body, half way between round and oval in cross-section, is covered in small, exceedingly rough scales and a most distinct lateral line starting high up at the top of the gill cover and ending midway into the tail root.

The head is quite neat relative to the zander's size, slightly flattened at the top with a pair of strong jaws, into which are set (one very good reason to use a wire trace) a galaxy of small teeth plus four large canines at the front – two in the top, two in the lower jaw. With these stabbing teeth, the zander grabs and quickly cripples its prey.

The zander's fins, especially the dorsal, are large. The dorsal is separated into two, just like the perch (hence their

During windy, overcast conditions, zander will feed at almost any time of the day, especially in heavily coloured waters. David Wilson caught this silvery fish on a small ledgered deadbait. Note its double dorsal fin, the first spiked and flecked, and that cold, opaque eye.

similarity), the first consisting of strong spikes and the second comprising soft rays. Both, incidentally, are liberally marked with dark flecks. These markings also cover the tail, which is forked and sometimes coloured a pale yellowy-orange. The anal, pelvic and pectoral fins are almost translucent and virtually devoid of any pigment.

Body colour can vary quite dramatically, possibly more so than any other freshwater species. For instance, zander inhabiting waters that are permanently and thickly coloured will appear quite drab; grey to buff coloured along the back down to the lateral line and then pale gold below, with a creamy white belly. Those living in clear water might even show a mixture of blue and steel-grey along the back with several vertical bars of dark blue down to the lateral line, with sides of metallic silver and pewter and a silvery white belly below.

The strange eye, opaque and rather cold, is large, indicating that zander are well equipped for hunting their prey in coloured water and during the hours of darkness.

FEEDING

Although young zander feed on invertebrates such as daphnia and shrimps, and are even occasionally caught on maggots and worms (as is the odd whopper) they do

become almost entirely predatory from around 6 in to 8 in long, consuming much smaller fish, including their own kind and the fry of any species present. Mostly they keep close to the bottom, hunting collectively as a pack, and are particularly active during the low-light conditions of dawn and dusk, and throughout the hours of darkness. This is not to say that during bright sunshine they do not feed, because they do intermittently, but with nowhere near the same kind of aggression. During poor light they have better vision than their prey, and the zander knows it.

Shoal fish in the 4–6 in range are the perfect diet (and bait size) for adult zander, but they take much larger bream and roach. In so far as fishing for them is concerned, however, it is wise to use only small baits, otherwise a large proportion of zander runs will be missed on the strike.

REPRODUCTION

Zander spawn in the early spring during quite low water temperatures and afterwards predate heavily on their own fry. The transparent eggs are laid in the shallows among gravel or the fibrous matts of sub-surface tree roots like those of the willow, or around the stems of reeds and rushes. Incubation takes up to 2 weeks, and once hatched the fry live on their yolk sac before commencing a diet of zooplanktons.

LOCATION

In both still and flowing water, wherever they have the choice, zander will invariably choose to occupy the deepest and darkest spots. Moreover, zander use sub-surface features for ambushing their prey, and any sudden drop-off from shallow to deep water, such as where the bottom shelves steeply away from dense beds of marginal reeds and rushes, or between the supports of road bridges should be immediately considered as potential zander hot-spots (see fig. 1.22).

Really low road and railway bridges spanning narrow drains and rivers are among the best locations of all due to the much-reduced light values beneath, even during the hours of daylight. In fact, the mere presence of a bridge spanning a drain that runs featureless for mile upon mile makes it the obvious spot to expect zander. Large pump-pools, where the water is regularly transferred from one drain to another, are usually productive spots because regular pumping will keep a deep hole clear in the lower pool, much to the liking of zander. Wide confluences where one drain joins another also hold great attraction for zander, no doubt because of the increased populations of small fish that gather there.

Small overshoot weirs or sluices that continually cascade water from streams, ditches and storm drains at a higher level into the main drain, no matter how small and seemingly insignificant, hold the key to potential zander hotspots. The tumbling, well-oxygenated water attracts massive shols of fry which, in turn, attract predators.

If there is one kind of weather pattern guaranteed to make zander active – often throughout the entire day – and produce a run virtually at any moment between dawn and dusk, it is during gale-force winds. It might be that strong surface movement accompanied by overcast conditions make small shoal fish mass closer to the bottom, making

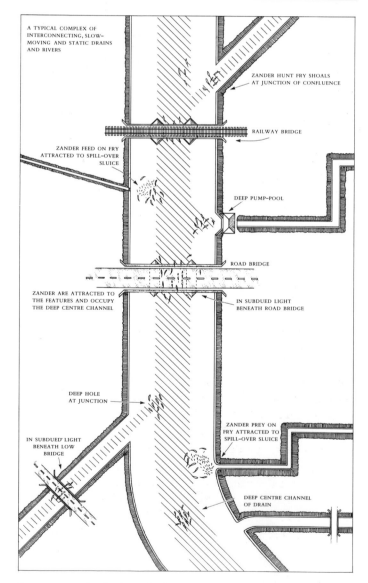

A TYPICAL COMPLEX OF INTERCONNECTING, SLOW-MOVING AND STATIC DRAINS AND RIVERS

ZANDER HUNT FRY SHOALS AT JUNCTION OF CONFLUENCE

RAILWAY BRIDGE

ZANDER FEED ON FRY ATTRACTED TO SPILL-OVER SLUICE

DEEP PUMP-POOL

ROAD BRIDGE

ZANDER ARE ATTRACTED TO THE FEATURES AND OCCUPY THE DEEP CENTRE CHANNEL

IN SUBDUED LIGHT BENEATH ROAD BRIDGE

DEEP HOLE AT JUNCTION

ZANDER PREY ON FRY ATTRACTED TO SPILL-OVER SLUICE

IN SUBDUED LIGHT BENEATH LOW BRIDGE

DEEP CENTRE CHANNEL OF DRAIN

FIGURE 1.22 *Fenland zander location*

them more attainable to the zander, or that zander are motivated into a searching, feeding mood by the strong sub-surface tow created by strong winds. After hours of inactivity, it is no coincidence when several runs happen in quick succession within minutes of a strong flow starting up, regardless of light intensity at that time.

In lakes and gravel pits, all the deepest, darkest areas, especially those where deep water is shaded by over-hanging trees, are the most likely zander hotspots. The shoals become particularly tightly packed in cold condi-tions, so an exact knowledge gained from careful and extensive plummeting of the water being fished will prove an enormous benefit.

Though zander are cold water predators, they become very localized when water temperature really drops and severe weather sets in. So if you wish to catch them consistently, concentrate throughout the autumn and during settled bouts of really mild winter weather.

This is exactly what a small fish sees a moment or two before the zander opens those hideous jaws. Note the four large canines, used for stabbing and immobilizing prey.

Zander are particularly suited to wide, deep drains such as the Middle Level and Great Ouse Relief and Cut-Off Channels, where packs of zander roam the centre channel and provide good autumn sport.

DISTRIBUTION

The zander has now been legally (and illegally) spread throughout much of southern England into both river systems and stillwaters. It is, however, absent from Scotland and Ireland. No doubt one day, certainly within the next few decades, every suitable river system will contain them. I have used the word suitable with delibera-tion because the species prefers sluggish, coloured water with low visibility, and does not fare well in fast, clear-flowing rivers. Inevitably, through its own choice, the zander will not spread everywhere within the British Isles.

The species covers most of Europe and southern Scandinavia, and two species – the walleye and sauger – are both prolific throughout the USA and Canada. In the Russian states lives a similar species, plus other, very much smaller zander-like freshwater fish that weighs only a few ounces, even when fully matured.

The zander is also present in North Africa, as I found out when fishing the dams of Morocco. No doubt introduced as a food source (and very good eating it is, too) by the French during their occupation.

CHAPTER TWO

HABITATS

RIVER HABITATS

MILL AND
WEIR POOLS

STILLWATER HABITATS

By far the quickest and most accurate way of locating a fellow human being is to knock on his front door. And believe it or not, there are many instances in freshwater fishing when exactly the same routine can be followed, simply by putting your knowledge of natural history to good use in recognizing particular plants or trees living both in and out of the water.

Watercraft, particularly the study of water plants, can be almost a hobby in itself, because if you learn which habitats particular species are attracted to, you have located them. Moreover, certain plants prefer either a soft or hard bottom strata and will only live happily in a certain depth band. Therefore, within a few minutes of arriving beside a summer's lake, for instance, which you have not previously seen, let alone fished, you will be able to formulate a fair idea of the depths over much of the lake, the bottom strata, and even where if present, certain species are most likely to be situated.

Taking this a step further, as small waters like ponds and pits, streams and small rivers, are microcosms of much larger sheets of water, and because each will contain similar features, similar plants, and be overhung by similar trees, you will be able to relate fish to their habitats wherever you fish.

RIVER HABITATS

Trees

Of all natural habitats, those provided by trees are the favourite of chub, barbel, perch and big roach. Overhanging alders, willows, chestnuts, ash, beech, blackthorn and hawthorn bushes, elders and the like, not only provide shade over the water under which fish love to lie, but in addition their root systems sometimes create caverns which go far back into the clay banking.

Undercut banks

Most undercuts do not consist just of a vertical hollowing of the banking, but are horizontal caverns, not unlike a rabbit warren. They have a long shallow entrance that opens out into a large chamber immediately below the fringe of fibrous sub-surface tree roots.

The bright red matting of willow roots, for instance, upon which many species love to spawn, grow from 1 to 3 ft below the surface. Beneath this matting two dozen chub or a group of barbel may well be hiding in a cavern without the slightest chance of being seen.

This, of course, is how chub, for instance, are suddenly able to perform disappearing tricks when they have been scared, leaving the noisy or clumsy fisherman totally perplexed. Some undercuts reach so far into the bank (up to several feet) that if you were to stand on the very edge of the bank beneath the tree and peer down, the chub might very well be behind you. Naturally, undercuts can usually be expected on the outside of acute bends, where the water comes sweeping round and is continually eeking away at the soil beneath the tree roots. They exist also beneath trees (particularly alders and willows) overhanging perfectly straight sections of bank, and beneath weir sills, lock cuttings, wooden pilings and so on.

Overhangs and rafts

During the summer months trees also provide a never-ending supply of food in the way of falling insects from above. Those whose lower limbs are submerged and have collected flotsam and silt over the years, form a dark, impenetrable cavern that is capable of housing a large number of resident barbel.

BEST HABITATS – RIVERS

	trees	overhangs	rafts	fallen trees	marginal plant cover	bullrushes	weedbeds	road and rail bridges
Barbel	•	•	•	•		•	•	•
Bream								•
Chub	•	•	•	•	•	•	•	•
Grayling						•		•
Perch	•	•	•	•		•		•
Pike		•		•	•	•		•
Roach	•	•	•		•	•	•	•

This lovely piece of the Hampshire Avon may look drab, but numerous fish-attracting features exist. Overhanging willows in the foreground hold chub among the entanglement of sunken branches. The slow run close into the bank, where matted brown rushes overhang, is favoured by roach and the odd large pike. Dace and grayling occupy the fast bubbly water in the drop-over weir where the river's course divides. Further downstream, where the river narrows around deep, acute bends, a shoal of perch is in residence.

In large and small rivers, particularly where mature willows and alders overhang acute bends, expect the banking beneath to be undercut, carved by the force of water during flooding. In these dark caverns species like chub and barbel may hide during bright sunshine when the water is crystal clear. Chub also love to lie immediately below the water-lapping foliage in readiness to pounce upon juicy titbits like caterpillars as they fall upon the surface.

That there is a pecking order for occupying the choicest swims is beyond doubt. Pike also love to lie among the entanglement of submerged branches. What better ambush point from which to attack a passing shoal of roach or dace.

Marginal plant cover

Marginal caverns formed beneath rafts of floating sweet reed grass, sedges, dense beds of watercress, and so on, have enormous capacity for hiding species like chub, roach and pike. It is along the banks of clear-flowing rivers prolific in sweet reed grass that you can walk for mile upon mile fish-spotting, and come to believe that there is next to nothing worth catching in the entire river. In fact, all the better, wiser fish are well out of sight beneath the first 2 to 6 ft of floating raft, most of which looks like part of the bank until you try walking on it. A 5 ft wide by 100 yd long raft of floating sweet reed grass can obscure a very large number of fish.

During the summer months when cut weed collects around the trailing edges of a willow, the holding capacity of the habitat could easily double, resulting in quite disproportionate-sized groups of barbel occupying an area little more than a few square yards.

Fallen trees

Before the drainage department of the local river authority performs their 'jobsworth' and removes trees which topple during gales or because of old age, make sure you capitalize on the situation. Within days (sometimes hours) of a large tree crashing into the river, fish will take up residence. And it has been my experience that the largest trees will contain the largest concentrations of chub and barbel. Moreover, the snaggiest spot within the honey-comb of sub-surface passages created by the sunken woodwork invariably harbours the largest specimens.

Unfortunately, this particular plant can drastically narrow a river due to the sediment which gathers around its enormous root structure and which eventually is claimed back by the land. It does, however, tend to keep whatever channel is left to a reasonably uniform depth, often with as much water below the leading edges as there is in mid-stream: a good point to remember for both summer and winter, especially during heavy flooding.

Though the careless angler who walks heavily on marshy ground will rarely see chub, for instance, as they slide out from beneath overhangs to move up river and feed, it is the mixture of diffused light and tranquillity which makes the chub and roach feel safe beneath overhanging vegetation. During undisturbed daylight hours chub especially love nothing better than to lie facing the flow on the very edge of the overhang, or even a few inches beyond the trailing edges in clear water, on the look out for titbits brought downstream by the current or food dropping into the water from the land. However, they can melt away very quickly.

Water crowfoot sprouts from the gravel bottom in long, wavering beds, topped by erect, daisy-like white and yellow flowers. Species like barbel and chub adore clear runs between the weedbeds and the shade they provide. Large depressions are also favoured during the summer months by small groups of very large river bream because current pressure is, to a large extent, offset by the weedbeds immediately upstream.

Bullrushes

The true bullrush only grows in a firm, gravel bottom, and its tall, tapering, onion-like, blue-green stems grace the surface of the river in irregular-shaped clumps or beds, slightly bowed and gently quivering in the pull of the current. Bullrushes line the shallows in depths up to 3 ft and colonize shallow bars, even in the middle of the river-bed, and sometimes in huge clumps attracting perch, roach, grayling, pike, chub and barbel. In fact, above all others, this plant attracts barbel like bees to the proverbial honey-pot. The barbel feed on snails and eggs, plus a whole host of aquatic insect larvae that adhere to the base

of the tough, perfectly round stems and upon the harvest of freshwater shrimps that scurry from one patch of stems to another.

Bullrush stems provide an interesting network of corridors and passageways along the bottom, with clean gravel or sandy runs between them – the perfect habitat, providing sanctuary from harsh light and bankside disturbances, and with a readily available larder of food on tap. So whenever you find bullrushes, even if only a few isolated patches in a river where they do not commonly grow, expect to find either chub, pike or barbel. Even during the winter months, when all that can be seen is a few broken stems protruding from just above the surface, barbel will not be far away. During flood time they gather behind what is left of the previous year's bullrush stumps for protection out of the main flow. When the river runs cold, low and clear, providing little else in the way of natural cover, barbel worm their wiry bodies right in between the dead and decaying stems, venturing out into open water only during low light conditions and at night, and occasionally for the thoughtful fisherman who introduces a regular stream of loose feed such as casters, maggots or worm fragments, from a position a long way upstream so as not to alarm them.

Long, flowing weedbeds

I use the word 'weed' here only as a rough description because plants like the water crowfoot, of which there are several varieties, with their delicate daisy-like flowers, are amongst the most beautiful of flowering aquatic plants. The potomogeton pondweeds also grow in long, flowing beds, providing a mass of tough, bright green leaves, beneath and between which species like chub and barbel love to hide throughout the summer months. So do not immediately discount distinctly open parts of the river barren of obvious bankside habitat features like over-hanging trees. Down there close to the gravel bottom, beneath the mountain of greenery, in a world of silence and much reduced light, even on the brightest day, you can find chub, often in the kind of numbers you would consider absolutely impossible when viewing the same stretch of river from the bank through polaroid glasses.

Only in the early morning around dawn and again in the evening will chub choose to leave their habitat, rising to lie immediately below the surface to take advantage of hatching aquatic insect life.

Those who regularly fish-spot for barbel know only too well how one minute a clear run between flowing weed beds appears to be completely empty, and the very next the current sways the tail end of the weed mass momentarily to one side, revealing beneath it the shapes of numerous barbel that are then covered again just as quickly. If you are not concentrating, such happenings can seem like a mirage.

Road and rail bridges

Despite the thoroughness and expertise of civil engineers, the power of flowing water can never be underestimated, which is why many species are attracted to these man-made habitats.

However, much depends on the formation of the river-bed both up and down stream, the angle of the main flow to the bridge, the depth beneath and, of course, the construction of the bridge itself. Those resting on steel or concrete pillars, for instance, are likely to support at least a small group of barbel or chub, which shelter behind the pillars and in the undercuts eroded by the continual force of the water pushing against the concrete footings.

Where the river narrows to pass beneath a bridge, this in

subdued light, even during the brightness of a summer's day, are by far the most productive swims for bream and barbel I have ever fished. The occupants of such a swim are willing to feed at any time.

Bridges spanning the river on a bend are well worth exploring. A deeper run is always dug out on the outside of the bend beneath the bridge by the force of the current, and this is where species like chub, roach, grayling or barbel will be lying. Such swims also produce during times of heavy flooding because the occupants move across to occupy the slacker water on the inside of the bend close in to the bank.

Canoe observation

Strange though it may seem, most species are far less intimidated by someone's presence actually in or on the water than by that same person crunching along the bank. So if you own a canoe, put it to good use during the close

Just look at these mouth-watering swims between the old and new bridges spanning the majestic River Severn at Atcham. Wonderful fish-holding habitats are created by the line of trees, where chub and barbel reside beneath overhanging foliage and down below in the dark, deep runs beneath the supports. Such areas attract shoals of roach, perch and pike, with a population of eels in every crack and crevice eeked from the foundations by current erosion.

This quiet section of the River Shannon immediately upstream of Meelick Loch in souther Ireland contains a totally unspoilt river habitat, supporting massive shoals of large bream, which browse the centre basin. Rudd are prolific to over 2 lb and work just outside the marginal fringe of tall reeds and bullrushes, while tench meander through the beds of common yellow (Nuphar lutea) *and white water-lilies* (Nymphaea alba).

itself creates a faster push of water and thus will attract species like chub, grayling and barbel. Ancient brick road-bridges spanning wide rivers are more liable to attract than modern constructions. This is because time will have eroded the brickwork at river-bed level and created the odd undercut.

Bridges that are very low to the water, guaranteeing

season and during the middle of summer when levels are low and the water is crystal clear. Be careful, of course, not to upset other river fishermen by paddling through their swims.

Searching a river course by canoe is the most accurate method of location I know next to scuba-diving, and is by far the quickest way of ascertaining the whereabouts and numbers of chub, barbel, roach or bream, etc., in a previously unexplored part of the river. Providing you sit quietly with minimal paddle movement, fish will permit the canoe to come quite close before moving position.

Extremely long sections of the river, and even entire stretches between mills several miles apart, can be covered in a comparatively short space of time with the help of a fellow fisherman, two roof racks and a double canoe. The secret is to deposit one car at the downstream mill, before driving the canoe to the starting point well up river, where the second car is left. You can then go happily with the flow, allowing the current to drift the canoe close by all the obvious habitat swims, knowing transport is waiting for you at the other end. It is then a simple matter to pick up the second car.

Mill and weir pools

Of all habitats, weir-pools (and I use this word to cover both mill and weir pools because both have sluice gates) are the absolute tops. The mysterious, ever-changing pattern of surface currents is your visual guide to where species like roach, rudd, barbel and bream are lying below, bellies pressed close to the bottom. So take time to study the current direction carefully, looking in particular for runs of fast but steady water. Then use a heavy plummet to acquire an outline of the pool's bottom contours and its make up – gravel, silt, weedbeds, and so on.

Chub always feel happy about the extra depth of water above their heads, and the fact that the surface is broken by strong currents. To them it is as much sanctuary as the thickest weed-beds or submerged branches. Should the water flatten off during low levels, or the sluice be temporarily closed by the mill owner, the crafty chub will slink beneath the sill or work its way up into the pool under the mill house itself. Many old mills, whether still working or not, contain a dark cavernous sluice (completely hidden from view) into which water tumbles from above the mill in order to work the machinery. This is sometimes referred to as the 'turbine pit'. The largest chub of all are attracted to such mysterious sluices, which explains those rare one-off captures of giant chub, the size of which few anglers believe, quite simply because they are so rarely seen in the river proper. The goliath chub, of course, has been there all along. Hidden from view and leading a sedentary life during daylight hours, it only ventures into the open river under the cloak of darkness.

In the summer months, especially during low water levels, the shallow bars, deep holes or runs and weedbeds are usually plainly obvious when you look through polaroid glasses. In some pools it is even possible to pinpoint visually groups of barbel hugging the fast, gravelly runs at the tail end of each flush. They love that extra pace of the water, which roach or bream, for instance, do not. They will move deeper into the pool once winter arrives, of course, but summer observation fixes so many pieces of the jigsaw together and stands you in good stead when the river runs coloured and these natural features cannot be seen. As all weir-pools are different in size, shape, depth and positioning of the operative sluices, each has its own very special and definite character.

During the hottest part of the year, when the levels of dissolved oxygen throughout the entire river are correspondingly low, bream congregate in weir-pools, and even occupy the fastest runs. Being of slim profile when viewed head-on, they can in fact happily hold station against considerably faster currents than you would expect. So search for the shoals through polaroid glasses (even in turbulent water) from midday onwards when the sun is at its highest to pinpoint their exact location. The occasional rolling bream can be expected at dusk or dawn in the slower parts of the pool during summer and autumn, but in general fast-water bream tend not to porpoise with anywhere near the same regularity as those inhabiting slow-moving rivers and stillwaters.

Once winter sets in, do not expect any visual pointers, even from resident weir-pool bream. They will be down on the bottom in a deepish, comfortable part of the pool where the flow is slowest along with the roach shoals.

Pike will also be present, including, towards the latter part of the season, one or two whoppers. Perch also love the larder of food found in weir-pools and tend to occupy the slow, deep eddies to the sides of the working sluices, especially where the banks have been reinforced with wooden or steel pilings.

STILLWATER HABITATS

Sunken/overhanging trees

The presence of carp should always be expected beneath overhanging branches and those which actually trail the surface, because they love a roof over their heads during the hottest, brightest part of a summer's day. Whole trees or large foliage-covered limbs actually sunk below the surface provide fabulous hot spots all year through not only for carp but tench, rudd, perch, eels and catfish.

Sunken willows and alders in particular sprout, enormous, fibrous root structures which are teeming with aquatic insect larvae. They provide fish with both food and a retreat where the light from above is always diffused. It is no coincidence that the biggest specimens in small waters choose to live in the snaggiest habitats.

Reeds

Tall species of grass such as the common reed (often referred to as the Norfolk reed because it is commonly used for thatching in that county), cannot grow in really soft silt, or it would soon be uprooted in strong winds. So reeds grow thickest where the bottom is generally of a firm structure, such as in gravel, marl or clay.

During the early season the reeds with green, round stems, which may each grow to 10 ft high, can often be seen 'twitching', 'clanging' or 'swaying' when there is no wind, as species like rudd, tench, bream or carp either brush the stems as they move between them, or remove crustaceans and aquatic insect larvae such as the caddis grub.

Reed lines also play host to pike and perch, which love to lie in ambush between the upright stems.

Fallen and overhanging trees provide both cover and a prolific food source to many species in stillwaters. Eels and catfish make their homes among the sub-surface limbs and fibrous roots, while pike and perch use the tangle of branches as ambush points. Carp are attracted beneath lapping and sunken willow branches both summer and winter, while throughout the warm months, the splashy rises of rudd sucking in flies from the surface is a regular occurrence.

Reed mace

Another reed with a liking for a firmish bottom in which to anchor its thick, fibrous roots is the greater reed mace, best known for its large, brown, cigar-like seed heads. Often called the bullrush (wrongly), the reed mace and the lesser reed mace (a slimmer plant) both attract tench, carp and bream in numbers, particularly during the early season

BEST HABITATS – STILLWATERS

	sunken/ overhanging trees	reeds	reed mace	lilies	sweet reed grass	soft weeds	sub-surface features	scum lines
BREAM		•	•	•	•	•		
CARP	•	•	•	•	•	•	•	•
CATFISH	•							
EEL	•							
PERCH	•	•		•	•	•	•	
PIKE	•	•		•	•		•	
RUDD	•	•		•	•			•
TENCH	•	•	•	•	•	•	•	

when water temperatures are high. The fibrous-matting type roots at the base are much favoured by spawning fish, which regularly return throughout the following days to mop up their own and the spawn of others.

Beds of reed mace which make the best hot spots are those with their roots in marginal depths of between 2 and 3 ft. Because the stems do not grow so close together as those of the common reed, even large tench or carp may just pass between without so much as a shudder on the brown seed heads. So keep a sharp lookout for tail patterns, or bubbles on the surface amongst the stems.

Bullrushes

The true bullrush with its dark green, distinctly onion-like stems, tapering gradually to a fine tip is more commonly found in flowing water. However, it does grow happily in fertile, clear-watered ponds, lakes and pits, where the bottom is guaranteed to attract a prolific colony of freshwater shrimps – and thus tench and carp during the summer months.

Experienced pike fishermen also know that during the winter pike love to lie in wait among the rotting stems.

Sweet reed grass

This tall, rush-like marginal prefers a soft bottom where its creeping rootstock form such a dense mass you might be led into thinking you are treading on dry ground, until your boot suddenly fills up. It hangs out over the margins with as much as 3 to 4 ft of water beneath the dark floating canopy, and is much loved by tench, bream and carp. They can be caught directly under the rod tip when patrolling amongst the extensive sub-surface rootstock, which harbours delicacies such as midge larvae, leeches, snails, beetles, caddis and the like.

Soft weeds

These, the submerged oxygenating plants like Canadian pond weed, hornwort and mill foil, can pose enormous problems in clear water where, due to the maximum penetration of sunlight, they grow rampant. And generally speaking the smaller the pond or pit, the more rampant and the more problematic they become. It's often possible to observe bubbles from tench for instance (feeding down on the bottom, beneath the weed) rise to cluster tantalizingly on the surface without there being a way of getting the bait down to them. To a much lesser extent this also happens with carp.

Both species are naturally attracted by the overhead protection and diffused light that these soft weeds provide,

Every gravel pit fishery is entirely different. The drag-line digs deeper when removing the richest mineral seams, leaving long troughs or gullies. Location of these and other depressions or holes by careful plummeting of the bottom will provide the most likely guide to the patrol routes of species like tench and bream, and where shoals of perch and roach are most likely to be in residence. Find the latter, and you will find pike also.

and of course to the larder of aquatic insect larvae attached to their stems.

Surface plants

Most species, particularly tench, rudd and carp love to occupy areas beneath lilies. The attraction is a roof over their heads, diffusing the light and obscuring enemies. In such places tench especially always feel comfortable to browse and feed in their characteristically ponderous, lazy way, even through the heat and brightness of a summer day, when they abandon more open swims as the sun starts to rise high in the sky.

To tackle thick lily beds with inadequate tackle or even the wrong type of outfit (such as a fast-taper rod instead of one with a forgiving, cushioning action) could be asking for trouble. What proves invaluable, however, is an understanding of the structure of stems and roots beneath a mass of floating pads and flowers, because, in addition to the species already mentioned, perch and pike are also attracted to the diffused light beneath surface plants. Artificial lures worked on the surface between lily-pads provide an exciting way of catching summer pike.

While there are numerous cultivated varieties of coloured lilies available only a handful of clubs or owners plant their fisheries with them. This is a pity because it's impossible to make a stillwater fishery look too beautiful, and to sit

Surface plants such as lilies attract carp, rudd and tench, providing natural food such as aquatic insect larvae and snails plus their eggs, which cling to the undersides of the pads, and most important of all, subdued light. This pretty lake is planted with a range of cultivated varieties in addition to the common yellow lily with its distinctive cabbage-like sub-surface leaves.

fishing with pink or dark red lilies dotted amongst a carpet of velvet-green pads is a delightful experience.

There are no less than five commonly found 'natural' lily type plants: the common yellow water-lily, sometimes referred to as brandy bottle due to the distinctive shape of the seed head, which forms once the petals have shed; the common white water-lily (the white alba lily); the dwarf pond lily: broad-leaved pond weed; and amphibious bistort.

Fish adore the *common yellow lily* because of its soft, cabbage-like, sub-surface leaves, amongst which they love to browse. Most anglers often refer to this plant simply as 'cabbages', especially in certain river systems where the pads and flowers rarely reach the surface. Boating activity can be responsible for this, as can, to some degree, excessive depth. It is one and the same lily, nonetheless.

In shallow lakes, however, particularly those with a bottom layer rich in nutrients, the sheer growth of both sub-surface cabbage and floating pads can present a daunting prospect when you are thinking of extracting specimens.

Second in both size and root structure density to the common yellow lily comes the *white alba lily* and the cultivated (coloured) hybrids. Due to their very much smaller rhizomes, thinner stalks and complete absence of sub-surface greenery, there is naturally more room beneath the pads and beautiful flowers for fish to both hide and move about, although viewed from the surface the growth looks impenetrable.

The *dwarf pond lily* is not really a true lily, although its small, round green pads and buttercup-yellow flowers would fool most fishermen. The main difference between it and the true lilies is that it multiplies rapidly, not by sending up extra stalks and pads from the bottom roots, but by growing outwards in short bursts across the surface. It creates mini plants each with its own rootstock and flowerhead, every 6–10 in. At the end of the summer these little plants rot off and separate from the old main stem; they drift into the margins where a percentage take hold. And in the following spring, it all sprouts up again. This lily also spreads from the seed head once the yellow flowers die off.

One advantage of this plant, when you are trying to extract fish from a seemingly impossible surface covering, (see 'Raking') is that while the long stems and pads are tough and thick on the surface, there is little beneath the surface for tackle to catch on. A couple of square yards of floating jungle may be supported underneath by only half a dozen thin stalks.

Broad-leaved pond weed In some locations, especially shallow marl, clay and gravel pits, the oval-shaped green leaves (often noticeably crinkly along the edges) can clog the surface almost from bank to bank. It is easily recognizable by the erect, tight, pink seed heads. Also, from the hard bottom in which it prefers to root, the main stem can sub-divide two or three times before each individual plant reaches the surface. For this reason the density of foliage causes a problem only from mid-water upwards. Like most surface plants, broad-leaved pond weed flourishes best in depths of between 2 ft and 6 ft. This is useful to know when you are reconnoitring new waters, because a reasonably accurate assessment of depths can be made wherever this plant covers the surface.

This applies also to *amphibious bistort* which is really a terrestrial plant that loves to have its roots in water, thus providing a floating canopy in depths up to around 3 ft. It, too, sports an erect, knotty, pink seed head, but the leaves are pointed and dark green. It will occasionally grow as a thick covering well out from the bank over gravel bars, but it is more often seen growing in thick clumps along the margins, sprouting on dry land and reaching out across the surface, exactly where you would expect to find tench and carp browsing.

During the heat of a summer's day, especially when fish feel vulnerable in clear water and are loathe to be seen out in the open, the best place to search is around surface-covering plants. However, don't take my word for it – go and explore for yourself.

Hidden sub-surface features

So much for locating fish by visually identifying those plants they most like to frequent, and in part treat as home. But what about lakes, ponds or pits which, for one reason or another, remain weedless for much, perhaps all of the summer – waters without obvious features where the fish might be anywhere. Gravel pits are renowned for their uneven sub-surface contours, created when the sand and gravel deposits were originally laid down following the last Ice Age. To harvest the maximum potential in minerals, aggregate companies dig deeper into the richest seams, thus creating gullies or holes once the pit has been allowed to fill from the water table.

It is along these deeper gullies, or in the holes and drop-offs that fish love to patrol. The bottom lay-out is to them as avenues, cul-de-sacs and road systems appear to us. Obviously, time spent carefully plummetting unknown waters to gain a mental picture of the bottom contours will prevent you wasting time when you are fishing. Make a sketch of each fishery you visit, and draw in the deeper areas so that you have a record for next time.

After spending numerous sessions at a particular pit, it will become obvious that tench frequent certain areas only at certain times of the day. In clear-watered pits, for instance, it usually follows that marginal ledges and gullies are favoured during low light levels such as dusk and dawn, when tench are feeding in earnest on natural food. As the light increases, they evacuate the margins in preference for distant deeps, where they may very well spend all the midday hours. Now this is not a rule of thumb, because tench in each water react differently, but wherever there is a complete lack of marginal cover or surface habitats, such as partly submerged overhanging trees or lily-type plants, it is a good yardstick.

Scumlines

Thick scumlines of pollen, twigs, leaves and other bits formed by the wind blowing from the same direction for several days are great attractors. Natural food including clouds of zooplanktons such as daphnia, plus the remnants of floating fishing baits, are all concentrated in a soup in one area. If this happens to be a shoreline already blessed with features like thick beds of marginal reeds or sedges, lilies or partly submerged trees, it could attract carp in surprising numbers and hold them there until the wind changes direction. On large 'featureless' waters, wind direction alone usually dictates where all small items of natural foods held in suspension near the surface will eventually be deposited. This is why varying areas attract carp only at certain times. These deposits often come to rest on the leeward side of islands and promontories just as silt in flowing water sinks to the bottom downstream and on the inside of bends where the current always slows down. And whilst the feeding bubbles of carp cannot easily be seen rising in these natural larders at great

Huge lakes can seem daunting initially, and the secret is to divide them into small, manageable areas. Pay attention, for instance, to scum lines where the wind blows surface flotsam and food to a particular shoreline; areas where dense reed or rush beds line the margins; and the entrances of feeder streams. Shallow bays with huge patches of lilies will attract rudd or roach, and in turn predators like perch and pike. Ultimately, you can search the bottom with a portable sonar unit like the Humminbird, which will provide you with an accurate plan of the bottom contours.

distances, fish often roll or jump completely clear of the surface when feeding actively and give away their position.

Look closely also for any large 'flat' or calm areas several feet square which suddenly appears amongst the waves. These 'calms' are caused by carp moving beneath the surface without actually breaking it. Such is the force created by their body displacement and powerful fins, the surface tension is 'flattened' long enough for it to be picked up through binoculars even at great distances.

Carp which cannot be seen through really heavily coloured water, even when they feed close in along shallow margins, also indicate their presence through water displacement called 'tail patterns'. These spiral up to the surface in minute vortexes when the carp stands on its head to feed, wagging its tail gently from side to side. Sometimes these 'tail patterns' are accompanied by feeding bubbles and even the fish's body breaking surface, but not always. All are visual indications not to be missed.

Depths

Carp are sometimes stocked into and caught from waters of great depth (20 ft and more) completely devoid of shallow areas. However, where they are given a choice of varying depths at which to feed (most waters), I would suggest they spend a much greater part of their time in less than 12–14 ft of water, rather than deeper water. This is because the greatest concentrations of natural food and choice plant habitats are produced in part by sunlight. And in excessively deep water, particularly if it is heavily coloured (old clay pits and the like), sunlight cannot penetrate down far enough to stimulate growth.

Many prime summer haunts will still hold carp throughout the winter months, particularly dense habitat areas where partly submerged trees and bushes overhang the margins into deepish water. Deep gullies or troughs in what are generally shallow lakes or pits are also certain to be holding fish.

The much deeper, 'dam' end of man-made estate-type lakes is the obvious choice in continually cold conditions. Even lily-beds (or what's left of them) maintain their attraction for carp despite the rotting stalks, and pads not being visible. Always keep a mental note (by lining up a particular tree or gate post on the opposite bank during the summer when the pads are up) as to exactly where the main structure of the plants are situated for winter attention. Carp will always be found among it along with groups of perch and the occasional big pike.

TACKLE

RODS

Float rods

To present the bait close in, and for tackling small waters (overgrown streams, especially), my choice would be a 12-footer. Conversely, to present the bait way out into deep water with a fixed float, a 14-ft model will pick up more line on the strike and thus convert far more bites into hooked fish. However, I must admit to using a 13-footer for something like 90 per cent of my float fishing, and so I will suggest that you follow the same course if you are uncertain about length and can afford only one rod.

Choice of action in float rods is between the snappy yet easy waggler action or a fast-tip action, which has a considerably finer tip section of somewhere between 20 and 24 in spliced into the top joint. Both models are perfect for use with reel lines of between 2 and 2½ lb, but most waggler rods can also be used with lines up to 4–4½ lb for long trotting with chub or barbel in mind, and float fishing for tench, etc.

Spliced-tip rods allow for a more sensitive, delicate approach when you are underarm casting at close range and for easing the bait downstream when stick-float fishing with ultra-fine hook lengths and tiny hooks. If you can afford both actions, then fine. If not, opt for a waggler-style rod, which should prove more versatile overall, taking both close and long-range techniques into account.

Weight is a factor to consider in a rod that you could be holding all day long. I much prefer those slim in profile, which cut easily through wind resistance and are extremely fast on the strike – a quality much needed when striking the shy bites that roach, rudd, dace and especially crucian carp can give at times.

The rod must feel comfortable beneath your forearm, with either a full cork or a cork/duplon-mix grip, and this brings me to the subject of handle length. While certain manufacturers still insist on over-long handles, resulting in up to 1 ft of the rod (in effective length) protruding behind your elbow and getting in the way, others produce an ideal length of between 22 and 23 in. I have a pet hate, also, against handles that are too thick and thus restrict fluent manipulations of the reel, the ideal diameter being somewhere between ⅞ and 1 in.

Rod rings should be stand-off to eliminate 'line stick' in wet weather, and they should be lined with either silicon carbide or aluminium oxide centres to alleviate unnecessary wear on fine lines. If you intend using a centre-pin reel, ensure there are two rings on the bottom joint between handle and spigot so that the thumb and forefinger of your free hand can easily draw line off for casting.

A snappy-actioned 13 ft carbon fibre waggler rod is the ideal all-round float rod. Coupled to a 2 lb reel line, there is sensitivity in the tip for enjoying dace, while lines up to 4½ lb test may be safely used for big bream, tench or chub like the 4-pounder John is about to net.

Ledger rods

When considering ledger rods for small species like roach, rudd and dace, there are three pointers worth bearing in mind: length, power, or rather sensitivity, and whether to opt for a model with a threaded tip-ring into which a swingtip, springtip or a quivertip (see Bite indicators, p. 97) can be screwed, or a built-in quivertip ledger rod. You could get both if you can afford it. Most quality, slim-profile ledger rods are now made from lightweight carbon fibre, which can be held all day long without fatigue. This

The best all-round choice in a ledger rod is the 1¼ lb test, carbon-fibre Avon, which can be used with lines up to 6 lb test and has a lovely all-through action.

allows you to hit more bites successfully while simultaneously enjoying maximum pleasure from playing even small fish.

For narrow fisheries, streams, canals and so on – in fact, all close-range work when a vast length of line is not going to be pulled through the water in order to ensure the hook is driven home – a 9 or 10 ft rod with a snappy, yet all-through action and a threaded end-ring to accept bite-indicator tips will do the job nicely.

Moving up the scale a little and thinking in terms of placing the bait (together with perhaps a medium-sized swimfeeder) distances of, say, up to 30 yd in both still and flowing water, necessitating a 3–4 lb line, I suggest a slightly longer rod (10–11 ft), again with a snappy action, which, under full compression, also bends into an all-through curve. This helps cushion the strike required (for line pick-up), yet stops small hooks from ripping out or fine hook links from snapping, while permitting the utmost enjoyment from playing even modest-sized roach, bream or rudd, and even dace.

In this medium-range bracket I would suggest a built-in quivertip model or a multi-tip, most of which come complete with two or three extra tips (stored in the handle) of varying sensitivity to suit different current strengths.

Lastly, and if much of your ledgering happens to be either at distance into deep, still water, or in exceedingly deep and fast rivers like the Severn, Norfolk's tidal River Yare, or in the lower reaches of the River Bann in Northern Ireland, necessitating feeders of up to 2 oz and a reel line of 4 to 6 lb, then choose the horse for the course –

an 11 to 12-footer with a medium-action, built-in quivertip. Many of these powerful models are referred to as Avon quivertips, and possess enough meat in the lower two-thirds to combat the fast water and subdue large chub and barbel living in rivers like the Hampshire Avon, coupled with a surprising degree of sensitivity in the finely tapered quivertip, permitting bite detection from the shyest roach.

The Avon Ryobi twin-tip ledger, which incorporates both standard (with a threaded end-ring) and built-in quivertip tops, is the ideal outfit if you regularly concentrate upon both fast rivers and big stillwaters, where versatility and a touch of power is required. The standard tip, for instance, may be employed without a tip indicator, when distance ledgering for specimen stillwater rudd, roach, tench, perch and bream, where a bobbin bite indicator fixed on the line between butt ring and reel is much preferred.

Alternatively, the standard-tip Avon may be employed, freelining or floating crusts down to chub, stret pegging for barbel, or presenting small livebaits beneath a float to perch. It is the perfect zander rod. And for laying on among marginal lilies for tench with a 6 lb line it has no equal.

Those who enjoy constructing their own specialist rods will find that a superb and most versatile quivertip rod can be made from an 11 or 12 ft, 1¼ lb test curve carbon Avon blank. This will cover all eventualities in running water from roach to double-figure barbel.

Cut it back by 24 in at the top and splice in a 24 in solid-glass tip. The best tips are arrived at by cutting back a 3 ft solid glass, rapid-taper donkey top from the thick end (and a little off the fine tip if you wish) until it protrudes from the top of the cut blank, leaving just 2 in inside, which alleviates any chance of a 'dead spot' (see fig. 3.1).

Gently file the end of the top joint after carefully removing the last 24 in with a fine-tooth hacksaw, and instead of gluing in the quivertip, simply pull it through slowly with a degree of firmness and turn gently until it 'locks'. Do not be over forceful or you will split the carbon blank. Once the joint has been whipped over, there is no chance of it slipping back down. Should you break the end of the fine tip at any time in the future (easily done), a replacement is easily sleeved in. To remove the broken tip, undo the whipping and hold the quivertip tightly. Gently knock the base of the top joint against a stone or wooden floor until it slides down inside the joint and can be pulled through.

To complete, whip on five or six small, one-leg, fuji, lined rings plus a tip and paint the last 20 in with two coats of matt white paint. This really makes it stand out, so even tiny bites are easily seen in poor light conditions, whatever the background.

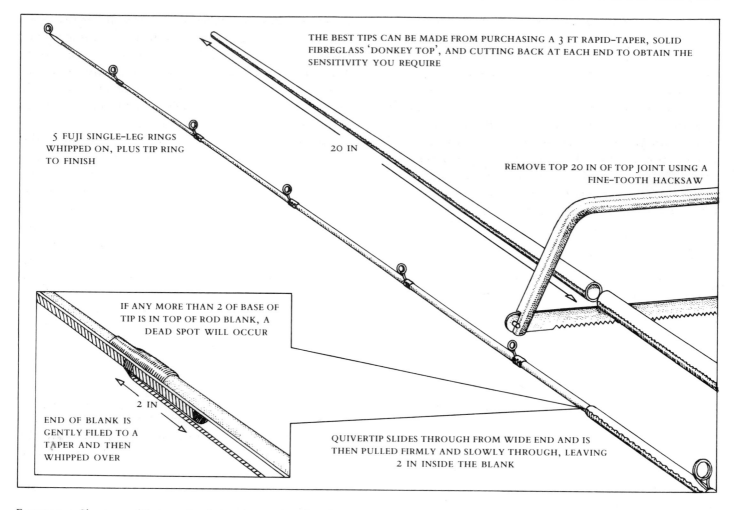

FIGURE 3.1 *Sleeving a solid-glass quivertip into the top joint of a carbon 2 pc powerful Avon-style rod blank*

Poles

There is absolutely no question whatsoever that when it comes to exact bait presentation beneath a float at distances of up to 40 ft out in still or running water (barring gale force winds), the pole is without equal.

Today, not only are poles longer, lighter and thus more pleasant to use, but due to the European 'elasticated tip', which acts as a built-in shock absorber to a fish pulling hard, much smaller and lighter terminal tackle can be used, compared to the running-line set-up of a float rod. The only disadvantage as far as top-line, reinforced carbon-fibre poles are concerned is expense. Consider all the various options at your local tackle shop (by handling them as though fishing), and go for as light and as rigid a reinforced carbon take-apart pole as you can afford.

While poles up to 14½ m (an incredible 47½ ft) are currently available (and no doubt the advance of match fishing technology will create even longer models), for most pleasure fishing a length of somewhere between 8 and 11 m should suffice.

You have the option of tying the line directly to the tip (flick-tip) of the pole, or cutting the tip back carefully using a fine-tooth hacksaw and adding a PTFE bush, through which runs high-stretch pole elastic. No. 4 elastic – incidentally – is perfect for catching species like bream, roach, rudd and dace (see Pole fishing, p. 162).

Top-of-the-range carbon poles come supplied with a 'top-two kit' – a duplicate of the top two joints (usually telescopic) – enabling one to be used as a flick-tip, the other cut back and elasticated. Also available from some manufacturers is a duplicate top-four or five section kit, allowing you to have at the ready (for a speedy change-over) a complete second, lighter or heavier float rig. You simply change the entire end of the pole at the fourth or fifth joint, and instantly start fishing with a different rig.

Much in vogue for catching smaller species at close range, which makes them particularly suitable for roach, bream, perch, rudd and dace, are the slim-line, super-lightweight carbon 'whips'. These fabulous tools are easily supported beneath the forearm just like a float rod, up to lengths of 6 m. Most are fitted with super-fine carbon flick-tips, onto which a tiny ring is glued. Except for the bottom two joints, whips are telescopic.

Having said all this, and taking into account the relative cost of top-quality carbon poles, you can still quite happily catch roach, rudd and dace at close range with a pole at a fraction of the cost, simply by purchasing an inexpensive hollow-glass telescopic model of 5 to 6 m. These 'cheapies' usually incorporate a solid-glass tip, to which you whip a loop of thick mono (20 lb test) or glue on a mini tip-ring. Telescopic poles up to 6 m can be held for quite some time supported by the forearm without undue fatigue, and while they are rather sloppy in action, this does act as a buffer when you hook into a 1 lb roach on a size 20 hook tied to a 1 lb test bottom. Conversely, they are equally good for bullying larger roach, rudd and bream hooked among heavy weed or lilies on lines of 2 and 3 lb test with hooks tied direct.

Pole tips

There are two ways of joining a ready-made-up float rig to the pole tip: either directly, to a small ring glued on to the end of the flick-tip (some tips already have these tiny rings fitted), or by doing away with the flick-tip altogether and constructing an elastic tip.

Flick-tip fishing is best when you are using reasonably large hooks and big baits, say size 14 to size 8 tied direct to 2–5 lb line, which in turn is tied direct to the tip-ring. However, as many situations using the 'long pole/short line' set-up demand super-fine hook-lengths down to a 1 lb bottom or less, and size 18–22 hooks that all too easily tear out on a direct line, an elastic tip acting as a buffer will prove indispensible. It takes only a few minutes to convert

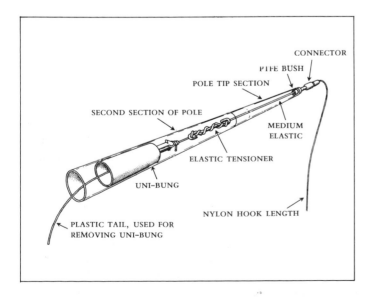

FIGURE 3.2 *Pole-tip elastic conversion using a standard pole-elastic kit*

the pole tip using one of the many kits available (fig. 3.2). You start by cutting back the tip carefully, a little at a time, so that the hollow PTFE bush fits in neatly. Use a fine-tooth hacksaw for this, and smooth the edges with fine glass paper or emery cloth. The rig connector will now fit inside the bush, but first tie on the elastic supplied with the kit and thread it down through the tip.

Into the other (wider) end of the second section, fit the coned 'uni-bung', to which the other end of the elastic is tied. The wide end of the plastic uni-bung may be reduced in diameter so that it fits neatly several inches up inside the second section, leaving the fine plastic tail protruding. To pull the bung out again for alteration to, or a complete change of, elastic you simply pull gently on the plastic tail.

Lastly, apply a few drops of elastic lubricant to the elastic to protect it against abrasion, and the tip is complete.

CARP AND PIKE RODS

Test curves

Rods designed and sold specifically for carp and pike fishing (usually in carbon-fibre) have a 'test curve' rating printed along with the manufacturer's logo immediately above the handle. This provides a guide to the rod's power and therefore suggested line strengths to go with it so that both rod and line stretch in harmony like one enormous elastic band. To find out the suggested line strength for a particular rod you simply multiply its test curve rating by 5. For instance – a test curve of 2 lb will result in an ideal line strength of around 10 lb. It is as simple as that. To find the lower limit of lines that can safely be used with a rod, multiply by 4 (8 lb test) and by 6 for the upper limit (12 lb test).

These figures of course offer only a general guideline, but there has to be a better yardstick than judging the power of a rod purely by its looks, and as yet no one has improved on the test curve principle. Incidentally the words 'test curve' relate to the strain (in lbs) required to pull the rod's tip into a quarter circle.

Action

In addition to the rod's power, its action must also be considered. Most rods fall roughly into one of three popular categories. Rods which bend progressively along their length, into a full curve are described as *all-through action* (fig. 3.3A). Those whose action is mostly in the upper half or tip section are called *medium tip action* (fig. 3.3B). Rods where only the upper tip really bends to any degree are called *fast taper* (fig. 3.3C). All-through

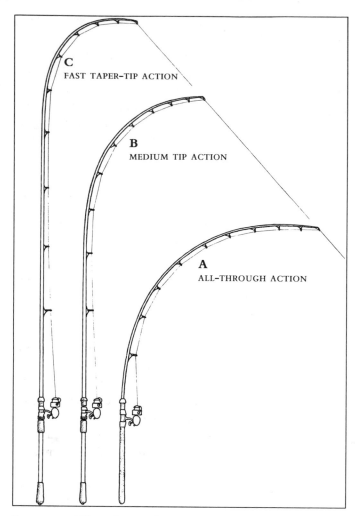

C
FAST TAPER-TIP ACTION

B
MEDIUM TIP ACTION

A
ALL-THROUGH ACTION

FIGURE 3.3 *Pike and carp rod actions*

action rods are great for carp, and for fishing at reasonably short range, say distances of up to 30/40 yd. Beyond this, for picking up the line and subsequently setting the hook into carp and pike when striking at greater distances, up to say 70/80 yd, a 'medium tip action' is the tool for the job. This is probably the most useful rod for both species and a test curve of around 2–2¼ lb is perfect. To cope with still greater distances, 80 yd plus (far more specialized fishing) a fast taper action rod with a test curve of 2½ lb or more is the tool for the job. Such a rod is also ideal for putting big eels or catfish on the bank. However, because a fast taper rod bends very little other than in the extreme tip, you need to be especially careful not to rip out the hook or snap the line when bringing a heavy fish to the net on the end of a short line.

Length

While two-piece 13 ft 'specials' are perhaps necessary for ultra-long-range carp fishing, most carp and pike rods are produced in either 11 or 12 ft models. For picking up line

at distance and for fishing into deep waters I would suggest that a 12-footer is absolutely ideal. For all close-range work, casting and playing fish beneath overhanging trees, fishing overgrown jungle-type swims, etc., the standard length of 11 ft is perfect.

Lure rods

While an 11 ft carp or pike rod can be used for lure fishing at a pinch, with continual casting it becomes extremely tiring to use after a while. The tiredness factor, together with the fact that the snappier action of a lure rod allows the artificial to be worked more attractively, makes an 8½ or 9 ft rod more pleasurable to use. Again, there is little reason for more than a comfortable length between reel stem and butt cap, so reject any rod which protrudes beyond the elbow.

Some manufacturers provide a choice of handle grips suited to both fixed-spool and multiplying reels. However, in the case of handles for multipliers, the stability given to the multiplier rod by a trigger grip built into the reel fitting makes for far more comfortable casting and retrieving than those without.

Though they are considered a highly specialized part of the rod manufacturing industry, the 5–6 ft single-handed, trigger-grip American bait-casting rods offer the chance of extra fun with pike and chub on artificials. Being stiff, these wand-like sticks are far better for imparting live action to artificials, especially surface-popping plugs and buzz baits, compared to the longer, traditional spinning rods, which tend to absorb much of your arm movement instead of transferring it directly to the plug.

Fly rodding

I have purposefully headed this fly rodding, as opposed to fly fishing rods, because catching chub, perch or pike for instance with the fly rod does not have to be limited to artificial flies. Certainly a dry fly, a wet fly or even a slow-sinking nymph will each catch chub in the right situation. But you can also use tiny spinners, spoons and plugs and have double the fun, by catching all three species and many more.

For traditional dry or wet fly fishing I would recommend a lightweight two-piece 9 ft carbon fibre rod with a snappy action, which has a line rating of 5/6. This means that it will effectively throw a size 5 double-taper line or a size 6 weight-forward. Dry flies are best presented on the double taper line because they land more gently on the surface, while wet flies and nymphs may be fished on both types. As a weight-forward line casts better into the wind and over shorter distances, I would perhaps suggest that if you were to go for just one line to cover all traditional fishing then a weight-forward size 6 floater is ideal.

For presenting small spinners and plugs to chub and perch I would recommend a 9½-footer with a 6/7 line rating and a weight-forward floating line from which 3 to 4 ft of the forward tip has been removed. Used in conjunction with a short (5–6 ft) cast to reduce the distance between the weight of the lure and casting weight of the fly line. Using the fly rod to propel spinners and plugs

accurately without danger to your being is then much improved.

To obtain maximum distance when pike-fishing and for the additional power, I suggest a 9½–10 footer with an 8/9 line rating. At the other end of the scale and to obtain the utmost pleasure from catching dace and roach on the fly from overgrown streams and small rivers, I scale right down to a 7½ ft carbon brook rod that takes a size 4 or 5 line.

REELS

Fixed spool reels

To catch smaller species of freshwater fish, I find that a lightweight, small-format fixed-spool provides the greatest pleasure. It should incorporate a roller in the bale arm to help minimize friction against fine lines, and run smoothly on ball-bearings. Models that come complete with two spools allow for a choice of 2 to 2½ lb test on one to cover most floatfishing, and on the other, 3, 4 and even 6 lb test (depending on the circumstances) for ledgering, freelining and heavy float fishing. The spools of most top-quality reels are now purposely designed to take just 100 yd of line without the need for unwanted and wasteful backing beneath.

The ideal size is between 1,000 and 2,500 – certainly no larger. Reels of a heavier, larger format are less complementary to fine lines in that the slipping clutch is invariably less sensitive. And if you play fish by adjusting and using the clutch (as opposed to backwinding), a smooth, super-sensitive clutch that reacts to small increases of pressure from the drag knob, one digit at a time, is imperative.

When stepping up in size to a reel in the 3000 to 4000 format and to a reel suitable for both carp and pike fishing, it should have a wide spool so that the line comes off in large loose coils, as opposed to tight coils which restrict casting and bait presentation. Also, the spool should hold enough line, say 200 yd of 8/10 or 12 lb test mono. A super-fast retrieve is not required; I repeat – not required. The playing of fish is much smoother with a reel of standard gear ratio. A sensitive clutch, however, is of paramount importance if, like me, you prefer to play fish using the clutch.

In recent years the tactic of tightening the clutch right down and backwinding to play the fish through the gears instead of the clutch has been popularized by many specialist anglers. I would suggest, however, that by learning to use the clutch for the purpose for which it was designed – by setting it properly so that the spool rotates

and gives line before reaching full load – remains the most efficient way of ensuring that a big fish takes no more line than you actually need to give. And for controlling fish hooked close to, or actually right in among snaggy swims, this is very important.

You simply tighten the drag knob until line can just be pulled firmly yet smoothly from the spool – no more, no less. This of course prompts the question, which type of reel is best: reels with a standard front-adjusting clutch (built into the spool itself), as in the legendary Mitchell 300 and 400 range of reels; or skirted-spool, rear drag reels, a format most manufacturers now seem to be producing. Skirted-spool reels do not allow line to slip down and become tangled between spool and the rotor housing; in addition, because the drag knob is situated at the rear or bottom of the reel, clutch adjustment even whilst playing a fish is found easier by the majority of fishermen. On the other hand, front drags are far less complicated; they have

Most modern, fixed-spool reels have skirted spools to alleviate line trap, and run effortlessly on ball-bearings. Models in the 1000 to 2500 format have particularly sensitive slipping clutches and are ideal for use with lines in the 2–6 lb range.

fewer parts to wear, and less torque on the system because only the spool turns and not the rotor.

Something that has become an important feature to carp anglers, however, in particular those presenting baits on heavy leaded shock or bolt rigs (see 'Bolt rig ledgering'), is the 'baitrunner' design patented by 'Shimano' which, through a trip lever, allows the spool to be completely disengaged from the drag system. Thus, a carp belting off is allowed to do so with the bale arm in the closed position as the spool rotates freely. There is even a separate 'spool drag' for when the baitrunner facility is in operation. Simply by turning the handle again the spool is returned to its pre-set drag and disengages the baitrunner lever.

Several reel manufacturers now build a 'baitrunner' or 'spool disengaging' facility into models designed for carp and pike fishermen. Though it is a fact that well-educated pike, wary of the slightest resistance when sucking up a static deadbait from the bottom, will quickly reject it even with the free spool facility set at its lightest tension.

For catching carp and pike, high gear ratios creating a super-fast retrieve are nowhere near so important as manufacturers would have us believe. In fact, techniques of wobbling deadbaits, plugging, spinning, and so on, are made more difficult by a fast-retrieve reel. Also, playing fish is more pleasurable with reels of standard gear ratios. So beware of merchandizing promises.

In recent years, reels fitted with long-nosed, tapered or 'coned' spools have become extremely popular among carp and pike anglers wishing to add extra yards to their casting range, and the super-smooth models by Shimano, Ryobi and Daiwa are particularly recommended for very long range work.

Closed-face reels

I rely on the centre-pin for close-range float work and long trotting. However, even if I did not, there would still be occasions when I would choose a closed-face reel in preference to a small fixed-spool. During extremely windy weather, the closed-face provides excellent control because the line passes through a hole in the totally enclosed face of the reel (hence the name), as opposed to flapping in coils around the bale arm as it can do with a fixed-spool reel. However, because the line angles around a steel pin during the retrieve, only lines between 2 lb and 5 lb test can be used effectively with it. The playing of big fish on heavier lines is hampered by the amount of torque transmitted to such a sensitive piece of machinery. Closed-face reels manufactured by Daiwa, Ryobi, Abu and DAM are recommended. These come available in both rear-drag and back-winding models.

Centre-pin reels

That centre-pins are technically far superior to both the fixed-spool and closed-face reels for long trotting is beyond question. Nothing can compete with the way in which a float can be used to 'ease' the bait slowly downstream along the river-bed with the line in a straight line from float to rod tip, in complete readiness for an instant strike. And no other reel can match that pleasurable, direct feeling of playing a fish with your thumb pressure gently braking the edge of the drum, ready to give line instantly should the fish suddenly charge off.

For many years now, in fact since my very early teens, I have preferred to use a centre-pin reel for float fishing, not only in rivers but for many close-range situations in stillwater when after tench, bream and carp.

Long-trotting enthusiasts who fancy switching from a closed face or fixed-spool reel over to the centre-pin can start at the more economical end of the scale by investing in one of the older secondhand models. Classics like the Trudex (my first centre-pin) Rapidex, Speedia or one of the fabulous Aerials originally made by Allcocks, are the reels to look out for, with the narrow-drum Match Aerial arguably the best of them all.

The Match Aerial is in fact currently being produced in small numbers through a specialist mail order service, after being unavailable for many years. It is a reel I love to use, especially with ultra-fine tackle. Another current centre-pin of quality is the Stanton Adcock, which runs superbly on ball bearings.

Making a line guard

A point worth mentioning about centre-pins is that unless you fit them with a line guard, you will experience all sorts of problems. During really windy weather, for instance, you will forever be looking down to free line that is flapping behind the cage, and this means that you lose concentration and take your eyes off the float.

It is easy to construct an extremely efficient cage-type line guard, the design of which fits both reels previously mentioned perfectly. As you can see from fig. 3.4, it is made from 18 gauge stainless-steel sprung wire (the sort tackle shops sell for making-up wire sea-booms), and can be adapted to fit virtually any make of centre-pin reel, although originally I designed it to fit the Match Aerial.

Start by shaping the wire into slightly more than a half circle fractionally larger than the diameter of the spool or drum, with 28 mm ends bent back at right angles, as in fig. 3.4A.

To form cross-bars, three 28 mm lengths of the same

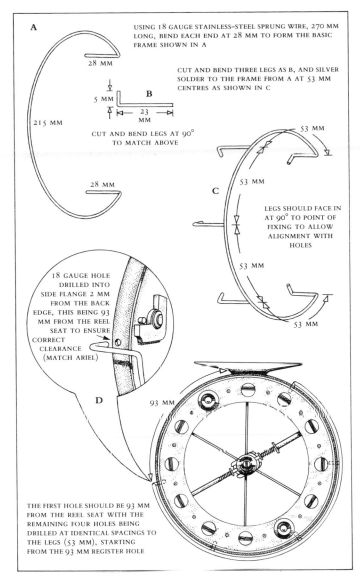

FIGURE 3.4 *Making a line guard*

wire are then silver-soldered neatly to the guard, as in fig. 3.4B. This is a task that most small engineering firms will do for a small charge. Insist that all solder joints are really smooth or the line will chafe on them. The ends of all five bars are then bent inwards at right angles (fig. 3.4C) and clipped off with wire cutters to 5/16 in long for fixing into the side flange of the reel's back plate once you have drilled holes to accommodate them (fig. 3.4D).

This job must be done accurately because the tolerance between back plate and spool is minimal, though more than enough for an 18 gauge hole to be drilled without the wire ends fouling the back of the spool. This job can be farmed out, and the local jewellers shop is the best place to go.

Provided that all goes well and the guard has been carefully made, being a half-circle of sprung wire it clips neatly into the holes and holds itself firmly in place.

Multiplier reels

For presenting lures on both standard and short American-style single-handed rods, and for piking on wild open waters such as reservoirs or the Irish and Scottish lochs, where fishing from boats into great depths at anchor, or trolling, puts greater demands on your tackle, the multiplying reel has much to offer. Indeed, the technique of trolling is almost impossible with a fixed-spool reel.

Top models nowadays are superbly engineered with lightweight duralium spools, friction-free level wind and magnetic cast control. But these features naturally affect the price, and I would even go so far as to say that unless you are prepared to invest in the right tool for the job do not buy one at all, because cheap multipliers will never allow you to enjoy lure fishing fully.

The Swedish manufacturers ABU lead the field with their range of Ambassador freshwater multipliers, closely followed by Shimano, Daiwa and Ryobi. Even the tiniest models (a real delight to use when matched to a bait-casting stick) will accommodate 200 yd of 10–12 lb test, and for boat-work on large waters, when lines up to 18 lb may be needed for fishing over rocks or into heavy weeds, both the ABU 6000 series and Ryobi's 12 hold more than sufficient, up to 300 yd.

In recent years, lefthand-wind multipliers have become readily available, which allows you to hold the rod in your strongest hand while performing the simple task of winding in with the other, just like fixed-spool reels.

Baby multipliers

The choice of baby multipliers to match single-handed trigger-grip lure rods is, unfortunately, rather limited in the lower to medium price bracket. To be more precise, it is non-existent. You have to accept that to fully enjoy American-style casting, a suitable multiplier will cost twice as much as a quality fixed-spool reel. Having said this, I certainly would not wish to be without my collection of baby multipliers, which includes trouble-free, magnetic casting-control models made by Ryobi, Daiwa and ABU. All are left-hand wind (the Ryobi is ambidextrous), and all are fitted with automatic level wind, so necessary for foolproof casting and, though tiny, each of the spools can hold up to 200 yd of 8 lb test, which makes them perfect for catching smaller predators on lures such as chub and perch, in addition to pike.

Fly reels

The requirements of a fly reel are considerably less than those of a fixed-spool reel. All that is needed is a singleactioned reel with a ratchet, capable of holding 50 yd of backing beneath the fly line. This is not to prevent you from running out of line when a fish goes charging off but because well-filled fly reels ensure that the fly line has less 'memory' and peels off in large, limp coils. You need look no further than the rimfly range made by Leeda or the lightweight magnesium models manufactured by Ryobi.

To take size 4 and 5 lines, the Leeda mini 50 fly reel and the Ryobi MG 255 magnesium are ideal, while size 6 lines are perfectly matched to the Leeda lightweight 60, and Ryobi MG 355 magnesium. For heavier lines in sizes 7–9 go for the Leeda 80, or the MG 357 made by Ryobi.

LINES

Contrary to all the advertising hype accompanying every new line as it arrives on the market, very little has changed with monofilament line during the last few decades. This is possibly because it is, quite simply, a commodity which can be developed no further. It is now as abrasion-resistant, as fine and as supple, with a suitable degree of stretch, as it is ever going to be. The plain truth is that if you pre-stretch monofilament of a certain test and diameter, it will become that much thinner and therefore easier to fool the fish with. But at what price – and this is what everyone seems to forget – because it will then have greatly reduced elasticity, and it is the elastic-band action, or 'stretch', of regular monofilament that permits the landing of big fish on light lines.

Remove the 'buffer', as has happened with so-called revolutionary, much thinner lines (which have been reduced to minimal stretch) and the line parts just when you don't want it to: with the fish thumping away beneath the rod tip on a short line, about to be netted.

Having said all this, low-diameter pre-stretched monofilament does make excellent hook lengths. A thinner line tied to the hook is bound to encourage more bites, especially when presenting floaters or fishing in clear water. Only when fishing at extreme range, however, (100 yd plus) would I ever consider filling the reel with a pre-stretched line; and then only because regular mono, due to its inherent stretch, inhibits hook penetration on the strike.

While match fishermen seem perfectly happy about using lines down to 1½ lb test on the reel, I am not. I prefer a greater margin of safety against breakage (and the possibility of harm to wildlife) between the terminal rig and the rod, considering the amount of wear monofilament suffers as it is continually pulled back and forwards through rod rings, often under severe pressure. Besides, only at the hook end does the diameter make any significant difference between bites and no bites. So I never fish with less than a 2–2½ lb test reel line, which is ideal when float fishing for species like dace, roach, perch, rudd, bream and chub.

Brands I can recommend for their reliability (for float and ledger fishing) are Sylcast, Siglon, Bayer Perlon and Maxima. Maxima is particularly useful for waggler fishing in stillwater because it sinks much more easily than other brands. Incidentally, to ensure any monofilament line sinks quickly, dab a drop of neat washing-up liquid around the spool every so often.

For most close-range ledgering after smaller species, I find 3 lb test a fine all-round choice, even when casting small feeders. But for bomb or swimfeeder ledgering into fast and deep swims for barbel or chub or into stillwater for tench and bream a 5–6 lb test reel line again provides that valuable safety margin. As hook lengths, low diameter and low stretch monofilament has much to offer, and I suggest a selection of spools in tests from 12 oz to 1½ lb is an invaluable addition to your tackle-box. Brands like Drennan Double Strength or Aikens Concept 2000 are particularly recommended. When pole fishing with an elasticated tip, for instance lengths down to 8 oz can be used with confidence due to the in-built buffer. With the flick-tip, on the other hand, it would be wise to stick to standard 'stretchy' brands.

For the demands of pike fishing (this also applies to carp, eels and catfish) the ideal monofilament line should be abrasion-resistant, supple and possess a reasonable degree of stretch to absorb the pike's lunges and tail-walking antics. Under no circumstances should you use pre-stretched and thus 'thinner' mono lines, which fracture all too easily just when you need elasticity in the line to prevent the pike making off, possibly with a set of trebles deeply embedded in its throat.

Continual lure casting, or punching deadbaits out long distances, tests monofilament to its limit, so always use a slightly heavier breaking strain line than perhaps you really need to give yourself an extra safety margin. Most top brands can be purchased in bulk spools, which works out considerably cheaper than buying 100 yd at a time, and allows you to change over to fresh line regularly.

For most pike and carp fishing requirements Sylcast sorrel in 9–11 lb test is very reliable. Other brands such as Bayer Perlon, Siglon specialist and Maxima are also recommended.

For trolling, when setting the hooks with a long length of mono behind the boat proves troublesome, and for presenting baits at great distances beneath a sail-type drift float, low-stretch dacron is worth considering. There are brands that float and can be easily lifted from the surface to alleviate a bow when drifting in strong winds. At long range (100 yd plus) the fact that dacron has less stretch than standard monofilament increases the chances of the hooks penetrating the pike's bony jaws.

The new cofilament mono lines that float permanently, like Siglon yellow, are excellent for distance drifting and for presenting floating baits to carp. When fishing in among snags for carp, big pike or catfish, step up the reel line to between 14 lb and 15 lb test. It is always better to be safe than sorry.

Incidentally, when winding new line straight on to the reel, I increase its suppleness by removing any coil caused by being stored on spools. This 'relaxing' process makes

fishing with brand new line a pleasure instead of a nightmare because the 'spring' has been taken out. After filling up the spool and fixing the reel to the rod, thread the line through the rings and tie a large loop on the end. Slip it over a gate post or something similar and walk 30 yd away.

Then wind gently down and slowly bend the rod into a full curve, holding it there for several seconds. Now point the rod at the fence post and wind until the line is tight to the reel with the rod straight. Walk slowly backwards a few paces 'feeling' just how much stretch there is in new monofilament. When it is really tight, obviously long before full elasticity is reached, hold it there for ten seconds. Afterwards, it can be wound back onto the spool nicely limp and ready for work.

HOOK LENGTHS

In addition to using both regular and pre-stretched monofilament for the hook length, as opposed to tying direct to the reel line, for both tench and carp fishing requirements (barbel also) the suppleness of braided dacron makes it a fine alternative.

In fact, all kinds of braided hook lengths are available from the standard black, low-stretch but incredibly supple

braided dacron (also available camouflaged and flecked) to the multi-strands like Gamastrand floss and Kryston, both of which separate on the bottom into numerous gossamer single strands. The latter gives fish greater confidence in accepting the bait with the advantage that the multi-strands return to one unit and full strength for striking and playing the fish.

KNOTS

Poorly tied knots, and knots of poor design, are one of the main contributing factors to fish being lost. I still see references in articles and books to the 'five-turn half blood knot' as being a suitable knot for tying eyed hooks to catch big fish like carp. Yet this knot can so easily pull or fracture under the kind of pressures involved.

As far as eyed hooks are concerned the the knot I put complete faith in is called the 'Mahseer knot', handed on to me by my guide, Suban, when after the legendary fish of that name in India. Its stength (see fig. 3.5A) lies in the fact that the end is trapped beneath two loops, instead of the standard half blood knots' one loop. For eyed hooks that are going to be used in the most demanding of situations the mahseer knot is unbeatable because it actually 'stretches' under full load instead of strangling the line.

With modern carbon hooks, which have particularly neat eyes, especially in the smaller sizes, the mahseer knot can prove rather bulky to tie. In this case, the seven-turn tucked half blood knot (fig. 3.5B) is both quick and easy to tie.

While both these knots are perfect for tying mono-filament, for dacron and other braids the choice lies

between two more popular knots. The 'palomar knot' (fig. 3.5C) is simple to tie and also creates minimal strangulation of the line. It is not an easy knot to manage with small-eyed hooks because the line has to be doubled into a loop and passed through the eye. Devised by the late Richard Walker and named after his son, the 'Grinner' knot (see fig. 3.5D) is far less constricting than the blood knots and technically more efficient because all five turns around the line are trapped against the eye, not just the end one.

Both of these knots are also good for tying multistrand floss, which is not the easiest material to deal with particularly if you work out of doors and suffer rough finger tips. However, provided you wet the length to be tied and keep it moist whilst bedding the knot down gently, both the palomar and the grinner work efficiently.

For tying spade-end hooks to the finest monofilament, it is worth learning to tie the simple knot in fig. 3.6, which requires no threading or special tool, and allows you to tie the smallest of hooks direct to the reel line or a lighter hook length or bottom quickly. It really is easy. If your fingers

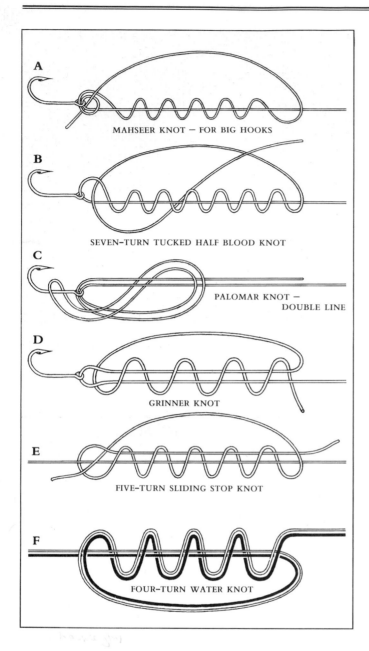

FIGURE 3.5 *Knots 1*

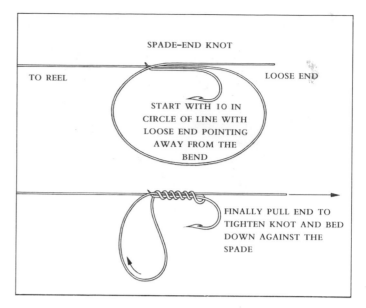

FIGURE 3.6 *Knots 2*

and eyesight will not co-operate, however, there are several excellent tools for tying on spade-end hooks, such as the matchman hooktyer.

For joining 2–3 ft of slightly lighter (finer) hook length to the reel line for trotting with small baits, or for making a simple fixed paternoster ledger, consider the four-turn water knot (fig. 3.7A). This reliable, neat and easy knot allows you to tie a weak bomb or shot link (so it breaks when snag fishing) to the reel line (fig. 3.7C); or a lighter hook link to the reel line for a finer presentation to finicky fish (fig. 3.7B); or a thicker ledger or swimfeeder link to the reel line which stands away from the reel line and alleviates tangles.

As an alternative to the four-turn water knot, use a tiny size 12 swivel (fig. 3.7D) as the junction, remembering always to tie both hook link and reel line to the same end of the swivel. Then, if the swivel breaks in half you are still connected to the fish.

By now it will be plainly obvious that running ledger rigs play absolutely no part in my fishing. They are, in fact, unnecessary and no more sensitive to a biting fish (except when ledgering for pike, zander, perch or catfish and you must allow a run to develop before striking) than the simple fixed paternoster, which, owing to the neat junction knot, creates minimal resistance and attracts nowhere near so much weed and bottom debris as swivels, booms and anti-tangle rigs.

An extremely useful knot I suggest you learn to tie – the simple sliding stop knot – is shown in fig. 3.5E. This is tied directly on to the reel line (using a 10 in length of the same) above a sliding float, which rises and locks at the depth at which the knot is tied. Remember not to trim the ends of the line too short. Around 1 in is a good length, so the ends fold when passing through the rod rings.

This knot is also used in conjunction with a small bead as a stop against which the controller float rests when presenting floating baits, and for casting with sliding pike floats. Again, a bead is used between float and the knot which may also be tied with a length of power gum which is softer than mono and slides through the rod rings easily.

Lastly for joining and making up pole rigs or for joining your reel line to the pre-tied loop of hooks tied to nylon, make a simple, double overhand (surgeons end) loop (fig. 3.8).

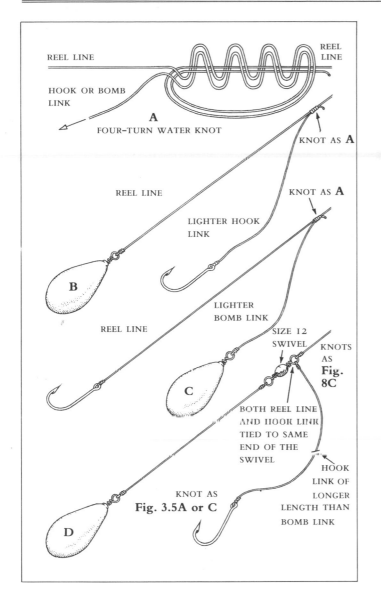

The knot connecting line to hook is invariably the weakest link in the chain. Used for beating huge mahseer in the swift-flowing Indian rivers, John now exclusively uses the mahseer knot for tying eyed hooks direct to monofilament.

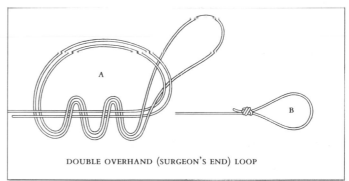

DOUBLE OVERHAND (SURGEON'S END) LOOP

FIGURE 3.7 *Knots* 3   FIGURE 3.8 *Knots* 4

HOOKS

To cater for all requirements in freshwater fishing you need a comprehensive range of both eyed and spade-end hooks from size 2/o down to the tiniest match hook. I stop at a size 22 tied to a low-diameter, 12 oz hook length. If I became involved in competition fishing on really hard venues like over-fished canals, then no doubt, in order to instigate bites, I would contemplate the use of tiny size 24 and 26 hooks tied to gossamer-thin, 8 oz bottoms.

In sizes 14 to 22 I use spade-ends exclusively, and the choice of pattern depends on several factors. With large baits such as stewed wheat, sweetcorn and bread crust presented on a size 14 or even a 16, if big roach, rudd or bream are the quarry and the hook is tied direct to, for example, a 2 lb reel line, I prefer a forged spade-end, such as Kamasan B640 or a Mustad 495. Conversely, for a size 14 or 16 tied to a 1½ lb bottom for presenting punched bread, casters or an elderberry to shy dace or roach, I choose lighter, fine-wire patterns, such as the micro-barb Kamasan B520 and B620 or Drennan carbon match hooks.

From size 12 upwards, I use eyed hooks tied direct to the reel line in the majority of cases. For big roach and rudd, bream, tench, chub and barbel, where line strengths of between 2 lb and 6 lb are used, the Drennan chemically etched round-bend, straight-eyed, carbon specimen hook is perfect for all baits, from particles such as sweetcorn to a large lobworm or lump of bread flake. Throughout the entire size range they are relatively light in the wire so as not to overweight the bait, but are forged strongly enough.

Going up in hook strength with reel lines of 6 lb and heavier, when the quarry is a big tench, barbel or carp, my favourite pattern is the Drennan super-specialist, a really strongly forged pattern, which can be used with confidence in all the smaller sizes. For instance, a single corn kernel on a size 12 tied direct to 4 lb or even 5 lb test is quite in order, as is, say, a single caster on an 18 or 20 tied direct to 2 lb test (the only occasion when I use a small eyed hook rather than a spade-end.)

I also use this pattern with complete confidence when fishing among snags or dense weed and presenting larger offerings: sizes 4 and 6 for whole prawns and cockles or small dead fish, cheese paste, worms and so on; and sizes 8 and 10 for crust cubes and flake, luncheon meat cubes, tares, corn or maize presented two or three up, and so on.

For those occasions when offering whole lobworms, squid, livebaits, mussel, and so on, when a long-shank hook is preferable, the Mustad O'Shaughnessy 34021 pattern in sizes 10–2/o fits the bill admirably.

Treble hooks

From the start I must say that while I prefer to fish lures with barbs on the hooks, for all live- and deadbait pike and zander fishing I use only semi-barbless trebles. Semi-barbless means that one barb is left on one prong only of the treble, for holding on the bait, leaving the two barbless hooks for hooking. Reliable makes include the Partridge outbends, the Drennan carbon semi-barbless, and the Eagle Claw in-turn point (which needs to be doctored by flattening two of the barbs with pliers or forceps before use). Hook removal is much easier with semi-barbless hooks, especially if you are presenting static deadbaits, when the occasional deeply hooked pike is inevitable.

For really heavy work, Partridge make a super-strong treble hook which, though rather thick in the wire, can safely be used even on lines up to 20 lb test for the occasional situations that demand extra-heavy gear.

Making wire traces

Trace wire is available in two types: cabled alasticum, which is easily workable, and can be twisted by hand around the eye of the treble or swivel (fig. 3.9A and B); and the slightly more springy, yet finer-diameter wire, such as Drennan bronze-tinted Seven Strand, or Marlin Steel which is available in green or brown (fig. 3.9C). Both require crimping with narrow-gauge ferrules (such as Drennan 'slim crimps') for a neat, strong join.

The type and strength of hooks are, of course, no less important than knots, so never ever purchase cheap hooks.

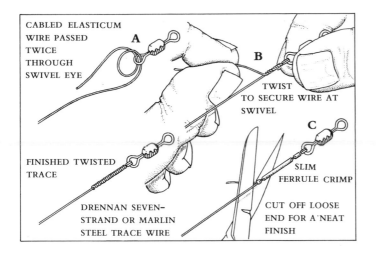

FIGURE 3.9 *Making traces*

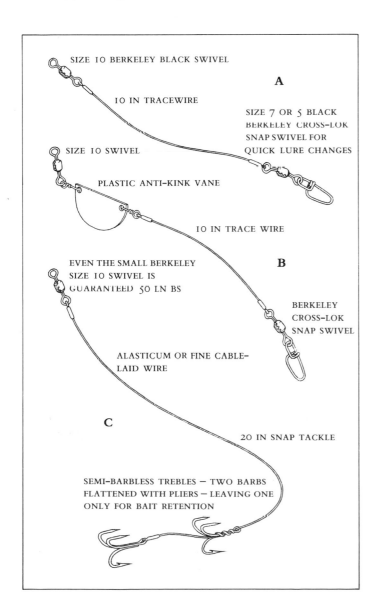

FIGURE 3.10 *Traces*

Cabled alasticum in 15 lb test (it is available at 10–15, 20 and 25 lb) provides sufficient strength for both spinning traces and two-hook traces, more commonly called 'snap tackles' for pike and zander fishing.

Because springy brands are slightly narrower in diameter than cabled alasticum, for most pike fishing you can afford to step up to 20 lb test to provide a safety margin. For zander I use 10 lb wire, but for eels step up to 15 lb with just a large single eyed hook.

To make a simple 10 in spinning trace with cabled alasticum (longer traces have the habit of kinking prematurely and are not necessary for working lures), pass the end through one eye of the swivel and through again, making sure that the end comes out through the coil (see fig. 3.9A). After pulling tight, firmly wind the end of the wire around itself as in fig. 3.9B, using thumb and forefinger. A 1-in long end is quite sufficient with alasticum because its strength lies in the fact that the wire has been passed twice around the swivel eye and trapped. To ensure that the prickly end of the cabled wire does not catch on the reel line, firmly give a few quick turns with thumb and forefinger in the direction in which it was wound, to bed it in.

When trace-making with the finer, springy wire and slim crimps, follow exactly the initial procedure in above for the holding knot, then sleeve on a slim crimp and gently squeeze at each end with a pair of pliers or forceps, before trimming the end off (fig. 3.9C).

Repeat these simple procedures at the other end of the trace to add a snap-type swivel for quick lure changing (fig. 3.10), and your trace is complete. Berkely's snap swivels are the best type to use in all situations because they are guaranteed to take specific loads. They are available in dull black, and the size 10, which is perfect for all traces, has a loading of 50 lb. Berkely cross-lok snap swivels are at least twice the price of others, but are infinitely superior. Sizes 7 or 5 are best for changing lures easily, especially when your fingers are cold. Fig. 3.10B shows a trace to which a plastic anti-kink vane has been added to alleviate line twist when using spinners.

To make a standard snap-tackle trace using a brace of trebles, follow exactly the procedure above, depending on the type of wire. For nearly all my pike fishing, I find size 8 hooks more than adequate. I step down to size 10s if presenting small deadbaits such as sprats when zander fishing.

I usually make the traces of my snap tackles 20 in long for a specific reason (unless float paternostering, when a shorter trace has less chance of tangling). Should the treble end, for instance, become kinked or frayed or one of the trebles badly bent through using forceps, I can snip it off and make it up again without even removing the trace from the rig, knowing that at worst it will be reduced to 15–16 in long, more than adequate for any pike. The wire simply passes through the eye of the up-trace treble, which can be held in any position (depending on bait size) by

wrapping the wire carefully five times around the shank (as in fig. 3.10C).

When using very small livebaits, two trebles are not really necessary so make the trace up using a single size 8.

FLOATS

In order to present the bait to a 6 in roach inhabiting an overgrown canal or farm pond, a sensitive antenna like a small stillwater green carrying just two No. 1 shots is quite sufficient. Conversely, to catch that same 6-in roach from the fast, deep waters of the River Severn or a large, windswept lake where you need to fish at distance, a bodied or loaded waggler carrying up to the equivalent of three swan shots is needed.

I am not suggesting that you need to become a walking tackle shop, but you should relate your float choice to the venues and conditions at hand, stocking up with the patterns most suited to where you fish.

Stillwater floats

For delicate bait presentation in ponds, small lakes and canals you require a range of fine-tipped antennas in shotting capacities from two No. 1s up to 3AA, plus a range of loaded antennas, or darts, for fishing ultra-light and on the drop in sizes two No. 4s to 2BB.

For fishing further out into gravel pits, estate lakes and even larger stillwaters, such as reservoirs and Irish loughs, the most useful float is the waggler. A range each of plain straight, tipped and bodied wagglers in sizes from 2BB up to 3 swans is indispensible and exceptionally versatile because you will also need these in flowing water. In addition, for distance fishing on stillwaters, a range of

loaded wagglers (almost self-cocking) that take minimal shot down the line, permit extremely sensitive presentation for both on-the-bottom and on-the-drop techniques.

I would also recommend that you carry in your kit a few stems of plain, unpainted peacock quill of varying thickness, for stret pegging for presenting a flat float when surface fishing for rudd, and for fishing the lift method for tench, bream and carp.

River floats

In addition to the three types of wagglers previously mentioned, I would suggest a series of trotting floats that are attached with silicon tubing at the top and bottom. At the lighter end, wire-stem stick floats or plain sticks, carrying from three No. 8 up to 3BB are superb for easing the bait through at close range in slow currents. I would also suggest at least one heavier pattern, such as a range of big sticks or balsa trotters carrying from around 3BB up to 3½AA.

For currents demanding still more shot to get the bait down and keep it there – weir-pool fishing and the like – a range of chunky-bodied, Avon-style floats carrying from 3 to 6AA, or the lighter Haskins cork on crowquill specials, are just the job. And for long trotting in shallow swims for chub, grayling and barbel, a range of chunky, thick-tipped chubbers carrying from one to five swan shots are ideal.

POLE FLOATS AND RIGS

Do not be misled into thinking that unless your float-box contains the latest in modern design, you will not catch. Roach, bream, chub, crucian carp, rudd and dace etc. are adequately covered by just five basic patterns. These, like all pole floats, are attached by threading the line through a tiny ring on the top of the body and at the bottom of the stem with a fine piece of silicon tubing.

Many pole floats have bodies based on an elongated heart shape. Those constructed with the wide end uppermost are more suitable for flowing water. Conversely, if the body is positioned upside down with the narrow part at the top, it is ideal for still or very slow-moving water because it creates less resistance to a biting fish.

Stillwater floats

For the most delicate, close-range, fine-line presentation in small waters, a slim-bodied, bristle-top range taking from three to six No. 12 shots is perfect. Going up in size, the next range should have a slim, reversed body with a shotting capacity from 0.05 gm up to 0.30 gm – perfect for use with the whip or with a long pole and short line.

For greater stability in still water, when you want a shotting capacity of between 0.25 gm and 1.50 gm, again choose a reversed heart or oval body with a slightly thicker tip so it can be seen easily at distances up to 10–12 m, even in a good ripple.

While the different pole floats in the local tackle shop may number hundreds, four or five basic patterns, each in a selection of sizes, some already made up on winders for convenience, should cover most requirements in both still and running water.

River patterns

I would suggest a round or heart-shaped, bodied wire-stem range with a shotting capacity of between 0.30 gm and 1.50 gm, plus a much heavier set taking from 2 up to 7 or even 8 gm. These bulbous patterns may look cumbersome and insensitive, but for holding back hard in order to ease the bait slowly along the river-bed in low water

temperatures during the winter months, and for the best presentation in strong currents, you do need a good-sized, buoyant body. As long as it is shotted right down so that only the float tip is visible above the surface until you start to hold back, even the largest-bodied pole floats provide sensitive and natural presentation of the bait.

For shotting these larger floats easily, invest in a comprehensive selection of olivette weights from 1 up to 8 gm. Being hollow, they are easily threaded onto the line and stopped 2–3 ft from the hook by a small shot, so your bait goes straight down to where it needs to be. It is then a simple case of adding just one or two small shots between the olivette and the hook to balance the rig.

Contrary to popular belief, it is not obligatory to own an entire boxful of pole rigs ready made-up on plastic winders, to cover every eventuality in both still and running water. The speed factor demanded by match fishing is, of course, responsible for this idea. It is comforting, however, especially when fingers are numb or the light is poor, to have a small selection of made-up rigs suitable for the fishing at hand. Remember to purchase plastic winders wide and long enough to accommodate the more portly, bulbous patterns of river floats.

When you are using tiny hooks, instead of tying on a new bottom or a hook length of fine mono plus a new hook every time a breakage occurs, followed by a re-adjustment of the shots, it makes sense to use hooks-to-nylon. As all come tied to bottoms of identical length, a quick 'loop to loop' change-over soon has you fishing again with little more than a small shot or two to adjust.

FLOATING CONTROLLERS

The controller is an indispensible piece of equipment for presenting both small and large floaters to surface-feeding carp and chub. It has a swivel at the top, plus a coloured tip for good visual location at distance, plus a weighted stem so it sits vertically in the surface film.

Controllers originated from the age-old spherical bubble float made from clear plastic, into which water could be put to aid casting. However, striking with bubble floats causes so much water displacement that much of the power never reaches the hook. It was for this reason, unhappy with commercially-produced controllers at that

time (now there are several good designs), that I devised my 'Tenpin' which, as its name implies, is shaped exactly like a bowling pin. Rounded and wide at the top, into which a size 10 Berkeley swivel is glued, it tapers down to a narrow wrist which consists of a weighted stem of brass, plugged into the balsa body. I required a weighted surface controller that could be flipped even underarm from banks suffering badly from overhead branches, up to distances of 30 yd or more. I am pleased to say even the small 'Tenpin' (there are four sizes) accomplishes this with ease (see Floater fishing).

PIKE FLOATS

Pike float selection depends on whether you want to support the bait off bottom on a free-roaming or pater-noster rig, drift it with the wind, suspend it with a sunk float above bottom weed, or merely use the float as a bite indicator when, for instance, presenting static deadbaits and you prefer watching a float to other forms of indicators.

Let us start with floats used for supporting deadbaits or livebaits off bottom and as a visual indicator. Size, and the resulting buoyancy, are most important because if too large a float is used, the pike feels resistance and ejects the bait. Moreover, when the pike sulks down on the bottom having grabbed, say, a roach livebait, and submerges an enormous, buoyant float that would perhaps be better sold as a navigational marker rather than as a pike float, every time the pike relaxes its grip for swallowing, the bait is immediately yanked away by the float rising back to the surface. So over-large floats not only inhibit runs from spooky pike, they prevent the bait from being turned.

My favourite float for close-range livebaiting is a 1 in diameter pilot float plugged gently to the line with 2 in of thin peacock quill (see fig. 3.11A). To most anglers this probably seems ridiculously small, because the bait actually submerges it every now and then. But that's the whole point. A small float allows baits up to, say, 6 to 7 in long to work naturally, attracting far more pike.

When supporting larger live- or deadbaits or fishing at longer range, there are numerous cigar-shaped pike floats to fit the bill (fig. 3.11B). The clear plastic zepplers and pikers made by Drennan are ideal, and are available in a variety of sizes. With a tube down the centre and a small eye at the base, they can be threaded on to the line or fixed bottom-end only as sliders or fixed floats.

For presenting a livebait above bottom weed, you require what is called a 'sunken float' such as the Drennan sub-float, which has a centre tube through which the line passes. Alternatively, a 1½- in diameter pilot float painted green or black will do at a pinch.

Loaded floats

For fishing deadbaits lying static on the bottom, when nothing needs supporting, the loaded or self-cocking float is ideal. Like most other pike floats, these come in a range of shapes and sizes from pencil slims to the bulbous-topped tenpin shape, depending on the range being fished and the subsequent visibility required (fig. 3.12).

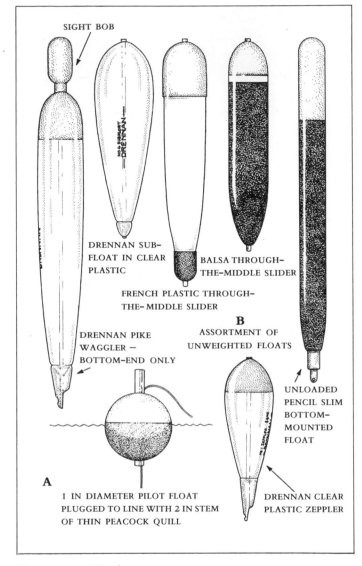

FIGURE 3.11 *Pike floats*

For good visibility at a really long range, floats with sight-vanes pushed into the top are most useful, and add little extra buoyancy.

For drifting both live- and deadbaits to far-off spots, beyond casting range, there are several sail-like drift floats available. The ET Drifter, for instance, has a long, counterbalancing wire stem going through the centre of a polyball body. The sail is then connected above the body and held in place with a rubber band. Spare sails in different colours to suit varying light conditions are available as extras.

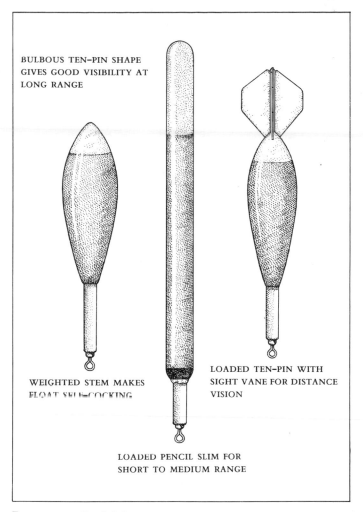

BULBOUS TEN-PIN SHAPE
GIVES GOOD VISIBILITY AT
LONG RANGE

WEIGHTED STEM MAKES
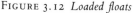
FLOAT SELF-COCKING

LOADED TEN-PIN WITH
SIGHT VANE FOR DISTANCE
VISION

LOADED PENCIL SLIM FOR
SHORT TO MEDIUM RANGE

FIGURE 3.12 *Loaded floats*

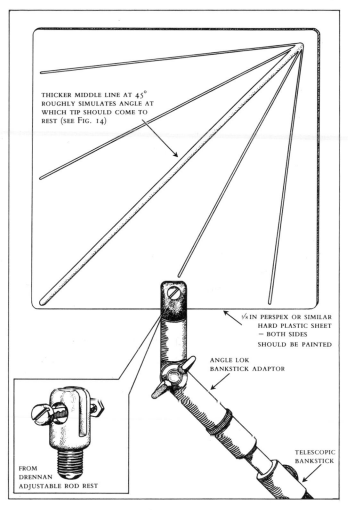

THICKER MIDDLE LINE AT 45°
ROUGHLY SIMULATES ANGLE AT
WHICH TIP SHOULD COME TO
REST (SEE FIG. 14)

⅛ IN PERSPEX OR SIMILAR
HARD PLASTIC SHEET
– BOTH SIDES
SHOULD BE PAINTED

ANGLE LOK
BANKSTICK ADAPTOR

TELESCOPIC
BANKSTICK

FROM
DRENNAN
ADJUSTABLE ROD REST

FIGURE 3.13 *Swingtip target board*

BITE INDICATORS

Swingtip

For the most sensitive bite indication when ledgering in still and very slow-moving water, for species like roach and bream choose a lightweight fibreglass swingtip of between 10 and 12 in. Ensure that the threaded silicone junction that screws into the tip-ring of your ledger rod is flexible but not floppy, and that the end ring at the tip is good quality and not liable to shred fine lines. A loaded (weighted) swingtip is required for slow-moving rivers, and when this starts lifting to current pressure against the line, change the swing for a quivertip.

A target board placed immediately behind the swingtip (once the tackle has been cast and the rod placed on rod-rests) will allow you to see the tiniest of tip movements (fig. 3.13). Target boards are also useful when watching quivertips in low water temperatures, when bites are liable to be tiny movements of between ⅛ to ¼ in. You can

easily make your own target boards or invest in one of the many commercial models available. Either way, it should be reversible (so the tip can be angled to the left or to the right) and accept the standard bankstick thread.

Quivertips

By far the most versatile bite indicator, the quivertip is available in a whole range of test curves from 1 to 3½ oz to suit current strengths from the slow draw on a canal, to a fast, deep run on the lower reaches of a tidal river where a 2 oz feeder is needed to hold bottom, and the most likely customers are barbel, bream or chub.

My preference for tip colour is all-white. This I can see easily against any background. Indeed, all my built-in quivertip rods have the top 16–20 in painted in two coats of matt white. A white tip is great if, like me, you prefer to illuminate it for night fishing with a narrow torch beam.

Screw-in, commercially-made quivertips, most of which have just a single ring at the tip, are best doctored by adding a small intermediate guide midway along so that the line is fully supported and follows the contour of the tip when it is under maximum compression.

Springtips

The springtip is a solid glass, tapered quivertip that passes through the middle of a 2 in long spring into a rubber moulding with a tip-ring thread. It can, in effect, be used as a fairly stiff quivertip. Or it can be used by pulling gently on the tip so that it leaves the spring but remains in the rubber joint, like a quivertip that hinges at the junction. Used like this it creates far less resistance to biting fish than the quivertip, and in still or slow-moving water is ideal for small fish like roach and dace.

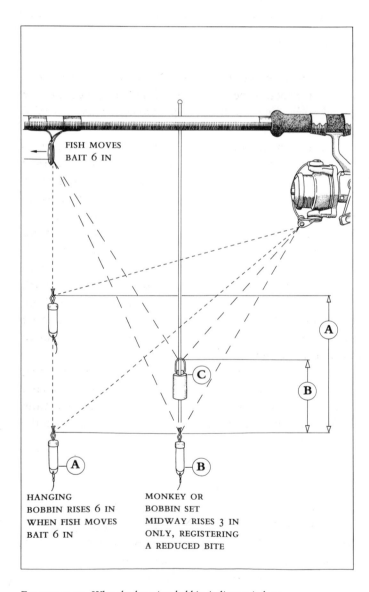

FIGURE 3.14 *Why the hanging bobbin indicator is best*

Bobbin indicators

Bobbin bite indicators, which clip onto the line between the reel and the butt ring and are retained by a cord fixed to the front rod-rest, are extremely useful in certain circumstances (fig. 3.14). I much prefer them for stillwater ledgering, especially at distance, when using large baits intended for tench, bream or specimen rudd and roach.

Daytime bobbins, which come complete with clip and retaining cord, such as the tenpin bobbin, are available in fluorescent red. The glo bobbin, which contains a luminous betalight element that lasts for 15 years, provides indication around the clock.

To counteract 'bobbin lift' in strong winds wherever there is a strong draw or sub-surface tow on stillwaters, simply pinch between one and three swan shots on the retaining cord immediately below the bobbin.

Coil indicators

When fishing for carp, catfish and eels, necessity sometimes calls for a visual indicator fixed between the butt ring and reel which is easily seen, easily attached, and which relates to both forward and drop-back bites. For years (some still do) anglers simply squeezed a piece of silver kitchen foil on to the line midway between butt ring and reel. Simple coil indicators (they can also be made from plastic piping in a variety of weights) are ideal for short freelining or ledgering sessions (see fig. 3.15).

Monkey climbers

The most popular of all carp indicators are, in effect, 'bobbins' on a stick which do not blow about in the wind, which makes them ideal when ledgering for most other species too. They are available in a variety of weights to counteract sub-surface tow and to indicate drop-back bites in certain circumstances. If a certain amount of your carp fishing will take place during darkness or in poor light, choose a monkey with a clear body that will accept a luminous betalight element. Monkeys which run super freely on a black (PTFE-coated) stick, aptly called 'grease monkeys', are worth the extra money as the body slides up and down effortlessly.

Bite alarms/buzzers

While monkey climbers work perfectly well without any electrical help in registering a bite when ledgering, they are used almost exclusively in conjunction with an electric bite alarm, or 'buzzer', for carp fishing. Used in conjunction with either a bobbin or monkey climber indicator buzzers

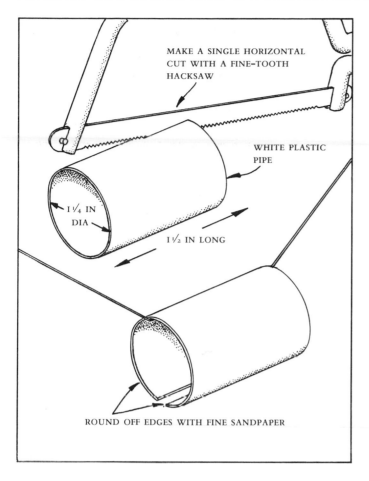

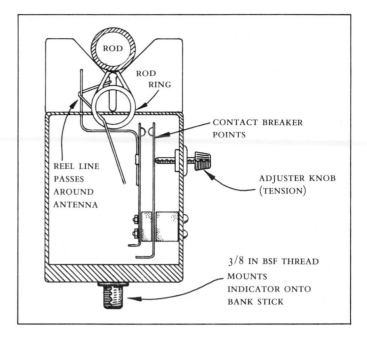

FIGURE 3.16 *Antenna-type buzzers*

FIGURE 3.15 *Coil indicators*

are also effectively used for tench, bream, perch, zander and pike fishing situations.

Antenna-type buzzers

These, the first design in buzzers ever marketed, are still popular because they fit nicely into the lower price bracket and work on the contact-breaker principle. When the line is pulled across the antenna, at the bottom of which is a breaker point, contact is made and the buzzer sounds in conjunction with a light-emitting diode for visual warning (see fig. 3.16).

The antenna can be tensioned or relaxed as required for registering twitches or steady pulls by simple knob adjustment.

Optonic bite indicators

These particular buzzer-alarms, which are in fact now almost standard gear amongst carp and tench enthusiasts, also indicate the speed at which line is being taken off the reel. For every ¾ in of line which travels across the sensitive 'wheel' a single bleep tone plus warning light is emitted, so you can instantly relate to the kind of bite,

whether it is a mere twitch, a slow run, or a scorching run. As the line rotates the wheel a tiny fan blade spigoted to the wheel with a fine spindle interupts the light beam of a mini photo electric cell

This system is available in various self-contained cordless compact forms, with or without volume and tone control, and with sensors (or heads) connected by wires to a sounder box which can be positioned several yards away inside a bivi so it effectively becomes an alarm clock.

All electronic bite alarms naturally become the front rod rest heads, for which the 'buzzer bar' was invented. Available in alloy or stainless steel there are buzzer bars to take two, three or even four rods (stick with two) which simply screw into the standard bank-stick thread. For both front and back rests (separate U-type screw-in heads take the rod butts) invest in a pair of telescopic bank sticks to allow for a variety of different marginal levels.

For the really hard banking of some gravel pits, reservoirs and the like, the rod pod is the answer. This is a complete rod set-up with a ground frame combining bank sticks and twin buzzer bars with an aerial bar located in the middle to take monkey climbers.

Drop-off/arm indicators

The simple drop-off or drop-arm indicator provides positive visual indication of a bite when ledgering for pike (zander also), whether the pike moves off and away with the bait or swims directly towards the rod.

The unit consists of a plastic-covered steel needle with a flexible junction of silicone tubing, plus a terry clip at one end (for fixing to the rear rod rest) and a 1½-in diameter orange polyball and line clip at the other. Upon tightening up after casting, the bale arm is opened and the line is fixed into the line clip.

When a pike runs towards the rod the arm drops back. And if the fish moves away, the arm lifts until the line pulls from the clip, whereupon the arm drops off and falls back – hence its name.

Mainly employed for pike fishing, though in big waters during rough conditions both zander and perch anglers also use them, drop-off, or drop-arm, indicators are by far the most visible. Coupled to electric bite alarms, there is no more effective set-up when ledgering for pike or presenting a livebait on a sunk float paternoster, which produced this immaculate 32¾ lb gravel-pit pike for Charlie Clay.

SUNDRIES

Bait-droppers and catapults

Bait-droppers that attach to the hook and deposit particle feed such as maggots, casters and hempseed straight down to the bottom, exactly where you want it in fast deep rivers, or both, are indispensible.

Wire-mesh models cost double the price of plastic droppers, but are far more durable and have in-built weight for a speedy descent to the bottom.

Because the accurate use of bait-droppers is obviously restricted to swims that are little further than one and a half rod lengths out, all distances beyond this should be covered by the catapult. You require two models: a medium-sized, soft pouch catapult with stretchy elastic for putting out maggots, hempseed, sweetcorn, and so on; and another with a larger, rigid pouch and more powerful elastic for propelling tangerine-sized balls of groundbait over distances beyond that which can be reached by throwing.

For catapulting boilies out a fair distance, invest in a specialized boilie catapult, which has powerful elastic and a small, moulded cup.

In slow rivers or stillwaters, the loose-feed catapult reigns supreme for ensuring that loose feed arrives on the bottom close to your hook bait.

David Wilson carefully removes a small hook from a colourful river perch using a barrel disgorger. These are available in both alloy and plastic in varying-sized heads to accommodate the tiniest spade-end, to medium-sized eyed hooks.

Bread punch

Of the numerous designs of bread-punch units available, I much prefer the pen type, such as the Seymo bread punch, which comes with four interchangeable brass heads, or the plastic Drennan bread punches. The latter consists of a set of four plastic punches with heads varying from 2 mm up to 5 mm in diameter, suitable for hooks in sizes 10 to 24. What I most like about these is the extra-shallow bowls, which really compress thick-sliced bread but only lightly compress thin slices – a feature that allows you to control the rate at which your bait descends through the swim.

Drennan punches are shanfered below the slot, so that when the hook is pulled through into the bread pellet and out, the point does not touch the bowl and so cannot become blunt.

Weed rakes/drags

If you are committed, either through lack of transport or local choice, to tench fishing in extremely weedy fisheries, some sort of weed-clearing device is essential if you wish to continue fishing throughout the summer.

For years tench fishermen have been wiring together (use 20 gauge galvanized wire) the steel heads of two garden rakes back to back, and tying on a long length of 'throwing' rope securely in the middle. This makes a cheap and most efficient tool for pulling out dense lilies or other surface plants and for removing rampant soft weeds such as Canadian pond weed or mill foil.

During the winter months there is no better time for

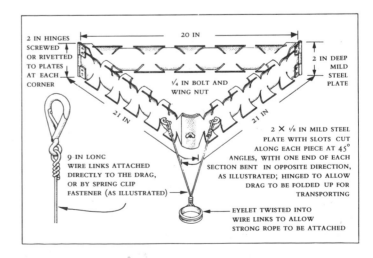

FIGURE 3.17 *Home-made weed rake*

constructing your own designer weed drag. An excellent pattern (fig. 3.17) handed down to me by my old friend Bill Cooper of Norwich has, over the years, proved to be most useful. It is light, well worth the trouble to make, and really cleans out a swim fast, whatever it happens to be clogged with.

Disgorgers

To remove a hook safely from any fish, whether a 3 in dace that has completely swallowed a size 22 hook, or a specimen tench or carp that needs a size 8, eyed hook eased gently from its throat, you need to be equipped with two items of tackle. A pair of long-nosed artery forceps between 5 and 8 in long, and a barrel-type plastic or alloy disgorger.

Roach, rudd and dace for instance, and especially bream, are delicate species, so be exceptionally careful of their throat tissue during hook removal. Always hold them firmly, but gently, with wet hands so as not to remove their protective mucus or slime, and refrain from any heavy prodding with the disgorger.

GLOVING AND UNHOOKING PIKE

In order to enjoy the freedom of wandering the bank with a lure rod, and even when bringing in a pike which has flying treble or hooks on the outside of its jaws, I forget the net altogether. I simply slip a strong, rubberized, industrial-type glove (always in the back pocket of my fishing waistcoat or tackle bag) on to my left hand and glove the pike out by the chin, unless both hooks of the snap tackle or lure are visible on the outside, in which case they can be flipped out easily with forceps and the pike set free immediately.

Provided care is taken, the technique of 'gloving' makes hook removal a formality. It should be done with a glove on the left hand (or the right hand if you are lefthanded). You gently slip your fingers into the pike's left gill opening and when half the hand is inside, clamp down against its left gill with your thumb (still on the outside) in a firm grip so that it is immobilized.

When you are confident that your left-hand (or right-hand grip for lefthanders) grip is secure, lay the pike on its back on wet grass or a dampened unhooking mat (when boat-fishing I use a sheet of ½-in thick dense foam over the floor boards) and slowly curl your hand. The pike has no option then but to open its lower jaw. Then remove the hooks with long-nosed artery forceps from the front, or gently through the opposite gill slit if they are well back in the throat.

Forceps between 8 and 12 in long are ideal, and whatever you do don't be afraid of your pike. Treat it with firm respect.

Sacks

As both carp and pike live a long life, and in popular fisheries will no doubt be caught dozens, perhaps even hundreds of times, you owe it to the fish and to the angler after you to return the fish without harm. This entails retaining it in a soft nylon sack of adequate proportions.

Sacks punched with numerous holes for the water to pass freely through are highly recommended. They come in various sizes (4 × 5 ft is ideal) with a draw-string top or long zip, and are black in colour which helps keep the carp quiet inside. Remember always to fully soak the sack before putting the fish inside, or some of its valuable body mucus will be removed, leaving it vulnerable to parasites and disease. Select a quiet shaded spot away from full sunlight and tie the retaining cord tightly to a bankside branch. Ensure that the fish has at least 18 in of water so it can fully submerge, and once again retain it for the shortest period of time only. Lastly never put more than one fish into one sack.

Unhooking mats

For the safe removal of hooks – safe that is for the fish, which can all too easily flap up and down on gravel banking and scrape itself raw – unhooking mats have been designed. For gravel pit fisheries in particular, renowned for stony banks which never grass over, these foam-filled unhooking mats are an absolute must for ensuring that the fish goes back in to the water in the condition in which it came out.

Weighing slings

Continuing the theme of disturbing the fish's condition as little as possible, it's just as easy to unscrew the landing-net top and hoist it on to the scales complete with tench, carp, pike or catfish to weigh it, remembering to deduct the net's weight afterwards. Should this prove impossible, have a large pre-wetted, soft nylon sling handy into which the fish can be gently moved immediately after unhooking. After weighing, take the sling into the water and hold it there to allow the fish to swim out under its own steam and in its own time.

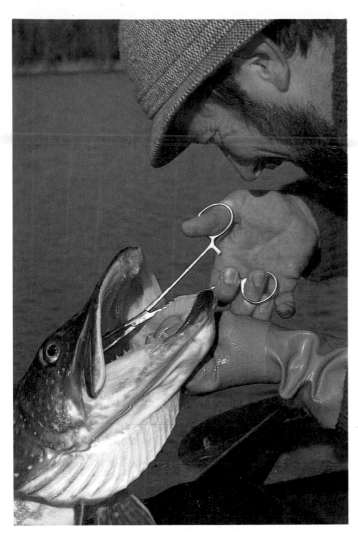

To unhook pike, simply sleeve an industrial (close-fitting) rubber glove onto your left hand and slip three fingers into its left gill opening. Now press your thumb hard against the fingers and gently curl your hand backwards. The pike has no alternative but to open wide, whereupon the hooks can be removed with long-nosed artery forceps.

Norfolk chub fisherman, Nick Beardmore, uses a landing-net that is perfect for most fish except the longer species like pike and catfish. It has a 24 in round frame fitted with a deep net of minnow-mesh sides and a micro base through which small shots do not fall.

Landing-nets

As even the largest roach or rudd for instance is unlikely to exceed 16 or 17 in in length (even a 2 lb roach will only measure around 14 in) a landing-net top of 18 in diameter is quite sufficient if only seeking the smaller species. There are many excellent, extremely lightweight designs on the market with triangle, round, bow and spoon-shaped frames, made from both plastic-covered alloy and solid glass or carbon.

In my local rivers Wensum and Bure, where roach are not uncommon over the 2½ lb mark, I may also catch chub over 4 lb, or the odd big bream or even a double-figure barbel, I hedge my bets by using a 24-in diameter round net, which engulfs them all. It is rather on the large side for most of the roach I catch, but not for specimen

roach and rudd caught after dark, when netting is far from easy.

My net has 24-in deep sides in minnow-mesh which alleviates the possibility of a good fish accidentally jumping or rolling out (as can happen with shallow-pan nets) plus a microbase for eliminating those awkward tangles that occur when shots drop through larger meshes.

To weigh a specimen simply unscrew the net-top and hoist it onto the hook of the scales, remembering to deduct the weight of the net afterwards. Transferring the fish to a 'designer' weigh-bag or sling only creates extra stress on the fish.

Traditionally, carp and pike landing-nets have always been triangular in shape with two arms supported in a preformed spreader block, fitted with a standard BSF ⅜th thread for screwing into any landing-net pole. A nylon cord stretched between the tip of each end keeps them slightly bowed, and thus the whole frame remains reasonably rigid. For several years I have used the North Western specimen net, which has strong hollow fibre-glass arms and is available in 36 in, 42 in and 50 in sizes. Frankly, having easily slipped two pike each of exactly 50 in (one a 30-pounder) into the 42 in carp model, I cannot see why anything larger, with its associated awkward manoeuvrability (especially in dense undergrowth), is ever required.

Twin meshes are extremely popular, and rightly so. The larger wall mesh allows the net to be steered easily through the water, while the soft nylon or micro bottom ensures that the fish's body mucus remains intact and that the terminal rig does not become entangled.

With regard to landing-net poles, I would suggest you purchase the longest and lightest model, in lightweight hollow glass, that you can afford. Telescopic models of up to 10 ft in carbon fibre are first class. There is nothing more frustrating than not being able to net a fish caught up in the fringe of marginal vegetation because the landing-net pole is too short, or because you cannot hold it when fully extended because with the net-top it is too heavy.

Incidentally, when flyfishing or stalking chub during the summer along small rivers and streams heavily overgrown I use a folding trout net with a telescopic handle, which clips neatly out of harms way on a D-ring sewn into the back of my waistcoat. Mine has a lightweight, 20 in, rigid aluminium frame and is more than adequate for the largest chub. The only alteration has been to replace its standard, large (trout) mesh for a soft micro net, perfect for coarse species.

Keep-nets

By far the kindest keep-net material is soft, black, nylon micro-mesh. Whether you choose round or oblong rings is not important, although rectangular nets have greater stability in shallow water and in windy weather. What is of paramount importance, however, is that you purchase the largest keep-net you can afford, because roach, rudd and bream for instance are extremely delicate species and quickly suffer from stress when crammed into small nets or nets with considerably larger meshes, through which their fins can poke and easily become split.

Wonderful keep-nets are available with built-in, angle-lock top rings in a rectangular format with 20 x 16 in rings, up to 13 ft in length, and round nets in both 18 in and 21 in diameter rings up to 11½ ft in length. My overall preference is for a round, 21 in diameter net, 10 ft in length, preferably with the protector net facility, which allows the entire catch to be released through the bottom of the net (without taking it from the water) by undoing a plastic clip on each side of the bottom ring.

ECHO SOUNDERS/FISH FINDERS

For the serious pike angler and any angler who wishes to know the depths and topography of his favourite fishery who regularly fishes from a boat, electronic wizardry is a great help, particularly when exploring large, previously unfished sheets of water that would otherwise take weeks of work with a plummet and sliding float rig. A good outline of the bottom contours can easily be made in a day using even a simple echo-sounder, marking the depths in ink on a drawing of the fishery.

There are two types of echo-sounders, though both work on the principle of sending a signal through a transducer down to the bottom and back.

Echo-sounders

The now outdated 'Seafarer' type provides an accurate account of depths as the boat moves along, whether propelled by oars or engine. By adjusting the sensitivity knob, objects situated between the surface and bottom do sometimes show up on the read-out band, but I have never been able to differentiate which is which, whether fish, weed or rubbish.

Fish-finders

With modern hi-tech sounders, fish location has become a fine art and new, more sophisticated models are appearing every year. Indeed, American charter-boat skippers who troll the Great Lakes in search of salmon for instance, could not possibly operate in such vast waters without ultrasonic fish-finders. A vast multi-million dollar industry would crumble, as would of course commercial fishing as we know it today.

The models I have used for several years now whilst down rigger trolling for giant lake trout in Canada, whilst locating the nile perch of Lake Victoria in Kenya, and of course when locating pike in the gravel pits, lakes and broads of Norfolk are made by Humminbird. These fabulous units (other recommended finders are manufactured by Lowrance) operate by sending through the transducer that clips on to the transom with a suction pad, ultra sonic signals at 5000 cycles per second down to the bottom and back. The read out then appears on the TV type screen in terms of a black outline, showing the surface line and bottom contours.

Whilst the bottom, weed beds and rocks etc show up in black, fish show up in red squares so there is never any question as to what is what.

Making mudweights

Steel mudweights are extremely expensive so why not make your own (which you can then take along and use wherever you hire a boat) by filling a couple of 2-gallon maggot buckets with concrete (fig. 3.18). To attach the rope bend a 10 in length of ¼ in mild steel into the shape shown so it protrudes from the bottom of the bucket when turned upside down on soft earth (make a narrow hole in the ground to take the wire), and fill with concrete to within 1 in of the lip. Within two days your mudweights will be ready for use after adding a suitable length of soft ½ in nylon rope to each at least twice the depth of anywhere you might fish.

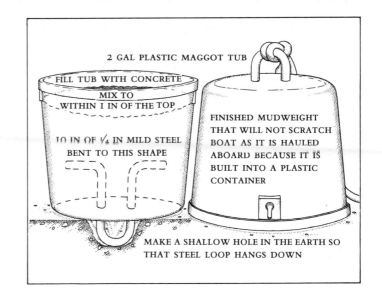

FIGURE 3.18 *Making mudweights*

BAITS

During my early twenties I worked several months for a printing firm whose premises overlooked a pretty little stream that ran fast and shallow through beds of bright green watercress. In those days the stream (it was in fact a feeder stream to the nearby River Lea) contained numerous shoals of immature chub to around 1 lb that basked in the sunshine during summer afternoons directly beneath the print room in which letterpress machines banged noisily away. And those chub very soon learnt to accept a rather peculiar daily diet.

For a precious 30 minutes at lunchtime the machines were switched off, enabling the lads to nip across the road to the 'chippy'. I can vividly remember that first occasion when I flicked a hot chip into the stream. Its sudden arrival on the surface just upstream from the shoal sent a dozen or so chub absolutely crazy. A second chip was flicked in and

disappeared with equal speed and another, and another, and so on. A new lunchtime activity was born, and soon everyone wanted to feed their fish and chips to those chub, which eagerly gobbled up anything and everything that was thrown in.

The moral of this story is two-fold. It illustrates perfectly the fact that (unless you scare them) most species are unlikely to refuse anything edible which falls in their direction. And it proves to the fisherman that fish can indeed be programmed, because within just a few days those chub were expecting their fish and chips at lunchtime. In short, pre-baiting is very worthwhile, whether it is just a few handfuls of hook bait scattered into the swim an hour before you actually fish, or whether you plan an organized pre-baiting programme to be executed over several days.

NATURAL BAITS FROM THE RIVER

There are numerous natural baits that can easily be obtained beside the river or actually in it. For this reason, it is always worth having a fine-mesh, rectangular aquarium net with you.

Crayfish

While collecting bullheads and stone loach in streams still running fast, clear and pure over a clean gravel bottom, you will also catch the occasional crayfish, the largest of our freshwater crustaceans, which in every feature looks like a lobster. Once, most rivers in the British Isles contained crayfish, and up until around the 1970/80s I would have urged you to try them for chub. As a summer bait, freelined into clear running water, their pulling power had no equal; however, this is not the case any more.

Unfortunately the saying 'when the crayfish disappear, the river won't be long afterwards', has come true all too often for minor rivers and streams in the past 20 years. Bore-hole water abstraction by farming and industry, greater quantities of treated and even untreated sewage, farming chemical run-off, each has taken its toll. Combined they have reduced clear flowing streams to ditches of effluent in which the crayfish is always the first to suffer. It is the barometer of pure water, and if a water you are fishing still contains numbers of crayfish, leave them be. Study the following pages covering the great diversity of fish baits that are available, happy in the knowledge that you are indeed privileged in having actually seen a live crayfish. Only in this way do they have a chance of survival.

Caddis grubs

Long before I purchased maggots, or 'gentils' as they were popularly called in those days, my hook baits were gathered from wherever I happened to be fishing. There are, in fact, over 200 different species of sedge or caddis flies inhabiting both still and running water, and it is their larvae, known affectionately as the 'caddis grub', which

As maggots are so readily accessible, most anglers would not dream of collecting caddis grubs nowadays. Nonetheless, they are a superb and entirely free bait, which is always available at the waterside.

chub, roach, rudd and dace (along with most other freshwater species) consume with relish. Most species of caddis construct intricate little homes of between 1 and 2 in long from pieces of wood, stone or sand, which act both as house and protection for one year, from the moment when the grub emerges from the egg laid by the sedge fly until the grub leaves its home. Once the pupa moves towards the surface in readiness for the last stage of metamorphosis, its body case eventually splits open and out crawls the sedge fly itself. It is a fascinating life cycle.

To gather a fresh supply of grubs, you simply rummage around in the shallows, lifting up large twigs and rotten branches and looking under large pieces of flint, etc., to which the grubs cling. If you peer intently through crystal-clear water, you can see them crawling awkwardly along the bottom with just their head and legs extended beyond their protective case.

To remove the succulent grub (noticeably larger than a white maggot), pinch its tail end to make the head and legs appear at the front. Then gently ease it out with thumb and forefinger. Present one up on a size 14, or two on a 12, and you have a superb, entirely free, natural bait that is there whenever you fish, just waiting to be harvested both winter and summer should you forget the maggots or simply wish to enjoy a piece of natural history to while away the time.

BANKSIDE NATURALS

Slugs

Although occasionally a perch or a pike grabs hold, if there is one bait tailor made specifically for chub from all those readily available and most effective throughout the summer and autumn months, it would be the slug.

Being weighty, slugs can be freelined long distances without additional shots, although they work just as effectively when ledgered on the bottom of a deep, fast pool or runs. Slugs can also be skate cast (in a series of skips just like skating flat stones into the sea) into awkward, mysterious spots beneath the low, overhanging branches of trees, where no other bait could be placed. Or they can be plopped in alongside long rafts of marginal rushes or sedges and retrieved in a twitching, popping mode just like a surface plug. They are the warm-weather chubbing bait par excellence. You nick a size 6 or 4 eyed hook tied direct to 6 lb test into one end of the slug – no more than is required for casting – leaving the entire point and barb exposed, otherwise the strike could be impaired and the hook not driven home.

Contrary to popular belief, it is not difficult to keep slugs prior to using them. All you need is an old aquarium filled with fresh vegetation on to which fits a weighted sheet of gauze. Kept in a cool, darkened spot (on the garage floor) and topped up with fresh inmates every now and then, you will always have a supply at the ready. The undersides of larger stones in garden rockeries, damp cellars, the bottom of piles of old cut logs, in fact any rotten, damp hideout, will provide the habitat that slugs require. Damp woodlands well away from farming chemicals, such as public parks and overgrown pathways, are the places to visit. The best times are at night after heavy rain, or during the early morning when dawn is accompanied by thick fog or mist.

Apart from being one of the most productive natural baits, an additional benefit with slugs is that they can be used to catch more than one chub.

Of the 20 different species of British slugs, only three are useful for chub fishing as they grow in excess of 2 in, and are thus heavy enough for casting. They are the common red slug, easily identified by an orange frill on the underside of its brown body; the black slug, openly adored by chub fanatics; and the great grey slug, a beautiful creature flecked with dark brown markings over a pale grey body.

Snails

The slug is really only a snail without a shell, and I have on occasion, when slugs have been impossible to find, used large garden snails to good effect. You crush the shell gently, pulling off most of the broken pieces, and hook the somewhat squashed snail as though a slug. It cannot be cast very far, but will be swallowed by the chub with equal relish.

Wasp nests

There is a certain something about the sweet and sickly smell that emanates from the grub-laden cakes of a wasp nest which drives chub wild. You can use the large, fat, white grubs singly or two up for trotting, and the mashed-up cake and grubs for groundbait, which works at any time in the season, even winter. The cakes (exactly the size of a round 2-pt bait tin) can be frozen until required. Or, and this is really a summer to autumn technique, large (50p-sized) pieces of cake heavy in grubs easily provide sufficient weight for freelining, just like presenting floating crust. A single grub fits nicely on to a size 14 hook and a piece of cake on to a size 6.

Actually, the grubs are not only relished by chub, they are a fine bait for roach, rudd and dace.

Of all natural baits, wasp grubs are the most difficult to obtain, and could be dangerous, so be very careful if you decide to take a nest. The best way of obtaining freshly killed nests is to pay the local fruit farmer a visit from around July onwards, when he will be busy destroying the nests heavy in grubs. Most local councils also run pest control units from which nests may be obtained. Or when you discover a wasps nest in the river bank, or in the garden rockery, you can even have a go at removing it yourself, but do be very careful. The local chemist will supply special preparations for 'killing' the nest with explicit directions. These should be followed exactly.

OTHER NATURAL BAITS

Lobworms

Many species, particularly tench, carp, barbel, chub, eels, catfish and perch are attracted to the distinct 'aroma' of animal baits, and especially those which wriggle like a big, juicy lobworm.

There is nothing like a supply of fresh lobworms harvested from a sopping wet lawn, the secret being to watch the weather carefully and only set forth after a prolonged spell of rain, and the local cricket pitch is the place to visit.

When the ground is really wet and the rain has dwindled to just a fine spray, or stopped completely, lobworms are more likely to be out of their holes, lying there on top of the wet grass waiting to be picked up. Incidentally, for those new to the art of worm stalking, do not rush about with a quartz halogen flashlight. Pick your feet up carefully as you walk slowly along (just like a chicken does) and use a wide-beam torch of medium power, otherwise every worm on the pitch will be halfway down its hole before you bend down. Lastly, to keep both hands free (one for the torch, the other for picking up worms) hang a 1-gallon plastic bait bucket around your neck at chest height.

Having tried presenting lobworms every which way over the years, I have come to the conclusion that hooking the worm once only through the head end is best (see fig. 4.1A). The worm can at least work naturally, and thus looks far more appealing than if it is double hooked. And fewer bites are missed through the hook point doubling back into the worm instead of into the fish's mouth.

Select hook sizes to match that of the lobworm. Huge snakes go best on size 4 or 6 hooks (tied direct to the reel line), while medium to small worms fit nicely on sizes 8 and 10. For long trotting, present a whole small lob on a size 10, or the tail end only on a size 12 (fig. 4.1A).

When presenting lobworms over really thick bottom weed to species like carp and tench inject the head of the lob with a little air from a hypodermic syringe so it floats tantalizingly above the weed, using a swan shot or two to compensate for its buoyancy (fig. 4.2). Lawn lobs keep best if packed loosely in clumps of sphagnam moss in a large bait tin.

Brandlings and redworms

There is scarcely a freshwater species that at some time or another will not readily accept these small, lively worms. Perch, chub, tench, bream, rudd and of course eels are particularly attracted to the brandling, which comes from

BEST BAITS – NATURALS

	brandlings	caddis grubs	casters	cockles	lobworms	maggots	mussels	prawns	redworm	shrimps	slugs	snails	squid	wasp grub
BARBEL	●		●	●	●			●		●				
BREAM	●		●		●	●			●					
CARP			●	●	●	●	●	●	●	●			●	
CATFISH				●	●		●						●	
CHUB	●	●	●		●	●		●	●	●	●	●		●
DACE		●	●			●								●
EEL	●				●		●		●					
PERCH	●		●		●				●		●			
PIKE											●		●	
ROACH		●	●			●								●
RUDD	●	●	●			●			●					●
TENCH	●	●	●	●	●	●	●	●	●	●				

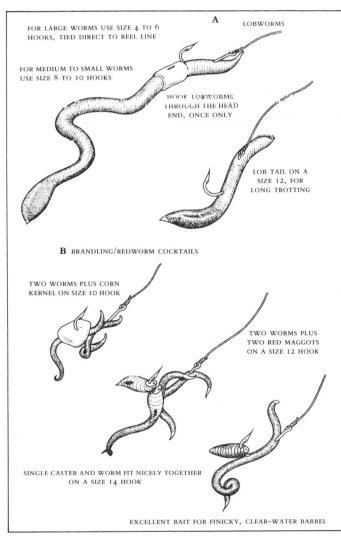

FIGURE 4.1 *Worms*

To gather a good supply of lobworms, visit the local cricket pitch at night following a heavy downpour. With a 1 gal bucket hung around the neck, one hand holds the torch and the other picks up the worms.

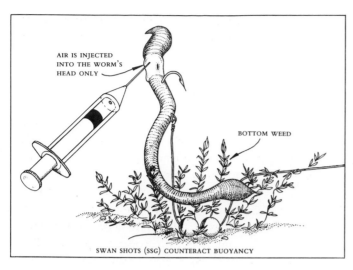

AIR IS INJECTED
INTO THE WORM'S
HEAD ONLY

BOTTOM WEED

SWAN SHOTS (SSG) COUNTERACT BUOYANCY

FIGURE 4.2 *Air-injected lobworm*

manure heaps and is easily identified by thin yellow rings
around its body and a yellow fluid inside. These worms
can be fished on their own or in bunches and they make
superb cocktail baits used in conjunction with sweetcorn,
casters, or maggots (fig. 4.1B). Brandlings are easily
obtained pre-packed in containers from tackle shops or
from manure heaps that farmers pile by the roadside.
Always have the decency to ask whether you can gather a
boxful, and few farmers will refuse.

Redworms are found in compost heaps, especially those
comprising rotting leaves and garden vegetation, and are
used in the same way as brandlings.

Mussels

Generally speaking freshwater mussels, and in particular
the largest – the well-known swan mussel – seem to grow
best of all in rich silty water, be they estate lakes, ponds or
pits. To open the clam-like shell, use a thin-bladed knife to
sever the powerful hinges holding the two halves together.
This reveals the orange meat inside – a food source which
carp, tench, eels and catfish just cannot resist.

Mussels live with their shell part-buried in the detritus,
feeding and breathing by continually syphoning water
through their system. They do in fact move rather more
quickly than one would imagine, with a keel-like foot
protruding from the bottom corner of their blunt end. In
thick silt they leave behind a definite furrow.

Gather mussels by pulling a long-handled garden rake
along the bottom through the margins. Some areas will be
far more prolific than others, so don't despair if you are not
immediately successful. In really muddy or silty shallows,
it's just as easy to roll your sleeves up and feel for them.
They can easily be kept alive for several days in a bucket of
water, but soon die and go off when left dry.

Whole mussels are best freelined, and result in the most
positive runs you are ever likely to encounter. Present
whole on a size 4 hook (larger for catfish, 2–1/0) and use
the insides from several other mussels for groundbait. Pre-
baiting a swim every other day with the insides of 20 swan
mussels could well provoke even difficult, well-fished carp
into a feeding frenzy. Try it and see.

Cockles

Whether tench and carp respond eagerly to cockles because
the orange meat reminds them of a baby swan mussel, I
cannot say. However, following a few days of pre-baiting,
cockles will have them climbing up the rod – or they will
produce absolutely no interest at all.

Buy them in bulk ready-boiled from the fishmongers,
and separate into smaller batches in polybags before
popping into the freezer for later use. Prior to freezing,
they can be coloured with the same powder dye used in
making carp baits.

Simply add a teaspoonful of dye to half a cupful of hot
water and pour over the cockles in a 2 pt bait tin. Colour
the cockles in 1 pt batches, stirring gently until they are
evenly coloured, then strain off excess dye before freezing.

Several other species are attracted to cockles – chub,
barbel, bream, eels and catfish. And because they are
usually left alone by small shoal fish, cockles really are
excellent for prebaiting.

Prawns and shrimps

Again, these are most cheaply bought in bulk (several pints
at a time) from the fishmongers ready boiled and peeled.
Split them into separate batches for freezing. As with
cockles, pre-baiting over a period of several days will
allow species like tench, carp, chub and barbel to acquire a
liking for the succulent meat.

In their natural grey-green, unpeeled state prior to
boiling, prawns can be effectively freelined (with the
addition of a shot or two) through clear water runs for
barbel and chub, which both gobble them up greedily.
Perhaps the natural prawn or shrimp reminds them of a
small crayfish.

Squid

Squid may seem a strange bait to offer freshwater species.
However, if they are purchased fresh from the market,
there is no finer bait for catching catfish. Large squid may
be sectioned along the body into strips and presented with
a length of one tentacle (although I doubt a catfish really
bothers about realism), while baby squid in the 4–6 in size

are perfect to use whole. Use size 2–2/0 hooks. A well-known secret on waters where both carp and catfish exist is that they catch far more carp than catfish.

Maggots

By far the cheapest and most readily available of all naturals, maggots have become the universal bait for most cyprinid species. Being small and grub-like in format and not dissimilar to one of the most common underwater naturals, the caddis larvae, small wonder maggots are instantly sucked in, converted to pulp by the pharyngeal teeth and swallowed. At this point, allow me to enlarge upon the problem of 'sucked maggots', which return as mere skins, having been squeezed of their creamy inner juices, because if this happens regularly you are not striking early enough.

If you move the lowest (tell-tale) shot of your float rig closer to the hook or shot the float tip right down until it is a mere blimp on the surface, you will see the bite earlier. Conversely, when ledgering, use a much shorter tail or hook length and strike at the tiniest indication of a bite. Plain, shop-bought maggots, which are bred from the second-most-common European bluebottle (the softer-skinned 'gozzer' maggots come from the most common bluebottle), are easily coloured with non-carcinogenic liquid dyes. Or they can be purchased ready coloured in red, green, yellow, bronze or mixed.

For most situations I place my confidence in a box of plain white maggots well-sieved of debris, to which fresh maize meal has been added to stop them from sweating. During the cold months of winter, however, when the water is particularly clear, with next to no natural vegetation visible, the stark white of a maggot does, I am sure, sometimes inhibit fish in accepting it. I am not talking about stunted rudd in a farm pond or a 500-strong shoal of immature dace crammed into the tail end of a weir race. Neither of these have the opportunity to be selective when they must always compete aggressively for food.

However, roach, chub or bream, etc. living in a river that, week in and week out, receives the attention of fishermen by the hundreds learn to be suspicious and extremely choosey. And I am sure in such circumstances that a bronze maggot is more readily acceptable. When seeking small fish in extremely cold, clear water a reduction in maggot size will sometimes produce more confident bites on light float tackle incorporating hooks in sizes 22 and smaller.

This is where either pinkies (the maggot of the green-bottle) or squatts (the maggot of a small house fly) can prove useful. Being lighter, squatts are particularly suited to on-the-drop fishing with an ultra-light terminal rig. Remember that fine wire hooks puncture far less than thick, forged patterns, which also, being heavier, make the bait fall quicker through the water.

It is not generally accepted, but maggots are just as effective for catching carp (including crucians) as they are for most other species. And in the vast majority of fisheries this is the problem – maggots are not selective enough. Everything from a plump gudgeon upwards has not the

Owing to their availability in plain white or various colours, shop-bought maggots are the most commonly used bait. They are particularly effective during the winter months, even for large fish when their metabolism slows down and they demand smaller food items.

Casters have become the supreme cold-water bait when float fishing for species like dace, roach, bream and chub. They are also much loved by barbel, and to deposit them on the bottom of fast, deep rivers, you need a selection of block-end swimfeeders.

slightest problem with even four maggots on a size 10 hook.

Casters

Casters are a superb bait for roach, dace, rudd, bream, tench, chub, barbel and carp. Under certain circumstances casters are a far more appealing bait than maggots. For the roach or dace in popular, clear-water fisheries that have been well and truly flogged with maggots, the caster will produce more bites and invariably a larger stamp of fish. I believe they are more appealing to cautious fish due to their inherent buoyancy, which, to some degree, offsets the weight of the hook and thus permits a more natural presentation.

The ideal way to get evenly coloured casters is to prepare them from slow-changing maggots in a room at a low temperature (the garage or garden shed are ideal), taking them off the ⅛ in wire riddle while they are still golden yellow. Place them in an open container in the fridge (other members of the family prefer you to have your own fridge for this) with a damp towel over them, which retards colour advancement. Alternatively, immerse the entire batch in a pail of water for a few minutes (skimming off any stray floaters), which halts colour advancement because it kills the animal inside. After draining off the water, put the casters into a polythene bag in the fridge. Use them within a few days, before they start to smell.

Present casters singly on size 18 hooks and smaller by piercing one end with the point and gently working the entire hook inside. When fishing two up on a 16 or 14, or in a bunch covering a size 12 or 10, the hook must go right through the shell, so be careful.

Caster cocktails, including maggots, sweetcorn, stewed wheat, elderberries and even bread flake and crust, are well worth experimenting with. Perhaps the most effective combination of all, winter or summer, is to trot or present a slowly falling caster through a swim loose-fed with hempseed. In cold, clear water conditions it is especially deadly for shy roach, dace and chub.

PARTICLE BAITS

Hempseed

Way out in front, in fact streaks ahead of all other particle attractor baits, is stewed hempseed. No other bait puts dace, roach, chub, tench and especially barbel and carp into a feeding mood so effectively or as quickly as these magical seeds. In addition, they are easy to prepare and use.

In stillwaters hemp can be scattered by hand into close-range swims or catapulted out, as indeed it can into slow-moving rivers. To deposit hemp accurately onto the bottom of fast and deep rivers, however, a blockend feeder is the answer. For fast and deep swims fished 'under the rod tip' the hemp is best deposited in position with a bait-dropper.

In complete contrast to maggots, which either carry on downstream with the flow and out of the swim or are eagerly devoured by small fish, hempseed gets caught up among the sand and gravel on the river-bed and generally only interests larger fish. So if you distribute a pint or two of hempseed on the bottom, unless barbel and chub eat it up immediately, it remains there until your target fish find it.

Attractor baits like maggots, on the other hand, have next to no holding power, especially during the warm months when nuisance species like minnows, bleak and dace are at their most active.

Preparation

To prepare hempseed, put it into a bucket with a rip-off lid and cover with boiling water. Press the lid down firmly and leave the seeds to stew in their own juices for a minimum of 24 hours, during which time they will expand and split. Surplus water can then be strained off, and the seeds will be very much darker, almost black, with tiny white shoots protruding. They are ready for immediate use.

Any surplus can be packed into polybags (a pint or two per bag) and popped into the freezer for future use.

Hempseed is usually best employed as the attractor for collecting and holding fish in the swim in conjunction with another bait on the hook. It works especially well when presented with other particles like corn, casters, maggots, tares, maple peas, elderberries, and even mini boilies. It is also very efficient when used in conjunction with larger offerings. A cube of luncheon meat ledgered or stret-pegged over a carpet of hempseed, for instance, is probably the all-time best catching combination for both barbel and chub.

Most carp fishermen would also put the attraction of hempseed at the very top of their bait list. For larger species like carp and barbel, hempseed used as hook bait can prove extremely effective when all else fails, if somewhat fiddly to present. The best way of making a

BEST BAITS – PARTICLE BAITS

	black eyed beans	borlotti beans	butter beans	chick peas	elderberries	haricot beans	hempseed	kidney beans	maize	maples	peanuts	stewed wheat	sweetcorn	tares	tick beans	tiger nuts
BARBEL					•		•		•	•	•	•	•	•	•	•
BREAM												•	•			
CARP	•	•	•	•		•	•	•	•	•	•	•	•	•	•	•
CHUB					•		•		•		•	•	•	•		
DACE							•					•		•		
ROACH					•		•				•	•	•	•		
RUDD									•			•	•			
TENCH	•	•	•	•		•	•	•	•		•	•	•			•

Stewed hempseed is, without question, the most effective loose-feed particle attractor bait. It can be used in conjunction with a maggot, caster, tare or an elderberry on the hook for roach and dace.

good mouthful is to string several seeds together on a fine hair with a needle, as in fig. 4.3A. I much prefer the softness of fly-tying thread for making the hair, which should be no longer than 1 in, otherwise fish are quite liable to become hooked on the outside of its mouth. Alternatively, you can use 1 lb test mono to make the hair.

Another method of presenting the stringer of seeds is shown in fig. 4.3B. This time the fine thread is tied to the eye of the hook and the seeds are sleeved on with the aid of a thin needle. The stringer is then wound tightly around the hook shank and down to the bend, where it is tied off. This produces a realistic bait, but is rather tiresome as a new hair must be tied to the eye each time when renewing the string of seeds. To ring the changes, other small particles like casters and tares can be mixed in with the hempseed hair stringer.

When using light trotting tackle for dace, chub and roach loose feeding with stewed hempseed should always be done sparingly, half-a-dozen seeds every other trot down is quite sufficient once the shoal is responding. In swims where hemp is rarely used, or has never been tried, it may take some time for the occupants to respond to this new-found food source, so be patient and be careful not to overfeed.

The problems arising from using hempseed as a hookbait include that of making it stay on the hook without impairing the strike, and attempting to hit those super-fast bites that invariably result in swims where hemp is used heavily. During the summer months especially, when roach and dace can be seen flashing through clear water as they rise with the speed of light to take the loose seeds there is the added problem of false bites. When this occurs, cut down drastically on the loose feed, or exchange the lower shots for a length of lead wire twisted around the line 1 ft from the hook and bent over at each end. The seeds may be hooked on by inserting the point of the hook into the base of the seed so that it comes out through the split (the seeds really do have to be well stewed and soft for this), or by pressing the bend of the hook into the split.

In truth, when trotting for roach, dace, chub and even barbel, it is best to loose feed only with hemp, and use a caster, maggot, tare, etc., on the hook.

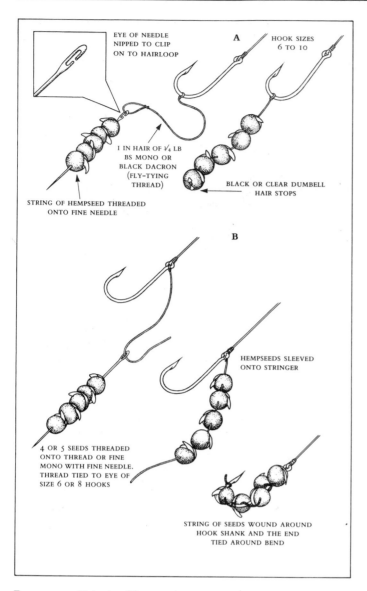

EYE OF NEEDLE
NIPPED TO CLIP
ON TO HAIRLOOP

A   HOOK SIZES
                     6 TO 10

1 IN HAIR OF ¼ LB
BS MONO OR
BLACK DACRON
(FLY-TYING
THREAD)

BLACK OR CLEAR DUMBELL
HAIR STOPS

STRING OF HEMPSEED THREADED
ONTO FINE NEEDLE

B

HEMPSEEDS SLEEVED
ONTO STRINGER

4 OR 5 SEEDS THREADED
ONTO THREAD OR FINE
MONO WITH FINE NEEDLE.
THREAD TIED TO EYE OF
SIZE 6 OR 8 HOOKS

STRING OF SEEDS WOUND AROUND
HOOK SHANK AND THE END
TIED AROUND BEND

FIGURE 4.3 *Hair-rigged hemp stringers*

Tares

As both loose feed and hook bait, these small, dark, hard seeds do not really have the same pulling power as hemp, but when used in flowing water for dace and roach, they come quite close. To make them soft, preparation is exactly the same as for hemp, except that I prefer to leave them stewing for 48 hours. One goes nicely on to a size 16 or 14 hook and comes cleanly off on the strike if softened enough in the preparation. As with hemp, loose-feed sparingly and experiment with hook-bait alternatives. Tares and elderberry is a winning combination. Tares are a fine attractor and hook bait for chub, carp and barbel.

Elderberries

Wherever an elder tree hangs out over the water, expect

the occupants of the swim beneath to respond to the soft, purple-black elderberries. Used in conjunction with loose-fed hempseed (or tares) elderberries are a wonderful trotting bait for winter roach and dace when the river is that distinct winter green. Both chub and barbel love them too.

If you gather berries in the autumn before they become over-ripe, you can bottle some and use them at any time during the season. Use a screw-top or preserving jar containing a diluted preserving solution of formalin or glycerine, and let small bunches of berries, still on their stalks, drop into it when you cut them with scissors from the main cluster. If you handle the berries individually they might spoil. Take time to rinse the preserving solution out of the berries with clean water before you use them as hook baits, and present one up on a size 16 or 14 hook.

Stewed wheat

During the warmer months especially, when most waters are loose-fed naturally with grass seed by the wind, not to mention wildfowlers who attract ducks to the margins by laying down a grain carpet, stewed wheat is a superb hookbait in both still and running water. It is in fact a much underrated bait, extremely effective for tench, bream and carp, and loose-fed stewed wheat will, in the clearest of water, instantly be taken by roach, rudd or dace.

There is certainly a special something about the nutty aroma of stewed wheat, which is prepared quite effectively in exactly the same way as hempseed except that, because the grains expand a lot, they must be covered with twice the volume of boiling water and are best left two days to stew. Once the excess water has been strained from the split grains, revealing the soft white insides, stewed wheat can be used at once or bagged up and frozen for later use. It is such a cheap, effective bait I can never understand why it is not more widely used. Present one grain on a size 14 or three up on a size 10 when you require a real mouthful on the hook to deter immature fish.

Sweetcorn

Whether fishing rivers or stillwaters just like wheat, sweetcorn is definitely a bait of the summer and a great alternative to bread in all its forms for seeking larger specimens. Of all the particle baits that attract tench and carp, sweetcorn is by far the most effective, whether ledgered or float-fished. One piece on a size 14 is about right, or three up on a size 12 or 10. It all depends on the size of the kernels.

For presenting a really good mouthful when fish are

spitting out the skins without registering a bite, simply thread two or three kernels up and over the eye of a size 8 hook onto the line above. Then slip three kernels on to the hook and slide the others gently back down again. It works wonders. Stillwater rudd and roach quickly respond to sweetcorn, as indeed do those fish that live in rivers. This applies particularly to chub and barbel.

If you intend using a fair amount of sweetcorn, it is cheaper to purchase it in large freezer packs rather than by the tin. Another benefit is that individual kernels in freezer packs are larger and not so soft. Sweetcorn lends itself wonderfully to the presentation of cocktail baits, so experiment by adding a caster or two, a tiny redworm, a couple of maggots, or even a small piece of bread crust.

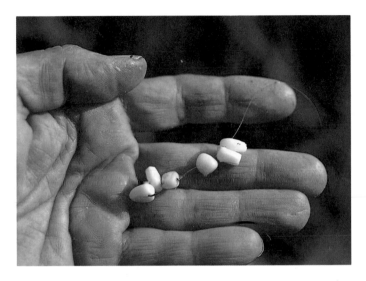

Sweetcorn is probably the most instant summer bait for tench, carp and barbel. Most other species love it too.

When fish are finicky in clear water or during the heat and brightness of a summer day, these little differences can create an instant response in them, leading to an exciting session.

On heavily fished waters, sweetcorn's effectiveness is reduced because everyone tends to rely on its pulling power, particularly early in the season. In this case, terminal tackle must be scaled down if you wish to stay catching on corn. It is not that fish stop eating it; far from it, all the loose feed certainly gets mopped up. They simply become suspicious of corn on the hook. You then have three choices. Rig up a short hair and present it off the hook (fig. 4.4E). Change its colour from yellow to red or orange (using a powder carp bait dye). Or stop using it altogether and change to another bait to see if you have more success with that.

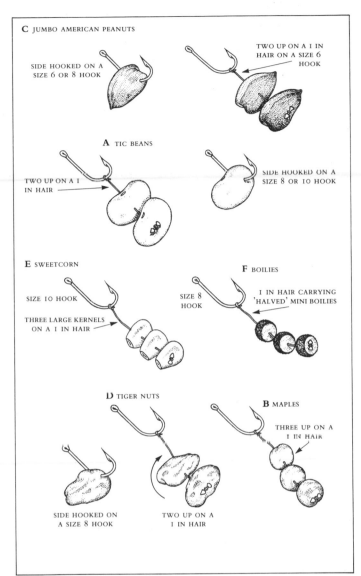

FIGURE 4.4 *Particle hook-bait presentation*

Tick beans

Though more commonly used as a particle bait for carp, there is no reason why, once softened sufficiently for hooking, this large, naturally dark-coloured bean cannot be used confidently to catch barbel. Its size permits a single bean to be presented on a size 10 or 8 hook, or two up on an 8 or 6. If refused repeatedly on the hook, rig two or three on a 1-in long hair (fig. 4.4A).

Maple peas

Maples are sold as pigeon feed in corn stores and pet shops, but once stewed this initially hard particle provides an ideal carp and barbel bait because, like tick beans, maples are impervious to the attentions of small nuisance fish that all too quickly consume the softer alternatives such as casters, maggots and sweetcorn.

Present maples singly on a size 12, or two up on a size 8. For educated fish, present on the hair rig (see fig. 4.4B). Both tick beans and maple seem to work best in conjunction with stewed hempseed as the attractor, so don't forget to add a handful to the loose feed. Prepare both as for hempseed.

Peanuts

I have enjoyed success with peanuts by catching roach, chub, barbel and tench on them – ledgered and floatfished. As my largest-ever carp of 33 lb 1 oz came on a peanut fished lift-style just a few feet out from the bank, I naturally rate them very highly indeed.

In fact peanuts are much loved by carp, and providing they are prepared properly will, contrary to popular belief, do the fish no harm. Put them into a tub with a rip-off lid, with plenty of space to spare. Cover by at least several inches of boiling water, to allow the nuts to expand fully. Fix the lid on tightly and leave for two days. Drain the excess water off and the nuts are ready for immediate use – or pop into polybags and into the freezer.

Standard-sized, ready-shelled nuts may be purchased reasonably cheaply from pet shops by the lb or in bulk. These are ideal for pre-baiting and loose feed. The much larger (and more expensive) jumbo-sized American peanuts make fabulous hook baits, one being nicely matched to a size 6 or 4 hook, and side hooked through either end

The colourful array of particle baits shown here, most of which are available either pre-cooked in tins or in dried form, represent just a small selection of offerings that will catch carp, tench, chub and barbel.

leaving the point and barb well exposed. Two nuts are best threaded on to a hair (fig. 4.4C).

Possessing tremendous inherent buoyancy, peanuts are great for fishing over and into thick weed. They tend to rest on top and remain visible to patrolling carp, unlike heavier particles which fall through and become hidden. Used over a bed of hempseed, American peanuts are a deadly bait whether float-fished or ledgered on a bolt rig.

Prepare the following particles (except red kidney beans) as for hempseed.

Black eyed beans are a rather bland salad bean excellent for tench and carp. With its distinctive black eye, it catches well and is most versatile. It is cheap to buy in dry form from health food shops (or in tins already cooked), and may be prepared to your liking. Stew as for peanuts adding colour and flavour as required. My favourite colours are dark red, brown, or orange, flavoured with caramel or butterscotch, but of course the permutations are endless. Present one on a size 8, two on a size 4 directly on to the hook, leaving the point and barb clear or thread on to a hair.

Chick peas. This round salad favourite, another excellent alternative for ringing the changes, is prepared, coloured and flavoured in exactly the same way as black eyes, or purchased pre-cooked in tins.

Butter beans. These flattish beans, largest by far of the carp particles, are tailor-made for fishing over dense weed-beds or thick silt. They are available uncoloured and pre-cooked in tins or may be purchased dry and then stewed, coloured and flavoured as all the other beans. Their size obviously permits the use of large hooks and even a single butter bean is heavy enough to freeline provided you cast gently.

Red kidney beans. If like me you adore 'Chili con carne', then this large, dark purple bean is no stranger. Carp love them too, whether presented over a bed of smaller attractors such as hemp or tares, or just as they are. As they need neither colour nor flavouring, simply buy them pre-cooked in tins and strain off the juices. Hook sizes 6 to 4 are ideal. To economize for regular pre-baiting, they can be purchased in bulk from health food shops and prepared in the same way as peanuts. Never be tempted to chew these beans unless they have been well stewed.

Borlotti beans also have the convenience of being available ready-cooked in a tin. Dark red in colour and slightly larger than a baked bean, individual beans should be side-hooked on a size 8 hook or presented on a hair two or even three up. Loose feed and pre-bait with the same, or use over an attractor such as hempseed.

Haricot beans. This, the most consumed bean of all when cooked in tomato sauce, is another 'change' particle bait. Buy tins of baked beans and drain off the sauce if you prefer them ready coloured, or buy a tin of plain haricot beans. One on a size 10 or two on an 8 does nicely.

Maize

Maize needs to be pre-soaked for a day in hot water and then pressure cooked for 20 minutes, otherwise it is too hard to use as bait. The prepared grain swells to twice its size, not unlike a giant but brighter grain of wheat (one grain to a size 8 hook is ideal). It is always much harder than wheat, however, and thus impervious to the attentions of small fish. Like wheat, it too may be coloured and flavoured although part of its secret is, I am sure, the

pungent, nutty smell. A superb bait for carp, tench and barbel.

Tiger nuts

You must prepare tiger nuts in exactly the same way as maize or they cannot be used as bait. To get carp really on to tigers may take several pre-baiting sessions, but once they have learnt to appreciate them, expect some fast action. Like peanuts they stay on well, and so can be reliably cast long distances. Tigers are also a great marginal bait. I present them two up on a size 4 hook beneath a length of peacock quill lift style (fig. 4.4D).

MANUFACTURED BAITS

Tinned meats

No serious carp, barbel, chub or tench angler should ever set off without a tin or two of luncheon meat in his tackle bag. It really is that good a bait, and while many will use only a particular brand of luncheon meat, chopped pork roll or ham, for the purpose of simplicity and not wishing to turn this chapter into a shopping guide, I shall treat all tinned meats firm enough to be cubed under the same heading. And that includes just about everything with the exception of corned beef, which is too crumbly.

However, there are very noticeable and important differences between one brand and another, and between one type of tinned meat and another. Some are fattier than others, which makes them more buoyant (useful when fishing over thick bottom weed). Others are more dense and so stay on the hook better and keep on the bottom in fast currents, reasonably impervious to the attentions of tiny shoal fish, which seem to be forever nibbling away. So experiment by trying different brands.

The secret of fishing using meat is to be happy about presentation and confident that your cube will not fly off the hook during casting, so learn to cut the meat into equal-sized cubes (using a fine, long-bladed knife) no longer than the shank of the hook being used (see fig. 4.5A). It is then a simple matter of pushing the hook through the cube and easing it out the other side without splitting the meat. Ease the bend of the hook into one of the corners and gently pull on the line (fig. 4.5B). The hook becomes hidden from view and easy to cast. And as the meat is soft, the hook will easily pull through the bait and into the fish on the strike.

When fish repeatedly refuse meat on the hook, present it on a 1-in long, fine hair, which gives them greater confidence (fig. 4.6). The shape can be changed to an

oblong when the cube becomes familiar to the fish and they can be seen to react against it. Alternatively, cut the meat into mini cubes and present three or four on a hair (fig. 4.6).

Meat in skins

As an exploratory trip to the chilled meat counter at the local supermarket or delicatessen will immediately prove, there is a wonderful, almost endless, choice of sausage-type (skinned) meats, and species like tench, chub, barbel and carp love them all.

In a narrow format there are chippolata sausages, spicey sausages, tinned sausages both large and small, and even

The variety of tinned and sausage-type meats available from the local delicatessen or supermarket is enormous. All are loved by tench, carp, chub, barbel and catfish.

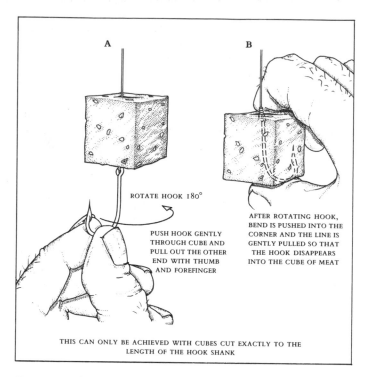

A

B

ROTATE HOOK 180°

PUSH HOOK GENTLY
THROUGH CUBE AND
PULL OUT THE OTHER
END WITH THUMB
AND FOREFINGER

AFTER ROTATING HOOK,
BEND IS PUSHED INTO THE
CORNER AND THE LINE IS
GENTLY PULLED SO THAT
THE HOOK DISAPPEARS
INTO THE CUBE OF MEAT

THIS CAN ONLY BE ACHIEVED WITH CUBES CUT EXACTLY TO THE
LENGTH OF THE HOOK SHANK

FIGURE 4.5 *PVA stringer rig, and hair-rigged cube baits*

*Many smoked and highly spiced meats made from turkey, beef and pork,
and available in skins and tins, have a long shelf-life, and can, for
convenience, be kept in your tackle bag.*

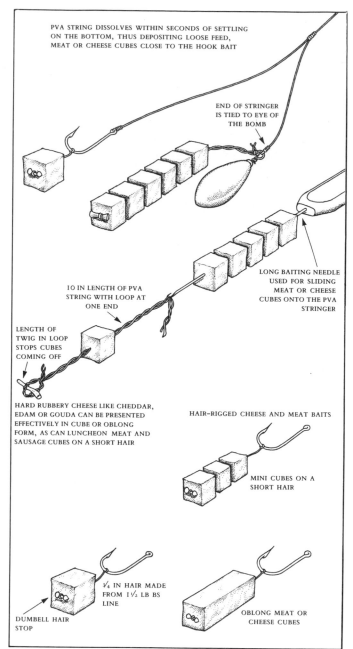

PVA STRING DISSOLVES WITHIN SECONDS OF SETTLING
ON THE BOTTOM, THUS DEPOSITING LOOSE FEED,
MEAT OR CHEESE CUBES CLOSE TO THE HOOK BAIT

END OF STRINGER
IS TIED TO EYE OF
THE BOMB

10 IN LENGTH OF PVA
STRING WITH LOOP AT
ONE END

LONG BAITING NEEDLE
USED FOR SLIDING
MEAT OR CHEESE
CUBES ONTO THE PVA
STRINGER

LENGTH OF
TWIG IN LOOP
STOPS CUBES
COMING OFF

HARD RUBBERY CHEESE LIKE CHEDDAR,
EDAM OR GOUDA CAN BE PRESENTED
EFFECTIVELY IN CUBE OR OBLONG
FORM, AS CAN LUNCHEON MEAT AND
SAUSAGE CUBES ON A SHORT HAIR

HAIR-RIGGED CHEESE AND MEAT BAITS

MINI CUBES ON A
SHORT HAIR

¼ IN HAIR MADE
FROM 1½ LB BS
LINE

DUMBELL HAIR
STOP

OBLONG MEAT OR
CHEESE CUBES

FIGURE 4.6 *Presenting cubed meat*

small cocktail sausages, all of which may be cut into ½-in
sections and securely hooked through the tough skin. For
loose feed, either scatter a handful of sections cut to the
same size into the swim every so often, or, if you are loose
feeding with stewed hempseed as the main attractor, dice

clearest of water, instantly be taken by roach, rudd or dace.

The larger sausage types, up to 3 in in diameter, such as
garlic-based German sausage, smoked sausage, black
pudding and so on, are best presented by removing the
outer skin and cutting into cubes or oblongs of the desired
sizes with a thin, long-bladed knife.

PASTES

121

PASTES

Soft protein pastes

The same milk-based protein ingredients as are used in boiled baits, mixed with water, flavouring and colouring, make exceptionally fine paste baits for tench and carp. The main reason for boiling is to produce a protective skin around the bait which irritating, unwanted species cannot pick at (boilies were first created for carp, remember). So if your lake is not rampant with shoals of paste-nicking shoal fish, allow the fish to sample large soft paste baits either float-fished, freelined or ledgered.

A piece of paste the size of a 50 p coin, covering a size 6 hook and flattened so it flutters slowly down and settles gently on top of any soft weed, is absolutely ideal. To pre-bait, introduce a few dozen paste pieces into several adjoining swims (so all the local residents see them) every other day over a period of a week or two. Then start using them on the hook. You could be amazed at the pulling power of soft paste. To make the paste really buoyant, so it rests ever so gently on top of weed, use a couple of ounces of sodium casenate in the base mix. A good formula to start with is equal proportions (say 4 oz each) of calcium casenate, wheatgerm, lactopro and soya isolate, plus water and your choice of flavour and powder colouring, all kneaded together to produce a soft but slightly rubbery texture.

Trout pellet paste

By far the most effective bait available in pellet form – manufactured in various sizes from fry crumb to ½ in diameter holding pellets – are those produced for the sole purpose of rearing trout and salmon. Formulated in various proportions of fish meal, oils and binders, *trout pellets* are effective as a surface attractor in their floating form, and as a sinking loose-feed crumb in the smallest sinking size. *Salmon fry crumb*, which have a higher oily fish content and are much darker in colour are especially attractive to fish.

To convert this effective bait into a paste, put into a bowl and wet (without oversoaking) with hot water. Leave for 30 minutes to allow all the water to be absorbed, and then knead into a stiff paste adding cornflour to blot up any excess water. For added attraction (although these pellets are a complete food in themselves) Bovril, marmite, or Phillips yeast mixture (a bird tonic) may be mixed into the paste, which can then be popped into a polybag and put in the freezer for later use.

Cheese paste

Another great paste for catching tench, carp, chub and barbel, can be made by mixing together equal parts of grated cheddar cheese and mashed bread. Start by soaking several slices of stale bread in cold water, and after squeezing out the excess, knead until you have a creamy paste. At this point, add the grated cheese and continue kneading until it has an even, fairly stiff consistency. Any type of hard cheese can be used to make a paste, although cheddar is best.

It is well worth taking time to evaluate the huge variety of cheese available at the local supermarket. Some brands of processed cheese, for instance, can be kneaded and used as a paste without any additions, or cut into cubes with a

	bread	bread paste	catfood paste	cheese paste	meat in skins	meat, tinned	sausage-meat paste	soft protein paste	trout pellet paste
BARBEL	•			•	•	•	•		•
BREAM	•	•					•	•	•
CARP	•		•	•		•	•	•	•
CATFISH			•			•		•	•
CHUB	•	•	•	•	•	•	•		•
DACE	•	•							
ROACH	•	•							
RUDD	•	•							
TENCH	•	•	•	•	•	•	•	•	•

BEST BAITS – PASTES

fine, long-bladed knife and presented on a short hair rig, in exactly the same way as cubed meat (fig. 4.6).

Wherever nuisance species are prolific, the best way to deter them is to use rubbery cheese such as gouda or edam, either cubed or cut into oblongs.

Sausage-meat paste

Plain sausage-meat, either beef or pork, purchased by the pound from the local butcher, makes a fine bait for barbel, chub, tench and carp. It is far too sticky to be used on its own, but you can make it into a firm paste by kneading cornflour into it, and this can be used for both hook baits

and loose feed. Sausage-meat paste can be popped into the freezer for future use.

Cat food paste

Tinned cat foods are available in dozens of different flavours which potentially all make excellent paste baits, that tench, carp and catfish find attractive. Stiffen with cornflour and some wheatgerm until firm enough, and then test in a glass of water to see how long it will last without disintegrating. Add a small quantity of wheat gluten to act as a binder in brands which are difficult to work with.

BREAD

When thinking in terms of catching larger-than-average tench, bream, chub, dace, even barbel roach and rudd, including the real monsters, or if you wish simply to evade tiddlers that continually gorge themselves on maggots, then both winter and summer look no further than a thumbnail-sized piece of soft white bread flake from the

inside of a really fresh loaf hiding a size 8 or even a 6 hook.

My preference is for ready-sliced loaves packed in polythene bags, which seem to stay fresh longer. However, to be fully confident when using bread flake, and that after a short while you are not simply sitting there with a bare hook because the flake has disintegrated, use only fresh white doughy bread. You can certainly help bread flake stay on longer by compressing it really hard around only the hook shank, between thumb and forefinger, while masking the point and barb with the thumb of your other hand. This ensures that the flake remains fluffy, hiding the hook. Penetration on the strike is then never impaired.

Flake also works well when used in a cocktail. To the bend of the hook try adding a grain of wheat, two maggots or casters; to increase buoyancy for fishing into or over heavy weed, add a piece of bread crust (fig. 4.7).

In all its forms, fresh white bread is a wonderfully attractive bait that generally sorts out a better-quality fish. During the winter months, when rivers run clear, there is no finer offering than a thumb-nail sized piece of bread flake.

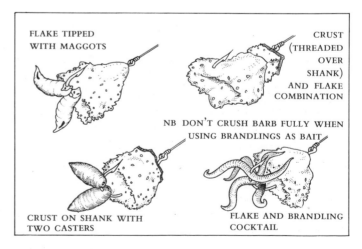

FIGURE 4.7 *Bread combinations and cocktails*

Breadcrust

As with flake, use the crust from a new loaf. While it will not stay on anywhere near as long as flake or paste, because of its greater buoyancy, there are numerous occasions when crust scores over all else.

As for actual cube size, remember that crust swells to at least half as large again once wet, so choose the hook size accordingly. A balanced bait of an oblong of crust along the shank and maggots or casters or even flake on the bend, for instance, permits a wonderfully natural on-the-drop presentation.

Bread paste

To ring the changes from flake and crust when after quality-sized chub, bream, roach and rudd, try a lump of creamy white bread paste, which is easy to make from all your old stale bread scraps. In fact, it is impossible to make a good paste from new, doughy bread because it is too soft and moist.

Start by removing all the crusts (the bread needs to be at least four or five days old) and hold the bread under the cold water tap for several seconds. Next, knead it (with clean hands) until all the stickiness disappears and the paste becomes pliable without lumps. Wrapped in a damp cloth, bread paste will stay fresh for at least 24 hours, and can be frozen for future use.

Punched bread

Fresh, white, sliced bread is the best to use when punching out pellets. Don't forget to take along a rigid board to press the bread against.

GROUNDBAITING

The very term groundbaiting can, I admit, seem rather misleading to the uninitiated. Handfuls of sweetcorn or stewed wheat thrown regularly into the swim as loose feed is a form of groundbait. However, as far as this book is concerned, let us think of groundbait as bulk preparation of a cereal base to which various ingredients are added, including fragments of the intended hook bait.

Mashed bread

Whether using punched bread while floatfishing, or a large piece of ledgered bread flake, by far the best groundbait is mashed bread. For this, use stale bread of at least 5 or 6 days old and soak it for a couple of hours in a bucket of water. After straining off the excess water, squeeze and mash the bread (hence its name) between your fingers into a fine pulp.

Prior to throwing it into the swim, squeeze the mash again and mould it into the size of balls required. Naturally, the tighter you squeeze and mould the mash, the further it sinks before breaking up into a cascade of attractive feed. If you merely desire a cloud to complement the use of tiny, punched bread pellets when canal fishing for small roach or rudd, keep the mash on the sloppy side and introduce it in tiny balls. At the other end of the scale, when bream fishing for instance, to stiffen the mash groundbait so it quickly descends to the bottom of deep, fast swims, add maize meal, bran or even dry breadcrumbs, plus a few fragments of the bait if you are not using bread on the hook.

Incidentally, mashed bread may even be packed into polybags and popped into the freezer for future use. A bag is then removed on the evening prior to a morning's fishing and left in the sink to thaw out overnight.

The reason for the success of well-mashed bread is that even when it is introduced all day long it never overfeeds the fish. This is because it separates into thousands of small, fluffy pieces which, if not eaten, soon pass downstream and disintegrate. There is no other attractor possessing even similar qualities.

Whether used for filling the entire open-end feeder, or simply as a plug at each end, lightly dampened coarse breadcrumbs are ideal. Don't over-wet them, or the feeder will clog and fail to release its load on impact with the bottom.

Bread crumbs

For bream fishing, plain breadcrumbs mixed with just enough water to hold them together makes the perfect base. To stiffen the mixture for throwing, I recommend that you add 2 pt of pearl barley per bucket of bait, plus several handfuls of the intended hook bait, such as worm fragments, maggots, sweetcorn, casters or stewed wheat, once the crumbs have been dampened. As an alternative to pearl barley, which really locks the crumb together and takes the balls of groundbait down quickly, try flaked maize. Looking rather like industrial cornflakes, flaked maize is a great binder, especially when using sweetcorn on the hook because it comes from maize's sister plant and has that similar, golden-yellow colour and distinctive aroma. The bream will be very much quicker on to your hook bait.

Lighter groundbaits

Lighter mixes that break up quickly and attract rather than feed are made from fine breadcrumbs, to which water is added slowly, a little at a time. Use a shallow mixing-bowl or groundbait tray for this job, and keep fluffing the crumbs about with your spare hand while adding the water from a maggot tin with the other. If it is prepared perfectly, a handful of this lighter mix, squeezed together hard, will go straight down and only break up on the bottom. Yet if it is squeezed gently, it will separate beautifully into an attractive cloud the moment it hits surface.

I have my own preference for making a similar, lighter cloud-type groundbait, again with fine breadcrumbs. I am not fussy whether they are white or brown, and it allows me to use up any old casters that are beyond redemption as hook baits. I do not care whether they are floaters, or how much they stink (indeed I even think that stinking casters add more attraction), I grind them to a pulp a handful at a time over the groundbait tray, using their juices to dampen the breadcrumbs while adding millions of brown caster-shell particles for visual effect. It makes a really super cloud groundbait to which a little water may have to be added. Try it and see.

Feeder groundbait

Whether ledgering for roach, tench, or bream, by far the best groundbait for use with wire, cage-type feeders, is a

The secret with breadcrumb-based groundbaits is in the mixing, which is more easily done in a shallow tray or a large cut-down bowl. Water is added a little at a time and the crumbs fluffed around for an even distribution so a ball holds together when squeezed firmly.

very lightly dampened mix of coarse bread-crumbs, to which a few fragments of the hook bait should be added. This mixture explodes and scatters only upon reaching the bottom, not prematurely.

An even better method, but one which can only be used with plastic open-ended feeders, is to fill the middle of the feeder with loose-feed hook baits and plug each end with dampened, coarse breadcrumbs. It takes a few seconds longer than filling cage-type feeders, but deposits more hook-bait samples on the bottom.

PRE-BAITING

Pre-baiting is often a prerequisite for catching bream that inhabit large, deep and wide rivers and huge stillwaters. Even during the summer months the shoals are seldom scattered evenly like currants in a well-baked cake, and unless you have attracted a shoal or two in advance, you could be fishing several hundred yards away from the nearest bream.

If I were contemplating fishing for bream in a large expanse of water not regularly fished, where the bream have not become used to the introduction of free food along the margins of certain areas, I would plan a pre-baiting campaign. If the shoals are numerically strong, with individual fish on the large side, I would introduce a bucket of groundbait laced with hook-bait fragments into the chosen swim every other day for a week. This I would do at dusk so as not to attract the attentions of diving water-birds and other anglers. In the meantime, I would keep a very close eye, with binoculars, on the swim each morning for signs that the bream had located the food – the occasional porpoising fish or the sight of bubble trails littering the surface – before thinking about starting fishing.

In complete contrast, to attract the attention of, say, a small group of large bream that are clearly visible in a deep hole or junction – swim on a small, clear-flowing, weedy river, all you need do is introduce a couple of handfuls of stewed wheat, sweetcorn or mashed bread each evening as dusk falls.

DRAGGING AND RAKING

Opinions vary as to when is the best time to drag a tench swim; or if to drag it at all. Some say the evening is best before a dawn start, some say immediately prior to fishing. Having taken good hauls after dragging at both times, I am not really fussy. However, I would perhaps bend towards the latter view on the grounds that I won't have missed any tench attracted to the area during the night which have subsequently departed, bellies full of free feed.

It is necessary to understand what is achieved by raking out a clear patch of water amongst dense weed, apart from allowing the fish to move about more freely, because the effect can prove three-fold.

Firstly, the sound waves attract tench (the most curious of fishes) to the area like bees to a honey-pot. Secondly, they have a nice surprise when they arrive because all the tiny, single items of food which they normally have to grub about to find are conveniently presented – along with your loose feed. Lastly, the thick cloud of silt which might be held in suspension for up to several hours depending upon water temperature and the number of tench which arrive in the swim and keep it churned up, makes them feel more secure.

If you own a pair of chest-waders, and your favourite tench lake is neither too deep nor too silty, take along a long-handled garden rake and give the bottom, whether weedy or not, a good raking. I wish I had a fiver for every time during high summer that I have stripped down to my underpants and got in to clear a swim of its weeds, or simply to churn the bottom up. Neighbouring anglers might hand out a few old-fashioned looks, but their faces soon change when they see your rod bending a few minutes later. And don't be afraid to get out there and give the bottom a good going over at any time of the day, especially when the sun is well up, sport has stopped and the tench have retreated into the thickest weed. It cannot do anything but improve your chances to stir up the debris on the bottom. See p. 101 for instructions on making a simple weed-drag.

FLOATERS

Breadcrust

On heavily fished waters floating crust is considered to be very old hat, and thus an ineffective bait for carp. Nevertheless, it still has pulling power and will catch in new fisheries and in fast, well-stocked carp waters where competition for food among the fish is always high. Use the tough crusts cut from either a white tin loaf or French bread.

I once asked a friend who is a baker to bake me half a dozen loaves dyed black with powder colouring, because the carp I was after at the time were scared by the whiteness of ordinary bread. And very effective the *black flake* and *black crusts* proved too. Give it a try.

BEST BAITS – FLOATERS				
	bread crust	cat biscuits	Pedigree Chum mixers	sunflower seed
CARP	●	●	●	●

Pedigree chum mixers

These, the most popular and certainly the most versatile of floating carp baits, can also be coloured and flavoured in addition to using them straight from the box. Being small and square, they catapult well, are relatively cheap if purchased in bulk (3.5 kg bags), and fairly impervious to the attentions of small nuisance fish. To prepare mixers for hooking, hold a double handful under the tap so they are all wet and pop straight into a polybag. Twenty minutes later they will have absorbed the moisture, and will be easy to hook without disintegrating whether you side-hook one, or thread two or three on to a floating hair rig (see 'Floater fishing', p. 169).

My favourite way of 'doctoring' mixers is to gently heat a batch for a couple of minutes in a frying pan containing a liberal covering of garlic butter. And there are countless permutations for spicing them up once carp noticeably become suspicious of them in their plain form. Experiment and have some fun.

Cat biscuits

Cat biscuits also make wonderful floaters for carp. They come in all sorts of shapes too, ovals, stars, rounds, even mini fish shapes. Pet food supply stores offer them in bulk in both meat and fishy flavours. Prepare in exactly the same way as 'mixers' for easy hooking.

Sunflower seeds

Sunflower seeds, which require soaking for a few hours for ease of hooking, are perhaps an unusual but nonetheless effective floater, possibly due to their high oil content.

Baits for catching carp off the surface are cheap, readily available and easily catapulted. Have a good look round in the supermarket, or better still, pay the local pet-food shop a visit.

Whenever I sweep out the cockatiel aviary and dump the entire mess of loose seeds on to the surface of the lake closest to the house, the carp are up on the top and mopping them up post haste. Only soak those required for hook baits.

Boilies

Floating boilies are a bait which small, unwanted species like rudd and roach cannot peck to bits, and as such are the most selective of all floaters, whether side-hooked or presented on a hair.

Offer just one large (18–20 mm) boilie, which really stands out amongst a scattering of small attractor floaters such as cat biscuits or chum mixers; or a floating boilie of any size amongst a small scattering of others of the identical colour and size (see 'Controller fishing', p. 168).

If you cannot find pre-made floaters in the tackle shop of the size, colour and flavour desired, simply put a batch of regular, sinking boilies into a shallow baking tray and pop into a pre-heated oven for a few minutes. They should all then float. Experiment to make perfect.

BOILED BAITS (BOILIES)

I have purposefully left boiled baits, or 'boilies' as they are affectionately known, until the end of this chapter. They are not the panacea for catching carp easily that certain bait manufacturers would have us believe. However, boilies

are extremely effective, and are a most selective bait for carp and tench because nuisance species cannot deal with them. Either their pharyngeal teeth are not powerful enough to crush the outer skin enabling the soft insides to

Ready-made boilies have been marketed since the 1980s and are available in a staggering variety of colours, flavours and sizes. Most brands have a long shelf-life, and a packet or two can have a permanent place in the tackle bag.

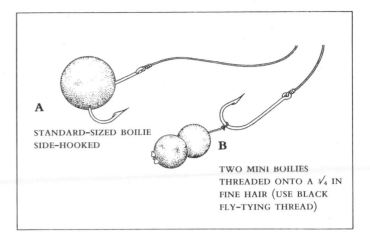

A
STANDARD-SIZED BOILIE
SIDE-HOOKED

B
TWO MINI BOILIES
THREADED ONTO A ¼ IN
FINE HAIR (USE BLACK
FLY-TYING THREAD)

FIGURE 4.8 *Hooking boilies*

be swallowed (which is the whole idea of wrapping a protective skin around the bait), or their mouths are simply too small.

It is said that there is nothing new in fishing and at times this fact is really brought home. For instance, one of the most famous carp baits of yesteryear, though seldom used nowadays – par-boiled potatoes – was in reality nothing less than a boilie years ahead of its time. But then, huge paste baits made from millet flour and boiled to enhance the natural gluten so as to make the surface rubbery and thus impervious to unwanted species, were concocted in India at least 100 years ago by those who sought the legendary mahseer. And now anyone can walk into even a non-specialist tackle shop and be spoilt for choice by the sheer amount of varying sizes, colours and flavours of boiled baits on offer, both frozen and shelf life.

Shelf-life boilies are certainly the most convenient of manufactured baits. You simply need to choose a size from minis up to gob-stopper, 20 mm ones, select a flavour and colour which hasn't seen much use on the water in question, and give them a try. There is no wonder flavour or magic boilie, so don't waste your time looking for one.

Consider (and ask the salesman about) the bait's density and whether it will lie lightly on top of weed or fall through. Think about various colours and how they will relate to the colour of the bottom the bait is presented over. Will they blend in naturally or stand out? Think about the flavour. Do you want one which is used regularly on the water you fish because the carp have become accustomed to it, but also possibly scared by it through being caught too many times? Or is an entirely new and unknown flavour more likely to score once several pre-baiting sessions have accustomed the carp to a different food source?

These are the questions you should consider when purchasing pre-made boilies, and if you are not entirely happy then simply make you own. Bait suppliers not only provide all the component parts, they also give suggested recipes.

Boilies can be side hooked or presented 'off' the hook on a hair rig (fig. 4.8) to spooky fish.

PREDATOR BAITS AND LURES

Predatory species eat all kinds of waterbound creatures. Chub, zander, perch and eels, for instance, consume crayfish, worms, newts, frogs and toads in addition to small live and dead fish. Catfish and pike also go for fully-grown waterbirds like dabchicks, moorhens, cootes and mallards. However, as far as serious fishing is concerned baits fall into three distinct categories – live-baits, dead-baits and artificial lures.

LIVEBAITS

As there is nothing in the way of scales and fins that pike and catfish will not eat, one might say that any small fish will suffice as a livebait. However, some species look better, work more attractively, and last considerably longer as an active bait than others.

Availability is the main consideration when it comes to choosing bait fish. As there is continual pressure on stocks of shoal fish from pollution, farming chemicals, years of poor fry recruitment owing to inconsistent weather patterns, and so on, the first question any conservation-minded fisherman must ask himself is a controversial one. Can the fishery that I catch bait fish from afford to lose a dozen or two small shoal fish in order to catch for instance a pike or two which are then returned? Because sooner or later (and in small fisheries it takes but a couple of years) the delicate balance between predator and prey can be irreversibly upset. It is also wrong to ruin the enjoyment of float fishermen by removing all the small roach from a fishery for use as livebait. So only take livebaits if you are certain that it will not affect the sport of others.

Minnows

Whether you obtain them from the gravel shallows with a minnow trap, or simply scoop out a bunch by swatting the water with a large, small-meshed, landing-net, minnows are great baits for chub, barbel and perch.

Hook only once through the top lip or through both nostrils with a size 6 or 4 tied direct and freeline your minnow or trot it down clear runs between beds of streamer weed. It is equally effective when ledgered static on the bottom of deep runs or weir pools etc. or cast beneath overhangs and then retrieved erratically.

Bullheads and stone loach

Although these bottom-dwellers are seldom taken on rod and line, they are common in most rivers, brooks and streams, and they will be hiding beneath every large flint, housebrick or item of junk which litters the bottom in clear-flowing water.

Simply place a net upright and hard against the bottom immediately behind any likely-looking hideout, and then gently lift the flint or brick upwards and to one side so everything beneath is washed downstream by the current straight into the net. For a holding can, you can use a 1-gallon bait bucket, which can be hung on the belt thus keeping both hands free. When enough bait has been

Hook small fish with one prong of the bottom treble in the pectoral root and one prong of the upper hook in the top lip (use semi-barbless trebles) to ensure maximum manoeuvrability and maximum attraction to predators.

	bleak	bream	bullhead	chub	carp, crucian	carp, common, mirror	dace	eel, baby	gudgeon	lampreys	minnows	perch	roach	rudd	stone loach	trout
BEST BAITS – LIVEBAITS																
BARBEL								•		•	•					
CHUB	•		•				•	•	•	•	•				•	
EEL	•						•		•	•	•				•	
PERCH	•	•	•	•			•	•	•		•	•	•	•	•	•
PIKE	•	•		•	•	•	•	•	•			•	•	•		•
ZANDER	•	•		•			•	•	•			•	•	•		•

gathered, and only ever take enough for your own needs, they may be kept for a few days in a water butt or an aquarium with an aerator.

Bullheads and loaches can be trotted beneath a float in weir pools, ledgered on the bottom in deep, fast runs, or used as deadbaits and 'twitched' beside rafts and overhangs using freeline tactics. A size 4 hook through the top lip or nostrils secures them well for casting and banging into species like perch and chub.

Brook lampreys

Brook lampreys are seldom longer than 6 in and never leave freshwater. They are generally found (whilst turning over the bottom looking for other natural baits) clinging to the underside of large stones or boulders, but while in their infant stage they live semi-dormant in soft silt or mud in a blind, toothless state measuring 3–4 in long.

They are most likely to be found in numbers amongst deep silt and mud banks such as are found immediately behind bridge supports or beneath tree roots and are not dissimilar to a small eel, perhaps with a touch more beige or buff yellow.

Lampreys can be trotted beneath a float or freelined with the addition of a single AA or swan shot, and are just as effective when being retrieved. Present them on a size 6 or 4 tied direct, hooked once only through the mouth.

Baby eels

Better known as elvers, and at 3 to 4 in long only slightly thinner than a young lamprey, young eels are also fabulous natural baits for chub, barbel and perch. Elvers are best collected with a fine-meshed net at night from mill and weir pools, where they collect around the sluices on their upstream migration by the thousands throughout the summer and early autumn. Pick the right night and one scoop is all you will need. Gently hook once only through the head or through the middle with a size 6 or 4 hook tied direct, and freeline or present beneath a heavy trotting float. Though a bait few anglers bother to use, elvers provide one of the most prolific natural food sources throughout the summer and autumn to several predators including brown trout and sea trout.

Gudgeon and bleak

Both of these species attract well, the gudgeon because it is constantly on the move sending out distress signals to predators, and the bleak because of its highly reflective silver enamel colour. These are good close-range baits which, owing to their small size, invariably attract equally

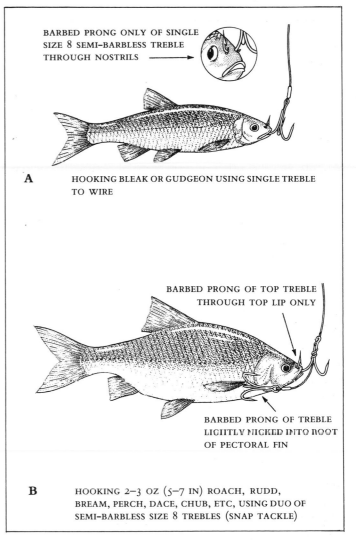

FIGURE 4.9 *Hooking livebaits*

small pike. Both, however, are superb baits for perch, zander, eels and chub. Present on a single hook tied direct to the reel line when seeking perch and chub, while for zander and pike use a wire trace (fig. 4.9A).

Dace, rudd, roach, chub, bream and perch

Of these, the rudd is the best to use in shallow, weedy waters because it automatically works the upper water layers near the surface. The chub is probably the strongest of the group and lasts longer. There is no truth whatsoever in the old wive's tale that pike will not eat perch because of their spiky dorsal fin. Perch are gulped down greedily just like other small fish, and they make a fine, active bait not only for pike, but zander and big perch too. Really small baits should be presented on a single treble to wire (fig. 4.9A).

Purely with pike in mind the ideal size for casting, controlling the bait, and for the ease with which they can be turned in the pike's jaws, are fish in the 5–7 in (2–3 oz) bracket. Really large livebaits are not only wasteful, but unnecessary. More runs are missed with large livebaits than for any other single reason, because small pike grab and subsequently make a mess of quality fish that they have little chance of swallowing.

Everyone has their pet method of presenting livebaits, and I am no exception. I believe that by inserting a duo of semi-barbless size 8 trebles as illustrated in fig. 4.9B (one in the top lip, the other in the pectoral root), the bait is allowed maximum freedom to roam; and when engulfed, at least one of the trebles is pointing in the right direction for positive hooking.

Crucian, common and mirror carp

Small, chunky carp in the 4–6 in range are very strong workers and will keep active for hours. A size 8 snap tackle suffices for all pike fishing techniques.

Trout

Rainbow trout for use as livebaits are readily available from fish farms. They come in various sizes, usually at very competitive prices. They are strong workers, and because their use does not affect the balance in coarse fisheries, they are perhaps the ideal livebait. Those fish that are 5–6 in long are nicely matched to a size 8 snap tackle for pike, while 3–4 in trout make great perch and zander baits.

Fish movement

You must be sure to check the local river authority rules concerning the transfer of all bait fish from one water to another, whether trout from a farm, or cyprinid species caught from one river system for use in another. To be absolutely certain, catch your livebaits only from the water in which you are fishing.

DEADBAITS

All predators are certainly able to distinguish between freshly killed and long-term frozen baits. Their smell is totally different even to humans, and there is nothing more attractive or effective than a freshly killed deadbait. However, particularly during cold winter spells, we are not always permitted the luxury of catching and using small fish on the same day. You can ensure that they are at least as fresh as possible by tapping each on the head and wrapping it individually in cling film or a mini polybag and putting straight into the freezer. Baits which break down after a couple of casts when wobbled, or disintegrate during a powerful distance cast, are useless.

It really is worth taking time and trouble to gather or purchase deadbaits and store them correctly. Freezing

down a dozen or so fish in one lump all covered in slime and twigs and loosely wrapped in newspaper, for instance, apart from being sloppy, is a complete waste of good fish.

All of the cyprinid species mentioned under livebaits work well when presented dead, either static or wobbled. My preference when wobbling for pike, for instance, is a silver, firm-bodied fish like roach, rudd, dace, chub or rainbow trout, which are particularly tough. Small grayling can well withstand constant casting, but at the very head of the list for durability is the freshwater eel. Catfish, zander and pike simply adore them.

Eels

In most river systems eels are easy to catch during the summer on maggots or worms. If you do not fancy catching them, there is a ready source available wherever dragline dredgers are operating in lakes or rivers. Those clearing out rivers are more productive, even if only because the bottom silt is usually stacked up along the banks. It is then simply a matter of wading through the silt, sifting it for eels. If you can catch the dragline when it is actually working, so much the better. Within seconds of the shoe depositing its load on the bank, eels can be seen wriggling out all over the place.

Eels between 8 and 14 in long are perfect for pike baits. The shorter ones are best used whole for wobbling. In fact,

BEST BAITS – DEADBAITS				
	eels	*octopus*	*seafish*	*squid*
CARP		●		●
CATFISH	●	●		●
PERCH	●		●	
PIKE	●	●	●	●
ZANDER	●		●	

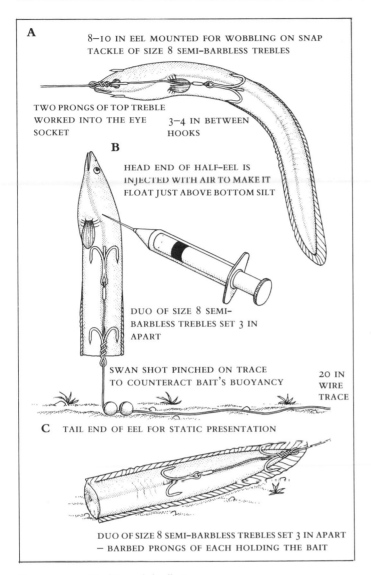

A 8–10 IN EEL MOUNTED FOR WOBBLING ON SNAP TACKLE OF SIZE 8 SEMI-BARBLESS TREBLES

TWO PRONGS OF TOP TREBLE WORKED INTO THE EYE SOCKET

3–4 IN BETWEEN HOOKS

B HEAD END OF HALF-EEL IS INJECTED WITH AIR TO MAKE IT FLOAT JUST ABOVE BOTTOM SILT

DUO OF SIZE 8 SEMI-BARBLESS TREBLES SET 3 IN APART

SWAN SHOT PINCHED ON TRACE TO COUNTERACT BAIT'S BUOYANCY

20 IN WIRE TRACE

C TAIL END OF EEL FOR STATIC PRESENTATION

DUO OF SIZE 8 SEMI-BARBLESS TREBLES SET 3 IN APART – BARBED PRONGS OF EACH HOLDING THE BAIT

FIGURE 4.10 *Hooking eel deadbaits*

I have wobbled all day with just three or four eels, and taken several pike on each without the baits wearing down or breaking up. And they look so life-like if mounted with two prongs of the top treble worked into the eye socket and the bottom one set 3 in down the body (fig. 4.10A). Cut the longer eels in half for static presentation. Head or tail end? I am certain it matters little to the pike, at least not in my local waters where an enormous number of eels are consumed by them.

For a change, try offering the head end injected with air from a hypodermic syringe, or insert a length of foam strip so it rises tantalizingly out of the bottom silt (fig. 4.10B), with three or four swan shot midway along the trace to hold the eel down. This is a great way of ensuring that the bait rises above a silty bottom or blanket weed where non-buoyant baits could become hidden from the pike's view. The tail end is best offered lying static on the bottom, rigged as in fig. 4.10C. Incidentally a 3–4 in section of eel

ledgered static on the bottom (use size 10 trebles on the wire trace) is an electric bait for zander.

Eels are a fabulous natural bait, free, and you can take as many as you like without upsetting anyone, or anyone else's fishing.

Seafish

Owing to their pungent and most distinctive smell, many species of seafish make excellent deadbaits. The effectiveness of sprats, herrings and mackerel, for instance, is well known. However, while the occasional good zander has come my way on herrings and even perch on twitched small smelts, generally speaking it is the pike that really relates to sea deadbaits.

If fishing a water where the pike rarely see the angler's bait, I would still put my faith in a fresh herring above all

When fresh, the herring is arguably the most attractive deadbait of all. When it is cut in half diagonally, the oily juices permeate the water quickly.

else. On the fishmonger's slab, look for the bright red eye and crimson gill filaments, and those golden scales that easily come away from the flanks (when the bait hits the water) and scatter down in a shower of stardust to settle all around the bottom. What could possibly be more attractive to a foraging pike?

In addition to being wobbled on light tackle (a size 10 snap tackle is ideal), sprats are great to use as a loose-feed attractor. Try chopping a few into halves or quarters and scatter around a larger deadbait presented static on the bottom.

Probably the all-time favourite is the half-mackerel, or to be more precise the mackerel tail. It should be presented on a duo of size 8 or 6 trebles, with the uppermost one worked into the sinewy muscles of the narrow tail root, and the bottom one 3 in away (fig. 4.11).

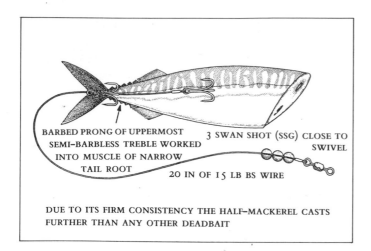

FIGURE 4.11 *Mackerel tail*

distinct aroma, they are great attractors. Other softish deadbaits that are best offered as statics are sardines and sand eels.

Oddities

Other oddities from the sea that are well worth trying, especially in hard-fished waters where the pike probably know the names of the species used to catch them better than fishermen, are baby octopus and squid. Presented static (very tiny squid can be electric when wobbled) just like a herring, these really do produce, not only pike but catfish and carp too.

A friend of mine has achieved no small measure of success in recent years with uncooked turkey pieces. Yes – turkey pieces. Working in a turkey processing factory, he has access to scrap chunks and these in the coloured waters of the Norfolk Broads are regularly snapped up from the bottom when presented static. Pike obviously recognize a mouthful of good, wholesome food on the bottom and swallow it. After all, pike eat ducklings and the body of a duckling without feathers is not so different from a chunk of turkey.

Even a small, dead rodent, a rat, mole or mouse found by the waterside, is worth a try so long as it is fresh. So be prepared to keep a very open mind.

The half-mackerel will cast further than any other deadbait, and for stillwater fishing there is no need to add extra lead, in the way of bombs, to the line. Simply pinch three swan shot on to the trace immediately below the swivel to give the pike a little something to pull against. In recent years, pike fishermen have discovered that almost any small seafish will catch pike and this opens up an exciting new field.

Durable seafish that are particularly firm in the body, and thus best suited to wobbling, are small 'joey' mackerel, scad (horse mackerel), red gurnard and mullet. I also like the cucumber-smelling smelt for wobbling. It is readily available in flat freezer packs from most tackle dealers, although this fish does tend to break up rather easily.

Smelt are better as a static bait because, owing to their

Colouring deadbaits

Deadbaits can be coloured easily using either neat liquid food colouring or the powder dyes used for making carp baits. Neat food colouring straight from the bottle can be

A comprehensive selection of deadbaits for pike fishing, comprising both coloured and natural small freshwater and saltwater species. Squid is well worth trying for pike, catfish, eels and carp.

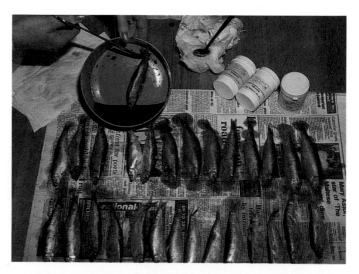

To colour deadbaits, first blot off the excess water with newspaper. These small, fresh herrings have been coloured with some powder dyes that are used for making carp baits. Grip the fish's tail with forceps and swish it around until the colour is even.

applied by brushing it on both sides of the fish and leaving it to dry. Prior to brushing the colour on, be sure to blot off excess water with a piece of kitchen roll. Powder dyes are used by adding a spoonful of dye to half a cup of water and mixing in a shallow dish or 2 pt bait tin. It can be brushed on, or the bait's tail can be gripped in a pair of locking artery forceps so it can be swished slowly around until both sides are evenly covered. Wrap the coloured baits carefully in cling film and store them in the freezer until required.

ARTIFICIAL LURES

An artificial lure is something which, when pulled through the water, irritates predatory fish like pike, zander, catfish, perch and chub into attacking and grabbing it, through hunger, territorial aggression or just because it feels so inclined. Lures are constructed from metal, wood, rubber, plastic, feathers or fur and fitted with large single, treble or even multi-treble hooks. Some are heavily weighted, others are buoyant, while many combine the action of floating and diving through built-in alloy or plastic vanes. Some are drilled with holes for water to gurgle through, whilst others have an inbuilt rattle from a chamber containing a ball-bearing. Some have propellors to churn the surface, and some are fitted with flapping arms. Lures are designed to throb, gurgle, nose-dive, deep-dive, wriggle, jig, flap, sink slowly, float upwards slowly, dive fast, vibrate, twitch, rattle, pop and pulsate. The weedless varieties may even be confidently retrieved through thick weed-beds.

Each has a very special part to play through its unique and individual action, and the fun of catching pike especially, with artificial lures lies in trying them all so you know what each is capable of doing, the depth to which it works and the speed at which it can be retrieved. You will then have an answer to match whatever mood the pike is in, regardless of the depth at which it lies.

There are in fact so many thousands of different artificial lures available today from patterns old and new, split up into several different categories, that it is impossible to list them all, but the following selection should give the predator angler a more than reasonable armoury. To start with, let us return to where it might have begun, to the ordinary, yet deadly 'spoon'. This is my own standby wherever I find myself fishing in a new water.

Spoons

Made from hammered copper sheeting, brass, chrome plated steel, aluminium, even heavy plastic, the spoon usually comes fitted with a treble at one end and a swivel at the other, both joined by split rings.

Because of its weight, the spoon is great for casting into the wind and can even be used as a plummet, employing the count-down method of allowing one second per foot of descent from the moment it hits surface until the line goes limp when the spoon touches bottom.

As it does not spin, but wiggles or wobbles from side to side against the water pressure, there is no need for an anti-kink vane, because spoons do not create line twist. They can therefore be retrieved at almost any speed. For coloured water, a slow retrieve allows time for the pike, perch or zander to home in and grab; whereas in extremely clear water, pike especially are loath to follow unless the pace is fast and variable. It is as though they enjoy the chase. The spoon shape is roughly oval, although bar types are decidedly more elongated.

Lengths of 3–6 inches suffice for most situations, (2–3 in for perch and zander) although for trolling huge lochs or loughs spoons of up to 10 in long are necessary. These may appear large, but what is a 10 in fish to a 20 lb pike.

One of the most effective spoon shapes is the bar type or ABU Toby, which incorporates angled fins at the rear and

This collection of spinners, spoons, spinner baits and buzz baits covers predator fishing from a weed-covered surface down to 20 ft or more. Success with artificial lures comes from knowing the function and capabilities of each and building up your collection according to the kind of waters you fish.

is available in numerous lengths from 2 to 6 in and from 10 to 40 grams. I also love ABU's Atom, a deep-sided, ribbed spoon that has a red plastic teaser attached to the split ring of the treble, and the UTO, a large, unique spoon that has a treble fitted at both ends.

Of the weedless varieties, the ABU Favourite and the Dardevle weedless are terrific, and come fitted with sprung wire guards that protect the large single hooks from catching on aquatic vegetation no matter how thick.

As for colour, I tend to be rather old fashioned, preferring plain gold, brass or silver. Combinations of coloured spots, stripes, even two tones, will have their day so it pays to carry a variety.

Spinners

These vibratory lures differ from spoons in that the blade or spoon revolves around a weighted bar or stem, to which the hook is connected. To alleviate line twist, you need to incorporate a plastic anti-kink vane when making a 10 in wire spinning trace.

Spinners such as the Voblex, which is a fabulous lure in the larger sizes, particularly for perch, are unique because the rubbery head in front of the blade acts as a built-in anti-kink device. The American 'Dardevle' spinners made by Eppinger overcome line twist in a most simple way. The wire stem for a distance of ⅝ in in front of the blade is bent almost at right angles.

Spinners attract because they emit tantalizing vibratory pulses or buzz while 'flashing', as though a small fish is passing by. Most are of the blade type – an oval or heart-shaped blade spins at high speed around the shaft. Brass or silver collars, brightly coloured beads, deer hair, plastic skirts, feathers and even latex rubber help to stir the fish's predatory nature, as in the Flying C made by the Kilty Lure Co. Better known as the 'flying condom', this large spinner incorporates a long, oval blade, revolving around a long shaft covered in thick latex available in several colours. This spinner is a hit with salmon anglers because, owing to its long shaft, it hooks well, and I have used it most successfully for pike, chub and big perch.

A proportion of fishermen still stay true to the well-proven makes of spinners such as the 'Mepps' and Ondex, the latter in all probability being the all time best perch spinner ever invented, and catches lots of chub too. ABU's 'Droppen', and even the Devon minnow which, although considered a salmon lure, does catch a lot of pike and perch. Devons are available in metal for deep-lying fish in heavy water, and in wood for a buoyant retrieve just off bottom. For this an up-trace lead is incorporated. The lead, not the lure, bumps over the bottom; the lure spins attractively above it, missing all the rocks and other snags.

Spinner baits

Although spinner baits are an American invention, evolved from spoons and spinners for the downfall of the large-mouth bass and other sunfishes, in certain situations – heavily coloured water in particular, where visibility is minimal – they are fantastic catchers for pike and perch. This is due to the tremendous vibrations emitted from the large single or two small blades connected to the top of the v-shaped shaft. At the bottom of the shaft, behind a leaded head, is attached a large single hook inside a pulsating, squid-like plastic skirt. Both blades and skirts are inter-changeable, and available in a galaxy of colours, and the skirt helps to make this lure quite weed-free. Two spinner baits in particular are recommended, Barries Buzzer and Double Buzzer made by Ryobi Masterline.

Unfortunately, the large single hook is nowhere near so successful for hooking pike as for black bass, and I always wire on a size 6 treble to the bend of the single. This converts a much higher proportion of 'hits' into pike on the bank, although the additional treble does ruin the lure's weed-free properties.

There are numerous variations of the spinner bait in a whole range of sizes; some even come fitted with latex rubber fish as opposed to the skirt. Those which incorporate a lead-headed jig with a sleeve-on plastic worm are particularly effective and great fun to use on a light outfit, not only for pike but chub and perch too.

Buzz baits

These are top-water lures with a similar v-shaped but much shorter top shaft than spinner baits. They also incorporate a propeller, which churns the surface film. Some come fitted with double, opposite-rotating propeller blades creating massive surface displacement – guaranteed to bring even deaf pike out of the weeds and up to the top for an attack. And that is the secret of buzz baits, pike and big chub cannot resist their irritating audacity. I particularly like Eppinger's Buzz 'n' Devle, which incorporates a spoon and weedless hook. It can be yanked through the toughest surface vegetation without hang-ups, and produces the most glorious, spectacular attacks.

Plugs

Lastly, we come to all those marvellous creations in wood, high-density plastic, nylon, aluminium and copper known as plugs. There are several different types, but for convenience sake I shall group them as floaters, floating divers, and sinkers that dive, because the ability to identify each type and understand how it works provides the secret to catching on plugs.

Floaters

Pure surface floaters or 'poppers' are great for bringing any predator, pike and chub especially, out of or away from its cover and up to the surface for an attack. They stimulate interest in the thickest covering of surface plants, such as lilies, by the way they gurgle, plop and splutter. The best-known surface plug is the Heddon Crazy Crawler which, by means of its hinged arms that are activated by the retrieve, flip-flaps like a swimmer doing butterfly stroke. One of my favourites, also made by Heddon, is the Torpedo, which is equipped with churning propellers at both front and rear. Worked in short, sharp pulls, this lure really gets pike hopping mad. The Creek Chub mouse, which sports a stiff bushy tail, is another firm favourite.

Incidentally, it is not difficult to convert floating divers such as Ryobi's Mugger or Shakespeare's Big S range into pure floaters that simply pop and gurgle. Saw gently through the diving lip using a fine-tooth hacksaw and gently rub in a drop of rapid, hard-setting waterproof glue to fill in and smooth over. Any single or double-jointed floating diver can be doctored in this way if your fishing demands a greater selection of floaters than is available from the local tackle shop.

Floating divers

These extremely versatile plugs float and gurgle when pulled gently, but then dive when the retrieve is stepped up due to the angled vane or lip under the chin. They come in all sorts of shapes and sizes, in both single and double-jointed formats. The faster you retrieve, the deeper they dive; and whenever you pause during the retrieve, the plug starts to float back up to the surface.

There is an easy way of telling whether a particular model has been designed for shallow or deep diving, and this is by the size of the diving vane. Those with enormous lips such as Bill Norman's Deep Big N, Heddon's Timber Rattler or the Kwikfish King Kranky, can be quickly cranked down to 10 ft or more. In fact, the term 'crank bait' is the apt American name given to floaters which dive deep when being retrieved fast.

Floating divers that contain a steel ball-bearing inside a hollow chamber, and thus rattle and emit sound waves, are the most effective within this range. The Ryobi Mugger and Shakespeare's Big S range are both well proven pike and chub catchers, as are Rapala's Shad Rap and the Shad Rattler from Mirrolure. An unusual plug, in that its tiny vibratory blade protrudes from its rear, is the famous Heddon Big Bud, which only dives a few feet but really does bring out the worst in pike. They just have to attack it.

These boxes contain surface poppers, floating divers and sinking divers. Don't be afraid to ask your tackle dealer which does what.

Helin's 'flat fish' lures, the laziest of floating divers, can be retrieved extremely slowly due to their 'distinct' banana shape, which creates enormous water resistance. They are therefore particularly suited to coloured water and for pike and perch that need time to home in on their food.

Sinking plugs that dive

Plugs that sink by themselves can be counted down towards the bottom at a rate of roughly one second per foot of descent, just like big spoons, so in effect they help you to plummet the depth as you fish. Some have rattles for extra attraction, and most come fitted with much smaller vanes or lips than floating divers because their weight is enough to take them down to the desired fishing depth. They will then dive a few extra feet when retrieved. These plugs are great for reaching pike lying close to the bottom in really deep water beyond the comfortable depth workable with floating divers, say depths well in excess of 10–12 ft.

Rapala's Magnum sinking plugs are considered to be the finest lures available, especially suited to trolling. They are strongly built with good-quality trebles and come in a variety of weights and metallic colour combinations, with body lengths up to 7 in. For general work, Rapala's countdown sinking and double-jointed sinking plugs are really great. ABU make superb sinking plugs too, and I particularly recommend the Killer balsa sinkers, which come in a variety of colours in both single and double-jointed formats, up to 20 grams in weight and 6 in in length.

CHAPTER FIVE

TECHNIQUES AND RIGS

FLOAT FISHING
IN STILLWATER

FLOAT FISHING
IN FLOWING WATER

PRESENTING
FLOATING BAITS

LEDGERING
IN STILLWATER

LEDGERING
IN RUNNING WATER

PREDATOR RIGS

FLYFISHING

FLOAT FISHING IN STILLWATER

To enjoy modest size species like perch, roach, rudd and bream, where possible I would always choose to present the bait beneath a float rather than by ledgering, due to the fact that the tiniest bites can be struck and the bait can be offered in a most natural manner anywhere between the surface and the bottom of the water being fished.

To catch fish from small stillwaters, or when the shoal is fairly close into the margins of large lakes and pits, there is nothing to beat the joy of light float fishing using a 13 ft waggler-style rod and a 2 lb reel line.

BEST TECHNIQUES – FLOAT FISHING IN STILLWATER

	multi-purpose antenna rig	loaded dart on-the-drop	zoomer rig	tipped peacock waggler rig	loaded peacock waggler/slider rig	bodied waggler/driftbeater rig	float fishing from a boat	flat float/laying on rig	float fishing	lift method	float ledger rig	pole float rig
BREAM	•		•	•	•	•	•			•	•	•
CARP			•					•		•	•	
WILD CARP			•					•		•	•	
PERCH	•	•	•	•	•						•	
ROACH	•	•	•	•	•	•	•			•		•
RUDD	•	•	•	•	•		•			•		•
TENCH		•	•	•	•	•	•			•	•	

LIGHT MULTIPURPOSE ANTENNA RIG

I suggest a simple multi-purpose rig as shown in fig. 5.1A incorporating a fine-tipped antenna (such as a stillwater green or blue) holding between 2 no. 1 for calm water or taking up to 3AA for windy conditions. The stability provided by the body allows you to shot the sensitive tip down to the merest 'dot' so the tiniest bite registers.

Plumb the swim carefully so the bait just comes to rest on the bottom once the two shots have settled. A bite can be determined at any time throughout the bait's descent (as in fig. 5.1B), or once it comes to rest on the bottom. Should the majority of bites happen 'on the drop' because the shoal (most typical of summer rudd) is situated in the upper water layers, then move the float down and try these higher levels. In really deep water, say 10–12 ft or deeper, the 'layer' at which the shoal holds may change at any time, so when bites slow up try different levels until you relocate the main shoal. Remember to cast well beyond the area being loose fed and dip the rod tip beneath the surface while cranking the reel handle a few turns in order to sink the line. This is a most important procedure for all stillwater float fishing, otherwise any slight draw or chop on the surface will drag the rig and thus the bait along unnaturally.

If the bait is not taken on the drop, but lies untouched on the bottom for several minutes, one ruse that sometimes instigates an immediate response from lethargic bream in particular, is to wind the float quickly towards you, a foot or two at a time. This momentarily whisks the bait attractively upwards, allowing it to freefall again.

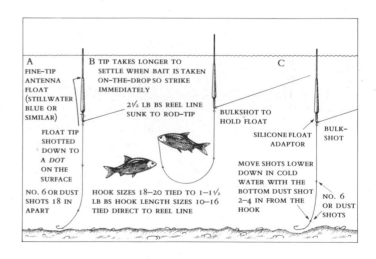

FIGURE 5.1 *Light, multi-purpose stillwater rig*

Light baits, such as a single caster on a size 20 hook, fall much slower and thus more naturally on a finer hook length. Even roach to 2 lb and bream up to 3 lb can be comfortably handled on a 1-lb bottom, so experiment whenever bites are not occurring but you are certain fish are in the swim.

When bream are packed tightly together, feeding in earnest from the carpet of groundbait or loose feed on the bottom, lack of space may prevent them from moving off with the bait and providing you with a sailaway bite on the float-tip. Instead, with their bodies angled downwards and their protrusible mouths fully extended, they hoover up food and right themselves to chew on the spot.

By far the best shotting pattern to indicate this kind of bite is to slide both shots down to within 4–6 in from the hook. The bait is now anchored and presented lift-style –so that when a big roach, hybrid or bream sucks it up and rights itself, thus dislodging the shots, the float-tip rises in a glorious lift. To encourage more deliberate float-tip indications, do not be afraid to juggle about with that all-important distance between hook and bottom shots to see what works best.

In really cold water conditions move both dust shots lower down with the bottom (tell tale shot) one just 2–4 in from the hook and strike at the very slightest indication no matter how insignificant (see fig. 5.1C).

Water clarity in this huge, deep gravel pit has compelled this tench fisherman to use a super-sensitive antenna float rig baited with a single caster.

From a pre-dragged and groundbaited swim, Bob Nudd accounted for these plump tench using a loaded dart float rig, most bites actually coming 'on the drop' as the bait wavered down those last 4 in to the bottom.

LOADED DART 'ON THE DROP'

When purposefully presenting the bait 'on the drop' to rudd or roach working the upper water layers during the summer months, especially shoals patrolling tight up against marginal reeds, along the opposite bank of a canal, or a reed promontary reaching out into the lake etc. use a small loaded float like a zoomer or a 'dart' which sails through the air ahead of the bait as in fig. 5.2.

The secret when fishing on the drop is to catapult the loose feed out and cast over it immediately so that both bait and feed sink simultaneously.

With heavy baits use no shot on the line but a single caster or maggot may need the addition of a dust shot midway between float and hook. The bait is quite liable to be sucked in any second from the moment it hits the surface. So be ready.

Tie hooks in sizes 10–16 direct to a 2 lb reel line for baits such as bread flake and sweetcorn. To achieve the slowest-possible descent with small baits like casters or punched

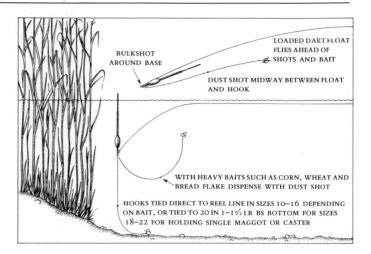

FIGURE 5.2 *Dart rig for fishing on the drop*

bread use a 1–1½ lb test, 20 in hook length and fine-wire hooks in sizes 18–22.

THE ZOOMER RIG

This is a deadly float rig with species such as tench, big bream and even wild carp for placing the bait close up to reed-lines or against lily-beds in clear water conditions, where bites materialize only if the bait is presented among the habitat (fig. 5.3A). Simply rig up an onion or zoomer with the bulk shot at the base of the float. After plummeting the depth accurately, pinch on a BB shot around 5 in from the hook, so it comes to rest just on the bottom. Then, because the float precedes the hook and shot, you can allow it almost to bump against the reed-line before stopping the cast, knowing the bait will angle back down through the water to settle mere inches away from the leading reeds, in full view of patrolling fish.

This method also pays dividends on even-depth, clear-watered lakes and meres where dinghies or punts are used (fig. 5.3B). If beds of marginal reeds, rushes or sedges are the only cover, that is where the fish will be. Row up quietly to within practical casting distance and position the boat side-on to the reed-line.

As the float cannot be wound back with the rod tip held

beneath the surface to sink the line (which would only bring the bait away from the reeds), take along a small (medicine) bottle of neat washing-up liquid and dab a finger-full over the spool every so often. The line will then sink willingly and instantly, after which you can very gently tighten up without pulling the float away from the reeds. Hold the rod whenever bites are expected.

Keep catapulting fragments of loose feed like sweetcorn, maggots, casters or worms along the reed-line for a distance of several yards either side of the float, and fish might be encouraged to work the area all day long.

As a last resort when bites appear to have finally dried up once the sun rises high in the sky, try this favourite old all-or-nothing ruse. Row over to reeds and with an oar spend 15 minutes clouding up the bottom silt. Then return to your anchorage and commence fishing. It is particularly effective with the ever inquisitive tench.

Though the float may be light, this is certainly not a light-tackle method. You will need all of a 6 lb test line to subdue even modest-sized fish of 2–3 lb.

'TIPPED' PEACOCK WAGGLER RIGS

For presenting the bait to species like perch, roach, rudd, bream and tench in stillwaters where casting distance or choppy conditions immediately rule out the light rigs

already mentioned, the float to use is the tipped waggler. It can be shotted to offer the bait on the drop or at any depth from a few feet beneath the surface to hard on the bottom.

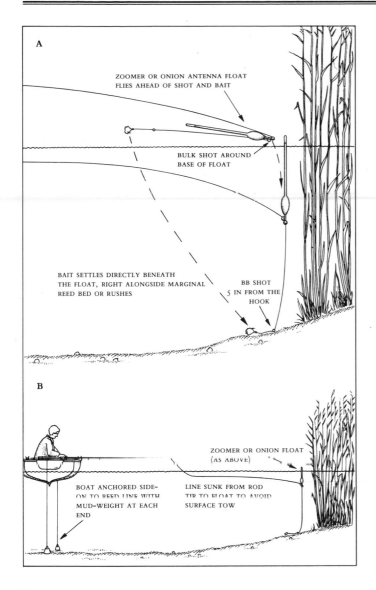

FIGURE 5.3 *Zoomer rig*

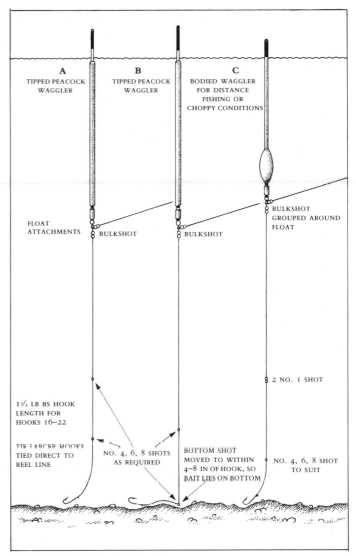

FIGURE 5.4 *Tipped peacock waggler rigs*

A good general rig is shown in fig. 5.4A, with the bulk shot required to reach the swim grouped around the float so that it casts like an arrow, leaving two small shots down the line near the hook. If you plumb the swim carefully so the bait just touches bottom at the end of its fall bites on the drop will register by the float tip failing to settle in its final position, and at any time afterwards when the bait touches bottom. When fish occupy the lower water layers, the bait might need to be nailed to the lake-bed to indicate a bite. If so, then fish slightly over depth and juggle about with the lower shots, ensuring the bottom one is somewhere between 4–8 in from the hook (as in fig. 5.4B). This is an excellent general shotting pattern for bottom feeders like tench and bream.

At all times remember to overcast and wind the float back over the shoal with the rod tip below the surface to ensure that the line is sunk.

For the often long and continual casting involved in waggler fishing in stillwater, I increase the reel-line strength to 2½ lb test and use a 14 ft rod for long-distance work. Otherwise a 13 ft suffices. To facilitate a quick change, the swivel, push-in float attachment allows you to alter from a tipped to a straight waggler (to improve visibility at distance) and for rough conditions, select a bodied waggler for greater stability (fig. 5.4C).

When offering large baits like a bunch of maggots, sweetcorn, stewed wheat or breadflake etc. then tie hooks direct to the reel line (see Hooks). But for a more delicate approach especially in clear water use a 1½ lb hook length and hooks in sizes 16 and smaller for maggots and casters.

Unless shoals are truly enormous (its so easy to overfeed rudd and roach) keep loose feed to hook bait fragments only, regularly introduced by catapult as opposed to heavy helpings of cereal feed. A few small balls to get them interested is fine but thereafter loose fed casters or maggots on the little and often principle will do fine.

The only exception to this is when the swim is full of bream, when you may need to keep cereal feed going in to hold them.

Incidentally, one of the problems encountered whilst after the better-quality bream in a swim full of mixed sizes, where small bream plus roach or rudd occupy the upper water layers, stems from an over-sensitive shotting pattern, which allows smaller fish to intercept the bait on the way down.

To remedy this rearrange the shotting load to take the bait straight down to the bottom on to the noses of the larger bream. Simply move half the bulk shots from around the float and group them with the lower shots just 10 in from the hook.

LOADED PEACOCK WAGGLER/SLIDER RIG

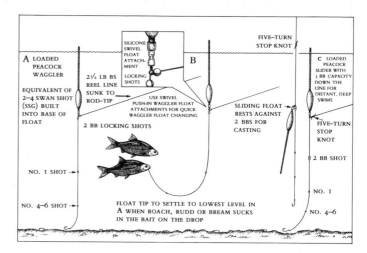

FIGURE 5.5 *Loaded peacock waggler/slider rig*

Ballyquirke Lake is typical of many stillwaters in southern Ireland that are only inches deep in the margins and slowly deepen off further out. The float enabling these anglers to catch roach at distances of 30 yd plus is the loaded peacock waggler, which is best fished as a slider in depths of over 8 ft.

To reach distant deep water the peacock loaded waggler due to its built-in weight at the base (the equivalent of 2 to 4 swan shot wagglers are available according to distances required) will get your bait there and, because so little shot is required, will allow the bait to be presented delicately.

As can be seen in fig. 5.5A and B, it is shotted in exactly the same way as the tipped waggler to register bites both on the drop and on the bottom. In really deep swims during the summer months when roach and rudd especially occupy the upper water layers, start with the float set to just three feet deep say and deepen off a foot or so every

cast until bites come. The 'loaded waggler' is a great float to use 'slider fashion' for bream where depths in excess of 10–12 feet present problems with the fixed float. For a loaded slider that accepts an additional shotting of 3BB down the line for instance (as in fig. 5.5C) split this up into three groups 18 in apart above the hook so the float rests against the 2BB for casting.

Remember not to close the bale arm immediately after casting in order for line to peel off as the lower shots take the bait down through the bottom of the float. Remember also that once the slider knot hits against the bottom of the float, bites on the drop will be indicated if the tip fails to settle at its lowest position on time. It will in fact settle in three increments. When the 2BB's hang, when the no. 1 shot hangs, and finally when the no. 4 or 6 shot hangs. So learn to count each down accordingly, striking instantly at anything out of the ordinary.

BODIED WAGGLER OR 'DRIFTBEATER' RIG

If you want to float-fish for species like tench that are actively feeding considerably further than say a couple of rod lengths out, particularly in windy weather, the line must be sunk or the float will drag under. This means you cannot strike upwards and immediately rules out the simple 'lift rig' using a length of plain peacock quill.

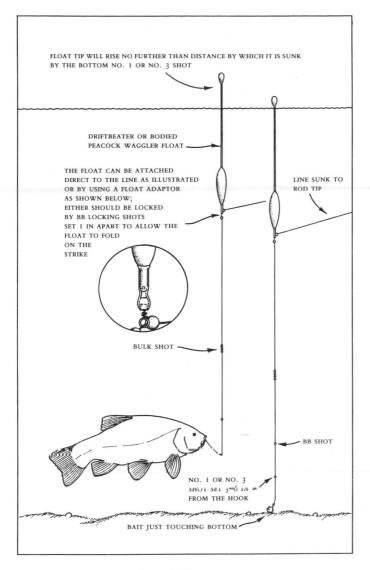

FIGURE 5.6 *Bodied waggler or driftbeater rig*

Renowned for his float-fishing expertise, Dave Thomas helped to popularize the waggler during the 1970s. For the bream occupying a distant swim he has chosen a bodied waggler rig to beat wind-drift on a huge lake near Silkeborg in Denmark.

To reach greater distances, you require a float taking a fair shotting capacity – anywhere from 3AA to 2½ swan shot – and this means using a bodied waggler or a driftbeater. The float is locked by a BB on both sides, with the bulk shot set at mid depth, leaving a small shot (no. 1 or no. 3) to go near the hook, and a BB between it and the bulk shot (fig. 5.6).

To facilitate a quick change of float as surface conditions alter, use a swivel float attachment into which the float can instantly be pushed or removed. Lift bites on this rig are obviously not going to make the float come flying out of the water. However, with the bottom shot close to the hook, if the float is 'lifted' the float top will rise the same distance as it is sunk by that shot. So, after casting and winding the rig back over the swim with the rod tip beneath the surface to sink the line, memorize the level of the float in the water when the tip eventually settles once the BB shot is 'hanging', and by how much more it sinks when the bottom shot hangs the bait just on the bottom.

In all probability most bites on this float rig will consist of a slow disappearance of the tip; you reply with a strong scything, sideways strike, keeping the rod tip low to the water to pick up maximum line and put the hook home. Gentle lift bites will occur, so watch for the tip rising.

FLOAT FISHING FROM A BOAT

The enjoyment from going afloat to catch species like roach, rudd, tench and bream in both still and running water is enormous. It is often the only way to tackle bream shoals that inhabit areas completely unapproachable from

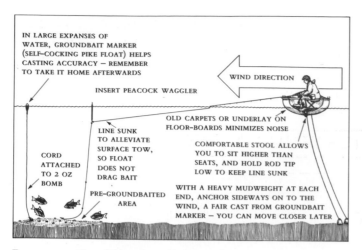

IN LARGE EXPANSES OF WATER, GROUNDBAIT MARKER (SELF-COCKING PIKE FLOAT) HELPS CASTING ACCURACY – REMEMBER TO TAKE IT HOME AFTERWARDS

WIND DIRECTION

INSERT PEACOCK WAGGLER

OLD CARPETS OR UNDERLAY ON FLOOR-BOARDS MINIMIZES NOISE

LINE SUNK TO ALLEVIATE SURFACE TOW, SO FLOAT DOES NOT DRAG BAIT

COMFORTABLE STOOL ALLOWS YOU TO SIT HIGHER THAN SEATS, AND HOLD ROD TIP LOW TO KEEP LINE SUNK

CORD ATTACHED TO 2 OZ BOMB

PRE-GROUNDBAITED AREA

WITH A HEAVY MUDWEIGHT AT EACH END, ANCHOR SIDEWAYS ON TO THE WIND, A FAIR CAST FROM GROUNDBAIT MARKER – YOU CAN MOVE CLOSER LATER

FIGURE 5.7 *Float fishing from a boat in stillwater*

This bream fisherman, anchored in a noted hot-spot just inside Wroxham Broad at one of the entrances where it joins the River Bure, presents a bunch of maggots on the bottom beneath a tipped peacock waggler rig.

the bank. Such is the situation on my local Norfolk Broads, for instance, most of which are surrounded by peaty, swampy margins with thick beds of tall reeds. Being largely underfished, these areas obviously contain shoals that rarely see a baited hook and invariably provide consistently good sport.

Boat-fishing also permits tempting, overgrown backwaters and other inaccessible parts of river-systems well away from all the popular areas to be reached. So if you own a suitable car-top dinghy, or dinghy plus trailer, or can arrange to hire one give boat-fishing a try.

You need to be very well organized in a boat (fig. 5.7), and the first consideration should be a pair of heavy mudweights on adequate-length ropes for keeping the boat anchored in windy conditions. There is nothing more irritating than suddenly to drift away from a feeding shoal because the mudweights are too light.

Sound carries very easily on water, and one slight klunk on the gunnel or seat can be heard by fish hundreds of yards away, so be especially quiet when rowing up to a potential swim prior to lowering the mudweights. Be very deliberate and slow in all your movements from stowing the oars to preparing nets and bait buckets. Take time to make the rods up, and arrange all the large items neatly in the boat either before you set off, or long before you reach the swim. Take along an old piece of carpet or carpet underlay to cover the floorboards, as this will minimize noise. Several hours spent in a boat encourages fidgeting, which in turn creates still more vibrations, so take along a comfortable folding-chair if there is enough room in the boat. If not, use a pad of thick foam on the seats, which in most boats tend to be rather on the low side.

If you are sitting high above the surface, you will be able to control the float more comfortably and effectively, as you can dip the rod-tip and sink the line to counteract surface drift. And exact float control is imperative when

out in a boat, facing the elements. Remember that if you keep too tight a line between float and boat, whenever the boat moves back and forwards on the anchor ropes, the bait will be pulled unnaturally along the bottom. For this reason, and assuming the surface will be broken (flat calms for most of the day are quite rare), by far the best rig is the tipped peacock waggler set-up in fig. 5.4. The lift method in fig. 5.4C can usually only be used effectively in really calm conditions, and even then you need to hold the rod to counteract the pull off the boat.

To ensure good sport from an early-morning start if your quarry is bream or tench, try rowing out to pre-bait the swim the night before (see 'Pre-baiting', p. 125), not forgetting to mark the swim in some way. It is surprising just how far out you can be when you make a calculated guess as to the exact position of the swim when you return to a large expanse of water, even when you go to the bother of lining up one feature with another on shore. You can construct a marker from a length of cord, with a 2-oz bomb tied to one end and a loaded (self-cocking) pike float on the other end. Drop the marker over the side of the boat once you have scattered the groundbait about. In the morning, as you approach the spot, use binoculars to look for signs of fish movement, or their bubbles, over the groundbait. Be sure to position the boat sideways-on to the wind (with a mud-weight at each end) at a reasonable cast length away from the marker so as not to spook the fish. If during the session the bream are feeding so confidently you feel the boat could be repositioned a little closer, simply lift the mudweights at each end and use the wind to drift silently forwards.

It is always better to fish from further away to start with, because you then have the option of moving closer later, rather than anchoring too close and scaring the fish initially. Don't forget to take the marker home at the end of the session.

When anchoring in rivers, you should anchor bows-on to the current. To do this, put down the bow mudweight first (if alone in the boat, this is the easier way round), and let out at least several feet more rope than the depth requires. Once the boat comes round to settle steadily lower the stern weight on a fairly tight rope. When the flow is too strong for you to use standard waggler techniques, use the stret-pegging rig shown in fig. 5.25, or simply swap over to a quivertip set-up (see 'Quiver-tipping', p. 175).

THE FLAT FLOAT (LAYING ON) RIG

When tackling dense reedlines along your own bank, either from wooden staging or from marshy ground, it is a waste of time to cast out over the reeds and expect species like tench and carp to feed in open water, unless the water is well coloured. They are much more likely to be mere feet away, working through the reeds or rushes.

Such swims demand a stealthy approach and to sit or kneel a few feet back from the waterline with a bait hanging right beneath the rod tip just 2 to 3 yd out, where fish will be feeding between the stems. Ledgering is an option, but invariably spooks large, deep-bodied, patrolling species such as bream, tench and carp. Even if the sound waves of a heavy lead going in doesn't scare them, the line stretched 'hauser' fashion from bait to rod tip most certainly will. They simply fade away when they sense the line or bump accidentally into it, and promptly vacate the area in blind panic.

Neither occurrence is likely to produce a specimen in the bottom of the net, but the problem is easily solved by the flat float rig shown in fig. 5.8. The float is not cocked because if it was, water displacement caused, for example, by a carp's tail, could move the line and dip the float momentarily (the float sometimes twitches when fish are in the swim, enticing you into striking when there is not a bite). When a fish does move off with the bait, however, the float sinks from view as the line from bait to rod tip straightens.

The rig is simplicity itself to construct. Attach 1 in of peacock quill (a tiny waggler will do nicely) to the line with a silicone rubber band at each end. After tying on the hook, set the float well over depth so that at least 3 ft of line lies along the bottom. Then fix on a small shot (a No.

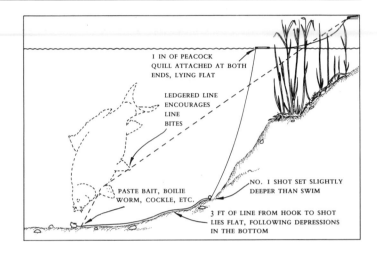

FIGURE 5.8 *Laying on*

1) below the float, slightly deeper than the swim. The rod can then be placed in two rests. Alternatively, it can be held.

Fishing right in among marginal stems means that pre-baiting is not really necessary because the fish are already there. However, you will need to creep about in order to catch them at such close quarters. Just scatter a handful of bait fragments among the stems every so often (worms, cockles, bread flake, boilies etc.) to keep fish moving through the swim.

Although the float may be light, this is certainly not a light tackle method. You will to relate line strengths to the species expected. For tench, bream and modest-sized carp, 6 lb test should suffice. For carp into double figures and larger, opt for a 10–12 lb reel line coupled to hooks of suitable size and strength.

FLOAT FISHING FOR CRUCIAN CARP

To catch crucians regularly, a very carefully shotted light float rig is imperative, the best floats being a fine tipped antenna or a short, narrow-diameter length of peacock quill fished in 'mini lift' style. The object is to see those tiny bites for which crucians are renowned and which often barely register on the float tip (fig. 5.9B).

For this reason the single shot (a no. 1, BB or AA depending on float size) should be not more than 2 in from the hook. Try moving it even closer, to 1 in away, because sometimes this alone can make all the difference between seeing bites and not. The secret, after casting in and tightening up so the float cocks, is to wind down even further so the tip is just the merest 'blimp' on the surface. Strike the slightest movement.

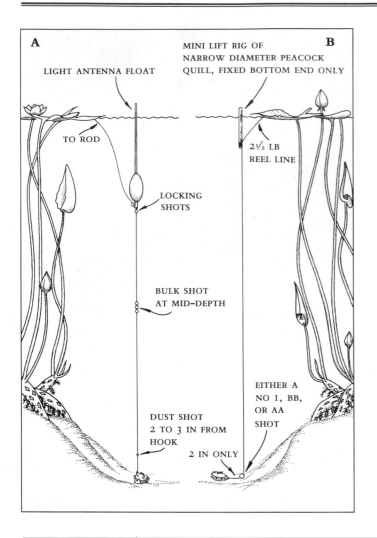

FIGURE 5.9 *Float fishing (left) and mini-lift rig (right) for crucians*

When crucians are really feeding confidently, denoted by clusters of small bubbles regularly rising to the surface, the float might even lift completely out of the water and lay flat, as the carp tilts its head up after sucking up the bait and dislodges the shot. Or the tip will sink positively as the crucian characteristically runs along the bottom. But far more bites will barely register on the float, so you need to hold the rod throughout and be eagle-eyed.

To stand a better chance of hitting bites from crafty crucians which just lie on the bottom blowing the bait in and out, rig up a light antenna float with a dust shot 2–3 in from the hook, the bulk shot set at mid depth (fig. 5.9A). After carefully plumbing the swim, adjust the float so the bait is literally a fraction above the bottom. As with the lift rig, strike at the slightest movement on the float tip. Remember to keep loose feed or small balls of ground bait going in on the little-and-often principle, and they might be encouraged to feed all day. A ruse always worth trying when they are particularly dour is to gently wind the float in 6 in at a time, which makes the bait lift upwards enticingly and gently fall down to the bottom again. Baits which are inherently buoyant like breadflake or casters, or which are expected to move such as worms, work best when 'twitching' in this way to encourage bites.

Incidentally, both these rigs work effectively for tench which are biting particularly shyly.

THE 'LIFT' METHOD

The lift method (note the peacock quill float resting against John's landing-net) has become synonymous with summer tench fishing.

No other float-fishing technique has been so exhaustively described as the famous lift method. Yet even now, almost 40 years since the Taylor brothers first popularized the method back in the 1950s with their huge catches of tench from the lakes at Wooton Underwood, the vast majority of anglers still get it wrong because they fail to grasp the basic principle of the lift. Once and for all let me explain how this great technique actually works.

The lift is particularly successful with, and suited to, the tench as a species because of the way in which they stand on their heads to suck in bottom-fished baits (see 'Feeding'). They then return to an even keel while chewing the food and spit out the hook because it is indigestible. This is why an angler whose lift rig is incorrectly shotted (the shot being too far away from the hook) will reel in time and time again with empty maggot skins on the hook, without seeing the slightest indication of a bite.

The essence of fishing the lift is to set the float (a length of peacock quill or commercial waggler) a little overdepth, attached bottom end only with a piece of silicone tubing

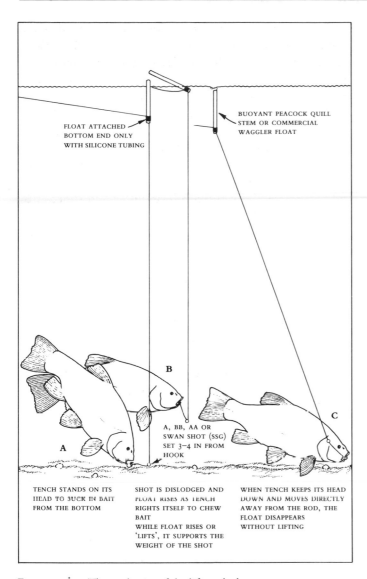

FIGURE 5.10 *The mechanics of the lift method*

Youngsters especially love the excitement of watching the float perform its drunken ritual of slowly falling over flat. They catch quality fish too, as young Jonathan Todd proved by beating this superb 15 lb common carp on only 6 lb test.

and *not* locking shots. I'll say that again: *not* locking shots. You do not want any shots anywhere near the float. All the shot loading, a BB, an AA, or a single swan shot (depending on casting requirements) must be fixed just 3–4 in from the hook (see fig. 5.10A). When the tench sucks up the bait and rights itself, thus dislodging the shot, the float starts to 'lift' (hence the method's name) and may even fall flat. But more importantly: while it is 'lifting' it is helping to support the weight of the shot. Of course, once the float lays completely flat (fig. 5.10B) the tench is fully supporting the weight of that shot and could eject the bait. This is why you should always strike as the float 'lifts'.

Some anglers suffer a mental block at this stage; because the float is still visible they do not consider the bite worth striking. You cannot risk waiting for such a positive indication because the tench will probably drop the bait in the meantime.

If, however, from the moment it sucks up the bait the

tench keeps its head down and carries on going directly away from the rod, the float without any pre-warning whatsoever (occasionally it might 'bob' first) will simply disappear as in fig. 5.10C. And this is the beauty behind the lift method – it allows you to interpret exactly what is happening down below.

When bites are expected at regular intervals you will convert considerably more (even the tiniest lifts and dips) into tench in the net if you hold the rod throughout. It may only take a split second to reach down and grab the rod set in rests, but the tench can blow the bait out even quicker. Besides, striking immediately allows you to bend the rod into a full curve and apply sufficient pressure against a tench hooked beside potential snags and to get it well under control before it can retaliate.

There is another advantage in holding the rod when fishing the lift. By gently moving the bait along the bottom you can encourage difficult tench to make a quick decision and grab the bait. This works especially well when the bait is presented over a clean bottom – either silt, mud or gravel – because as you slowly give the reel handle half a turn (providing the line is tight from float to rod tip) the inherent buoyancy of peacock quill will help the shot move along the bottom. Initially it will go under as you start to wind but will pop up again a second or two later. In the meantime, a tench may be aroused by the bait's sudden audacity in moving away, and make a sudden grab for it, resulting in a very quick 'lift' or 'dip'. If you are holding the rod you can strike these bites instantly, producing tench which would otherwise not be caught.

Tench can invariably be induced into feeding by bait movement, especially with baits which move anyway like maggots and worms. And there is no better way of moving the bait while remaining ready to deal with an instant bite than presenting the 'lift' rig.

For 'twitching' the bait over an uneven bottom, use a longer (and thus more buoyant) peacock quill than the shot requires. For example, if it is set shallower than the swim depth, the float should cock but with a good 2 in above the surface. Then reset it so that it is slightly over-depth and cast out, gently tightening up until only 1 in of the tip is visible (fig. 5.11A). You will know the set-up is correct when you wind down too much and the float lifts the shot along the bottom and keels over. Just tighten up again, as this is exactly what it is supposed to do (fig. 5.11B).

The lift can be used effectively with most baits (except really large mouthfuls), and sometimes it pays to juggle about with the shot, moving it a little closer to the hook or a little further away than the recommended 3–4 in. When tench are especially shy in clear water conditions, I use a single BB (it is almost impossible to fish the lift effectively with a smaller shot) pinched on just 2 in from the hook and select a short, super-slim length of quill.

This super-sensitive rig is great for bugging the

Tench and carp bubbling contentedly in the margins between beds of lilies are not too happy about a 2 oz lead landing among them. This is where float fishing techniques, and in particular the lift method, are so effective.

'bubblers', tench which are rooting just beyond the marginal lilies quite close in, where the bubbles of individual fish can be identified. Make a calculated guess as to which direction the tench is heading and cast a little to the right or left of where bubbles last erupted. Keep casting to rising bubbles until an instant bite occurs.

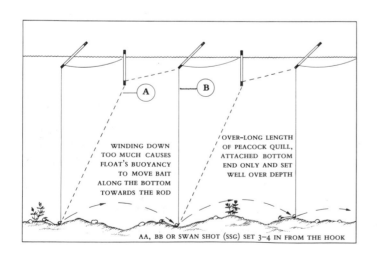

FIGURE 5.11 *Using the lift rig to twitch the bait along an uneven bottom*

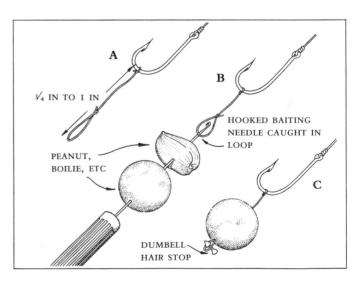

FIGURE 5.12 *Adding a hair to a hook on a lift rig*

Wilson cannot believe he has finally cracked a 30–33 lb 1 oz carp on a simple lift rig, 'lowered' into 3 ft of clear water close beside a marginal fringe of yellow iris. The bait was a single peanut, hair-rigged onto a size 4 hook tied direct to 11 line.

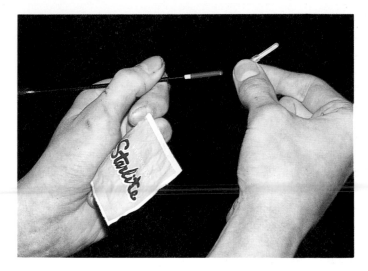

Float fishing for tench, bream or carp at night is now easy, thanks to these extra bright 'starlight' luminous elements. They push onto any waggler-style float via a sleeve of silicone tubing.

When bites are not forthcoming, but fish are obviously in the swim attracted by the loose feed, you can make the hook bait more appealing and easier to suck up without the tench feeling the initial weight and presence of the hook by threading the bait on to a 'hair' (fig. 5.12).

Because an upward strike is imperative with the lift method to pick up the slack created by the tench lifting the bait and shot, it can only be used as a close-range technique. If you want to float-fish for tench which are actively feeding considerably further than say a couple of rod lengths out, particularly in windy weather, the line must be sunk or the float will drag under. This means you cannot strike upwards, or continue to use quite the same rig, so no longer can just a single shot be used.

Carp and bream also stand on their head to take a bait from the bottom, as indeed do large rudd. The lift method is therefore successful with all these species. Particle baits rigged on a hair, fished in conjunction with the lift method, is a deadly way of getting wily old carp, for instance, to bite.

Lift float fishing at night

Tench and carp that inhabit very clear waters, or lakes and pits where marginal cover is sparse, are more inclined to feed close into the bank under the cloak of darkness. They then become nicely catchable with the lift method. Use a peacock quill fitted with a luminous element so that you can see the float easily.

For fishing close in just beyond the rod tip, and regular sessions at night, it pays to invest in a 500/600 micro-lambert (the most powerful) betalight luminous element,

which is easily glued and whipped into the top of a peacock stem (fig. 5.13A).

For the occasional night trip, and for fishing out well beyond the rod tip, use a luminous 'starlite' chemical element which is very bright. It is easily slipped on to the tip of the peacock quill with a short length of clear tubing which comes supplied with the element (fig. 5.13B).

These wonderful inventions come in a choice of three sizes. They consist of a clear plastic tube containing two chemicals which, once you bend the tube and shake, mix together and become luminous for about eight hours.

As bites at night tend to be far more positive than those experienced in the daytime, resist the temptation to wind the float tip down so only the merest tip is visible, or you will be forever striking at ghosts. By all means hold the

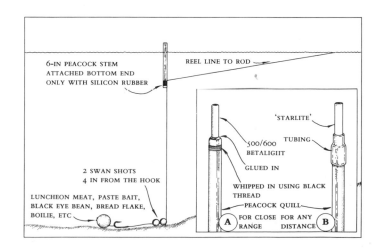

FIGURE 5.13 *Lift float fishing at night*

rod to capitalize on bites when they are occurring frequently, but when times are slow, try to relax by positioning the rod close to hand, supported horizontally on two rests.

Wherever there is a slight draw on the surface, the float might be slowly dragged under. Simply push the back rod rest down a little to angle the tip of the rod upwards, thus lifting sufficient line off the surface for the float tip to reappear. You will gradually learn these little tricks. You will also quickly discover to switch on a torch *only* when it is absolutely necessary (such as when the line is tangled) because night vision is instantly ruined by torchlight.

The lift/bolt rig

To adapt the basic lift method into a 'shock' or 'bolt rig', with or without the bait presented on a hair for carp simply pinch 4 or 5 swan shot instead of the usual two (fig. 5.14). This invariably stops nuisance fish like bream and tench from pushing the bait about and giving false bites. Be prepared to hold the rod all the time because it is rather tricky fishing, especially with the bait close to lilies or beside jungle swims. When a carp grabs the bait and instantly panics off, it feels the extra shots as the hook pricks home and it moves at incredible speed.

6-IN PEACOCK QUILL STEM

TO ROD

BOTTOM END MOUNTED

BAIT SIDE-HOOKED OR
HAIT-MOUNTED AS
REQUIRED

4 OR 5 SWAN SHOTS (SSG)
4 IN FROM THE HOOK

FIGURE 5.14 *Converting the lift into a bolt/shock rig*

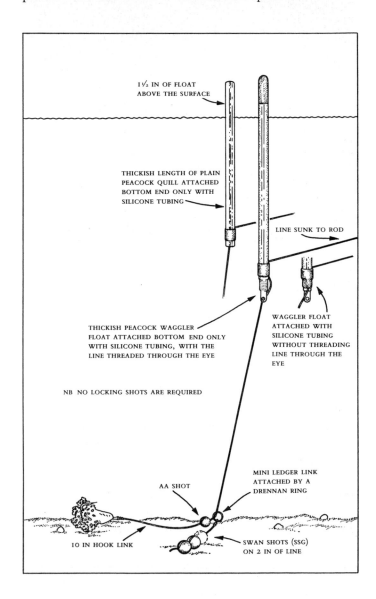

1½ IN OF FLOAT
ABOVE THE SURFACE

THICKISH LENGTH OF PLAIN
PEACOCK QUILL ATTACHED
BOTTOM END ONLY WITH
SILICONE TUBING

LINE SUNK TO ROD

WAGGLER FLOAT
ATTACHED WITH
SILICONE TUBING
WITHOUT THREADING
LINE THROUGH THE
EYE

THICKISH PEACOCK WAGGLER
FLOAT ATTACHED BOTTOM END ONLY
WITH SILICONE TUBING, WITH THE
LINE THREADED THROUGH THE EYE

NB NO LOCKING SHOTS ARE REQUIRED

MINI LEDGER LINK
ATTACHED BY A
DRENNAN RING

AA SHOT

10 IN HOOK LINK

SWAN SHOTS (SSG)
ON 2 IN OF LINE

FIGURE 5.15 *Float ledger rig*

FLOAT LEDGER RIG

When contemplating float-fishing for roach, perch, rudd, bream or tench at distances beyond the casting potential of the previously mentioned lift, bodied waggler or drift-

beater rigs, it makes sense to take all the shots off the line and put them on a mini ledger link stopped 10 in from the hook (fig. 5.15). With this float ledger rig, extremely long

A slab-sided, double-figure bream in the net for John from a Norfolk gravel-pit complex. The successful method was float ledgering with a long, straight peacock waggler rig, and a size 10 hook baited with three kernels of sweetcorn.

Pole fishing should not be limited to tiddlers. Even medium-sized tench are easily manageable with a little patience. Having located tench, Robbie Robertson finds the successful method is a single caster presented just above the bottom weed.

distances can be covered and the bait can be presented into areas where the ledgered bait is not practical, such as swims 40 yd out where a ledgered line cannot be sunk because of a large patch of lilies between the swim and the bank. The float ledger is also the best rig for presenting a static bait in extremely windy conditions, when either surface pull or underwater tow continually belly the line and submerge the tip of a delicately shotted float rig.

Strangely, in rough weather bites are invariably quite bold, and I can recall several outings when even using three or four swan shots on the mini ledger, large fish such as bream and tench have moved them and actually given a lift bite. Most registrations, however, will consist of a positive sinking of the float tip, so ensure that enough of the tip is visible so that you can see this easily at distance – about 1½ in should do.

POLE FLOAT RIGS

Because the line can be held immediately upwind of the float without its being dragged under or off course and thus affecting bait presentation in distances of up to 30–40 feet out, the degree of sensitivity gained from pole fishing has no equal. Only in extremely gusty conditions or when

you fancy a change is it pertinent to sink the line and change tack to waggler fishing or ledgering.

The renowned 'short line-long pole' method where only 5–6 ft of line exists between float and pole tip is arguably the most deadly of all match fishing techniques. Tackle

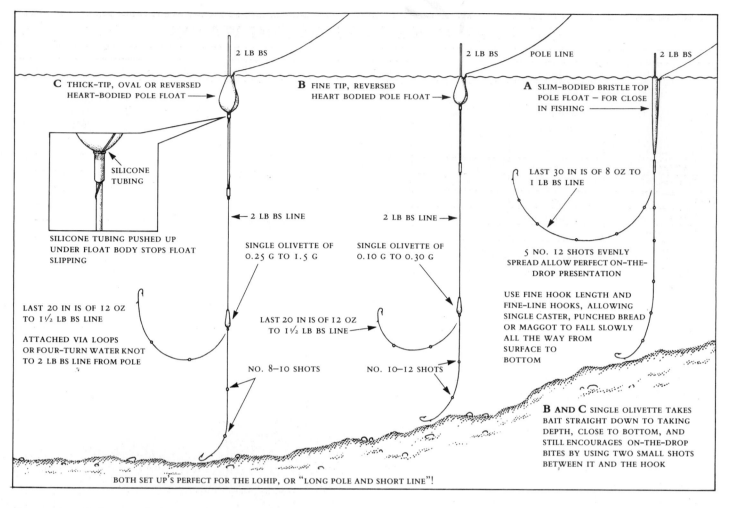

FIGURE 5.16 *Stillwater pole-float rigs*

rigs are not really so different from running line set ups except that shots are not used close to the float.

To offer a small bait caster or maggot on the drop to summer rudd which love the warmer upper water layers or to super wary roach or dace in a clear water canal, the set up in fig. 5.16A is perfect. If a bite does not happen on the drop or when the bait has been touching bottom for a while it is easy with the pole to move the float (and thus the bait) several inches either to the right or left, or whisk it up off the bottom a couple of feet and let it fall again or lift the rig completely out, flipping it straight back in again to encourage bites on the drop. Plummeting of the swim is critical during the winter months when the fishes metabolism has slowed down and bites are gentle dips of the fine tip. Most will come in that narrow band of water immediately above the bottom and so that is exactly where your bait needs to be all the time. The rig in fig. 5.16B is ideal because the single olivette takes the bait straight down and the two tiny shots between it and hook will still register any 'on the drop' bites. When fish are situated a fair way out into very deep water two things are important. A float tip thick enough to see easily and a heavy enough olivette to take the bait straight down to the feeding zone (as in fig. 5.16C). Again by using two tiny shots between the olivette and hook 'on the drop' bites will register by the tip not settling properly so watch it like a hawk. If the occasional specimen roach or rudd is on the cards and superlight tackle is imperative to initiate bites then use the elasticated tip set up (see Pole Tops).

Hit and hold tactics

Certain types of summer venues on stillwaters dictate that if you want quality fish you must present the bait in among or alongside thick beds of tough lilies. For the inevitable hit-and-hold tussles which follow, a 5–6 m telescopic glass or glass/carbon-mix pole can be wound up nicely into a cushioning bend, dispensing with the need for shock-absorbing elastic. Such a tool may be held single-handed and supported along the forearm like a rod, and its soft action is your buffer and insurance against breakages. An unpainted quill is fished in the simple lift method.

FLOAT FISHING IN FLOWING WATER

BEST TECHNIQUES – FLOAT FISHING IN FLOWING WATER

	waggler fishing	stick float fishing	big stick/ balsa trotter	long trotting	stret pegging	pole float
BARBEL	●		●	●	●	
BREAM	●				●	●
CHUB	●	●	●	●	●	
DACE	●	●	●	●	●	●
GRAYLING		●	●	●		
PERCH	●				●	●
ROACH	●	●	●	●	●	●

WAGGLER FISHING

Wagglers have neat bottom eyes permitting a speedy change from one float to another with the help of a silicon float adapter, which is sleeved on to the line. In addition, by grouping the bulk shot either side of the waggler, locking it in the desired position (remember to leave a gap between the shots), not only makes it cast accurately, like an arrow, but ensures that the float easily 'folds' flat to the line on the strike and so does not impair hook penetration on the strike.

A 2 or 2½ lb reel line is perfect for most waggler fishing used in conjunction with 13 foot waggler rod and a simple shotting pattern for slow currents.

The waggler/lift rigs (slow currents)

Use of the waggler in running water provides a choice between anchoring the bait to the bottom or presenting it trundling slowly over the river-bed at current pace. And for both methods the straight peacock waggler is best, because unlike the insert waggler, whose tip is drawn under too easily, its inherent buoyancy allows small baits to be trundled smoothly over an uneven bottom without the tip dragging under and registering false bites.

For dragging small baits like casters or maggots along the bottom in very slow currents in search of dace, roach, chub and bream group most of the bulk shot around the float, which should be set at least 1 ft over-depth. Then dot several small shots at equal distances (say, every 18–20 in) down the line, finishing with a dust shot (fig. 5.17A). For the best presentation in windy weather, sink the line as

John slips the net beneath a 6 lb River Shannon bream that accepted a bunch of maggots trotted around a slow 6 ft deep eddy, beneath a 5AA straight peacock waggler rig.

though fishing in stillwater and strike sideways. In calm conditions ensure that the line floats, allowing reasonable slack and a distinct bow from float to rod tip so that the bait is not drawn inwards and away from the feed line.

For those occasions when species like bream refuse to accept a moving bait and show interest only in one lying static, put your faith in the lift method (fig. 5.17B). By adding a starlight luminous element to the tip of the waggler good catches of bream can be made at night by fishing 'lift style'.

I particularly enjoy using the waggler to present small baits like maggots and casters to chub in the smaller rivers during the winter, when the weeds have gone provided

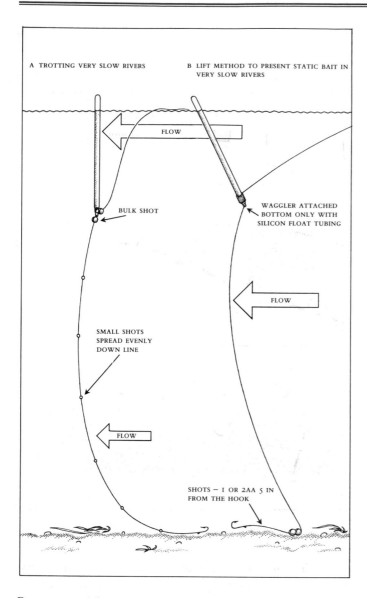

A TROTTING VERY SLOW RIVERS

B LIFT METHOD TO PRESENT STATIC BAIT IN VERY SLOW RIVERS

FLOW

BULK SHOT

WAGGLER ATTACHED BOTTOM ONLY WITH SILICON FLOAT TUBING

FLOW

SMALL SHOTS SPREAD EVENLY DOWN LINE

FLOW

SHOTS – 1 OR 2AA 5 IN FROM THE HOOK

FIGURE 5.17 *The waggler in running water*

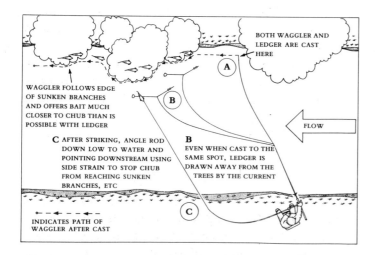

BOTH WAGGLER AND LEDGER ARE CAST HERE

A

B

WAGGLER FOLLOWS EDGE OF SUNKEN BRANCHES AND OFFERS BAIT MUCH CLOSER TO CHUB THAN IS POSSIBLE WITH LEDGER

C AFTER STRIKING, ANGLE ROD DOWN LOW TO WATER AND POINTING DOWNSTREAM USING SIDE STRAIN TO STOP CHUB FROM REACHING SUNKEN BRANCHES, ETC

B EVEN WHEN CAST TO THE SAME SPOT, LEDGER IS DRAWN AWAY FROM THE TREES BY THE CURRENT

FLOW

C

INDICATES PATH OF WAGGLER AFTER CAST

FIGURE 5.18 *Using the waggler to present the bait to winter chub beneath overhanging and sunken trees*

that the flow is not too strong. In clear, low, cold water conditions when chub in shallow rivers tend to pack beneath definite habitat swims like overhanging or sunken willows and are loathe to leave such protection, there are times when, unless the bait is teased into spots no ledger could ever reach directly under the edge of the branches, you won't catch any chub.

With the float set to present the bait just off the bottom it is cast a few feet upstream from the trees (fig. 5.18A) and allowed to be carried downstream unchecked alongside the branches. Any attempt to keep a tight line, as with the ledger (fig. 5.18B), will draw the bait away from the fish.

Loose feed should be kept to a minimum initially and should be catapulted well upstream to allow for current speed. If bating with a single caster or maggot, stewed hempseed or tares are excellent loose feed attractors, but feed sparingly in very cold conditions. Just half a dozen seeds every other trot down will suffice.

Waggler in steady medium-paced-to-fast swims

To offer a moving bait in deep rivers of medium pace or deep eddies in weir-pools, choose a waggler carrying a fair shotting capacity when seeking big fish like chub and barbel.

For ease of casting, and to hit the same line consistently, do not be afraid to rig up a really big, thick peacock waggler that takes plenty of shot. Between 5AA and 6AA. For long, medium-paced swims where there is time for the bait to find its level slowly, bulk most of the shot around the float, leaving room down below for a couple of No. 1s and a No. 4 20 in above the hook (see fig. 5.19A). In order every so often to mend the bow that forms between rod-tip and float as it is carried downstream unchecked, grease the line above the float with mucilin. The bow is impossible to mend if the line is sunk.

If the bottom is clean, smooth sand or gravel, the float tip may be shotted reasonably well down. Where the river bed is uneven, however, leave a good 1½ in of the tip above the surface, encouraging the buoyancy in the peacock waggler to drag the bait over the river-bed without the tip being submerged. When a barbel or chub grabs the bait, you will be in absolutely no doubt of a bite. In really clear water, the hook link can be reduced to make spooky fish bite, but no lighter than 2 lb test. Remember to keep feeding exactly the same line with the catapult on every cast to ensure that barbel move over the bait at some point along the swim. A loose feed mixture of hemp and casters works well in clear water with double caster, caster and maggot or double maggot on the hook.

To waggler-fish fast swims, shallow or deep, I prefer to bulk most of the shots at around two-thirds depth, with a

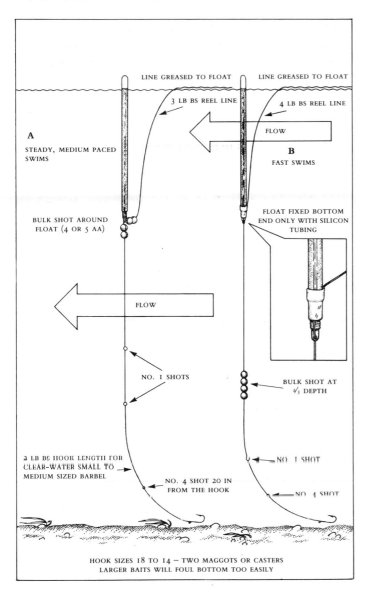

FIGURE 5.19 *Waggler fishing – peacock waggler rigs*

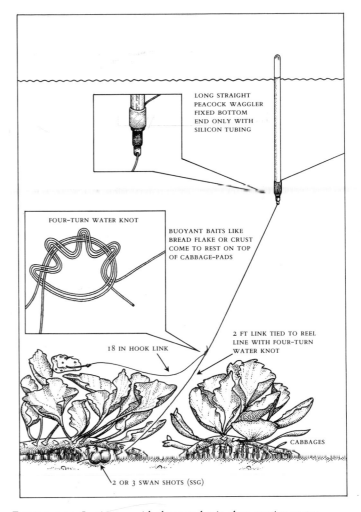

FIGURE 5.20 *Laying on with the waggler in slow-moving water*

No. 1 and a No. 4 between them and the hook (fig. 5.19B). The float is not locked to the line in the normal way, but held tightly by silicone tubing. I also feel happier switching over from a 3 lb to a 4 lb reel line in stronger currents – and ensure the line for at least 5 or 6 yd above the float has a liberal coating of mucilin.

Laying-on with the waggler

This technique is ideal for catching roach, bream and tench from deep, slow-moving water. It permits the bait to be presented 'laying-on' over bottom weeds such as the sub-surface cabbage of the yellow water-lily, instead of falling through them and thus being hidden from feeding fish.

You need a very long waggler to fish this method effectively. The swan shots (fig. 5.20) are not responsible for cocking the float, so you can use as many as you like to

aid casting and provide the weight necessary to carry them down through the cabbage leaves to the river-bed. Tighten up quickly after casting so that the waggler cocks with a good inch of the tip above the surface. This ensures that the very last thing to settle is the bait, which will rest in full view on top of the cabbages, where the fish can see it. A large piece of fresh, white bread flake, pinched tightly in just one small area along the hook shank, comes to rest extremely gently. Also effective is a balanced offering of crust on the shank and flake on the bend. Even better still is a ½-in cube of plain bread crust tipped with a single maggot to make it gyrate.

Fishing the stick float

The reason for fixing top and bottom is purely one of control. As the line is not actually threaded through any part of the float, changing from one to another is indeed accomplished in a matter of seconds. But overall it is the sensitivity in control of the stick float and subsequent finesse in presentation of small baits like casters, maggots,

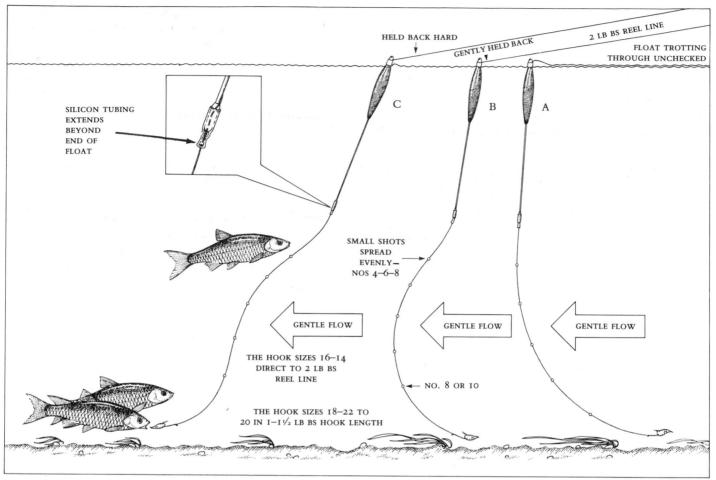

HELD BACK HARD

GENTLY HELD BACK

2 LB BS REEL LINE

FLOAT TROTTING
THROUGH UNCHECKED

SILICON TUBING
EXTENDS
BEYOND
END OF
FLOAT

C   B   A

SMALL SHOTS
SPREAD
EVENLY –
NOS 4–6–8

GENTLE FLOW   GENTLE FLOW   GENTLE FLOW

THE HOOK SIZES 16–14
DIRECT TO 2 LB BS
REEL LINE

← NO. 8 OR 10

THE HOOK SIZES 18–22 TO
20 IN 1–1½ LB BS HOOK LENGTH

FIGURE 5.21 *Fishing the stick float*

hempseed, elderberries and tares, which sets the technique apart. Fishing the stick float should be considered a technique which only really works effectively at short range – a length of one and a half rod lengths or a distance beyond which loose feed cannot accurately be thrown by hand.

As soon as you try to control the float if cast any further, as it is taken downstream by the current it will be pulled away from the line being fed and at which the shoal is lying. So first and foremost think of presenting the stick to roach, dace and chub occupying marginal and close range swims only. Beyond this – use the waggler.

Consider the basic shotting pattern of the wire stemmed stick float for instance in fig. 5.21. Sometimes bites happen when the float is trotted along, set overdepth and completely unchecked (fig. 5.21A). More bites are usually instigated however by constant light fingered control of the stick float. Bites also happen when gently holding back

Using the stick float to present casters down a narrow run between thick weed-beds on Norfolk's River Wensum, Dave Batten proves the method's effectiveness.

(fig. 5.21B) which momentarily speeds up the bait's forward movement. And by holding back hard for several seconds (fig. 5.21C) whisks the bait away from the bottom to flutter enticingly ahead of the float.

For a really slow, search of the swim, particularly effective in cold water conditions when roach for instance are loathe to give chase, slightly overshot the float so that if left to trot through unchecked the tip would actually disappear. But of course by gently controlling and holding back on the tip it keeps just above the surface to instantly indicate the very slightest and most hesitant of bites. A single bouyant caster presented slowly just above bottom in conjunction with hempseed fed very sparingly is a wonderful winter combination for chub, roach and dace. An elderberry or tare on the hook plus loose fed hemp, is also a winner (see Baits).

BIG STICK/BALSA TROTTER RIG

For presenting the bait to big roach, chub or barbel hugging the bottom of deepish swims where the pace is steady I like the sensitivity of big sticks and balsa trotters. I even step down to a 3 lb reel line if there are no snags or marginal rushes and reeds.

The shotting load can be spread evenly in three or four groups (depending on swim depth), with a small shot, a No. 4 or 6, between the lowest group and the hook (fig. 5.22). Try slightly overshotting the float so that you can ease back gently (as though stick-float fishing for roach) all

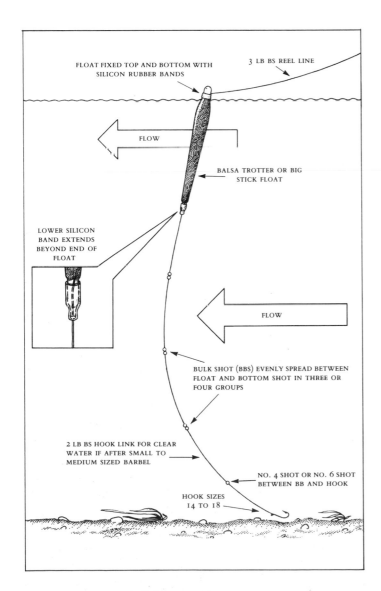

FIGURE 5.22 *Big stick, balsa trotter rigs*

A wonderful way to catch barbel, grayling, chub and specimen roach is to wade carefully out into a shallow river so that the float (a balsa trotter) can be guided directly downstream to a shoal. A bait pouch dispenses with the need to continually open and close bait tins.

the way down the swim with a fairly controlled line from rod to float tip. Do not be afraid to set the float well over-depth so the bait literally bumps bottom all the way down the swim. Bites are invariably a bold sinking of the tip which looks exactly like the bottom.

If the water runs crystal clear and bites on a heavier set up do not happen, be prepared to step down to small hooks, sizes 16 and 18 on a 2 lb bottom, as long as you have room to play a barbel should you hook one without the problems caused by nearby snags. I am talking here about small to medium-sized barbel, up to 4–5 lb. If there is any chance whatsoever of a specimen barbel inhabiting the swim, my advice is to stick with heavier tackle capable of landing it.

LONG-TROTTING RIGS

When using a 2½–4 lb line and long trotting the smaller rivers for big roach, grayling and chub, I use the simple rig shown in fig. 5.23, which incorporates the stumpy chubber float.

Because it has such a wide tip and is easily seen even at distances of up to 30 yd, and because for its size it carries a good shotting load, this float is ideal. In fast water there is no point whatsoever in messing about with complicated shotting rigs, especially in water less than 4 ft deep. Simply put the entire shotting load within 1 ft of the hook, so the

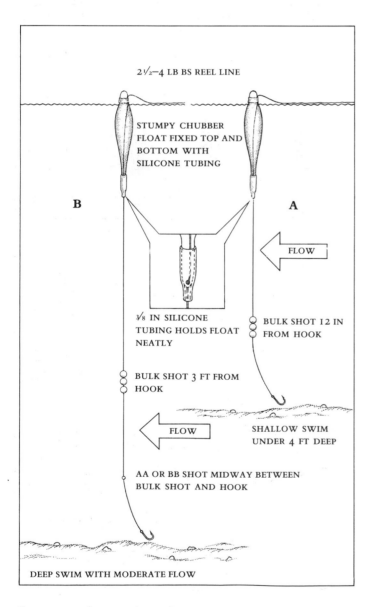

FIGURE 5.23 *Long-trotting tactics*

When he meanders along the winding course of clear-flowing rivers, using a long-trotting rig to search the fast, shallow runs preferred by grayling, David Wilson uses a float that carries plenty of shot, like a loafer or chubber, fixed tightly to the line with silicone tubing top and bottom.

bait is presented right down there just above bottom (fig. 5.23A). In swims of considerable depth where the pace is moderate, bunch the bulk shot within 3 ft of the hook and pinch on a BB or an AA in between (fig. 5.23B).

I prefer to slightly overshot these chunky floats and keep a fairly tight line as they are taken downstream by the flow; alongside overhanging trees, around the back eddies in weir pools, through deep centre channels, around acute bends overhung by willows and so on. It is very much a moving game whereby carrying the minimum of tackle, I can offer the bait to fish inhabiting numerous interesting and demanding swims along the river's twisting course. If roach and chub are the quarry I avoid all areas of heavy turbulence and extreme shallows, preferring the long, easy-paced glides where experience suggests they are most likely to be shoaled up. With grayling in mind, however, no run, no matter how fast, turbulent or rocky, is passed without running the float through a couple of times. This is such a good probing, searching, exploring method, and works best during mild winter weather when with the weed growth gone, fish keep permanently on the look out for food items brought down to them by the current.

For attracting roach and chub there is nothing to beat mashed bread as loose feed in coloured water, with either flake or small cubes of crust for the hook. In clear water, on the other hand, particularly when you are after grayling, maggots or casters have the edge. Grayling, especially, love trotted brandlings.

In classic barbel rivers, which are quite shallow and thus easy to wade and where shoals hug the clean gravel and sandy runs between beds of long, flowing streamer weeds, it is an absolute joy to catch barbel and chub by long trotting. You get the best results by climbing quietly into the river in thigh boots or chest-waders (a sound invest-ment), and wading slowly to an upstream position, from which the bait can be trotted almost directly downstream. This permits excellent presentation because the float is not dragged off course when it is controlled or held back. The bait can be trundled down in a natural way along the desired line by gently breaking the float's passage and occasionally swinging it upwards by holding the float back hard momentarily.

As the barbel feeds from the bottom and the layer of water immediately above the river-bed where food particles are washed along by the current, your bait needs to be presented either dragging bottom (only possible where the river-bed consists of clean sand or gravel) or within a few inches of the bottom. Any higher and it will ride above the barbel's head, out of its feeding zone. In the summer months when the water runs both warm and crystal clear, barbel will take, and can sometimes be observed, moving upwards and across the flow to intercept loose-fed casters

In the deep run beneath this road bridge, the barbel and chub fall to trotted baits and to a stret-pegging rig presenting the bait anchored to the bottom close to the clumps of rushes in the foreground.

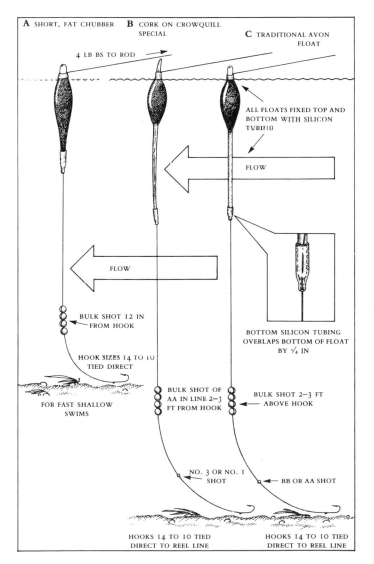

FIGURE 5.24 *Long-trotting rigs*

and maggots as they fall and tumble downriver. Such occasions are responsible for those unmistakeable bites that drag the float quickly beneath the surface within a second or so of your holding it back to waver the bait upwards. Generally speaking, however, barbel want their dinner to move slowly along or just above the river-bed.

Ideal baits for trotting are the big four, maggots, casters, worms and bread, with sweetcorn bringing up the rear. As for ledgering, I rate hempseed highly for loose-feed attraction and often put a couple of handfuls into the top of each swim when long trotting, prior to following through with a bunch of maggots or casters, plus loose-feed helpings of the same every other cast. It's only fair to state that at no time when trotting for barbel should you expect to enjoy a bite every other trot down, as you might when roach fishing.

It goes without saying that when wading, an indispensable item of tackle is the bait pouch or apron, and so too is a tackle waistcoat. There is nothing more infuriating than having to make frequent trips back to the bank in order to change floats or hooks.

I generally opt for a trotting line of around 4 lb test, and I have already mentioned my preference for trotting using a centre-pin reel. This I use in conjunction with a 13 ft, carbon waggler rod, but for tackling swims with particularly heavy weed, bullrushes or an extra strong flow, I increase the power to a 12 ft, 1¼ lb test curve, carbon Avon, which harmonizes nicely with a 5 lb or 6 lb test line.

Really shallow, fast runs are most effectively fished with a short, fat float (long floats could easily spook the barbel) such as the chubber, with all the shot bulked 12 in above the hook (see fig. 5.24A). Keep running the float through unchecked, inching it up the line on each cast until the bait is dragging bottom so hard that the float pulls under. Then pull it down a shade and commence fishing. This is a far easier method of finding the depth than plumbing the entire length of the swim.

In deep, steady runs where extra shots down the line are imperative for presenting the bait smoothly and trundling it along in a natural manner, I use cork on crowquill floats. These specials take up to 6AA and are best rigged with most of the bulk-shot loading set in a line 2–3 ft above the hook with a No. 1 or a No. 3 between the float and the hook (see fig. 5.24B) – this rig is very simple but most effective.

When the water is deep and swirling, the float to use is the traditional Avon. Its bulbous, oval body and thick tip permit maximum shotting capacity for a stable trot through and ensure that the bait searches slowly, close to or actually along the river-bed (fig. 5.24C). To achieve the correct depth, follow the procedure for chubbers. In really long swims, however, of 20 or 30 yd, it is not uncommon to find a raised lump on the bottom that would present the bait too high throughout most of the trot if it is set to the shallowest depth. The remedy is to hold back hard on the float just before the hump or similar obstruction (such as a weed clump) to ease the end tackle over it and then continue the rest of the run through.

STRET PEGGING

One of the most effective and fascinating close-range float-fishing techniques to use in flowing water is the art of stret pegging. It is a combination of float ledgering and laying on that ensures the bait is always accurately placed and lies perfectly static on the bottom.

So long as the intended species occupy a deepish run close into the bank beside man made pilings alongside marginal sedges or reeds, natural laybys and so on, then almost regardless of the flow, stret pegging is indeed the only way of watching a float with the bait layed hard on. It is a superb method both summer and winter especially during exceptionally cold conditions when fish are loathe to chase a moving bait. As can be seen from fig. 5.25A the float (a short length of unpainted peacock quill) needs to be fixed top and bottom and set considerably deeper than swim depth so the current forms a bow in the line between float and the bottom shots. This to some extent relieves the pressure on the float enabling it to lie flat and the bait to remain static with just a single BB, AA or swan shot (depending on current force) pinched on the line 5–10 in from the hook.

When the flow is too fast for a single shot to hold bottom then construct a 'mini ledger' using a small ring plus 1 in or so of thick line, to which a swan shot or two are added, as in fig. 5.25B.

If seeking species like dace, perch, roach and bream, reel line is 2½ lb test (in conjunction with a 13 foot waggler rod) and when I use this technique for catching specimen roach or bream hooks in sizes 8–14 are tied direct for baits like breadflake and crust or stewed wheat etc. When after modest sized fish and there is a need to step down much lighter such as in clear, cold water conditions add a 20 in length of 1½ lb test hook length enabling hooks in sizes 16–20 holding smaller baits like maggots and casters.

Always sit looking down river and make the cast downstream and across so the rig swings inwards (fig. 5.26). Put the rod on two rests with the tip angled upwards so no line actually lays on the surface or the float may be

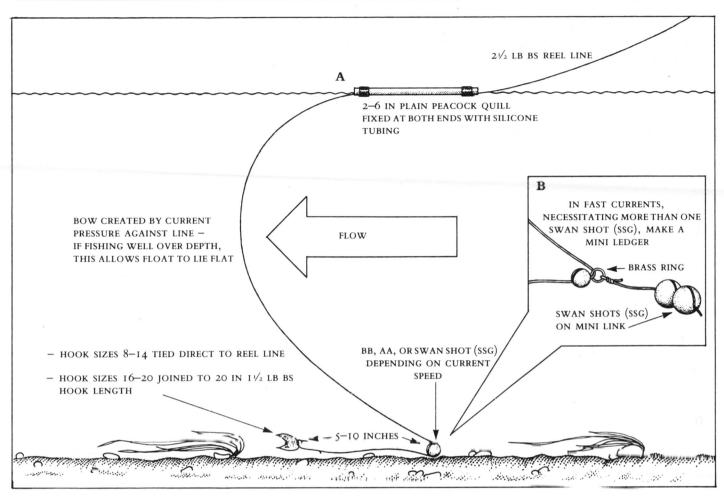

FIGURE 5.25 *Stret-pegging rig*

swept around. Most bites are positive with the float simply gliding under, sometimes preceeded by a gentle twitching or shaking. When presenting breadflake, introduce a few balls of mashed bread well upstream allowing for current speed so it comes to rest close to the hook bait. With maggots and casters simply use a bait dropper to deposit them with accuracy in strong currents or deep water.

For larger species like chub and barbel, line strength is increased to 5–6 lb coupled to an 11–12 ft, 1¼ lb T/C, Avon-style rod. To combat stronger currents, larger, more buoyant floats are imperative, along with mini ledger rigs or a blockend feeder to anchor the bait static on the bottom (fig. 5.27).

Stret pegging is a great flood water technique when rivers run tea coloured and lap the banks and most species seek out all the choice slacks or move into the mouths of sidestreams where they join the main river. To attract roach, dace, bream etc. put down a couple of bait droppers full of maggots or casters and follow in with your stret pegging rig. In mild weather you will not wait long for a bite. In cold weather if the maggots come back sucked to mere skins without any noticeable registration

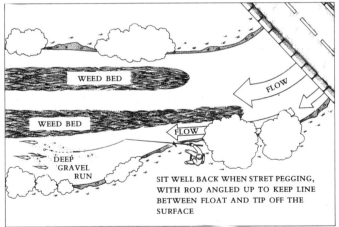

FIGURE 5.26 *Stret-pegging tactics*

on the float, reduce the hook length to just 3 or 4 in.

Lobworms really sort out quality roach, chub and barbel when the river is in high spate. Loose feed by scattering a handful of broken worms into the swim several yards upstream of the point where you intend them to settle close to the hook bait. To fool easily spooked chub and barbel, try presenting the bait (meat cubes, corn etc.) on a hair (fig. 5.12, page 148).

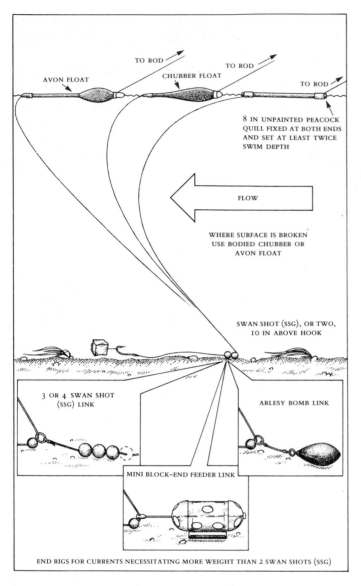

FIGURE 5.27 *Heavy stret-pegging*

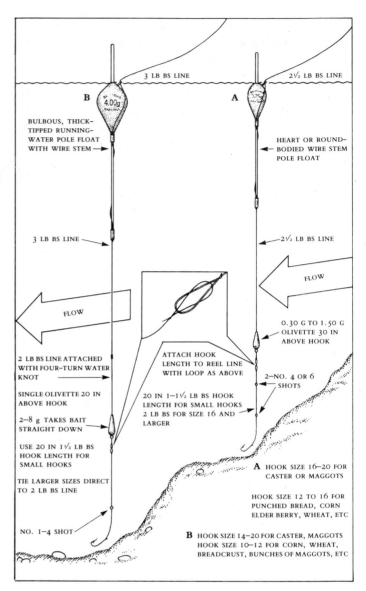

FIGURE 5.28 *'Long pole, short line', or to-hand rigs*

POLE FLOAT RIGS

To present the bait at reasonably close range or in gentle currents, the rig in fig. 5.28A, utilizing a heart or round bodied wire stem float carrying somewhere between 0.030 and 1.50 gm, will cover most situations. Presentation is of course far superior with the long pole/short line technique providing species like roach or dace are situated no further out than, say, 11 metres.

There will be numerous occasions – when trotting the float way beyond the pole tip alongside trailing branches in the opposite bank of a small river for instance or fishing along the centre bowl of a canal into water 12–14 ft deep, demands that you fish with a full pole length of line out. So that when you swing in a small fish or the hook for rebaiting it comes directly 'to hand' – hence the expression.

When fishing into really deep water, the 'to hand' method is extremely effective and much quicker than unslipping the pole after each cast to unhook or rebait although with an excess of line between float and pole tip, the sensitivity of the presentation can be impaired in strong winds. When presentation to hand becomes totally impossible, think about swapping over to the waggler or a feeder outfit. Or try drawing the shoal closer in by feeding along a shorter line so the long pole/short line method can be employed.

The beauty of using the pole in running water is that you can hold back gently on the bulbous-bodied float to slow the rig down and trundle the bait naturally through the swim really close to the bottom, like the loose-feed fragments. Choose the size of float required to combat the current speed (always go heavier rather than lighter), and a simple bottom rig as shown in fig. 5.28B to deliver the bait straight down to the feeding zone, which if after bream or roach is that first foot of water immediately above the bottom. Fix the single olivette around 20 in above the hook, with a No. 1 to No. 4 shot midway between. If the shot is moved closer to the hook, this will sometimes improve bite registration, so do not be afraid to move it around.

If you find groundbaiting with accuracy rather difficult when fishing at 9–11 yd out, try touching the surface with the pole tip and use this as a marker when employing the 'long pole/short line' technique. Loose feed such as maggots, casters and hempseed are always best catapulted (leave the pole tip in the water, freeing both hands for catapulting). To ensure that it arrives around the hookbait when trotting in really deep water, either lock the casters or maggots up in a small ball of firmly-squeezed bread-crumb groundbait (see Groundbait) that won't break up until it touches bottom, or use a small wire-mesh bait dropper. The latter are really effective for loose-feeding bait such as casters and maggots, except when you are using an elasticated tip (see Baitdroppers).

When easing the bait slowly through the water, concentrate on holding the pole really steady so that the float is not lifted or jerked. This is best achieved by holding it either across your knee or with the butt end lodged between crotch and seat, your strongest hand supporting it in front at arm's reach. This sounds more painful than it is, and it adds a couple of valuable feet to the pole's maximum distance with the fixed line.

Deep, flowing water

Fig. 5.29 shows two simple but heavy rigs for catching species like bream and roach/bream hybrids living in deep, flowing water where the bait needs to be taken straight down to the feeding zone immediately above the bottom and offered very slowly or even static.

In order to combat deep water and these strong, steady currents, monstrous bulbous bodied pole floats with wire stems and carrying anything upwards from 5 to 10 grams may seem over the top but they are perfect for the job. Using anything less would not allow the bait to be presented slow enough. The object being to get the bait straight down to the bottom, then easing back gently on the big float as the bait runs through. You will see from fig. 5.29A that all the weight is locked up in the single olivette fixed just 20 in above the hook, with a no. 1 or 3 shot set halfway between.

When the flow is simply too strong or the bream only

want a static bait (a complete lack of bites suggests this) dispense completely with weight on the line by adding a 6 in link of heavier line, as in fig. 5.29B.

For this method I prefer the flick tip and tie the rig directly to the small ring glued into the end. If big bream are expected then the rig should be made up on 6 lb test, with hooks from size 14 to 12 tied on a lighter 2 foot length of 3 lb test. Larger hooks, size 10 and 8 are better matched to 4 lb test and when bream are being cautious.

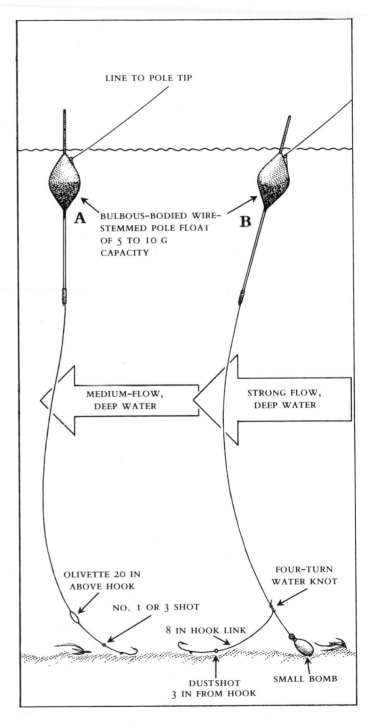

FIGURE 5.29 *Pole fishing*

PRESENTING FLOATING BAITS

BEST TECHNIQUES – FLOATING BAITS					
	freelining in rivers	*floating worm*	*flat peacock quill*	*controller fishing*	*anchored floater*
CARP	●	●		●	●
CHUB	●	●		●	
DACE	●		●	●	
PERCH		●			
ROACH			●	●	
RUDD	●		●	●	

FREELINING IN RIVERS FOR CHUB

Some would say the most exciting way of catching chub during the summer, when weed-beds furrow the surface and make other methods impractical, is with floating crust or wasp cake. For close-range swims a completely free line treated with mucilin so it floats easily and does not hinder the bait's passage downstream is all that is required. A fairly large hook is best for crust, and a size 6 or 4 (depending on bait size) is ideal. There is more than sufficient weight in a 10p-sized piece of crust for casting and if you think not, simply dunk it momentarily.

Floating crust

To entice chub up to the surface, away from the cover of weed-beds or overhung hideaways, and to persuade them to suck in crusts confidently, sit or crouch well upstream of the swim and introduce a batch of loose crusts into midstream every couple of minutes. Half a dozen at a time will do nicely. Don't worry if the first few batches are ignored (you need at least a couple of large tin-loaves for a morning's crusting), it is all part of the ritual or game anglers and chub play with each other. Sooner or later up will come a huge pair of lips, and in a huge oily swirl down will go one of the crusts, then another and so on. Float your crusts down until each crust disappears when it reaches a certain spot. Then put your hook in the next crust. It is just like floater fishing for carp, probably the most heart-stopping technique of all.

When the first swim dries up because too many chub have been removed or you botched the first strike and put them all down, wander downstream following your batches of previously uninspected crusts, some of which by now will have attracted chub in other spots.

Charlie Clay knows all about the art of concealment, as he demonstrates while freelining bread flake and floating crust through a streamy run close into the bank of the beautiful upper Wensum.

Wasp cake

As an alternative and wonderful change bait to floating crust, try fishing in the same way with wasp cake.

It has a sweet, honey-like smell to which the chub quickly becomes addicted. Once aroused, chub will charge several feet through clear water to intercept a piece of floating cake ahead of other shoal members. It is therefore a most selective bait because as long as your cast puts a piece of cake alongside a noted specimen, unless you strike too early it is as good as in the net. As with bread crust, always wait for the fish's lips to close, for it to get its head down beneath the surface and the line to tighten before banging home the hook. A 5–6 lb line is mandatory.

THE FLOATING WORM

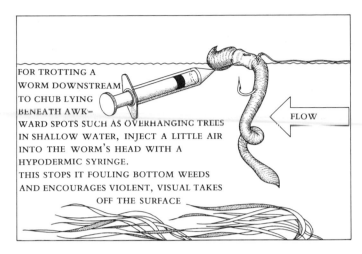

FIGURE 5.30 *The floating worm*

Carefully inject a little air from a hypodermic syringe into the head of a large lobworm to make it float tantalizingly on the surface (fig. 5.30) and you have a wonderful way of tempting at least three species. In stillwaters, among lily pads and around the lapping branches of overhanging willows, both perch and carp will quickly gulp in a floating, gyrating lob, whether it is freelined using its own weight or transported to the swim with the aid of a small controller float such as the tenpin.

Chub love them too, and the floating worm is a great bait for tempting those educated, well-fished-for specimens, living in popular stretches of a river that always seem to hole up in the snaggiest, most inaccessible spots. Simply drift the worm downriver, using the current to peel line from an open pool, taking it over weedbeds etc., into the shallowest runs beneath overhanging trees; and

David Wilson has every right to be pleased with this plump chub, having deceived it with a floating worm from the incredibly clear, weedy and shallow water of Hertfordshire's River Lea.

then give a gentle twitch when the chub have it in their vision. This technique produces the most fabulous, aggressive, visual takes from the surface. However, you need to be quick off the mark to extract a good chub from an entanglement of branches, using a heavy-hand, hit-and-hold technique. A 6 lb test line is therefore imperative.

THE FLAT PEACOCK QUILL RIG

When roach and rudd especially, are working the upper water layers during the summer months and more interested in sucking in food literally from the surface, make up a 'flat peacock quill' rig (fig. 5.31) with the shots fixed at both ends of the float and strike when it glides 'across' the surface as opposed to going under. It is a rig which creates the minimal resistance to surface takers and a fascinating way of catching both small and specimen sized rudd.

At close quarters it is often possible to watch the bait being sucked in and forget the float altogether. Just remember not to allow too much of a bow to develop between rod tip and float, otherwise striking could be

impaired. A good dubbing of mucilin on the line will ensure it floats well allowing you to 'lift' and mend the line every so often.

To loose feed, catapult fragments a little in front of the rig and slowly draw your hook bait among them. Casters are perfect bait for this technique but make sure you use all floaters or you might discourage the rudd from surface feeding. Loose feeding with scraps of breadcrust catapulted well upwind also attracts rudd and when they start splashing and nibbling at the bread use a small cube of breadcrust on the hook.

This rig also works well in really shallow rivers for dace and chub, both of which are partial to floating casters.

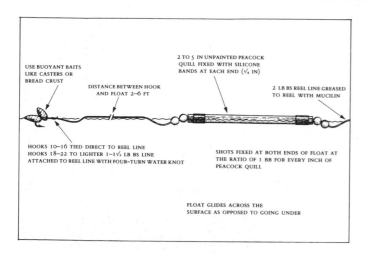

FIGURE 5.31 *The flat, peacock-quill rig for surface fishing*

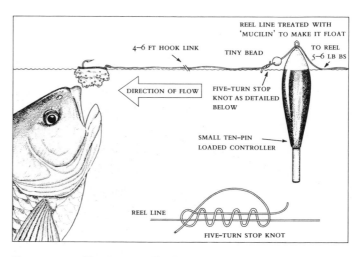

FIGURE 5.32 *Floating controller fishing*

CONTROLLER FISHING FOR CHUB

To drift floating crust into distant swims without the current bellying the free line into an unstrikable situation, the answer is to thread on a small loaded controller (like the ten-pin) which adds weight for casting (smaller baits such as casters can then also be used). More importantly, it allows the line to be mended occasionally while the bait

When weaning carp onto surface baits, wait for them all to come to the surface and feed confidently before putting one on the hook. You can then offer your floater to a particularly desirable specimen.

floats downstream. Stop the ten-pin 4 to 6 ft above the hook with a nylon stop knot and small bead (fig. 5.32).

Stop the ten-pin 4 to 6 ft above the hook with a nylon stop knot and small bead (fig. 5.32).

Floater fishing in stillwaters

Except for small overgrown lakes and pits, in which freelined crusts can be placed or drifted alongside bushes or sunken trees close to the chub's hideouts, the loaded controller offers the most effective way of getting the bait out to chub patrolling the surface. Loose attractor crusts should be catapulted well upwind around the float and the entire batch allowed to drift naturally with the wind or surface pull.

Keep paying out line as though trotting. Every now and then lift any bowing line off the surface with the rod held high, and lay or flick it upwind so that it is reasonably straight again. When fishing really large waters you have to decide on a point beyond which striking would be impaired because of the possibility of pricking and losing a chub. So strike the crust off and retrieve for a new cast.

Never wind the crust back across the surface. Only pike fall for such lack of thought, while the chub become craftier.

MARGIN FISHING FOR CARP

To catch carp slurping down floating baits like crusts or mixers which have either been scattered amongst the marginal growth or drifted there with the wind, there cannot be a more simple rig than using just the hook itself.

If the fish are directly below the rod tip, lower the floater down so it rests on the surface without any slack line lying on the water. Hold the rod loosely yet expectantly with the reel's bale arm closed (the clutch properly set), and in the

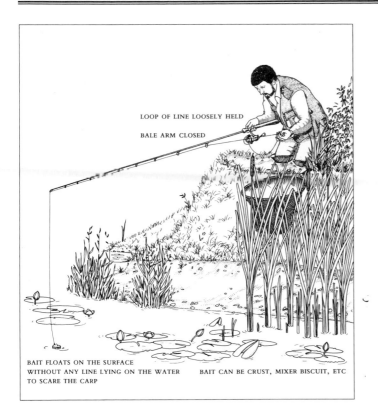

FIGURE 5.33 *Margin fishing (daytime)*

FIGURE 5.34 *Margin fishing (dusk onwards)*

other hand hold a loop of line pulled from between butt ring and reel (fig. 5.33). This you let slip through your fingers when a carp closes its mouth over the bait and submerges with it, before whacking the rod back to set the hook.

Many carp anglers would rate this particular form of marginal floater fishing as the most exciting technique of all and I would certainly not give them an argument. It is extremely satisfying, but demands tremendous stealth simply crawling into a position where a bait can be lowered amongst patrolling surface-feeding fish.

When surface activity is slow and the appearance of carp is not expected until the light starts to fade (either due to weather or clear water conditions) quietly set the rod on two rests, again with the bale arm closed, and instead of holding the loop of line between butt ring and reel, hang on a lightweight coil indicator. A cylinder of silver foil is perfect (fig. 5.34).

When fishing this method over marginal lilies, wind the bait so it comes to rest alongside the pads and lay the line over them (fig. 5.35). Don't for a moment imagine the carp cannot see even small floaters presented in this way. They are looking up into bright light, and can even identify the form of a floater resting completely on top of a lily pad. On numerous occasions I have witnessed carp knocking pads to dislodge a seemingly invisible (to them) unreachable floater. And they are not satisfied until such food is in their stomachs.

When using pieces of floating bread-crust over pads, or drifting them across the surface in open areas, if carp are suspicious of the floating bread use a crust/flake cocktail. Start by sliding a piece of crust up over the eye of the hook and then squeeze on a giant piece of flake. Slide the crust down again and gently squeeze a part of the flake on to the crust, thus 'locking' them together. Hopefully they will hold together until a carp investigates and 'knocks' them apart, whereupon the flake will slowly start to sink. At this point the carp can stand it no longer and promptly

FIGURE 5.35 *Fishing over lilies*

sucks in the flake. Watch the line carefully and hit any positive movement instantly.

One of the most suspicious and difficult of all carp to hook on floating crust is the grass carp. Rarely do they gulp the bait in and go charging off. More often than not,

they simply hold the crust between pursed lips for several seconds before swallowing it and turning away. Be sure that the bait has completely disappeared before striking to this type of bait, or you risk pulling the hook away and missing the fish.

Working the margins for carp offers unparalleled excitement. Try not to show your head and shoulders above the screen of bankside shrubbery and you will catch fish with surprising ease.

Using a small dog-biscuit floater presented with a loaded tenpin controller float, this young fisherman uses the all-through action of a 1¼ lb test curve Avon rod and a 6 lb line to subdue a superb 12½ lb common carp.

CONTROLLER FISHING FOR CARP

When carp will only accept floaters presented further out because the water along the margins is either too clear, too shallow or both, making them feel vulnerable, casting weight is required in the form of a self-cocking controller (see 'Tackle') like the 'ten-pin', which is available in four sizes. Rig up the ten-pin as shown in fig 5.36. Loose-feed floaters like small biscuits, boilies and so on can all be catapulted into any given area alongside features, and the hook bait deposited accurately among them. Or better

still, cast out the controller and hook bait well up wind; then catapult the loose feed around it, allowing the floating food to drift down wind whilst playing out line from an open (well-filled) spool.

Carp are invariably more wary of accepting surface baits once they have associated them with danger than they are of bottom-fished baits. But by fishing as light as you dare, using much finer line than normal, for instance 6 lb test instead of 10 lb test if conditions permit, and by fishing

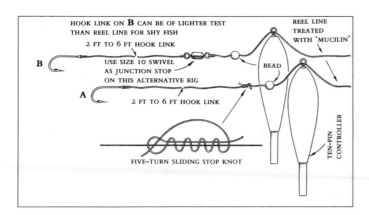

FIGURE 5.36 *Floating controllers*

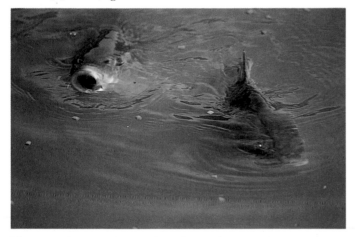

There is nothing too choosey about the way in which these two mirror carp are munching through a batch of dog-biscuit floaters. However, when they eventually wise up to floaters presented straight on the hook, offer the bait on a fine hair rig.

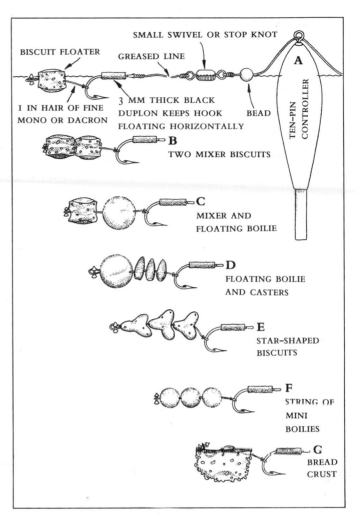

FIGURE 5.37 *Hair-rig floaters*

during periods of low light at dusk, dawn or even well on into darkness, most problems can be solved. Carp refuse the bait because they can see the line and hook, or because the bait behaves unlike all the free offerings around it due to the weight of the hook and drag from the line. Carp prove this time and time again by mopping up all the free floaters, but not the one on the hook. The problem is not so much getting them to accept floating food but to accept the hook bait. Even familiar unattached baits like pieces of bread crust are taken down, maybe not so quickly on waters regularly fished, but disappear they eventually will. Particle baits create far less suspicion, and sooner or later one will be sucked in, provided carp respond.

In contrast to bottom baits, at least it's possible to actually observe the reaction of carp and consequently do something about the way in which the bait is refused. Anything and everything is worth trying. Go for a much longer hook link to create less drag; or smaller hook; two floaters instead of one, which provides greater buoyancy; grease or even degrease the hook link, and so on.

If all else fails, put your faith in the hair rig (fig. 5.37) and offer the bait off the hook. There are all sorts of variations worth trying along these lines. Go down in hook size: try two or even three floaters on the hair instead of one; or a cocktail, one biscuit and one boilie together on the same hair, a boilie and casters, and so on.

Because the line actually passes through the top of the controller, when a carp moves away with the bait the line will visibly tighten and 'lift' across the surface. Hold the rod all the time with the bale arm closed ready for action. Straighten any bow in the line formed by wind drift, leaving just a little slack so as not to scare interested fish through resistance. Keep your eyes fixed on the float's red top and identify your hook bait amongst the loose ones, striking on sight if you suddenly see it go without the line actually moving or whistling through the float.

THE ANCHORED FLOATER

Ron Smith presented a brace of mini boilies on an anchored floater rig to tempt this modest-sized mirror carp.

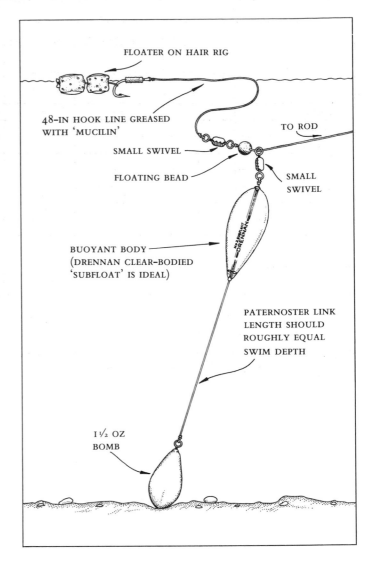

FIGURE 5.38 *Anchored floater for distance fishing*

The answer to distance problems is the *anchored floater* presented on a sliding, buoyant paternoster rig (fig. 5.38). When the rig lands and the bomb touches bottom, the buoyant float body rises up to the swivel and supports the reel line just a couple of feet below the surface with the bait floating nicely above. Tighten up gently with the rod set horizontal in two rests, ensuring the line is sunk, and clip on an indicator, such as bobbin or monkey climber. Keep the bale arm closed. When a carp sucks in the floater, the reel line runs freely through the paternoster swivel, up goes the indicator and you are in business with a hefty strike to pick up any loose line. For this kind of long-range floater fishing, keep your eyes peeled on the area of the hook bait so you can anticipate a probable run, and scatter loose floaters around the anchored hook bait.

LEDGERING IN STILLWATER

BEST TECHNIQUES – LEDGERING IN STILLWATER							
	freelining	*swingtipping*	*quiver-tipping*	*distance ledgering*	*twitcher hitting*	*snaggy swim rig*	*bolt rig*
BREAM		●	●	●	●		
CARP	●					●	●
CATFISH	●						
EELS	●						
ROACH		●	●				
RUDD		●	●	●			
TENCH	●	●	●	●	●	●	●

FREELINING

If you spend any time at all observing carp for instance and how they relate to a baited hook, you will soon understand why the simple method of freelining the bait without any foreign bits on the line (floats, shots, bombs, tubing, etc), other than the hook, is the most sensitive method of all. Unless the carp picks up the line with its large pectoral or pelvic fins, or brushes up against it and does a runner, it will trundle confidently off with the bait.

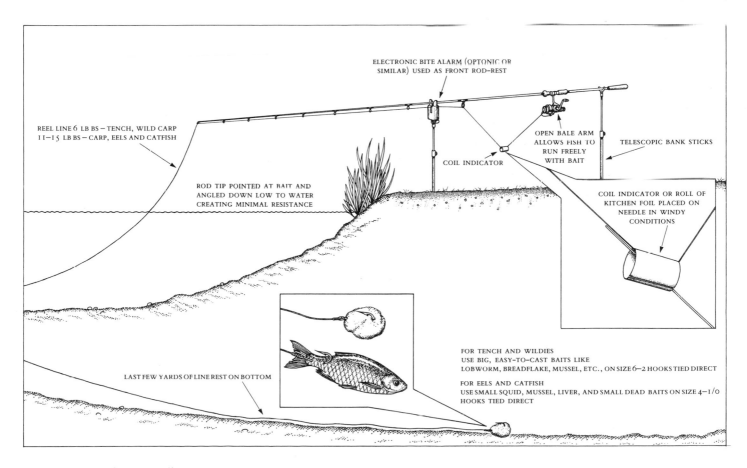

ELECTRONIC BITE ALARM (OPTONIC OR SIMILAR) USED AS FRONT ROD-REST

REEL LINE 6 LB BS – TENCH, WILD CARP 11–15 LB BS – CARP, EELS AND CATFISH

ROD TIP POINTED AT BAIT AND ANGLED DOWN LOW TO WATER CREATING MINIMAL RESISTANCE

OPEN BALE ARM ALLOWS FISH TO RUN FREELY WITH BAIT

TELESCOPIC BANK STICKS

COIL INDICATOR

COIL INDICATOR OR ROLL OF KITCHEN FOIL PLACED ON NEEDLE IN WINDY CONDITIONS

LAST FEW YARDS OF LINE REST ON BOTTOM

FOR TENCH AND WILDIES
USE BIG, EASY-TO-CAST BAITS LIKE
LOBWORM, BREADFLAKE, MUSSEL, ETC., ON SIZE 6–2 HOOKS TIED DIRECT

FOR EELS AND CATFISH
USE SMALL SQUID, MUSSEL, LIVER, AND SMALL DEAD BAITS ON SIZE 4–1/0 HOOKS TIED DIRECT

FIGURE 5.39 *Freelining in stillwater*

With two freelined baits strategically placed, one close into the margins, the other beside a bed of lilies some 30 yds out, a catfish angler waits patiently for a run despite the bright sunshine.

Large baits heavy enough in themselves to disguise the hook and neutralize its weight, such as the insides of a whole swan mussel, a lump of trout pellet paste or a lobworm, are each also heavy enough to cast accurately from a well-filled spool without added weight. Freelining is therefore a method which can only be practised at close range where species like carp, catfish, eels and tench are attracted to natural habitats.

Anglers who have only ever float-fished for tench, using light float tackle in heavily fished waters and straining their eyes for those tiny dips or lifts of the float tip in order to strike, would not believe the way in which tench run off with a freelined bait. But then, with an unweighted bait they have no reason to be fussy. They simply suck it in and move off looking for the next meal, lifting the line in a glorious, unmissable, almost carp-like run.

If immediate bites are expected, do not bother with indicators. Hold the rod and keep your eyes glued to the bow in the line from rod tip to surface. If not, hang a lightweight foil indicator on a 2 ft drop between butt ring and reel, after positioning the rod on two rests with the tip pointing directly at the bait (fig. 5.39). Whack the hook home just before the indicator slams against the butt ring.

With minimal resistance on the line, the tench is just as likely to swim towards the rod and give a 'drop back', whereupon the indicator suddenly falls to the ground. This is a good reason for always keeping the bale arm closed when freelining, enabling you to go straight into a 'wind-cum-strike' routine in order to pick up the line and punch the hook home.

When freelining into darkness or when tench activity is on the slow side, rig up an electric alarm in conjunction with the foil indicator so you can relax. You can certainly afford to, because bites are nearly always positive.

When freelining for eels, carp and catfish at night, in addition to stepping up line strengths to 11–15 lb test, it is wise to leave the bale arm open. This allows the fish to make a positive run, peeling several feet of line from the open spool. You then close the bale arm and strike the hook home.

SWINGTIPPING

Conceived by Jack Clayton of Boston to identify the shy bites of Fenland bream, the swingtip is, in theory, the most sensitive ledgering bite indicator ever invented and works with equal effect when ledgering for other species like roach, rudd and tench. Because the swingtip screws into the tip-ring and hangs down in front of the rod, resistance to a biting fish is minimal compared to quivertips, ledger bobbins or monkey climbers. And in certain circumstances, shallow water in particular, bite amplification sometimes occurs; a long swingtip will move further than the distance a fish pulls the bait.

It is important to remember that swingtips are only effective in still and very slow-moving water. In fact to counteract even the slightest current, you need to use a loaded swingtip to which weight has been added. For most stillwater situations, except when strong winds rip down the lake or pit causing a heavy undertow, a standard, lightweight swingtip is ideal.

Swingtips are great indicators to use when bream-fishing on hard-fished waters. They are also good for registering bites that occur on the drop within seconds of the ledger bomb or feeder hitting the bottom – a common occurrence during high summer, when bream tend to layer off bottom above the feed. The best rig (as it is for all bream ledgering) is the simple fixed paternoster. For this, join a 3–5 ft lighter hook link to the 3–4 lb reel line 2 ft above the bomb or feeder, which should be tied direct to the line using a four-turn water knot (fig. 5.40).

After casting, put the rod in the rests quickly and tighten up to the bomb, watching that tip like a hawk. It will slowly drop backwards after each turn of the reel handle until the line is reasonably tight from bomb to rod. A bite on the drop is easily registered by the tip failing to ease back when it should, because a bream (or another species) has sucked in the bait and stopped the process.

Buoyant baits such as casters, or a caster and maggot

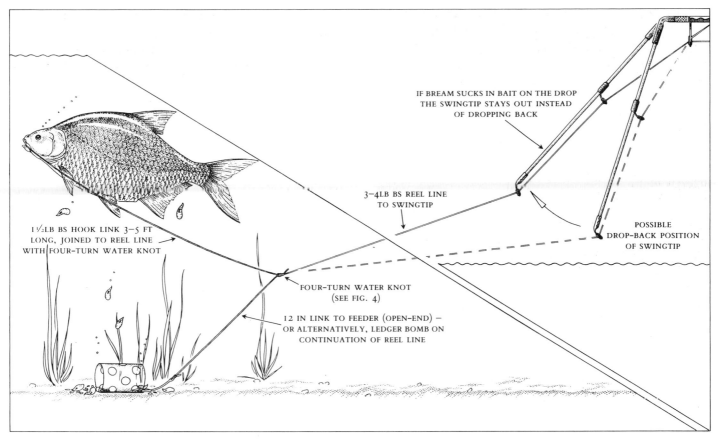

IF BREAM SUCKS IN BAIT ON THE DROP
THE SWINGTIP STAYS OUT INSTEAD
OF DROPPING BACK

3–4LB BS REEL LINE
TO SWINGTIP

POSSIBLE
DROP-BACK POSITION
OF SWINGTIP

1½LB BS HOOK LINK 3–5 FT
LONG, JOINED TO REEL LINE
WITH FOUR-TURN WATER KNOT

FOUR-TURN WATER KNOT
(SEE FIG. 4)

12 IN LINK TO FEEDER (OPEN-END) –
OR ALTERNATIVELY, LEDGER BOMB ON
CONTINUATION OF REEL LINE

FIGURE 5.40 *(Above) Fishing on-the-drop in stillwater with the swingtip*   FIGURE 5.41 *(Below) Striking when swingtipping*

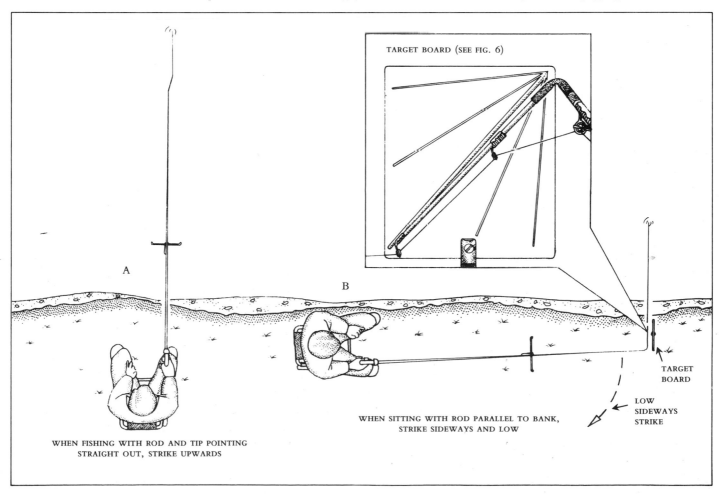

TARGET BOARD (SEE FIG. 6)

A

B

TARGET
BOARD

LOW
SIDEWAYS
STRIKE

WHEN SITTING WITH ROD PARALLEL TO BANK,
STRIKE SIDEWAYS AND LOW

WHEN FISHING WITH ROD AND TIP POINTING
STRAIGHT OUT, STRIKE UPWARDS

Dave Thomas has every reason to be over the moon with this fine 1¼ lb roach and 7 lb bream caught from a deep lake. They were only part of a haul made on a chilly winter's day using a swingtip bite indicator.

cocktail, are excellent for on-the-drop fishing. To engineer as slow a fall as possible, use a long, light hook length – about 1½ lb test – and a small, fine-wire hook. Because they are so small and light, size 20 and 22 hooks holding a single maggot fall very slowly indeed.

Once the bait has settled on the bottom and a fish moves directly away from the rod with it, the tip will respond in a positive upwards movement. Often straightening out horizontal with the top joint. On other occasions, the tip will rise or suddenly fall no more than ¼ in; treat these as positive bite indications, as though float-fishing. After all, if the float-tip with just ¼ in showing above the surface suddenly disappeared, you would strike and expect to hit into a fish. Ledgering, like float fishing, is all about using the correct indicator for the occasion, and interpreting each movement correctly.

When bites are coming thick and fast, do not bother

with rod-rests. Get used to holding the rod handle comfortably beneath your forearm with the tip pointing directly at the bait (fig. 5.41A). Bites become much easier to see if you allow the rod-tip to angle downwards so that the swingtip is just an inch or so above the surface. Then strike upwards in one smooth, sweeping action. Any abrupt movement could wrap the swingtip around the rod-tip if you miss the bite. When bites are not happening with regularity, or it is too cold to hold the rod and concentrate, or bites are barely discernable movements, set the rod on two rests at an angle parallel to the bank and use a target-board positioned immediately behind the tip. Bites, even tiny indications, show up surprisingly well, and to strike you simply ease the rod from the rests in one long, sweeping sideways pull all the way backwards, pulling the line through the water as you would a waggler on a sunk line, not lifting it up against the surface tension, which greatly reduces the effectiveness of the strike (see fig. 5.41B).

Consistent accuracy in casting is imperative when swingtipping, so on every cast concentrate on putting the bait into the feed area. The only exception to this is when the swim is so full of moving bream that line bites occur on almost every cast. Possessing such incredibly deep bodies and large fins, bream cannot help but pick up the line when they are tightly packed. The swingtip might suddenly flip up and drop back with equal speed – obvious line bites these – or it could straighten out, to all intents and purposes like a positive bite. Line bites from roach and rudd are rarely experienced, but from bream they are a very real problem.

Eventually you will learn to distinguish between liners and genuine bites, but whenever you strike and miss what looked to be a positive bite, don't waste time winding in to inspect the bait. Drop the rod-tip immediately after striking and allow the rig to settle again. Besides, now the rig will be closer to you, in a less populated part of the shoal where line bites should be minimal. In fact, casts made to where you consider the outer edge of the feeding shoal to be, as opposed to the centre, are a good plan of attack. You experience less bites, but they are invariably positive lifts resulting in hooked bream, instead of the constant irritation of liners. In addition, bream hooked on the perimeter of the shoal and bullied quickly away will never spook the others, whereas a big fish hooked from the most dense part of the shoal and then played for several minutes through the others while they are trying to feed, might just unsettle them.

QUIVERTIPPING

Generally speaking, bites in static water are not going to register on the tip as boldly as those in running water, so opt for a finely-tapered, super-sensitive tip. If using screw-in tips, one of 1½ oz test curve is suitable, although in extremely cold weather a step down to a 1 oz tip will improve bite registration.

To alleviate wind disturbance, position the rod on two rests (I use a front one only and rest the rod butt on my right knee for a quick strike) with the tip just a couple of inches above the surface – where, incidentally, bites show up better. Angle the rod to either left or right (whichever is more comfortable) and follow through along the same line on the strike. If the water is very deep, strike upwards; if it is shallow strike low to the water (see fig. 5.42).

The end rig is the faithful fixed paternoster, with a bomb on the end if you wish to loose-feed by catapult or groundbait by hand only. Substitution of an open-end swimfeeder for the bomb, however, dramatically increases the chances of immediate bites because it deposits a pile of crumb and bait fragments right where it matters alongside the hook bait (see fig. 5.43).

Note how the hook length is tied to the reel line and varies in test according to the hook size. This in turn is dictated by the bait and to some extent by the species and size of fish expected. When using maggots, for example, start with a 3 ft hook link, but if they return sucked to skins without a bite registering, start reducing the hook link until hittable movements are seen on the tip. Sometimes species like bream and tench will run along the bottom with the bait and pull the tip slowly all the way round. At other times they chew the bait on the spot, showing only the merest indication on the tip, as will

Ledgering into deep gullies way out from the margins in really clear gravel pits is the most effective way of catching tench right through the day. A reduction in both hook length strength and hook sizes is imperative. This angler used a quivertip indicator, and continued to catch when the anglers on either side remained fishless.

immature rudd, bream and roach. When this happens, do not be afraid to reduce the hook length to somewhere between 6 and 10 in of 1½ lb bs, and hooks down to 18s and 20s.

You can often create a response by winding in gently a half or one full turn of the reel handle, should a fish think its food is getting away. And this ruse works especially well when baiting with worms. I am sure it is the gyrating movement of the worms, plus their internal juices, which really excite bream, rudd and tench. On

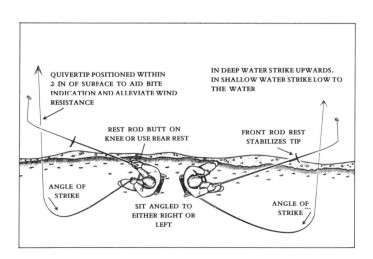

FIGURE 5.42 *Quivertipping in stillwater*

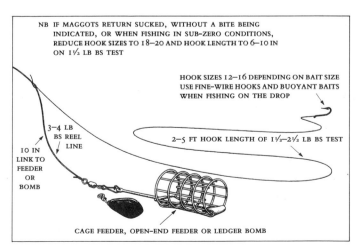

FIGURE 5.43 *Stillwater quivertip or swingtip ledger rig*

another day they might refuse worms, corn or maggots, and show interest only in fluffy, white bread flake. So always be prepared to experiment when bites are not forthcoming. Change baits, use cocktails and move the bait along every so often to goad them into grabbing hold of it.

Watch out for the tip slowly but decisively dropping back, a sure sign a fish has moved towards the rod and in so doing has dislodged the feeder. To encourage drop-back bites, use just enough lead on the feeder to enable you to tighten up after casting but not so much the bait will be dropped. The only situations on stillwaters when I would use more lead than is necessary are either to aid casting, or to get the bait down quickly through deep water, past the attentions of nuisance shoal fish like roach and rudd to the bream feeding on the bottom.

Whenever you can, get used to holding the rod and support it on the front rest only; and make sure the line will lift off cleanly at whichever angle you strike. This way, you can make small movements of the bait, and reply to snatchy bites, much more easily. Dampen the breadcrumbs going into the feeder only very lightly so they explode as it touches bottom, sending a cascade of attractive feed all around the hook bait. If the breadcrumbs are too wet they could clog the feeder, and remain inside it until you pull in for a recast. Loose-feed hook fragments can be added to the crumb, or you can sandwich a quantity of hook baits like maggots, corn or casters, or even finely chopped worms, between a plug of breadcrumbs at each end of the feeder (see 'Feeder Groundbait', p. 124).

When specifically quivertipping for bream at the start of the session it is a good ploy to lob out a few balls of groundbait (stiffened well for throwing) by hand to get them feeding. Then keep them interested and moving around within the area through the feeder's regular arrival carrying extra food, whether bites are coming or not. And this is the secret of feeder-fishing: consistency in casting accuracy and consistently introducing those tiny piles of free nosh. Bream really respond well to these tactics, as do most other species.

DISTANCE LEDGERING

When you are expecting to hit into tench and bream at distances of 40 yd plus in lakes and gravel pits, a standard ledger rod is not up to the task. This is particularly true with specimen bream, which are always difficult to hook. At this distance I use an Avon-actioned, 11 or 12 ft carbon rod of 1¼ lb test curve (see 'Ledger/Quivertip rods', p. 80–1) for maximum line pick-up, and a 6 lb test line. I also change bite indicators, switching to the ledger bobbin. This clips on to the line between butt-ring and reel, and falls harmlessly to the ground on a retaining cord, even when I make a hard, sweeping strike. For daytime ledgering I use the fluorescent-red tenpin bobbin, and after dark the luminous glo-bobbin, which incorporates a betalight element. The glo-bobbin can of course be used around the clock.

Whenever long periods of inactivity are likely – for example on waters where there is a low density of bream (often the case with 'big-fish-only' lakes and pits), or during the hours of darkness when long periods of inactivity are liable to occur – it is comforting to have an electric alarm incorporated into the set-up, and the Optonic indicator is ideal. An alarm, or 'buzzer' as they are called by carp anglers, allows you to appreciate fully the surrounding wildlife, and also to scan the surface away from the area being fished with binoculars for signs of bream activity. Indeed, I wish I had a £5 note for every bonus fish that has graced the landing-net as a result of winding in and placing a bait on top of a bream (or tench) I had seen breaking the surface. Watching a pair of bobbins (two rods are an advantage when covering a large area) for hour upon hour is not just dull; you are missing out on much of the pleasure that ledgering has to offer. This is a clear-cut case where electronic wizardry earns its keep. However, do not turn the volume up so loud that everyone on the next lake hears it. Apart from the irritation this causes to other anglers, you are also informing them of your success. Incidentally, to stop bobbins blowing about or steadily rising with the underwater tow and registering annoying false bites, pinch two or three swan shots on to the retaining cord immediately below the bobbin.

As for rigs, the faithful fixed paternoster ledger is still top of the list, but slightly changed. For distance ledgering, and for presenting baits over thick bottom-weed so they come to rest on top in full view, I use a bomb or feeder link of 4–5 ft and a hook link of around 16–20 in joined to the reel line with a four-turn water knot (see fig. 5.44).

Where only small numbers of large bream are present and regular helpings of groundbait not required, I usually put out a few balls by catapult and stick to a bomb ledger. On the other hand, where there are large shoals capable of continually mopping up loose feed and crumb groundbait, the open-ended swimfeeder is indispensable, especially when you are casting distances beyond accurate catapult range.

The further out you present the bait, greater will be the

This fantastic catch from the Joinery stretch of Ballyquirke Lake at Moycullen came to the feeder in conjunction with bunches of brandling worms, using quivertip bite indicators.

Having cast the second feeder rig intended for spooky specimen bream far out into the clear water of a rich gravel pit, Charlie Clay holds the ledger bobbin down while the line sinks in a straight line.

problems of setting the hook, especially a large hook, so remember to follow through on the strike in a full, scything movement, keeping the angle at which the line is lying beneath the surface. Remember that in really shallow water a low, sideways strike will pick up more line because it pulls it through the water as opposed to lifting it upwards against the surface tension (fig. 5.45A). On the other hand, when presenting the bait into deep-water swims, an upwards strike is more advantageous (fig. 5.45B).

Try to tighten up gently after casting, to sink the line fully, so that it settles in a straight line between feeder or ledger and rod tip, not in a huge belly. Then clip on the indicator. A little washing-up liquid dabbed around the line on the spool will help it sink quickly, so keep a bottle handy. In strong winds, endeavour to fish directly into the wind. Otherwise, pinch a swan shot or two on to the bobbin line to stop any underwater tow bellying the line between feeder and rod tip, thus reducing the effectiveness of the strike. Remember that if the line is not reasonably tight from ledger to rod, setting the hook becomes more of a problem the further out you fish. This may occur when

you are fishing over dense beds of soft weed if the rods are set too low to the surface. Bite indication will be hampered if the line actually rests on the weed, resulting in a much reduced movement of the bobbin. The remedy here is to set the rods as high as you can, keeping as much line as possible off the weed.

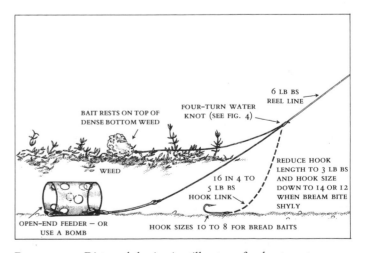

FIGURE 5.44 *Distance ledgering in stillwater – fixed paternoster*

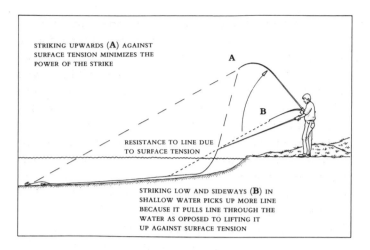

FIGURE 5.45A *Striking when ledgering* 1

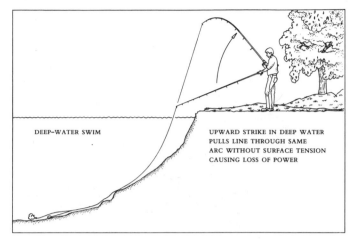

FIGURE 5.45B *Striking when ledgering* 2

TWITCHER HITTING

To capitalize on the tiniest of movements registered on bobbin bite indicators while ledgering for tench, John stands up and hovers over the rods. Twitcher hitting can, in bright conditions, produce a bag of tench from bites that raise the indicator barely more than ¼ in.

During high summer when tench are at their most active, but suddenly become preoccupied with loose feed deposited by the feeder, and as your casting becomes more accurate, concentrating good numbers of tench into a comparatively confined area, tiny twitch bites – 1 to 2 in lifts or drops of the bobbin – will become commonplace. This happens to a much lesser extent with bream.

Now is the time to reduce both the bobbin drop so that small movements are more noticeable, and the hook length to just 6 in enabling you to see bites much earlier, but retain the 10 in feeder link (fig. 5.46). Quite simply the tench are no longer moving away with the bait to another patch of food, they are consuming it on the spot. Bites

which merely lift or drop back the bobbin by ¼ in may seem to be the work of small fish instead of tench, but that is because they have become so preoccupied and so confident, with an excess of food spread around them, that they have little reason to move.

If on a standard hook tail (18–20 in long) you repeatedly reel in sucked maggots or sweetcorn skins, or your worms have had all the goodness crushed out of them, the bait must have been sucked back to the pharnygeal teeth, chewed for a while, and then spat out. It is wise to strike promptly at the slightest twitch or jingle of the bobbin once the twitching cycle begins – once you have shortened the hook length.

On calm days you can forget the bobbin altogether after tightening up, and simply watch the line itself where it enters the water, hitting the slightest lift or drop back no matter how seemingly insignificant.

If bites prove conspicuous by their absence, and you believe tench are still in the swim – as may be the case in the middle of the day when parts of the terminal rig look far more obvious in very clear water – it is time to reduce the hook length from 6, 5 or 4 lb to just 3 lb, and to step down in hook size, presenting smaller baits. While a number 10 hook holding four grains of corn or five maggots may be the taking formula at 6 am, by 11.30 am, when the sun is high above the water, those same tench may not provide you with a hittable bite until you offer them a size 16 holding two casters. When bites are not forthcoming, it is worth trying anything. However, don't be tempted to go down to a lighter hook length than the tench can be safely extracted with. Consider the weed growth, snags, and the general size of the fish expected and only step down accordingly.

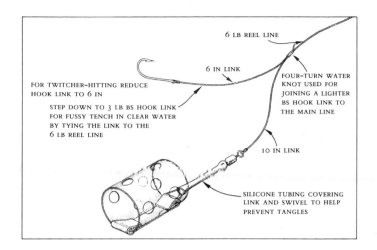

FIGURE 5.46 *Twitcher-hitting rig*

I like to try to stimulate bites by constantly changing hook baits (regardless of what has been fed in), from maggots to corn, flake to worms and back again. Occasionally a buoyant bait presented on the drop will bring immediate action simply because it's different. Or try offerings like casters and crust cocktails, casters and corn, flake and maggots, and so on. Never be afraid to experiment. Try twitching the bait in, pausing for 30 seconds or so between each half or full slow crank of the handle. This of course is suicidal in thick weed, but where the bottom is reasonably clean it is a deadly technique which often leaves you next to no time between twitches to reset the bobbin before it is yanked upwards.

As you might a float, try and relate movements of the bobbin to what is actually happening at the end of your feeder rig. For instance, wherever the bobbin jerks upwards a couple of inches and then suddenly falls completely slack in a glorious drop back, this is not the fish first moving away and then turning around and swimming back towards the rod, as you might be forgiven for thinking. It is the ledger rig tightening (as the bobbin jerks up) immediately before the tension reaches too much and the feeder is pulled towards the rod, whereupon the bobbin suddenly drops. The tench has in fact been moving towards the rod from the moment it picked up the bait. These are always definite bites, because the tench is not going to let go, and a long sweeping strike to mend the loose line nearly always connects.

SNAGGY SWIM RIG

In really overgrown waters where the ledger link may become snagged while trying to extract a big tench or bream from snags or weed-beds, I use a weak link or tie just a three-turn half blood knot, which will pull free at a certain pressure (fig. 5.47). Thus, using a junction swivel does have its advantages, including the option of being able to change the hook link from long to short or from lighter to heavier quickly without having to dismantle the entire end rig, using simple seven-turn 'tucked' half blood knots.

BOLT RIG TENCHING

The shock, or bolt rig was first devised for carp fishing, but also works well for wary tench. It is especially useful when fishing for tench which share carp fisheries, and which have been weaned on to carp baits, namely boilies and hard particles such as peanuts and black-eyed beans.

As can be seen from fig. 5.48, a rotten bottom is used on the bomb link, tied on to the main line with a four-turn water knot. If it snags up in weed you can continue to play the tench, losing only a 1½ oz bomb. Reel line is 6 lb (unless big tench are anticipated, in which case step up to 8 lb straight through) to a size 10 or 8 hook. If you always sit next to the rods (within grabbing distance) this method works best fished with a closed bale arm, although some may consider this rather risky. After casting and dunking the rod tip to lower the line along the bottom contours, support the rod in two rests, pointing it at the bait. Leave a slight bow between surface and rod tip before clipping on a bobbin or monkey climber half way between butt ring and reel, hanging on a 12 in drop. This scaled-down fixed-lead rig then catches tench in the same way as it does a carp which happens along and sucks in the boilie or particle.

As the bait is gulped back to the pharnygeal teeth for chewing, the tench suddenly (provided the hook and bomb links are not too long) feels the lead. It then quickly shuts its mouth and does a runner, forgetting the bait it was about to chew. Meanwhile, the hook is pulled down to the lips and jerked in by the fixed lead. When the line tightens a second later, with the tench 2 or 3 ft away and gaining speed, the hook is really banged home. While all this is happening (in a split second or so), the Optonic screeches a multiple bleep, followed by the rod trying to leave the rod rests. However, if the butt ring is jammed up against the Optonic, the rod will stay in place. You are then, without even having to strike, suddenly into a tench.

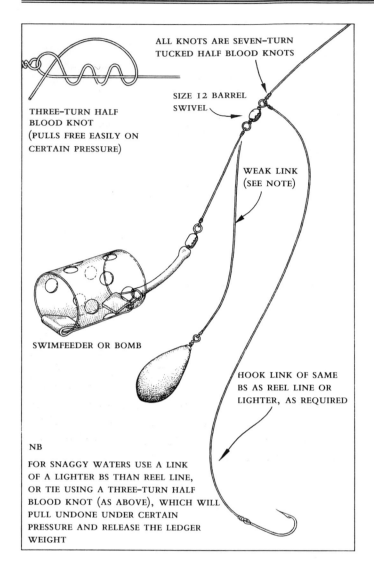

FIGURE 5.47 *Constructing a fixed paternoster using a barrel swivel*

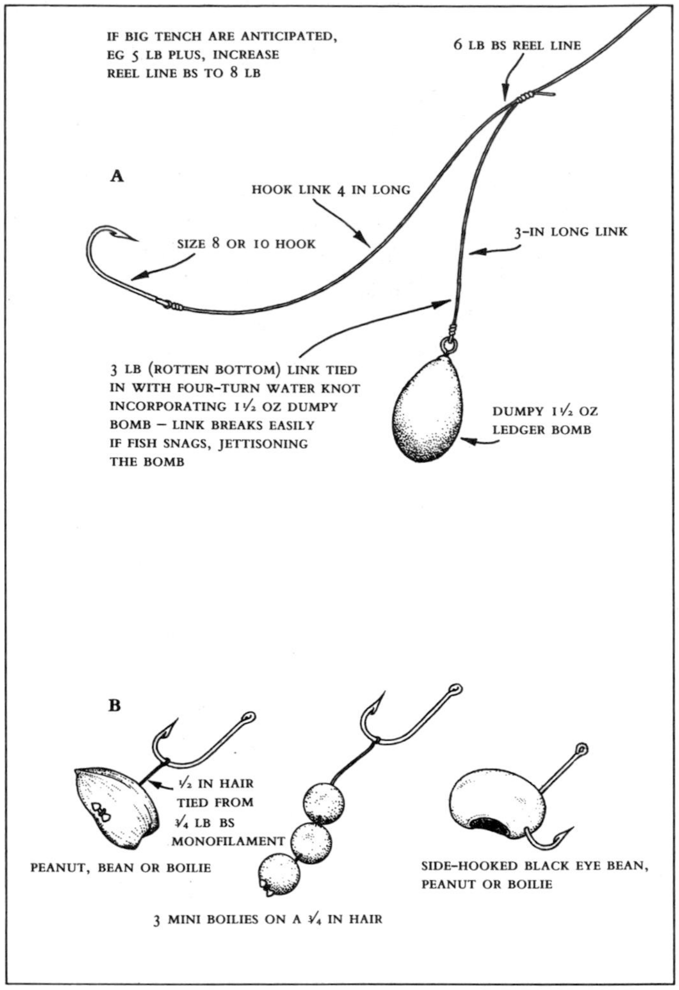

Left figure labels:

ALL KNOTS ARE SEVEN-TURN TUCKED HALF BLOOD KNOTS

THREE-TURN HALF BLOOD KNOT (PULLS FREE EASILY ON CERTAIN PRESSURE)

SIZE 12 BARREL SWIVEL

WEAK LINK (SEE NOTE)

SWIMFEEDER OR BOMB

HOOK LINK OF SAME BS AS REEL LINE OR LIGHTER, AS REQUIRED

NB

FOR SNAGGY WATERS USE A LINK OF A LIGHTER BS THAN REEL LINE, OR TIE USING A THREE-TURN HALF BLOOD KNOT (AS ABOVE), WHICH WILL PULL UNDONE UNDER CERTAIN PRESSURE AND RELEASE THE LEDGER WEIGHT

Right figure labels:

IF BIG TENCH ARE ANTICIPATED, EG 5 LB PLUS, INCREASE REEL LINE BS TO 8 LB

6 LB BS REEL LINE

A

HOOK LINK 4 IN LONG

SIZE 8 OR 10 HOOK

3-IN LONG LINK

3 LB (ROTTEN BOTTOM) LINK TIED IN WITH FOUR-TURN WATER KNOT INCORPORATING 1½ OZ DUMPY BOMB – LINK BREAKS EASILY IF FISH SNAGS, JETTISONING THE BOMB

DUMPY 1½ OZ LEDGER BOMB

B

½ IN HAIR TIED FROM ¾ LB BS MONOFILAMENT

PEANUT, BEAN OR BOILIE

3 MINI BOILIES ON A ¾ IN HAIR

SIDE-HOOKED BLACK EYE BEAN, PEANUT OR BOILIE

FIGURE 5.48 **A** *Bolt-rig tenching and* **B** *Hooking and bait alternatives*

The bait may be side-hooked, or, if the tench are particularly wary, sleeved on to a fine (¾ lb) hair just ½ in long. Invariably a single bait produces a better hooking ratio to bites, while a mini-string of tiny boilies may induce more offers. Once the hook baits are positioned, loose feed, and an additional attractor bait such as hempseed, can be scattered accurately around the area with a catapult.

MULTIPURPOSE CARP RIGS

For ledgering pieces of soft paste, cubes of meat, perhaps a couple of cockles, in diminutive waters where belt-off runs are neither expected nor desired, use a simple running link ledger as in fig. 5.49A.

Where a carp could go ploughing through weeds or snags, the ledger link, to which is attached a small bomb or swan shots, should be of a considerably lighter test than the reel line. Thus it creates a weak link which will break off when caught up in weeds, leaving the carp still connected to the main line.

For presenting pop-up baits, such as an air-injected lobworm or any of the floating baits (usually fished on the surface), fix on one or two swan shots 5 in from the hook to counterbalance the bait's buoyancy as in fig. 5.49B.

When fishing over dense bottom or blanket weed simply extend the ledger link to compensate, and use a heavier bomb for penetration down to the bottom (fig. 5.50). Experiment in the margins where you can see the rig working until you are happy.

Scorching runs are sometimes experienced with this

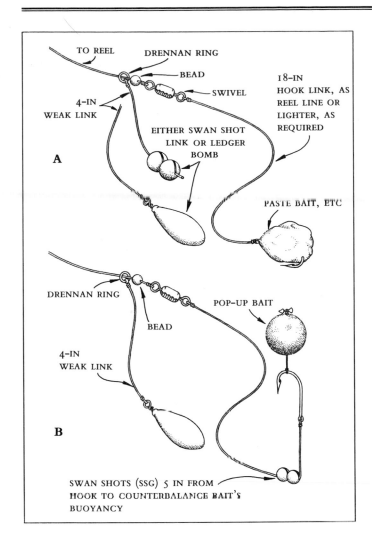

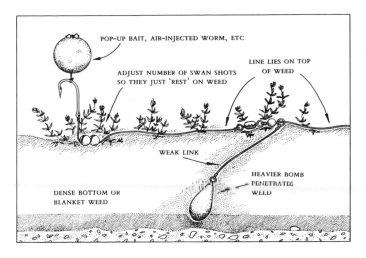

FIGURE 5.50 *A heavier multi-purpose rig*

set-up should the rig become hung up in weed. Generally, however, the indicator (monkey climber or coil) rises positively upwards, usually with enough time for an unhurried strike. Coupled to a buzzer the warning is quite adequate when sitting beside the rod. As I play fish from a pre-adjusted clutch, the anti-reverse is always on, enabling me at any point to grab the rod one-handed if necessary without the handle whizzing round.

FIGURE 5.49 *A multi-purpose rig – the running link ledger*

THE SHOCK OR 'BOLT' RIG

Now we arrive at what in recent years has become the panacea to catching carp: the *bolt* or *shock rig* ledger. Sadly, some anglers use no other technique because it is so effective. I have left the bolt rig until last because I wish you to treat it as a deadly method for catching difficult carp – carp which are so wary they won't provide enough indications on other methods of presentation for you to strike and hook them.

It's a fact that carp do not fall for the same tackle rig time after time. Bites which started out as slammers on simple ledger tackle soon become 'twitches', so imperceptible they are impossible to strike. And this is when the 'bolt rig' comes into its own. Using a heavy lead (1½ to 2 oz) which is felt by the carp just as it sucks the bait from the bottom back to its throat teeth for chewing, shocks that carp into closing its lips and doing a runner. In short it 'bolts off'. In the process it forgets about the bait and the hook is pulled home. The secret is in having exactly the right distance from lead to bait, which varies with different-sized carp.

A distance somewhere between 6 to 10 in from hook to lead is favoured. The bait (boilies and hard particles such as beans or peanuts, etc., work best with this method) can simply be side-hooked (fig. 5.51A) or slid on to a 'hair' (fig. 5.51B), providing the carp with extra confidence when it sucks it in. In each case the hook link can be of monofilament (reel line), black or multi-coloured dacron or braid or of floss which separates into numerous gossamer strands and becomes virtually in-visible on the bottom (see 'Hook lengths').

With dacron hook lengths, after tying the hook on don't clip the end off short. Simply tie in a small loop and use it as a 'built in' hair.

To stop the hook being blown away from the bait when a carp sucks it in, sleeve a short length of fine-diameter clear or black silicone tubing down the hook link over the eye and onto the shank, thus shortening the hair length (fig. 5.51C).

Note from fig. 5.51A that the (semi-fixed) 2 oz lead is

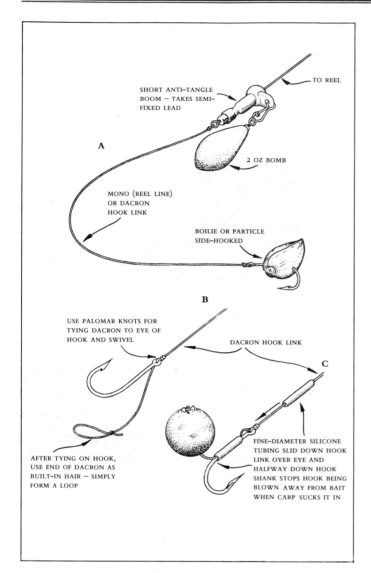

FIGURE 5.51 *The bolt or shock rig*

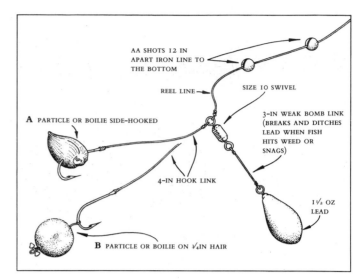

FIGURE 5.52 *A simple bolt rig*

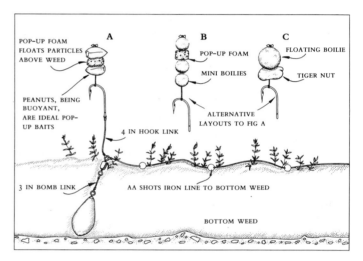

FIGURE 5.53 *A pop-up bolt rig*

attached to the clip of a short boom which threads on to the reel line above the hook link swivel and stops the lead from tangling. Keep your terminal rig as simple as possible (fig. 5.52). The short hook link and reel line are both connected to the same end of a tiny size 10 swivel, so that should it break in half you are still playing the carp, while the 'weak' bomb link is tied to the other end of the swivel. Lengths of both hook and bomb links can be varied to suit bottom or weed of varying types, but overall a hook link of 4 in and a bomb link of 3 in are ideal.

The beauty of this rig is that should a carp go belting off through heavy weed the weak link soon ditches the lead. It is also excellent for presenting pop-up baits on the hair rig above dense bottom weed (see fig. 5.53). If the bottom weed is deeper than the 3 in lead link, simply alter it accordingly. Note the three AA shots pinched at 12 in intervals up the line from the swivels, which iron the reel line to the weed or hide it in soft silt so as not to scare carp

as they approach the bait. To hide the reel line, dip the rod tip beneath the surface after casting, and with the left hand (assuming you are holding the rod in your right hand) gently pull the line until it is straight. Then allow a little slack from the reel and lift the rod horizontally on to the rests.

Contrary to popular belief, the line from bolt rig to rod does not necessarily need to be 'hauser' tight in order for the hook point to be driven home. The lead in conjunction with the speed at which a carp panics off are responsible for this. So wherever possible leave a slight bow in the line from rod tip to surface. This means the line close to the bolt rig will be lying along the bottom contours and not inhibiting carp in crystal-clear water from approaching the bait.

There is perhaps a better hooking rate once the carp has picked up the bait presented on a 'tight line' from lead to rod. But if a proportion of runs do not happen because the

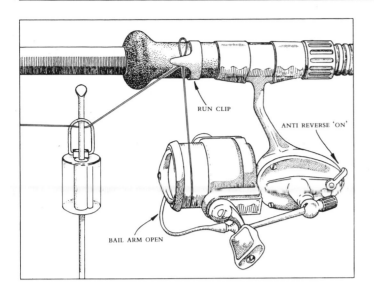

FIGURE 5.54 *Clipping up the line*

The shock or bolt rig used in conjunction with a bottle presented 50 yd out on a shallow bar accounted for this lovely carp.

carp sensed the 'bowstring line' and depart, it does not help you catch more fish.

Whenever there is a strong undertow in large waters, as in windy conditions, it is of course impossible to fish a gentle bow. Then it has to be a tight line 'clipped up' or nothing. At the reel end, after putting the line beneath the 'monkey', open the bale arm and neatly catch the line beneath a run clip fixed around the handle directly opposite the spool (see fig. 5.54). When a carp grabs the bait and promptly does a runner, line spews from the open spool while the monkey body drops a couple of inches, held there through the sheer speed of line evaporating from the open spool, while the buzzer screams its head off.

If using a reel with a bait runner facility, the bale arm will of course already be closed while the spool itself revolves. For both situations, a hefty strike is not required; indeed it could even prove disastrous. Simply close the bale arm by winding forward (which also puts the bait runner reel back into gear with a pre-set clutch) and gently bend the rod back into the fish when all is nicely tight. It is a very stereotyped and easy method to master.

In confined overgrown fisheries where the erection of rod rest set-ups, buzzers and monkey climbers could ruin the chances of carp even patrolling close by, let alone picking up a bolt-rigged bait, I fish in a very basic,

effective, if rather risky way. As I never leave the rod or rods (I occasionally use two rods, though for much of my carp fishing, because it is based on opportunity rather than patience, I use just one) after placing the bait accurately and ensuring the line is nicely sunk along the bottom I simply lay the rod down on the carpet of marginal plants. I use no rod rests or alarms, but the anti-reverse is on and the clutch is set a shade lighter than I intend to play a fish with when the time comes.

One minute there is nothing. The very next there is a furrow on the surface (if fishing shallow water) as a carp panics off, easily setting the hook and jerking the rod across the marginal plants in the process.

LEDGERING IN RUNNING WATER

BEST TECHNIQUES – LEDGERING IN FLOWING WATER

	freelining	*rod-top ledgering*	*quivertipping*	*quivertipping at night*
BARBEL	●	●	●	●
BREAM			●	●
CHUB	●	●	●	●
DACE	●		●	
ROACH	●		●	●

FREELINING IN STREAMS AND SMALL RIVERS

David Wilson brings a barbel gently upstream against the pressure of a fast, shallow run in an overgrown section of his local River Lea. In such clear water conditions at midday, an untethered bait has more chance of being accepted by many fish, so Dave chose to freeline a large piece of cheese paste slowly along the gravel bottom.

The art of freelining the bait in small rivers and clear flowing streams to catch quality roach and the odd sizeable dace is based upon concealment, and is most effective during the summer months when fish are really active. You need to creep and crawl stealthily about in order to get close to the quarry, so that you can flick the bait out a few yards – or even feet.

On open waters you can get away with using a 12 ft carbon float rod, but wherever the banks are heavily overgrown, and the most interesting and prolific diminutive rivers usually are, a long rod is an encumberance. My choice is a 10–11 ft built-in quivertip ledger rod. While you are not always watching the rod tip for indications, simply the line (as the word 'freelining' implies), the bait does at times need to be anchored on the bottom with a swanshot or two. And this is when the sensitive quivertip comes into its own.

All the weight for casting (pinching on a shot 12 in above light baits such as maggots is permitted) is of course in the bait itself, which will easily peel line from the spool providing it is full to the brim with around 2½ lb test. Do not forget to adjust the slipping clutch, because freelined large baits – and there is nothing better than a large lump of bread flake hiding a size 10 or 8 hook tied direct – really does sort out the better quality roach.

Groundbait is of course quite unnecessary. To get the fish interested, flick in a few hookbait samples every so often. Search all the likely-looking spots where you would expect roach to be in residence (see Location).

After pinching the flake on, 'dunk' it momentarily at your feet to make sure it sinks (dunking also makes it heavier), then flick it downstream, and allow the current to trundle it along the bottom. Keep a bow in the line from the rod tip to the point where the line enters the water and watch it like a hawk. It is your resistance-free bite indicator.

Even bites from 10 oz roach will look like a shark run. As the fish senses no fear from the food it is swallowing, due to a complete lack of terminal gear, it will grab it confidently, the line straightening in a ridiculously positive manner. If the roach decides to turn around and swim to a position at the rear of the shoal, the rod tip will even pull round. And if it chews the flake on the spot the line may only jerk forward momentarily once or twice.

In order to add chub and barbel to the species that may be caught freelining during the summer and autumn from both diminutive and medium-sized, clear-flowing rivers, a step up in tackle is necessary.

There is nothing to beat the versatility of an 11–12 ft, carbon Avon rod of 1¼ lb test with hooks tied direct. Such an outfit is capable of subduing a large barbel, yet permits enjoyment from smaller species such as roach and bream when they occasionally show up.

In trying to achieve maximum distance (to reach chub for instance, occupying a run on the opposite bank of a reasonably wide river) I occasionally punch the bait out with a double-handed cast. However, accuracy is more easily achieved by hooking the line over the ball of the forefinger to 'feel' the bait's weight) and casting with an underhand swing and flip. Provided that the spool is filled to the very lip, even with 5–6 lb test, the bait will fly effortlessly and accurately through the air until you 'feather' it down to land over the desired spot with the same finger. It is an art worth practising.

If you find this one-handed technique awkward or unsuitable, use the same underhand swing and flip, but hold a loop of line in your left hand (assuming the rod is in your right) and do a couple of pendulum swings with the rod tip pointing at the target to build up momentum before letting go. The key is confidence, and using a bait which is heavy enough – a large slug, lobworm, cube of meat, a large piece of bread flake or cheese paste, and so on. All are perfect for freelining.

Because the bait appears to be untethered and behaves so naturally fish are not concerned by the diameter of a 6 lb line or its colour, or even by a large, visible hook.

Although freelining for chub and barbel is most effectively accomplished by careful stalking along overgrown banks and manoeuvering yourself into a position from where a short cast can be made to fish lying between or beneath vegetation features, there are certain situations where wading is necessary. In diminutive, shallow, overgrown streams and rivers, you could easily frighten the fish long before a cast is made by taking to the water. In larger, overgrown and weedy, reasonably shallow rivers, where thick floating beds of potomogeton or water

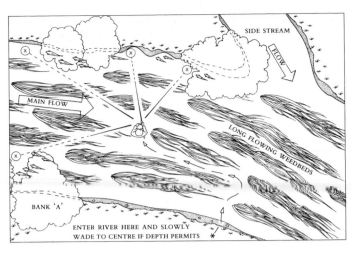

FIGURE 5.55 *By carefully wading into the centre of gravel shallows between weedbeds, you can offer a freelined bait to barbel and chub that are unapproachable from bank* **A**

crowfoot clog the surface during midsummer, or impenetrable bankside trees separate you from fish which are visible, wading permits several casts to be made into spots that are completely unapproachable from the bank. Consider the situation, for instance, in fig. 5.55.

In these choice lies you will naturally have to wait for the bait to reach bottom before a barbel grabs hold, whereas chub will strike from the second the bait hits the surface.

A common occurrence when freelining the bait directly upstream is for the line momentarily to fall slack. This is caused by the chub moving a few feet downstream, but then returning to its original position. This is just as 'positive' an indication as the rod tip going over, so strike immediately and strike hard, quickly levering the chub away from the sunken tree or bullrush bed behind which it is hiding and into which it will surely try to bury the hook. Chub are masters of not only ridding themselves of the hook, but also transferring it into the closest snag. Keep the rod well up and in a full curve from the moment the hook goes home.

Should the line quite suddenly fall completely slack, this is because a chub is actually swimming downstream towards you with the bait. Quickly crank the reel a few times to pick up the loose line before slamming the hook home. These bites often occur instantly, within seconds of the bait hitting the surface, so you need to be watching that line like a hawk even before you close the bale arm. The most instant bites of all come to natural baits such as a large slug skipped or skate-cast across weed-beds to where cut weed or debris collects around the trailing branches of overhanging trees; down into the swirling cross-currents and eddies where a side stream enters the main stream; into the gloom beneath the low, overhanging brickwork of a road or rail bridge.

ROD-TOP LEDGERING

During the cold winter months when the combination of low water temperatures, a clear river and bright conditions dictate that bites, even from chub, will be extremely tentative, the finely tapered quivertip will interpret every rustle and tap from chub.

A natural progression from freelining is to add weight to the bait, either for casting or for anchoring it down in a particular spot, or both, and watch the rod top for bite indication. Because of the water pressure of really fast runs, whether shallow or deep, in large powerful rivers such as the Severn or Wye, a 1 oz bomb or more may be required to nail the bait to the bottom. A similar situation exists in all rivers, even comparatively small ones such as the fast, swirling waters of weir pools where, unless the bait stays put until the chub or barbel locate it, the force of the current will simply wash it downstream to an unproductive area.

As with freelining, the ideal rod is the standard-top Avon, which should be held during the summer months when bites are liable to be quick in coming. Whether standing or sitting, hold the rod firmly with two fingers either side of the reel stem and your entire forearm supporting the handle. After casting, and once the ledger has settled in the desired spot, make a habit of hooking your forefinger (at the first joint) around the line. Once adopted, you will find this a particularly sensitive and comfortable way of keeping the rod still. There is nothing to stop you from using a front rod rest, which helps steady the tip, especially in windy conditions and extremely fast water. You will quickly come to recognize the line tightening across your forefinger as the rod tip knocks.

When you cast downstream, the rod tip will be pulled round if the fish moves downstream with the bait. If it simply moves across the current, however, the tip might suddenly relax or spring back immediately following a gentle knock.

When casting directly upstream use only enough weight to hold bottom so that when a fish sucks in the bait and turns around, the bomb is dislodged causing the line to fall slack immediately. These are great bites to hit, but remember that, as when freelining, you need to lift the rod back in a long, hard, sweeping strike to straighten the line and bang the hook home.

It is best to use the minimum amount of lead needed to hold bottom for ledgering downstream. It allows you to inch the bait down and across the bottom by raising the rod tip every so often in order to search the swim thoroughly (fig. 5.56). This imparts a certain amount of life to the bait and often promotes an instant bite. There are times when fish will only accept a completely static bait and times when, unless it is constantly on the move like the unattached offerings thrown in to attract fish, they will show not the slightest interest. So always be willing to experiment and to work the bait along. Don't sit there waiting for something to pull the rod in, although a barbel just might.

For heavy water ledgering a 5 or 6 lb line is ideal. Resist the temptation to make up complicated ledger rigs. Running ledgers with swivels, split rings and non-tangle tubing may look acceptable on paper, but in reality work no better than a simple fixed paternoster (see fig. 5.57). I would in fact say that as all the various bits tend to collect weed, running ledgers are inferior to the fixed paternoster described.

Simply tie on a 10 in length of mono (reel line), using a

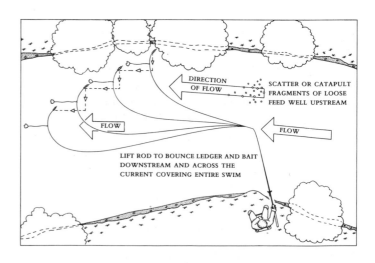

FIGURE 5.56 *Rod-top ledgering for barbel and chub*

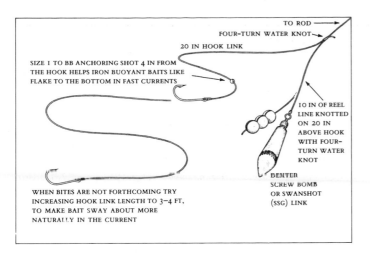

FIGURE 5.57 *Simple fixed paternoster*

four-turn water knot, 20 in above the hook. To this, fix either an Arlesey bomb or enough swan shots to just hold bottom. Swan shots are more practical because it takes seconds to either add or subtact one for fine adjustment. For currents requiring in excess of five or six swan shots, bombs are advisable. The brass screw design are good because they make a quick change of weight easy. Attention to little things such as continually changing the ledger weight to suit the current force of each swim as you move up or down river, may seem unnecessary, but will be reflected by more fish in the net.

Buoyant bait like bread flake does not always settle on the bottom in really strong currents; it tends to flap about and look unnatural. Sometimes fish gobble it up for this very reason, and at such times an increase in the hook length to 3 or even 4 ft will encourage more confident bites. On other occasions it is refused for the same reason.

Experiment by adding an anchoring shot just 4 in from the bait, which will ensure it settles statically.

Worms and hard baits such as cheese are ideal fast-water offerings. They stay on a large hook well, and withstand the attentions of unwanted nuisance species. Also worth trying, particularly during the autumn, is a small fish such as minnow, bleak, gudgeon or stone loach. Hook once only through the top lip or through both nostrils, and fish as any other bait. If little interest is shown when the fish is presented hard on the bottom, bump it downstream every so often by lifting the rod tip to dislodge the lead and lowering it again. And be ready for a really slamming take as you do so. Both barbel and chub grab small fish with considerably more force than they do paste baits. In weedy or particularly snaggy parts of the river don't bother to present the fish live. Tap it sharply on the head before casting and you won't have to worry about it hiding or swimming into snags. Alive or dead, it will be sucked in just the same. For additional bait ideas see the chapter on baits.

Whilst looking at both freelining and rod top ledgering techniques and the use of largish baits where indications of the line or the rod tip are likely to be most positive during the summer and autumn months, as the season progresses and much colder weather sets in, a different approach is required.

No longer will chub and barbel instantly respond to large 'moving' offerings. In low water temperatures especially smaller baits will be the order of the day which of course promotes much smaller bite registrations. And to identify smaller indications the finely tapered tip of the Avon Quiver tip rod is the answer (see Avon Quiver Tip/ Tackle Section).

QUIVERTIPPING

There are two important points to remember when using the quivertip in running water. Choose the most sensitive quivertip to match current strength in order that even tentative bites from small species will register (see Tackle). Secondly, use the minimum weight, whether swan shots, bomb or feeder, so that drop-back bites are always indicated. Smaller species do not have the strength to move a heavy bomb or feeder and indicate a drop-back bite on the quivertip so make sure you anchor the bait with no more weight than necessary.

Loose feeding/groundbait

You must also decide whether to introduce loose feed or groundbait or both, by feeder, or by hand. When fishing

clear flowing small rivers during the summer months, for instance, where swims and even the position of shoal species like dace, roach, bream and chub is clearly defined, the answer is to flick in a few fragments of hookbait every so often by hand or catapult – pieces of flake, stewed wheat, maggots and so on. Indeed, throw in too much free food and your sport might end prematurely, as it is easy to overfeed the fish unintentionally.

Through clear water it is sometimes possible to see how many fish there are in the swim and to observe how they react to free food. You can then regulate the feed exactly to match their mood and appetite. There is a problem of course, when ledgering in coloured water or into distant, clear-water swims, where the size of the shoal cannot be seen – which, let us face it, is most of the time.

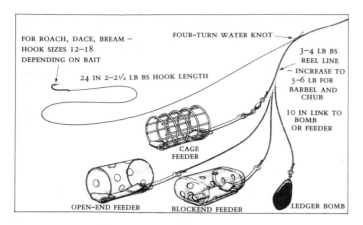

FIGURE 5.58 *Basic quivertip ledger rig for river fishing*

In large rivers where shoals of roach or bream, for instance, might number several hundreds rather than dozens, and competition for food is high, loose feed or groundbait deposited by swimfeeder with the hookbait each cast is imperative for constant sport. See fig. 5.58 for the various rig options.

Incidentally, when ledgering into deep water or for casting a feeder out 30 to 40 yd plus generally speaking I prefer the safety margin provided by a 4 lb reel-line. When barbel and chub are the quarry a 5–6 lb reel line makes more sense, while quivertipping slow moving or small rivers for dace, roach and perhaps the odd chub or bream a 3 lb reel line is quite sufficient. To keep a massive shoal of roach feeding in the fast, deep waters of Norfolk's tidal rivers Bure, Yare and Waveney, or the River Bann in Northern Ireland, you have the option of using a cage or open-end feeder packed with maggot- or caster-laced breadcrumbs, or a blockend feeder holding maggots or

Winter weir-pools are choice locations for coming to grips with very large roach, and quivertipping tactics with the bait anchored hard on the bottom are most effective when water temperatures are low.

casters only. On some days roach will respond better to the addition of cereals, some days they will not. If in doubt, stick to a blockend and loose feed only.

For attracting the roach, bream and chub living on the bottom of a fast and deep weir-pool into a given area, the blockend certainly reigns supreme. The cereal/open-end or cage feeder combination is more likely to scatter fish all over the swim because the crumb particles are so light that they disperse a long way. And in winter conditions, when you need to really concentrate the shoal into a small area, this could prove disastrous. And unless your casting is consistently accurate, the same thing will happen.

For dace and roach that inhabit really fast shallow swims, the blockend and maggot or caster combination is certainly more productive (use a small blockend for dace). It is worth remembering that in strong currents the blockend's load (even casters) will wash out much quicker than in slow currents. For fast water, therefore, choose a blockend with a limited amount of small holes for slow dispersal of the bait. This of course applies whatever the species. In slow swims, go for the reverse – a feeder well punched with large holes.

Incidentally, the 'spring tip' indicator is great in really gentle currents for shy biting fish especially dace when you need to step down to really fine hook lengths, and tiny hooks. Use in exactly the same way as the quivertip. In really cold conditions when bites are hard to define, use a target board.

Some feeder manufacturers offer weights of alternative sizes for their feeders. The Drennan Feederlink (a great blockend for slow-moving water), for example, has a plastic spigot at the bottom to which different weights of between ⅛ and ½ oz can be clipped. It is handy to have a supply of fold-over or strap leads in varying sizes from ½ to 2 oz so that any make of cage, open-end or blockend feeder, can be doctored to hold bottom regardless of current strength (fig. 5.59).

Rod positioning

Many anglers are unsure about which position the rod should be placed in when quivertipping in flowing water and the best positions are illustrated in fig. 5.60.

It is a fact that more drop backs will occur when casting way out across the flow in big rivers such as the Thames or Severn for instance to distant swims and the further out you fish directly across the flow, greater is the bow in the line (created by current pressure) between bait and quivertip.

Incidentally, when casting across river to swims beyond the accurate range of the catapult, the best way to introduce loose feed to attract species like chub and

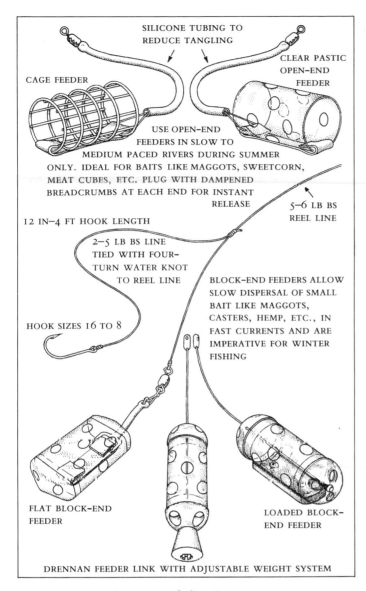

FIGURE 5.59 *Fixed paternoster feeding rigs*

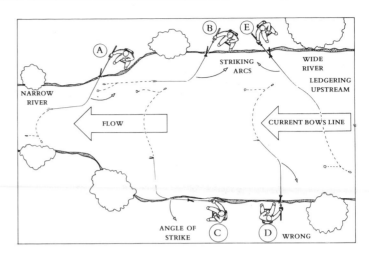

FIGURE 5.60 *Correct positioning of the rod when quivertipping in flowing water*

Quivertipping upstream

The advantage of quivertipping upstream is that on most rivers there will always be a percentage of swims that can only be tackled successfully by casting directly upstream against the flow, using just enough weight to hold bottom so that species like barbel and chub feel minimal resistance when moving off with the bait. Bites are sudden, dramatic drop-backs, the quivertip flipping backwards as the line falls completely slack.

Generally, a long, sweeping strike will drive the hook home, but odd occasions arise when you need to wind like mad in order to recover most of the line as the fish swims several yards towards you before you can make a successful strike.

Complete concentration on the finely tapered, solid-glass quivertip for gentle drop-back bites is, of course, imperative during sub-zero conditions. With his swim-feedered maggots placed straight out, note how Bob Nudd sits side onto and with the flow, enabling him to strike through the same angle at which the line is held by the current.

particularly barbel is with the aid of a large blockend swimfeeder. Five or ten minutes spent casting and recasting to lay a thick carpet of hempseed (including a few hook-bait samples) on the bottom of the swim at the start of a session is time well spent. Do not forget to enlarge the holes of the (pre-baiting) feeder with a pair of scissors so that its load washes out within a second or two of it hitting bottom. And do not worry about the splash it makes as it goes in. On most well-fished chub and barbel rivers, the occupants of the swim might even be rooting about among the seeds before you have finished the pre-baiting. Then again, well-educated chub and barbel may make you wait an hour or so before they move up into the swim and over the seeds. If bites do not materialize within a few minutes, do not be tempted into introducing more loose feed.

When upstream ledgering sit facing the river with the rod angled slightly upstream as in fig. 5.60D.

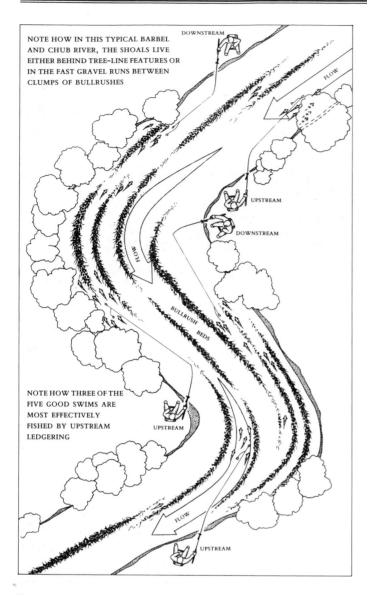

NOTE HOW IN THIS TYPICAL BARBEL AND CHUB RIVER, THE SHOALS LIVE EITHER BEHIND TREE-LINE FEATURES OR IN THE FAST GRAVEL RUNS BETWEEN CLUMPS OF BULLRUSHES

NOTE HOW THREE OF THE FIVE GOOD SWIMS ARE MOST EFFECTIVELY FISHED BY UPSTREAM LEDGERING

FIGURE 5.61 *Upstream ledgering*

Swims with excellent potential are ignored by many anglers because they cannot cast the bait downstream and across in the accepted manner, and loose feed thrown in is taken down by the current. Fig. 5.61 illustrates an example of a river in which barbel and chub occupy runs behind the tree-line features and in runs between bullrush beds. However, three of the five swims can be fished effectively only by ledgering upstream. Moreover, loose feeding with either a particle attractor such as hempseed or fragments of the hook bait, or both, is not as difficult as it may first seem. In most instances, the problem is solved by quietly walking upstream, parallel with the head of the swim, and catapulting the bait out a little upstream of the shoal.

If overhanging trees or tall beds of dense bullrushes prevent you catapulting in loose feed upstream, use a blockend feeder for depositing baits like hemp, casters or maggots; or make up a PVA (plastic vinyl acetate)

dissolving stringer and tie it to the bomb swivel, when presenting large offerings such as meat cubes or cheese paste.

Quivertipping for bream

Used in conjunction with an open-ended swimfeeder filled with dampened breadcrumbs, quivertipping is the most deadly and versatile method of ledgering for bream in running water, all season through.

For many fishermen, it has completely taken over from the swingtip in recent years due to the wonderful choice of specialist, built-in quivertip rods now available. For close-in work there are super-sensitive, 7–9 ft wands. At the opposite end of the scale, powerful 11–12 ft feeder rods are available. These are capable of detecting the tiniest bite on a finely-tapered tip from the swirling waters of a weir-pool, but have enough backbone to subdue any size of bream – and even a barbel should you hook one. If you do not wish to own lots of specialist rods, a 10 ft multitip quiver rod with a choice of three or four interchangeable tips (kept in the handle) is the answer (see 'Ledger rods', p. 80–1). However, whatever you decide upon, it is the very tip that you must keep your eyes concentrated on, and you must learn to interpret its every movement so that you can distinguish the difference between weed on the line, line bites, current pull and, of course, a genuine bite.

The main difference to consider between quivertipping in still and in flowing water is the influence of pressure on the line. In really fast currents, unless you support the rod in two rests with the tip up in the air to keep most of the line above the surface, the tip will be pulled right round by current pressure alone. This completely defeats the object of having a finely-tapered tip in the first place. Moreover, when current pressure becomes too great, the bomb or feeder will bounce off downstream and in towards the bank along the bottom, dragging the bait well away from the intended swim.

Coldwater chubbing

Using the quivertip to catch winter chub is all about understanding the river, and deciding where they are most likely to be shoaled up (fig. 5.62). For instance when the level is up and the water coloured, large areas of really shallow water unlikely to hold chub (except in full flood) are not immediately apparent to those unfamiliar with the river. Those who know it well of course don't both with these barren swims because they remember how the river was during the summer. And those who observe surface currents wherever they fish will, from the action of surface displacements, be able to distinguish between shallows and

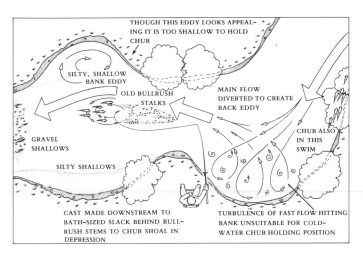

FIGURE 5.62 *Current patterns for chubbing in cold water*

Pick the right conditions, with the river fining down nicely after heavy flooding, coinciding with a mild spell, and large hauls of chub are on the cards. Quivertipped bread flake in conjunction with mashed bread groundbait was the winning formula used by John to account for this bag of over 20 fish, all between 3 and 4½ lb.

deeps. Remember how tiny vortexes of water are sent upwards when hitting the dying stalks of bullrushes sprouting from the gravel shallows. Well, the same spiralling and displacement occurs when fast currents hit the tiniest of pebbles. Thus gravel shallows are easily depicted on the surface by completely 'broken' water – despite the fact that through heavily coloured water the bottom cannot be seen.

Having said all this, for part of the day chub may very well choose to occupy the fastest, shallowest part of the swim, but on a 24 hour basis their requirements are consistant. They prefer to hold station in a quiet slack out of the main current force, but not so far away they cannot every so often nip out and suck in a juicy tit bit. Maximum food, for minimum effort aptly sums up the chub's outlook towards life. Of course in mild winter conditions chub are renowned for being continually on the move and will follow a food source (the anglers loose feed) from a considerable way downstream. But in the coldest of subzero weather and freezing winds the shoal will huddle

together, loathe to move very far. And when you decide to fish in these conditions, pinpoint accuracy is essential for success.

Low temperatures

Much depends on the daytime temperature and whether it increases a few notches or not. Some days chub might move several yards to a bait when the light values increase at around midday. While on another they will not budge an inch until dusk sets in. And then one solitary knock on the quivertip is all you will get. Sometimes the bait has literally to be bumped on their noses for baits to materialize.

QUIVERTIPPING AT NIGHT

Quivertipping is as effective throughout the hours of darkness in flowing water, as float fishing is in stillwaters. It is often also the best way of coming to grips with specimen roach, chub, bream and barbel inhabiting rivers that run very clear. I illuminate the quivertip with a narrow-beam torch set on the ground downstream of the rod, pointing upwards and out, so it shines only on the tip and not into my eyes or on the water (fig. 5.63). This is most important, because in clear water the fish might easily become scared.

All my quivertip rods are painted matt white (two coats) along the last 16–20 in to catch every bit of light. This

makes them easy to watch, even for hours at a time, and also improves daytime concentration on the quivertip in poor light conditions and against a broken background. If the rod is firmly set on two telescopic rests with the butt-ring hung up against the curve in the front rest (fig. 5.64), before the torch is positioned, the quivertip will then settle right in the middle of the torch beam every cast without further ado. As I keep a second, small torch in my jacket pocket, there is no need to move the one carefully positioned on the ground.

A second, and I think less effective, method of visual indication at night is provided by whipping a ¾-in section

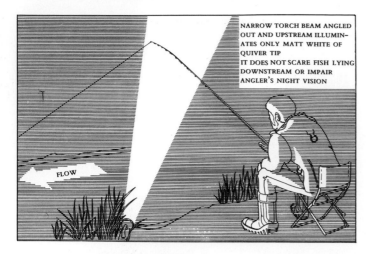

FIGURE 5.63 *Quivertipping at night*

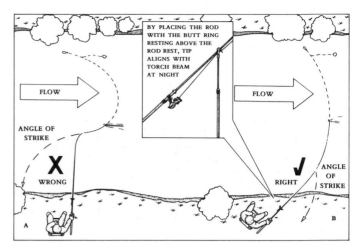

FIGURE 5.64 *Quivertip ledgering across the flow in larger rivers*

of silicone tubing on to the very end of the quivertip and pushing in a powerful betalight element (600 micro-lamberts), or a mini starlight chemical element, which is considerably brighter but lasts for only 6–8 hours (fig. 5.65). When fish are biting regularly, a luminous element on the end of the quivertip is quite sufficient. However, considering that there will inevitably be long periods of inactivity, coupled to occasions when bits of weed and other debris continually hit the line and register false bites, I find the torch-illuminated tip far easier to concentrate on.

At night always tighten up to the bait a little more than you would during daylight, so the tip has a definable curve. Drop-back baits then become apparent immediately.

When fishing new swims, it is well worth doing some pre-baiting to ensure that you do not waste a night's sleep.

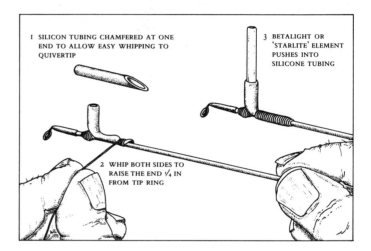

FIGURE 5.65 *Quivertipping at night*

PREDATOR RIGS

FREE-ROAMING MINI LIVEBAIT RIGS FOR PERCH AND CHUB

The secret in presenting a free-roaming livebait to perch or chub in stillwater, where there is no current to accentuate its movements, is to use a small float (like a pilot float plugged to the line with a stem of thin peacock quill).

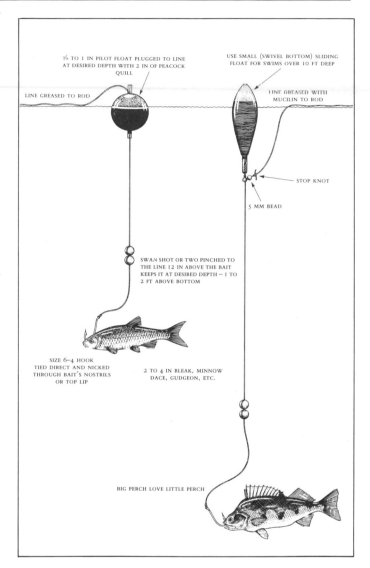

FIGURE 5.66 *Free-roaming, mini livebait rig for perch or chub — for use in still or running water*

Small livebaits worked beneath a float are a most productive and exciting method of catching perch and chub in both still and running water. When exploring rivers, trotting tiny fish like minnows or the fry of any small shoal fish beneath a float, a 2 to 3 swan shot chubber fixed to a 5 to 6 lb line both top and bottom should suffice. Set it to present the bait 1 to 2 ft above the bottom with the bulk shot set 1 ft above the hook.

For larger fish, such as a 2 to 4 in bleak, gudgeon, bullhead, small dace or lamprey, use a ⅞ in diameter pilot float plugged to the line with 2 in of fine peacock quill (fig. 5.66).

Use a size 6 hook for minnows and a 4 for larger baits, hooking them once only through the top lip or through both nostrils. Trot steadily downstream holding back every so often to waver the bait tantalizingly up and away from the bottom.

Summer live-baiting can produce hectic results, especially at the tail end of large weir pools and in the back eddies where perch and chub gather in large shoals. Trot the bait beside all the usual habitats along the opposite bank, remembering to let it swing across the current at the very end of the run so it finishes up in the margins along your own bank. Then retrieve it gently in slow pulls plus the occasional twitch, ready for a take at any moment.

Generally speaking that first run through the swim offers the most likely chance, so move on after giving each spot two or three casts. With this wandering, searching way of fishing, the opportunist always catches more fish.

When the float does suddenly shoot under and the line tightens, you are on your own. If you strike immediately you will pull the hook from a percentage of fish, and if you leave the run to develop you could still pull it out or have the bait returned minus its lower half. In short, there is no set formula guaranteed to hook chub and perch on live baits, which is why nowadays I strike as soon as the float goes in a long sweep of the rod. I keep it fully bent as the fish shakes its head, hoping the hook will find a purchase. If anything, winter live-baiting has the edge, and is particularly effective in very cold, clear-water conditions when jack frost has painted everything white and most other methods are less effective.

Sometimes small jack pike become a nuisance and every so often bite the hook off, which might just sway you into using a wire trace, but resist the temptation. Far fewer perch or chub will suck in the live bait as a result, and pike rid themselves of a large single hook unbelievably easily.

To present the bait in really deep water, say swims in excess of 10 ft, where the fixed pilot float inhibits casting, switch over to a small swivel-bottom sliding float (fig. 5.66) and remember to grease the line for several yards above the sliding stop knot to help control the bait. Remember also to wet the line with saliva before moving the sliding stop knot either up or down to accommodate a depth change.

Stillwater

The sliding float rig is, overall, a better option for presentation in stillwaters. For instance, if the depth is not known, you can use the rig (without bait) to plummet large areas prior to fishing, so that you can always work the bait in that all-important layer of water a couple of feet above the bottom. As only a small percentage of stillwater fisheries contain chub, it is larger-than-average sized perch in mind (1½ lb upwards) that are attracted by small, free-roaming fish close to the bottom. It is my favourite method for big perch throughout the summer and autumn, and in reasonably mild periods in winter. It works especially well whenever a good chop on the surface permits a large area to be explored. In extremely cold weather, however, I prefer to anchor the bait down in one place, and for this the perch paternoster livebait rig is recommended.

LIVEBAITING AND DEADBAITING IN STILLWATERS FOR CHUB

Where they can be seen charging into the fry shoals during the summer months, the usually enigmatic stillwater chub is at its most vulnerable to a freelined or float-fished livebait. They will take deadbaits too. Numbers of really huge specimen chub have fallen for large deadbaits such as whole herrings and half mackerel intended for a pike. A friend who regularly chub fishes some of the large, deep gravel pits adjacent to the River Thames near Oxford actually pre-baits for chub during the winter months with whitebait or freshly killed bleak.

A dozen or so free offerings are introduced close into the margins along a gradual drop-off every other night (grebes and cormorants clean them up if put in during daylight) for a week or more, followed by several consecutive sessions during darkness, fishing two rods with a freelined dead bleak on each.

To ensure the 6 lb line is not bitten through by the chub's pharyngeal teeth, the hook length is made from 10 lb test dacron to which a size 4 hook is tied. He does suffer wonderful catches of pike in an effort to locate these nomadic specimen chub, including the occasional whopper, but every so often a group of chub passes through the swim and one of them succumbs to the bleak deadbait on offer.

PERCH PATERNOSTER LIVEBAIT RIG

In very deep, cold water, when perch do not respond immediately, and may take their time approaching even a particularly lively bait, the most effective way of locating them is to anchor the bait close to the bottom in a selected area using the paternostered livebait rig (fig. 5.67). By employing a two-rod set up and continually re-positioning each bait every half hour or so until the action is initiated, you can explore a large expanse of water during a day's fishing. Remember to pinch a small shot onto the line a couple of feet above the end rig for the sliding float to rest against prior to casting, or tangles could result.

I find the bait works most attractively, and for considerably longer, if the single-eyed hook (tied direct) is gently slipped through the nostrils or once only through its top

lip, provided that the cast is an unhurried, gentle lob. Fierce casting encourages the livebait to fly off the hook, or become damaged by the time it arrives in the swim. As for bait preference, that old adage, 'the best way of catching a big perch, is by using a little perch', could not be more true. I also have much faith in gudgeon, which work attractively for hour after hour. Small roach, rudd and dace are good too.

A 1–1½ oz bomb tied to the 30 in link ensures that the bait works only in the lower water layers close to the bottom, and makes this rig perfect for snaggy or weeded spots in both still and running water during the summer, when a lively, free-foaming bait may either work away from the desired area, or become caught up in weed. It is

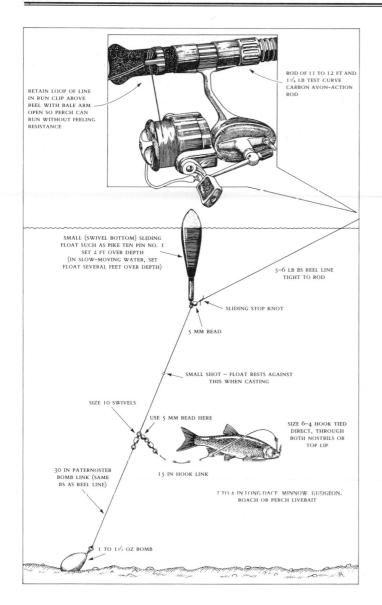

RETAIN LOOP OF LINE
IN RUN CLIP ABOVE
REEL WITH BALE ARM
OPEN SO PERCH CAN
RUN WITHOUT FEELING
RESISTANCE

ROD OF 11 TO 12 FT AND
1¼ LB TEST CURVE
CARBON AVON-ACTION
ROD

SMALL (SWIVEL BOTTOM) SLIDING
FLOAT SUCH AS PIKE TEN PIN NO. 1
SET 2 FT OVER DEPTH
(IN SLOW-MOVING WATER, SET
FLOAT SEVERAL FEET OVER DEPTH)

5–6 LB BS REEL LINE
TIGHT TO ROD

SLIDING STOP KNOT

5 MM BEAD

SMALL SHOT – FLOAT RESTS AGAINST
THIS WHEN CASTING

SIZE 10 SWIVELS

USE 5 MM BEAD HERE

SIZE 6–4 HOOK TIED
DIRECT, THROUGH
BOTH NOSTRILS OR
TOP LIP

30 IN PATERNOSTER
BOMB LINK (SAME
BS AS REEL LINE)

15 IN HOOK LINK

2 TO 4 IN LONG DACE, MINNOW, GUDGEON,
ROACH OR PERCH LIVEBAIT

1 TO 1½ OZ BOMB

particularly effective for exploring deep eddies, or beneath the main flush in weir-pools and in deep holes on the bends, because the bait stays exactly where you put it and works continually at the desired distance off bottom. To present the bait over a bottom covered in cabbages or thick weed, simply lengthen the bomb link to suit.

When fishing in stillwater, ensure that all the line from float to rod-tip is well sunk, or the float will be dragged under by the surface tow alone. When river fishing, however, the situation reverses, and to stop the float from being pulled under by the current, set it well over depth and angle the rod-tip well up on a front rest so that most of the line clears the surface. As perch are quite liable to eject the bait upon feeling undue resistance, once the rig is in position tighten up the float and slip a loop of line beneath a run clip or an elastic band on the handle immediately above the reel, with the bale arm left open. This allows a perch to run with the bait and peel line from the spool. However, do not wait too long before striking, or it may gorge the bait. There is no golden rule as to exactly when the strike should be made. When water temperatures are extremely low, perch invariably take time in approaching, grabbing hold and finally swallowing the bait. Indeed, the float may sink slowly, no more than a few inches beneath the surface. During mild spells however, perch could work the bait down within seconds. So if the hook fails to catch hold on the first strike, simply wait a little longer on each successive run before winding down and striking. Adopt a philosophical attitude in that it is always more desirable to miss, than initiate a deeply-hooked perch!

FIGURE 5.67 *Perch paternoster livebait rig*

PERCH AND ZANDER LEDGERED LIVEBAIT/DEADBAIT RIG

Zander

Zander spend the greater part of their life feeding close to the bottom, and ledgering is by far the most effective method of catching them in both still and running water. As can be seen from fig. 5.68 to enjoy sport with zander of all sizes, an 11–12 ft heavy Avon-action ledger rod is perfect, used in conjunction with a reel line of 6–9 lb test, depending on the presence of snags and so on. Where possible, endeavour to fish lighter rather than heavier, because more runs will result. If you are fishing waters where, in addition to zander, a really large pike is more than just an outside possibility, then a compromise of an 8–9 lb test line is the wise choice.

For minimizing resistance to a biting zander, the rod should be set in two telescopic rod-rests with the tip pointing downwards and directly at the bait. As there will inevitably be long periods of inactivity, it is comforting to employ an electronic bite alarm as the front rest, plus a visual indicator such as a greased monkey climber with a clear body. A betalight luminous element or a luminous 'starlight' can then be slipped into the clear body for those long night-fishing sessions. And on the majority of zander fisheries, night fishing greatly increases the chances of success with this predatory enigma, particularly the larger specimens, which are incredibly wary and shy in clear water conditions during daylight, unless the surface is broken by strong winds.

Even with the indicator set to hang on a drop of around 2 ft, zander bites are often extremely tentative and little more than slight jerks on the line that raise the monkey climber no more than a few inches at a time. These initial

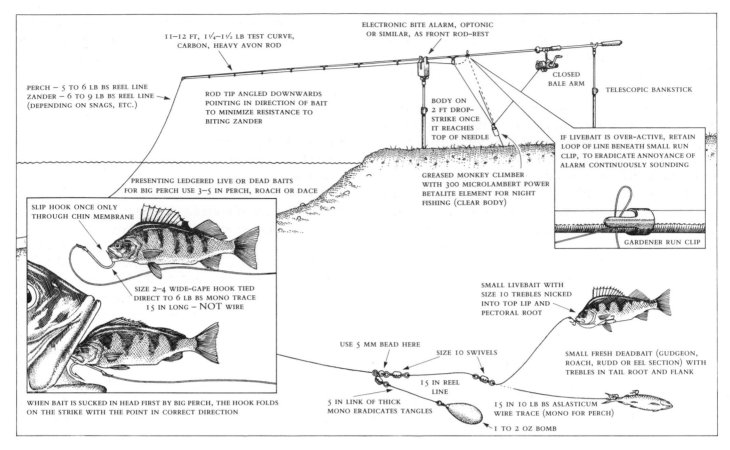

FIGURE 5.68 *Ledgered livebait/deadbait rig for zander and perch*

twitches do, at least, allow you time to anticipate further, more positive action. Nevertheless, only a small percentage of runs will eventually peel line from a free spool, as a pike does when making off with a live or deadbait, and my advice is to strike in a long, positive, backwards sweep of the rod as soon as the indicator hits the tip of the needle. This is one reason why I usually fish for zander with the bale arm closed. Again, if a big pike is more than likely, fish with an open bale arm and a loop of line in a run-clip on the rod handle, just in case.

When offering livebaits, I suggest you fix a tiny run-clip or an elastic band over the rod blank between butt-ring and indicator, which eradicates the annoying bleep–bleep from the bite alarm that is caused by the intermittent movements of an active bait, not zander. Obviously there is no need to do this when presenting deadbaits, unless river fishing against a strong flow.

For fishing in heavily coloured water, small freshly killed deadbaits (with the emphasis on 'freshly killed') are more effective than livebaits – my favourite zander baits being gudgeon, small roach and rudd, or a 3-in long eel section. Make a few slits with a knife along the flank on both sides to allow the bait's aroma to permeate the water, and mount it on a 15 in alasticum trace of no more than 10 lb test, holding a duo of size 10 trebles set 2 in apart.

The humble gudgeon is not only the bait par excellence for big perch, zander also accept them readily when ledgered on a livebait/deadbait rig. Use only small trebles on the wire trace set 2 in apart. Size 10 is ideal.

As can be seen from fig. 5.68, immediately above the trace swivel is a 15-in length of reel line with a running bomb (1–2 oz) link ledger above the second swivel, and a 'cushioning' bead between them. This set-up rarely tangles and is most sensitive to the tentative bites for which zander are justly renowned.

When zander are biting in a particularly finicky way, a good method of instigating action is to ease the bait (live or dead) gently along the bottom every few minutes by slowly cranking the reel handle a couple of times and resetting the indicator.

If using a two-rod set up (most advisable when after zander, because only very rarely is sport fast and furious), a large expanse of water can be grid-searched by casting out both baits to a particular spot, and inching each back every few minutes, then repeating the procedure along a slightly different tack with each successive cast. Alternatively, plan to keep one bait static-fished at short to medium range (10–30 yd, say) while searching long-range areas with the 'retrieved' bait technique. However, it is also true that there are times when zander reinforce the fishermen's belief that 'patience is a virtue'. The puzzle is in sorting out which plan of action will work on the day.

Ledgering live and deadbaits for perch

Much of what has already been said about ledgering for zander with live and dead baits also applies to perch, especially the common denominator of water clarity. In fact, I have only ever enjoyed good results with a ledgered deadbait in the deep and permanently coloured waters of old clay or marle pits, where the sediment is held in suspension, or in meres so rich in green or brown plankton that visibility is too bad for the perch to hunt by sight alone. And I am talking of inches here, not feet. When a perch can see its prey from 2 or 3 ft away, my confidence in deadbaits is much reduced and my thoughts switch immediately to presenting livebaits.

However, when offering a completely static deadbait, there is nothing better than a small, freshly killed little perch, which really does sort out the bigger perch of 2 lb

and over. What is more, I find perch of between 5 and 6 in long weighing perhaps 2 oz the perfect bait. If big perch are the quarry, do not mess about with minnows or gudgeon, which any perch of 6 oz upwards can manage with ease. Go straight for the very largest perch (and the odd pike, of course), which feel confident in sucking up a comparatively large deadbait from the bottom. Concentrate only on the very deepest swims, and from late autumn onwards throughout the winter months.

At this point we arrive at whether to use a wire trace or not, and from fig. 5.68 you can see that my preference is for a mono trace of around 15 in long made from the same 6 lb test reel line. In over 30 years of pike fishing using wire traces, I can only recall a handful of big perch that have been stupid enough to accept the bait, both live and dead. I am sure, on numerous occasions, perch have momentarily picked up static pike deadbaits from the bottom, only to reject them, resulting in dropped run after dropped run (while pike fishing) with seemingly little explanation. The truth is that any form of compromise means missing out on big perch in the net.

As can be seen from the perch/zander ledger rig, a run is registered by the monkey climber body rising slowly to the top of the needle. At this point resist all temptation to strike anywhere near as hard as you would for pike. Merely wind down to the perch until all is solid and bend the rod back into a full curve. This usually results in much head-shaking as it endeavours to eject the bait, so keep the line tight, which allows the hook to find a purchase – or the bait will simply pop out. It is that simple. Fancy multi-hook rigs are simply not worth the bother. A single wide gape size 2–4 eyed hook tied direct to the 6 lb mono trace and nicked through the chin will fold on the strike and be pointing in the right direction for the best chance of penetration whether offering a live or deadbait.

BASIC RUNNING LEDGER RIG FOR EELS AND CATFISH

The rig I employ when ledgering for eels and wels catfish is, in format, little different from my zander rig, except that I increase the reel line to 11–15 lb test (depending upon existing snags and the size of fish expected), and the rod's test curve to 2–2½ lb.

As can be seen from fig. 5.69, there is a 15 in section of mono above the trace with a swivel at each end, which stops the running bomb (¾–1 oz) ledger from tangling and possibly causing a fish to eject the bait. Incidentally, if actually fishing close to snags, construct the bomb link from much lighter mono than reel line (a rotten bottom) so it quickly parts company and ditches the bomb if it becomes snagged.

With catfish in mind (though, of course, in waters where they co-exist, eels are regularly caught when seeking whiskers because they are attracted to the identical baits) a 15 in bottom trace of 20 lb test mono is quite sufficient to withstand the abrasive action of numerous bristle-like teeth. The same might also be said of eels, except that every so often an eel will twist and squirm so violently that a mono trace becomes chaffed and eventually chewed through by the eel's teeth, which, in truth, are no more formidable than those of the wels catfish.

To be sure rather than sorry, construct your eel traces from 15 in of 15 lb test alasticum wire. You may well suffer the occasional refusal from a particularly choosy eel

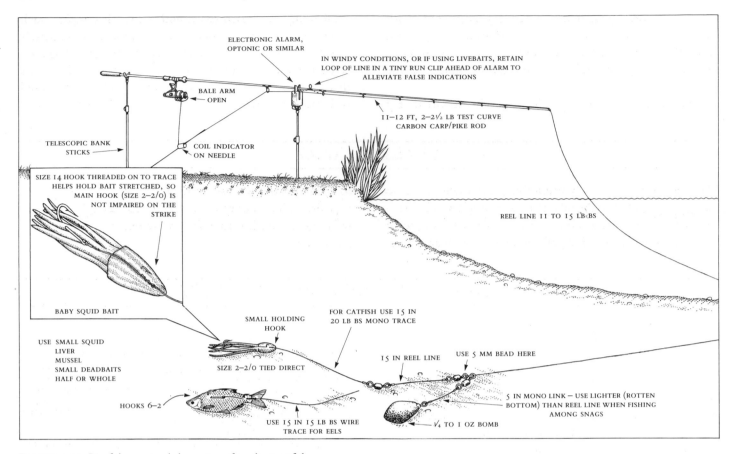

ELECTRONIC ALARM,
OPTONIC OR SIMILAR

IN WINDY CONDITIONS, OR IF USING LIVEBAITS, RETAIN
LOOP OF LINE IN A TINY RUN CLIP AHEAD OF ALARM TO
ALLEVIATE FALSE INDICATIONS

BALE ARM
— OPEN

11–12 FT, 2–2½ LB TEST CURVE
CARBON CARP/PIKE ROD

TELESCOPIC BANK
STICKS

COIL INDICATOR
ON NEEDLE

SIZE 14 HOOK THREADED ON TO TRACE
HELPS HOLD BAIT STRETCHED, SO
MAIN HOOK (SIZE 2–2/0) IS
NOT IMPAIRED ON THE
STRIKE

REEL LINE 11 TO 15 LB BS

BABY SQUID BAIT

USE SMALL SQUID
LIVER
MUSSEL
SMALL DEADBAITS
HALF OR WHOLE

SMALL HOLDING
HOOK

FOR CATFISH USE 15 IN
20 LB BS MONO TRACE

15 IN REEL LINE

USE 5 MM BEAD HERE

SIZE 2–2/0 TIED DIRECT

HOOKS 6–2

USE 15 IN 15 LB BS WIRE
TRACE FOR EELS

5 IN MONO LINK – USE LIGHTER (ROTTEN
BOTTOM) THAN REEL LINE WHEN FISHING
AMONG SNAGS

¼ TO 1 OZ BOMB

FIGURE 5.69 *Big-fish running ledger set-up for eels or catfish*

when contemplating making a meal of your bait mounted on wire, but at least you won't lose many once hooked. To complete the trace (whether wire or mono) thread on a tiny size 14 eyed hook before adding the size 6–2/0 wide gape, strong, forged, straight-eyed hook. Select sizes 6–2 for eels, depending on bait size, and sizes 2–2/0 for catfish.

There is a very good and important reason for this additional tiny hook sliding on the trace, because without it the bait will either shift position during the cast and mask the hook point when you strike, or wedge down over the gape the second you bend into the fish. It is there simply as a holding device for keeping the bait straight or stretched, and thus attractively presented. To hold the small hook in the desired position, simply wrap the trace around its shank a few times (as you would the top treble on a pike trace) before pushing the point and bend firmly into one end of the bait. The main, or 'business', hook can now be lightly nicked into the flesh of the bait with the entire gap and point clear for perfect penetration on the strike.

As most sessions in search of eels and catfish are planned 'all-nighters' (and should be, if you want the best possible chance of connecting with either), an electronic bite alarm as the front rod rests is imperative, as there will be long periods of inactivity. Always present the bait with the bale arm open, allowing a long, resistance-free run to develop

with the line retained beneath a lightweight coil or silver foil indicator slipped onto a needle to stop it moving about in the wind.

Also advisable when fishing in blustery conditions, and especially if presenting livebaits, is to retain a loop of line beneath a narrow-profile plastic run-clip or an elastic band fixed tightly around the rod in front of the bite alarm. This totally alleviates the nuisance of false indications, enabling you to relax until a genuine run occurs.

Invariably, lightweight indicators fall off as the line zooms upwards and starts to peel from the open spool. Now at this point, no amount of planning or advice can possibly prepare you for, or indeed have any bearing on, what happens next. One night you will close the bale arm while the line peels off in the most positive of runs, wait for all to tighten firmly, and promptly set the hook perfectly into an eel or catfish on the strike. On another session you are just as likely to miss screaming runs of a similar nature one after another.

In truth, there is no easy explanation. At times the culprits are, of course, either immature eels, baby catfish or even carp, each of which is liable to pick up a small squid or whole mussel, for instance, and do a runner. So do not despair. You can experiment by reducing bait and even hook size and try striking early the very second the indicator rises to the top of the needle. And this does definitely work, producing some very large and wary specimen fish in the process. On other occasions, you can allow the eel or catfish to run until it would seem to bury itself in the opposite bank, yet still fail to connect on the strike.

To enhance the chances of runs from eels and catfish, try pre-baiting the chosen swim with hookbait samples, such as chunks of raw liver, cockles, the insides of swan mussels or small, freshly killed fish, etc., every other evening for a week prior to fishing. However, do *not* pre-bait waters that are prolific in carp, pike or small eels, or you could well receive rather more action than you bargained for.

LIVEBAITING

There is good reason why using livebait to catch pike is so effective. By offering the pike an exact part of its daily diet – live fish – the presentation arouses far less suspicion and caution when the pike grabs hold of it, compared, say, to when it chomps on something alien and metallic such as an artificial lure, or even a wobbled deadbait, that does not try to get away. It is therefore more likely to keep hold of a live bait.

FLOAT-FISHED 'FREE-ROAMING' LIVEBAITS

Close-range rig

As can be seen from fig. 5.70A, my float rig for close-range free-roaming livebaiting is simplicity itself, incorporating one or two swan shot on the trace to keep the bait down, and a 1-in diameter pilot float plugged to the line with a thin, 2 in stem of peacock quill.

It is well worth taking time to grease the line above the float for 20–30 yd with solid mucilin (available in tins complete with felt applicator pad), to stop the line from sinking between rod tip and float. Otherwise, the bait's movements are hampered and it immediately becomes far less attractive. Apart from which, striking becomes impaired when the line is heavily sunk. But with the line floating nicely on the surface film, even small (5–7 in) livebaits can be encouraged to work long distances, and thus present themselves to pike over a greater area in either still or running water.

Because by its nature I consider free-roaming livebaiting to be a truly roving technique, I usually prefer to hold the rod in order to 'work' the bait, encouraging it to swim wherever I suspect pike might be lying. For instance, gentle pressure against the bait invariably encourages it to swim off in the opposite direction, so the bale arm is left open with just a gentle pressure against the spool with the forefinger. And whenever the line forms into a huge bow due to the bait's movement, current or wind direction, it is a simple matter (because it is well greased) to lift the line from the water without affecting the bait's direction and to straighten it.

Consider the typical pike river in fig. 5.71, for instance, where, due to careful use of the flow pattern to trot the bait downstream over choice lies, and delicate float control to veer it across the flow before retrieving slowly and trotting

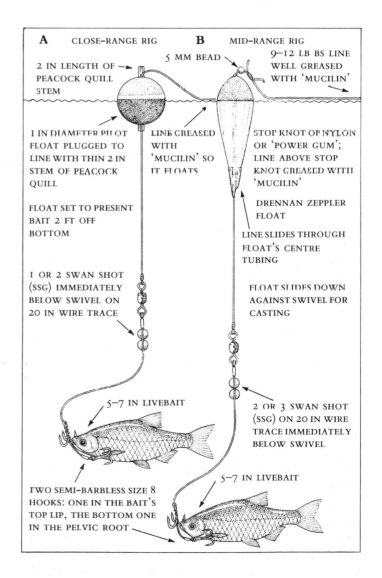

FIGURE 5.70 *Float-fished free-roaming livebaits for still or running water*

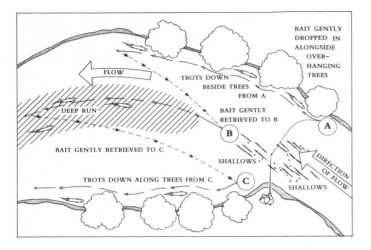

FIGURE 5.71 *On small to medium rivers maximize the area covered by each cast in order to preserve the livebait's strength and will to work*

down again, every pike has an opportunity to see the bait. Only one actual cast has been made, minimizing disturbance and maximizing the bait's freshness and strength, whereas continual casting would soon sap the bait's capacity to work.

In small to medium-sized rivers, pike (especially the larger, craftier ones) often succumb during that first all-important cast and trot through, provided the bait is set at an acceptable depth beneath the float, say 2 ft off bottom. When pike have learnt to associate the disturbance caused by an angler with danger, the chance of success diminishes with each successive cast.

It goes without saying, of course, that a careful approach up to the water is very important. Pretend you are chub fishing and show the pike equal respect. It is no less sensitive than other species even though it owns a mouthful of sharp teeth.

Striking

A few lines are in order at this stage about that age-old problem, when is the best time to strike a pike that has taken a livebait, because they do tend to hang on tightly, even to relatively small baits. Whereas with static deadbaits,

the pike seems to know that the bait is not going to put up a fight and it invariably sucks it straight back for swallowing.

With artificial lures you are compelled to strike immediately, quicker than the pike can eject it. But with livebaits a decision has to be made, and I am of the view that it is always better to strike early than late. To miss a small pike through striking prematurely is infinitely better than to deeply hook a big pike that has totally gorged the bait. And there is no way of telling what size of predator has grabbed your livebait. Adopt the view that if the hook comes unstuck on the strike or on the way in, the fish probably was not worth catching anyway. You will then suffer few deeply hooked fish.

The beauty of presenting relatively small livebaits is that as soon as the float goes positively under and away (often accompanied by a glorious swirl in shallow swims), you can close the bale arm and tighten down until the weight of the fish is felt, and then lean the rod back powerfully into a full bend and firm strike. Don't allow the rod tip to straighten at any time because when the pike senses danger it will open its jaws and shake its head from side to side in an effort to ditch the bait. Keep the rod well bent and continue winding so that when the bait does move, the hooks will be pulled home. Bear in mind that until the pike opens its jaws it is impossible for the hooks to catch hold, so tightly does it hold the bait.

When temperatures are low take along a small, fine-meshed aquarium net so that you do not have to search with your hands for a fresh livebait in freezing cold water. Its price more than compensates for the alternative of painfully cold hands.

Medium-range rig

For presenting the bait at greater depths or distances in stillwaters, or deep down close to the bottom of medium-paced rivers, an additional swan shot or two must be added to the trace, and this necessitates a larger float such as a Drennan Zeppler, which is available in various sizes, or a pike tenpin No. 2.

RUNNING PATERNOSTER LIVEBAIT RIG

Occasions will arise when the free-roaming livebait has less effect and you need to keep the bait in one spot. This happens when the water is well coloured, as in poor visibility the pike needs more than the usual amount of time to home in on the livebait. Free-roaming livebaits can even outrun a pike in heavily coloured water, and so the running paternoster rig is used (fig. 5.72). This rig is also

effective during extremely low water temperatures, when pike are liable to be considerably more lethargic. Again, presentation of the bait in one spot allows the pike time to investigate its movements. Alternatively, you may wish to anchor the bait in the middle of a deep hole on the bend of a river where continually trotting a free-roaming bait proves unsuccessful; or to present it during windy condi-

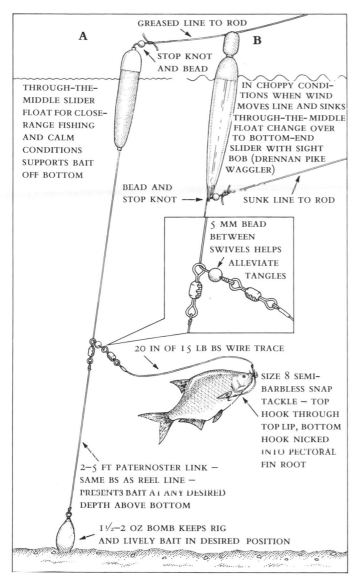

FIGURE 5.72 *Running paternoster livebait rig*

plummet. For instance, if after casting out and tightening up gently the float lies flat, it has been set too deep. And if it is taken beneath the surface it has been set too shallow. Ideally it should be set slightly deeper than the swim so that after tightening it remains upright and gently 'knocking' to the movements of the livebait. In case a violent, long run develops I like to fish with the bale arm open and a loop of line lightly clipped beneath a run clip or an elastic band situated around the handle immediately above the reel. A pike can then pull the loop free and take line from the open spool, but the livebait cannot. It is a simple yet effective ruse which works best with the rod set on two rests with the tip pointing at the float and angled upwards.

When fishing at distance or in strong winds, it is impossible to present a float-paternostered livebait with a greased line and through-the-middle slider. The wind bows the line and eventually pulls the rig away from the desired position. So you simply exchange the 'through-the-middle slider' for a bottom-only slider (such as the Drennan waggler pike float, which has an easily visible sight bob on the tip) and sink the line after casting – just as though you were roach fishing using a waggler float (as in fig. 5.72B), because exactly the same principles are involved. To ensure the line sinks quickly, keep a small bottle of neat washing-up liquid handy and dab a fingerful around the spool prior to casting. The bait can be presented at any depth from 2 ft off bottom upwards depending upon the length of the paternoster bomb link; you should allow for dense bottom weed or snags, and take into account pike that may be feeding among fry shoals, for instance, at mid-water. So increase or decrease the bomb link accordingly.

Before making each new cast and repositioning the bait, always make a point of inspecting the wire trace to ensure that constant bait movement has not kinked the wire. Badly kinked traces could easily fracture at the wrong moment, possibly leaving a set of trebles in the pike's throat. If in doubt, replace it with a new one. The cost of 20 in of wire to those who make their own traces is not worth thinking about (see 'Making wire traces' p. 92–3).

tions at various points along a deep gully in a gravel pit or lake without continually having to recast, as you would a free-roaming livebait.

As you can see from fig. 5.72A, the running paternoster is simple to construct, using the sliding float as a built-in

LEDGERED LIVEBAIT RIGS

Although livebaits usually work best when presented beneath floats and simultaneously provide immense visual enjoyment, there are situations which demand a ledgered bait because floats are impractical: for presenting the bait to pike on the bottom of deep, swirling weir pools, for instance, or pike occupying deep gullies far out in lakes or gravel pits, or during gale force conditions when any sort of float fishing is impossible.

Make up a simple running ledger as in fig. 5.73 with a 1–2 oz bomb clipped on to a 3 in anti-tangle boom stopped with a bead against the swivel of the 20 in snap-tackle trace. This gives an effective rig that casts well and presents the bait close to the bottom. To present the bait well off bottom to pike working the upper water layers, or to avoid the bait tangling with dense bottom weeds or snags, consider the benefits of the sunken float rig in fig. 5.74.

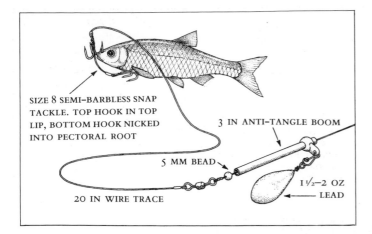

FIGURE 5.73 *Ledgered livebait rigs* 1

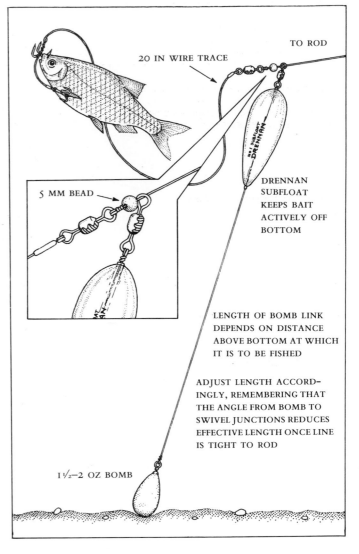

FIGURE 5.74 *Ledgered livebait rigs* 2

Again the set-up is kept simple, and is rather like the bottom end of the running float paternoster. Use a long bomb link with a Drennan clear plastic subfloat running free on the line. This rises and supports the livebait at the desired depth once the line has been tightened from reel to rig.

For bite indication when using these rigs, the drop-arm indicator is recommended because tension can be applied at the line clip to allow for constant pulling from the bait.

DEADBAITING

Big, fat old female pike in the majority of waters are far more susceptible to sucking up a static deadbait from the bottom than they are to chasing about after livebaits, particularly in heavily coloured waters where the pike's senses are geared decidedly more towards smelling out their food than sighting and chasing it. And so, presenting the easily located and taken 'static' deadbait has become the big-fish method in the majority of fisheries; except, perhaps, those clear-flowing rivers where the pike invariably show a preference for a moving bait.

THE FLOAT-FISHED STATIC DEADBAIT

In stillwater

The most enjoyable and effective way of presenting the static deadbait is beneath a float, because apart from minimizing resistance to a pike taking the bait (compared, say, to ledgering with a heavy bomb) a float also gives you something nice to watch. There really is nothing quite like observing the drunken antics of a deadbait float. It is almost possible to imagine what is going on down below by relating it to the movements of the float.

I prefer a sliding float with the line (greased above the float) passing through the centre for close-range work in stillwaters, where it won't get blown about and thus move the bait, as in the flat float rig (fig. 5.75A). For general fishing and most other situations, including really windy weather, consider the waggler-type rig in fig. 5.75B,

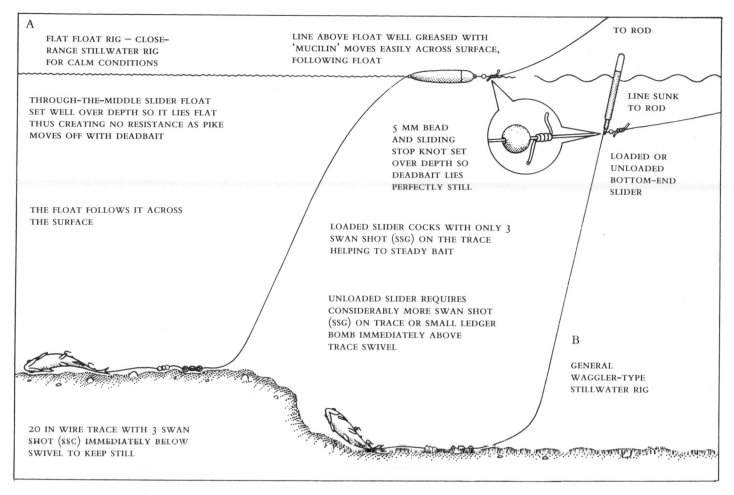

A

FLAT FLOAT RIG — CLOSE-
RANGE STILLWATER RIG
FOR CALM CONDITIONS

LINE ABOVE FLOAT WELL GREASED WITH
'MUCILIN' MOVES EASILY ACROSS SURFACE,
FOLLOWING FLOAT

TO ROD

THROUGH-THE-MIDDLE SLIDER FLOAT
SET WELL OVER DEPTH SO IT LIES FLAT
THUS CREATING NO RESISTANCE AS PIKE
MOVES OFF WITH DEADBAIT

LINE SUNK
TO ROD

5 MM BEAD
AND SLIDING
STOP KNOT SET
OVER DEPTH SO
DEADBAIT LIES
PERFECTLY STILL

LOADED OR
UNLOADED
BOTTOM-END
SLIDER

THE FLOAT FOLLOWS IT ACROSS
THE SURFACE

LOADED SLIDER COCKS WITH ONLY 3
SWAN SHOT (SSG) ON THE TRACE
HELPING TO STEADY BAIT

UNLOADED SLIDER REQUIRES
CONSIDERABLY MORE SWAN SHOT
(SSG) ON TRACE OR SMALL LEDGER
BOMB IMMEDIATELY ABOVE
TRACE SWIVEL

B

GENERAL
WAGGLER-TYPE
STILLWATER RIG

20 IN WIRE TRACE WITH 3 SWAN
SHOT (SSG) IMMEDIATELY BELOW
SWIVEL TO KEEP STILL

FIGURE 5.75 *The float-fished static deadbait in stillwaters*

where the line passes through the bottom eye and is sunk from float to rod tip just as in waggler fishing for other species in stillwaters.

The secret of presenting a deadbait beneath a float lies in ensuring that it remains absolutely static. Pike will then confidently suck it up, but not if the float is set too shallow causing the bait's tail to be monotonously lifted up each time the float bobs up and down with the waves. This is why I like to set the sliding float well over depth, whether it fishes flat or upright; at least twice as deep as the swim, so that at least a couple of feet of line lie along the bottom in addition to the trace and bait. In no way will the pike then feel any degree of buoyancy from the float as it engulfs the bait in its jaws. And as a result you will experience very few dropped runs using static deadbaits.

A static deadbait offered on the bottom produces a noticeably higher average-sized pike.

THE FLOAT-FISHED STATIC BAIT IN RUNNING WATER

In really slow-moving rivers use the general waggler rig in fig. 5.76 with a small bomb on the line above the trace to ensure the bait lies static. But for fast-running water,

because it lies flat and cannot be submerged by the flow, the close-range flat float rig (fig. 5.70, p. 199) is ideal so long as the cast is made directly downstream and the rod

Large, spooky pike living in hard-fished, clear-water fisheries – be they rivers or lakes – respond to static deadbaits with far more enthusiasm at night, as Bruce Vaughan knows only too well.

The sight of the red float-top suddenly sneaking across the surface of a lake or pit makes float-fishing a static deadbait an exciting method. Doug Allen caught this nicely marked double on a mackerel tail.

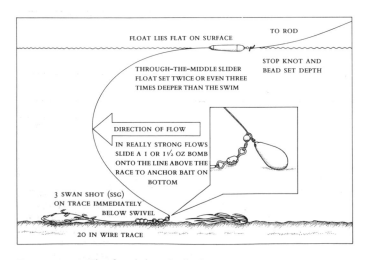

FIGURE 5.76 *Flat float-ledger rig for fast-running water*

tip angled upwards to keep the line off the surface. Those who like to stret peg for roach or chub during the winter months will know all about the mechanics of presenting a static bait with this method.

With both of these float rigs, after tightening up and positioning the rod on two rests set horizontally, the bale arm is opened and a loop of line clipped beneath an elastic band or run clip fixed around the handle. This is a safety measure against the occasional suicidal pike that really belts off with the bait, and of course against those unforgivable occasions when you failed to notice the float trundling away. We are all human, and there is no point in losing a rod and reel from the rests through sloppiness.

As when livebaiting, I prefer to strike straight away when presenting static deadbaits, on the basis that if it comes off it was probably a small pike anyway.

Half baits

I only ever use relatively small whole baits, say up to 7–8 in long – smelt, herrings and the like. In fact, for most static deadbait situations these days I much prefer to use half baits. I am certain that when cut in half the freshness and oily attractiveness of a deadbait permeates considerably quicker through stillwater, and a half mackerel is nothing compared to the size of the jaws of a 10 lb pike.

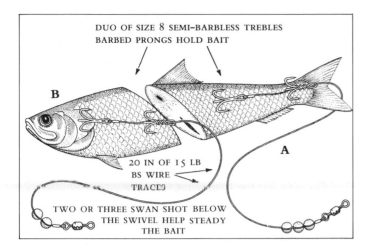

FIGURE 5.77 *Mounting half baits*

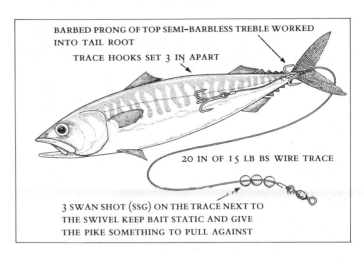

FIGURE 5.78 *Presenting a whole, static deadbait 1*

The best way of presentation is to cut the bait in half diagonally and mount it as in fig. 5.77A, using the standard duo (snap-tackle) of semi-barbless size 8 trebles.

Whole baits

When offering whole baits, fix the duo of trebles firmly into the tail root and along the flank as in fig. 5.78, with a distance of around 3 in between hooks. This allows the pike to swallow a good half of the bait before the hooks enter the throat tissue, and will result in few deeply hooked pike.

Pike do occasionally (after being caught on them several times) become suspicious of the static deadbait always lying flat on the bottom, and to buoy its head upwards by injecting it with air or inserting foam strip can produce runs from spooky fish (see fig. 5.79).

FIGURE 5.79 *Presenting a whole, static deadbait 2*

FREELINING AND LEDGERING FOR PIKE

When weather conditions, especially high winds, render float fishing impossible, or the deadbait needs to be cast long distances at which the float is impractical, say 50 yds plus, then a simple freeline or ledger rig is used.

I dislike using any appreciable amount of weight on the line (apart from three swan shot on the trace) when presenting static deadbaits, unless absolutely necessary. Heavy bombs lessen the sensitivity of the static bait, and because the line passes through while the bomb stays put (often creating a right angle of line between bait and rod tip) striking also could be impaired (see fig. 5.80A). Whereas with a freelined bait the line simply follows the route of the pike and is easy to straighten for a quick, positive strike (see fig. 5.80B).

Provided the bait (with just three, or a maximum of four

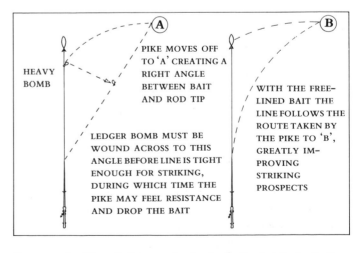

FIGURE 5.80 *The effectiveness of a simple, freelined static deadbait*

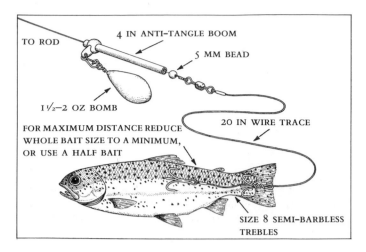

FIGURE 5.81 *Simple, distance static deadbait rig*

trace (as in fig. 5.81). Small, firm-bodied whole fish of between 4 and 5 in cast well and are not likely to break up.

Whether freelining or ledgering the static deadbait, bites are best registered on drop-off/arm indicators, which fit on the rear rod rests and clip to the line once the bale arm has been opened. As a precaution against deeply hooked pike, strike any indication of a bite immediately when ledgering or freelining.

Ledgering, again using the drop arm as bite indicator, is an effective way of presenting the static deadbait in running water. To minimize water pressure against the line, set the rod on two rests with the tip angled up high. Very often a definite 'knock' is seen on the rod tip (just as when ledgering for chub) as the pike sucks the bait up before moving off, at which point the line should be released from the indicator and the rod held. There then comes an eerie sensation as the line slips positively through the fingers in response to the run of the pike. But don't let it run too far. Close the bale arm and as soon as the fish's weight plus the current pulls the rod over into a full bend, whack the hooks home hard.

swan shot on the trace) can be cast to the desired spot (and a mackerel tail can easily be pushed 60 yd out), a freelined bait is best. If not, then rig up a simple ledger with the bomb attached to a 4 in anti-tangle boom sliding above the

FISHING AT NIGHT

Presenting static deadbaits during darkness is something worth trying on clear-watered rivers, lakes or pits which receive regular attention from pike fishermen during the day time.

Pike are certainly no different to all other species in that they become far less suspicious of baits offered them under the cloak of darkness. Pre-bait two separate areas so that, should the first fail to produce for any reason, after an hour you can move and try the next. In fact, if fishing at night starts to catch on, there is nothing to stop you pre-baiting and keeping several swims going.

Take along just two rods and start by placing one bait really close into the bank, with the second further out or deliberately next to a particular feature. Use simple freeline tactics with two or three swan shot on the trace next to the swivel, adding a bomb above the trace only to counteract a strong flow when river fishing.

For bite indication use drop arms or monkey climbers which incorporate luminous betalight elements, or simply illuminate the indicators with a wide-beam, low-powered torch laid on the ground away from the water and your line of vision.

WOBBLING DEADBAITS

Retrieving a small dead fish mounted head first on the trace so that pike assume it is alive and grab hold, is an extremely effective and exciting technique guaranteed to keep you casting and thinking all day long, just as in lure fishing.

It is also a very versatile, mobile method which provides total coverage of any given area. For instance, if you like to fish with a two-rod set-up to increase your chances in big stillwaters, but nothing is coming to the static deadbaits being presented on each, reel one in and cover the area in more depth by wobbling a deadbait in a grid-searching pattern. A total blank when pike are not moving around

and hunting out your static baits, can be turned into an exciting session by taking the bait to the fish through continually searching with a wobbled bait. This situation occurs most commonly in deep, coloured lakes and pits during long periods of low light values, such as day upon day of overcast weather. Unless you almost hit a pike on the head with a wobbled deadbait they simply do not move about much. The situation can, of course, change instantly if the weather does, when the strong rays of the sun penetrate deep, dark water. Suddenly pike are on the move, and in a short feeding burst several runs might come to previously untouched static deadbaits in as many

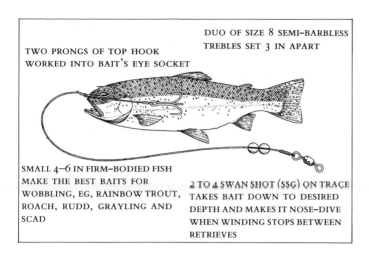

FIGURE 5.82 *Hooking a deadbait for wobbling*

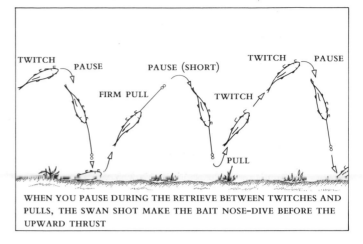

FIGURE 5.83 *Make your wobbled deadbait come to life on the retrieve by pulling and jerking it erratically*

minutes. Such feeding sprees, however, rarely last more than a couple of hours, and a switch to working the wobbled deadbait (still leaving one static on the bottom) could well keep pike coming to the net throughout the rest of the day.

To mount deadbaits for wobbling, fix the trebles so they are just 3 in apart by wrapping the wire around the shank of the upper treble, and firmly embed two of its prongs into the bait's eye socket. The bottom treble is nicked with the barbed prong only into the bait's flank along the lateral line (see fig. 5.82). The deadbait is now firmly rigged for casting and when retrieved will wobble attractively. When the top hook eventually pulls through the socket, re-rig on the other side.

For fishing over thick weed or in shallow water do not add any weight to the trace, but to keep the bait down close to the bottom where pike lie during the colder months you will need somewhere between two and four swan shot pinched on to the trace immediately below the swivel. It all depends on the depth and the rate at which you retrieve.

Where the bottom contours vary due to weed-beds, shallow bars, snags and so on, you need to retrieve the bait well up lest it catches, say, 3 or 4 ft above where you imagine the bottom to be. In lakes and pits of even depth where the bottom is clear, however, you can twitch the bait along, almost bumping pike on the nose. To do this, allow the bait to reach bottom before starting the retrieve. Then wind erratically, but very slowly; try to 'feel' what is happening down below. Keep the rod tip at an angle to the bait and watch it for any indication of a taking fish. Every so often give the tip a jerk or a twitch, followed by a couple of fast turns on the reel handle. Then pause, allowing the bait to nose-dive for a couple of feet before twitching it back up again (as in fig. 5.83). Remember that the swan shots hit bottom ahead of the bait, so if you lift it

quickly upwards you will not pick up much bottom debris. In the past this technique was called sink and draw because you allowed the bait to sink before drawing it up again.

Now for the strike. Do not wait for the pike to grab and then turn the bait in its jaws by giving it free line when you feel a 'take'. Pike react completely differently when snatching at a wobbled deadbait from when sucking up a resistance-free static from the bottom, when time is given. So unless you want the pike to drop the bait, whack it immediately by winding quickly down until you feel its full weight, and follow through with a long, powerful strike to put the hooks home, striking a second time to make doubly sure. At this point the pike tries to eject the bait by opening its jaws and shaking its head, so keep a good bend in the rod or the hooks will literally drop out.

Wobbling in running water

In slow-moving water, mounting and retrieving the wobbled deadbait is exactly the same as in stillwater and it is great fun to work the bait purposefully alongside regular pike hideouts such as overhanging or sunken willows and have it taken at the very place you imagined a pike to be lying. This is reading the water at its very best, and provides a mobile method of fishing where, with a pocketful of fresh baits, miles of winding river can be searched, wobbling beside all the 'feature' swims.

In deep, cold, fast rivers, however, where pike keep close to the bottom, a slightly different approach is called for, in the form of a 3 ft nylon kink joined to the reel line 1 ft above the trace (see fig. 5.84). A small bomb goes on the business end for bouncing along the bottom. A snap swivel allows for a quick change of bombs.

This rig ensures that the bait works just above the pike's

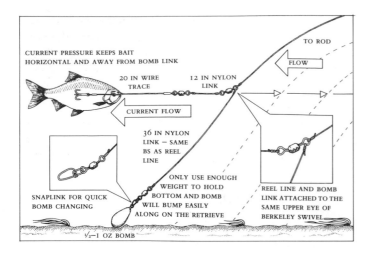

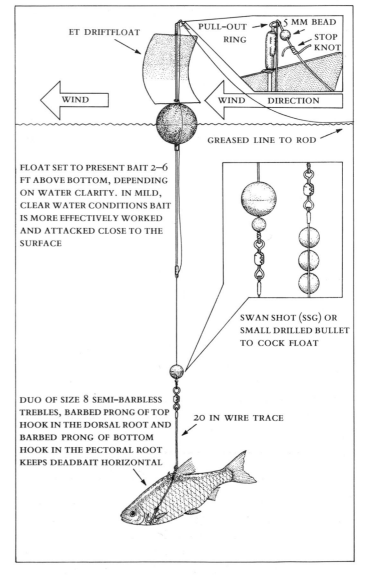

immediate field of vision, which is so important, especially in coloured water. Bumping the bait systematically across the bottom of a deep weir pool, for instance, can be great fun, resulting in some thunderous takes, and apart from ledgering the bait, no other method ensures the bait is actively presented just off bottom where the vast majority of cold-water pike will be lying.

As when wobbling in the usual manner, strike the minute the pike grabs hold, with a long, hard, sweeping strike, taking a step or two backwards to keep that rod fully bent, lest the fish manages some slack and ejects the bait.

FIGURE 5.84 *Wobbling in running water*

FLOAT-DRIFTING DEADBAITS AND LIVEBAITS FOR PIKE

Float-drifting deadbaits is a method which really works best and covers the maximum area from an anchored boat (see 'Boat fishing' p. 210), but may be used to good effect in large stillwaters fished from a headland when there is a strong wind coming from behind (see fig. 5.85). The line must be greased so that it floats well. Note how, by allowing a belly to form between rod tip and float, the same line can be held as the rig is taken down the lake (line must be given during this time from an open spool) until it comes to rest in the lee of the wind, having covered and possibly shown the bait to pike lying over an enormous area. Start by casting a short way out, and once the bait comes to rest downwind retrieve slowly (in case a pike takes the bait on the way in), then recast a little further out each time. Using the wind and waves to bounce the bait attractively about is a fascinating way of presenting a deadbait to pike, which in many cases assume the bait to be live due to its erratic action.

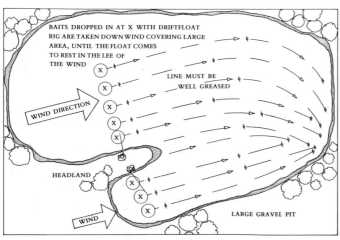

FIGURE 5.85 *Float-drifting deadbaits or livebaits*

FIGURE 5.86 *Driftfloat rig*

Presenting deadbaits and livebaits with the aid of a sail-type drift float is a great way of exploring vast areas of still water that are way beyond practical casting range, where the pike are rarely disturbed.

There are numerous sail-like drift floats now available, like the original ET Drifter shown in fig. 5.86. Note how the bait is presented horizontally to simulate the position of a live fish. It can be set to fish at any depth from within 2 ft of the bottom upwards, and in coloured water it is best presented closer to the bottom. In reality, however, taking into account a large area of water where, during the drift on a particular line or arc, depths of 10 to 18 ft of water may be encountered, my advice would be to set the float (easily rigged as a slider with bead and stop knot above) to fish the deadbait at 9 ft. It will then not foul bottom and has the possibility of attracting pike from almost every depth if the water is not too coloured. The beauty of drift-fishing is that as so much water is covered, action can come at any time from the moment when the bait is first plopped in to over 100 yd away. It is imperative when drift fishing to use a long, powerful rod and to have the spool of your reel full to the brim with fresh line, otherwise

the distance that you can cover will definitely be limited.

The best way of rigging the ET Drifter is with the line passing through the small, detachable ring on top of the stem and then through the swivel at the bottom of the stem, so the greased line floats easily on the surface throughout the drift. A sharp pull at the end of the drift, or indeed when a run occurs and the pike is struck, will release the line from the top ring, instantly converting the drifter to a waggler (bottom end only) for easy retrieval.

Drifting livebaits

The only difference is in swapping the deadbait for a small livebait. Remember to fix the hooks as described in the livebaiting section (p. 129), with one barbed prong of the top treble through the bait's top lip and one prong of the bottom treble nicked into its pectoral root – semi-barbless size 8s, of course.

Striking

When the float suddenly sinks to a pike which has grabbed the bait (alive or dead) 80 to over 100 yd away, it is not enough simply to wind down until the line is tight, and then strike. The amount of stretch in even 50 yd of 10 lb monofilament is enormous, and when contemplating setting the hooks successfully with twice as much line out, a new approach is required. In fact, there is no way of striking the hooks home when distance fishing. You simply point the rod at the pike, tighten up the clutch on your reel (so it does not slip under pressure and cause line twist) and keep winding like a person possessed until you feel the weight of the fish. And you keep on winding, and dragging the pike towards you, until it senses danger and opens its jaws to eject the bait. At this point, so long as the line is kept tight, the hooks should catch hold. A really big fish just may swim off in the opposite direction and help to pull the hooks home, but most pike will be led towards the rod for quite some distance. Once the pike's head-shaking routine has been transmitted up the line and the hooks are obviously well in, readjust the reel's clutch, keep the rod in a full curve and enjoy the fight.

BOAT-FISHING FOR PIKE

Echo-sounders are a great addition for locating the deepest areas of waters both large and small, but are not, a prerequisite for catching pike. Their use can come later, when you have learnt the fundamentals of boat-fishing. The same can be said of outboard engines. Huge waters apart, you will learn to understand and be at one with pike

fishing from an open dinghy far better by rowing quietly and positively, not aimlessly flitting from one area to another simply because getting there is easy with an engine.

It helps to divide the boat up mentally into two equal parts so that each angler has his own corresponding area of

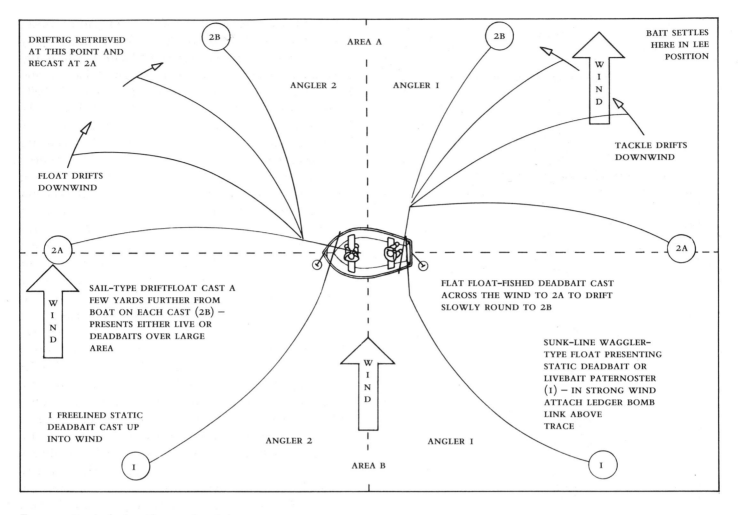

FIGURE 5.87 *Anchoring side-on to the wind*

water to fish, assuming that the weather permits an ideal mooring side on to the wind. This takes a little extra time and concentration, but the results are so much better than rowing out and simply lowering the mudweights over the side, as fig. 5.87 illustrates.

Both anglers have an equal area to work and search, regardless of methods used, with an invisible line drawn across the middle of the boat and water. When the wind is too uncomfortable for a side-on anchorage, or when even the heaviest weights will not hold, it is advisable to anchor bows into the wind (fig. 5.88). Start by lowering the bows mudweight and pay out at least twice the depth of rope so that whenever wave action lifts the bows, it does not bounce the mudweight (fig. 5.89A). Get it wrong (fig. 5.89B) and the boat will not hold position in strong winds. Once the long bows rope and mudweight are holding, put down the stern mudweight on a relatively short (steadying) rope. The imaginary dividing line between the anglers then runs down the length of the boat, through the middle from bows to stern, so each can fish out from his own side with a full 180° to cover.

You will see from the diagrams (assuming two rods are used by each angler) that each also fishes across the water without affecting the other so long as the invisible line is adhered to. This is important because it maximizes the potential pike areas around the boat in a whole 360° circle, and provides a mental picture of the divisions within the area for experimenting with various techniques.

Remember when out afloat on a huge expanse of stillwater (unless you are fishing towards the shoreline up against obvious pike-holding features like reed-beds and overhanging or sunken trees) that there is generally little indication of where the bait should best be placed other than depth. So if the bottom is of even depth over much of the fishery it pays to think in terms of taking a grid-searching approach with the emphasis on downwind, across wind and upwind areas in relation to the boat's anchorage. This permits the use of virtually any method from the freelined static deadbait to drift-fishing livebaits or dead-baits. You simply use the most likely method on the day, or indeed a whole variety of methods throughout the day, until one is successful, considering weather and water conditions as you would if bank-fishing.

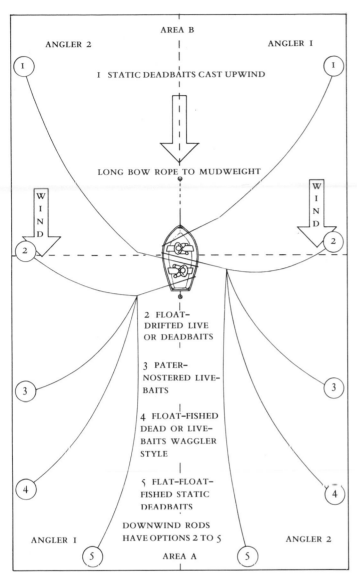

FIGURE 5.88 *Anchoring bows into the wind*

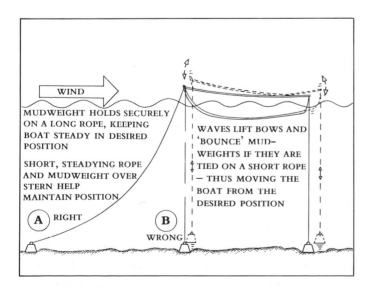

FIGURE 5.89 *Anchoring in strong winds*

For instance, consider area A in fig. 5.87, part of which, being in the lee of the wind, can be fished effectively by Angler 1 with a greased line and 'sliding flat float rig' presenting a static deadbait on the bottom. What is more, by casting slightly across the wind and flicking off a belly of line downwind, the bait can even be drifted along the bottom for a while and worked into lee positions far in excess of distances that can be cast. Angler 2 could fish likewise or work his part of area A with either live or dead baits beneath a sail-type drift float (see p. 208), starting with short casts and working progressively further out after each drift. Both anglers could also wobble deadbaits or lure fish as alternative 'active' methods within area A.

Area B, which incorporates both across the wind and upwind options, is rarely used to full advantage by most pike fishermen because, unless the line is well sunk below the waves when float fishing, the bait is whisked away far too quickly downwind, resulting in both baits being ridiculously close to each other. This is hardly conducive to searching the entire area effectively. In this instance a waggler-type (bottom end) 'loaded slider rig' is perfect for presenting a static, bottom bait across the wind. In really gusty weather use an unloaded slider and add a bomb above the trace to nail the bait to the bottom. Angler 2 could fish his B area with a freelined static deadbait by casting it directly upwind. It is worth remembering always to pinch three or four swan shot on the trace immediately below the swivel so that drop-back runs can easily be detected. Without a float to create valuable slack the pike must feel a certain amount of resistance when sucking up a freelined static deadbait, steadied with swan shot, which is why they invariably belt off at speed directly away from the boat. Then again, it could be that the pike just happens to be working an upwind course when it locates the bait and simply carries on in that direction. Certainly this can be verified on those really windy days when most runs come to the upwind rod. Strangely, such occasions are far from uncommon, which prompts me to suggest that there is far more to the upwind phenomenon than meets the eye.

In really choppy weather with white horses topping the waves, for instance, when it becomes pertinent to anchor bows into the wind, I become more optimistic about the upwind baits being taken, even when casting range is greatly reduced. Incidentally, for maximum distance when pushing baits into a strong wind, the mackerel tail, due to its density, is hard to beat. Half an eel (the head end) casts well too.

There is no doubt that, once anchored, it pays dividends to present baits with varying methods within a grid and wind division basis. Think of the boat as your very own piece of bank in the middle of the lake, with the advantage of also having water behind in which to search.

When searching huge, even-depthed lakes, broads, meres or pits, there are days when in complete contrast to anchoring, fishing on the drift will produce numbers of pike. I much prefer mild weather for drifting because pike are generally more active and respond well to baits on the move, either wobbled deadbaits or artificial lures. The secret is to row well upwind to the very top of the fishery and to work back with the wind, working baits on both sides of the boat as it drifts slowly along. Manoeuvre the boat so it starts side-on to the wind and to ensure it remains that way for drifting at an acceptably slow rate, tie a keep-net behind the boat at each end to act as drogues.

Special boat drogues are available for fly fishing trout reservoirs where drifting is a popular technique because it covers so much water. So if you intend doing any amount of drift fishing, invest in a specialized drogue.

When a hot area is located, quickly lower the mudweights and explore the area exhaustively before continuing the drift. It is a wonderfully effective way of locating pike in vast areas of water that are completely bare of visible features. Obviously you can only wobble deadbaits or work artificial lures with the one rod, but there is nothing to stop you using a second, 'sleeping' outfit by trailing a deadbait behind the boat. This often takes pike that follow lures in but sheer away at the last moment. Try it and see.

River boat fishing

Boat-fishing in running water is virtually the same as in stillwater, except that current pace and direction must be taken into account. Rivers invariably contain very definite habitats and pike-holding features or areas, and because they are easier to read, you can quietly anchor to full advantage, spending say an hour or so in each likely spot before pulling the mudweights and drifting with the flow downstream to the next likely area.

So that each angler enjoys both up and downstream lies,

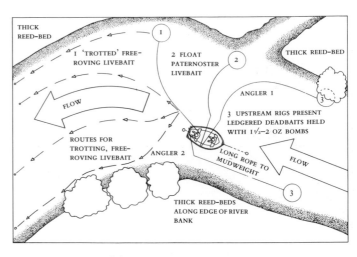

FIGURE 5.90 *Boat fishing on rivers*

consider the set-up in fig. 5.90, where the boat has been anchored bows-on to the flow, a rod's length out from one bank. Anchoring right in the middle is not only dangerous if other craft use the river regularly, it is invariably against the local river by-laws. Note that Angler 1 presents a ledgered deadbait on his upstream rod and a paternostered livebait on the downstream outfit, fished across the flow into the mouth of a confluence.

Angler 2 also fishes a ledgered deadbait on his 'sleeping' outfit, presented with the bale arm open and a loop of line trapped beneath a strong run clip or elastic band over the handle, so only the pull of a pike and not the current can initiate a run. His downstream rod presents a float-fished, free-roaming livebait trotted 2 ft off bottom, along different lines, searching across the river thoroughly. As change methods, both anglers could swap their livebait rigs for wobbled baits, artificial lures, or even static deadbaits when the river colours up after heavy rain and pike switch to hunting more by smell than a combination of vibrations and sight. Playing the waiting game with four static deadbaits from the one boat is then the best approach.

ARTIFICIAL LURE FISHING FOR PIKE

I say this quite without reservation: if you can catch pike (and any other predator) regularly from a wide spectrum of waters by fooling them into munching artificial lures constructed from quite alien materials such as plastic, copper, aluminium, steel, brass or wood, then by comparison every other technique should prove delightfully easy.

Without question, catching regularly on lures demands an optimum level of skill, and you need to have a fair idea of each fisheries character: the depths, the snags (otherwise it is costly for obvious reasons), the visible and non-visible

sub-surface habitats preferred by pike and so on. In other words, by pulling lures you enjoy a complete involvement with your quarry.

On a poor day when pike are unco-operative, the session could be put to good use by clipping on a heavy spoon and plummeting the depths all around the lake or pit for future occasions. By leaving the bale arm open after casting and using the countdown method (applicable to any sinking lure) of allowing roughly one foot in descent for every second counted, it is a simple and most enjoyable way of plummeting to obtain an accurate idea of the depth, plus

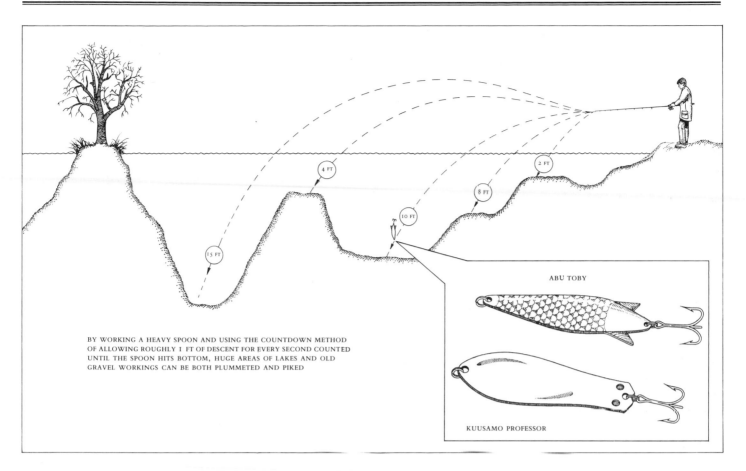

BY WORKING A HEAVY SPOON AND USING THE COUNTDOWN METHOD OF ALLOWING ROUGHLY I FT OF DESCENT FOR EVERY SECOND COUNTED UNTIL THE SPOON HITS BOTTOM, HUGE AREAS OF LAKES AND OLD GRAVEL WORKINGS CAN BE BOTH PLUMMETED AND PIKED

FIGURE 5.91 *Depth finding*

the exact whereabouts of shallow bars, plateaux, holes, gullies and so on (fig. 5.91). I favour heavy spoons for this wandering technique because they can be cast long distances, and flutter down to the bottom in an attractive way. Pike have grabbed hold so many times after just one turn of the handle to lift the spoon from the bottom at the start of the retrieve, that it cannot be coincidence.

Pike hear the spoon's arrival on the surface, and in clear water visually follow its route all the way down to the bottom, as they do with sinking lures. Throughout the retrieve hold the rod with the tip pointing at the lure, with just the slightest sideways deviation for twitching and jerking. If you hold the rod to one side, the hooks may not be driven home on the strike because of the incredible amount of stretch in monofilament. There is no chance of the line snapping with the rod pointing directly at the pike. Besides, when the hooks are felt to bite, you can raise the rod into its full curve and rely on the pre-set clutch to give line whenever the pike runs.

Occasionally, and this is more noticeable when you are fishing on a short line, pike will hit the artificial really hard and belt off all in one lovely, arm-wrenching movement, banging the hooks in hard as they turn. To facilitate hooking I doctor the trebles on most lures by gently

flattening all the barbs down, then hone each prong to a needlepoint with a file. This indispensible item I keep in the back pocket of my waist-coat so it is always at the ready. Lure trebles soon blunt from being continually retrieved through thick weeds, hitting the bottom and, of course, biting into the bone of a pike's jaw. And for the price of a good-quality file (which costs little more than just one lure), to fish with anything less than really sharp hooks is foolhardy.

A spoon is just one way of depth finding; an echo-sounder is the most effective but costly method (see p. 104). If you already fish a particular pike water for other species, you will no doubt already have a reasonable idea of its topography. The point is that many artificial lures have been designed not only to wiggle or dive or vibrate in a particular way due to their shape or weight, but to work in a particular depth band.

Take plugs, for instance, which fall into three basic categories: floaters, floating divers and sinking divers. It is pointless working a floating surface popper across 14 ft of cold water. In no way will the pike lying on the bottom shoot up and grab hold (fig. 5.92). By the same token, a sinking diver tossed into dense lily-pads, where it will become immobile after one crank of the reel handle, is equally useless. You really need to know the capabilities of

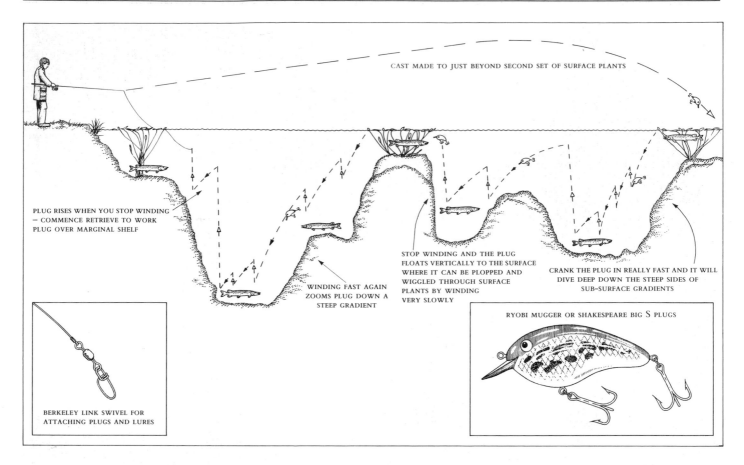

FIGURE 5.92 *Working a floating/diving plug above irregular bottom contours*

each and every artificial in your lure box, whether it floats, sinks or dives, and the respective depths to which each will dive on the retrieve; and, of course, their action (see pp. 133–5).

It is then a case of selecting a suitable artificial for the type of water or habitat at hand and making it come alive. For instance, and this applies particularly to clear water conditions, when a pike is following but will not hit, suddenly start speeding up the retrieve, making it faster and faster until you completely run out of water. It may well seem that time has run out, but then right at the last second the pike will make a lunge and grab hold with unbelievable speed. Do not chicken out and slow up over the last few yards or the pike will do the same and swim off disgruntled.

Conversely, when working lures deep down in coloured water the retrieve needs to be slow in order to allow the pike time to home in on it and grab hold.

Summer plugging

For imparting the most life-like action to surface plugs (and sub-surface lures), the best rod for the job is one with a snappy tip action (see p. 83–4). This is why the short, single-handed American bait-casting rods are so effective. Every single jerk and twitch is transferred to the artificial instead of being absorbed by the rod, as happens with soft-actioned, two-piece spinning rods.

With a surface lure, from the moment it touches the surface the retrieve should be as varied and as unusual as you can make it. Encourage it to gurgle by slamming the rod tip down to the surface. Jerk it, pause, twitch, gurgle again. Leave it static for a few seconds, jerk, twitch, pop, pause and so on. The variety of movements is as endless as the types of lures you can try. But be forever ready for that sudden hit by immediately whacking the rod back high to set the hooks and keep it high in a powerful curve, lest the pike's antics shake out the hooks. And for this it requires slack line. So play pike hard on artificials, giving line on demand, but begrudgingly.

Chub, perch and zander

Much that I have written about fishing for pike also applies to catching chub, perch and zander on artificials, because they behave in a similar way.

My favourite outfit is a 5½ ft, single-handed, American bait-casting rod coupled to a baby multiplier well heeled

On only his second trip afloat on massive Lough Corrib in the south of Ireland, John experienced a fabulous battle with this long, mean, 25-pounder caught with a copper spoon on the troll.

The action of spinner baits is attractive to perch, zander, chub and pike. If the large, single hook fails to connect on the strike, a much-improved hooking ratio is achieved by wiring on a size 8 or 6 treble hook.

with 8 lb test. This may seem heavy line, but it is an insurance against the odd big pike that might happen along and against the rigours of working lures through heavy weed. For the same reasons I connect the lure to a 10 lb, 6 in alasticum wire trace.

Any light-action spinning rod and small fixed-spool reel will suffice. However, on the baby American combo all chub seem like whoppers.

If worked erratically enough, any surface popper will persuade a chub into having a go. You impart the action by twitching it, popping, jerking, skipping it across the surface and so on.

Having said this, on numerous occasions when working artificials I have experienced chub coming up to grab hold of a plug that is simply being trotted downstream on the surface of a long run prior to being retrieved.

To obtain maximum enjoyment from working artificial lures, particularly for the smaller predators like chub and this splendid perch, invest in a short, single-handed, trigger-grip rod and a baby multiplier. On such an outfit virtually any pike feels like a monster.

Equipped with the bare minimum of tackle for an enjoyable 'hit and run' search along an overgrown river, John uses forceps to carefully remove a small floating plug from a chub while it is still in the water.

I have also used weedless crayfish imitations to good effect and I particularly love the action of buzz baits – a lightly-leaded jig to which a spoon and weed guard have been fitted, plus a propeller-type blade that churns the surface like a wounded fish. Where weed is not a problem, spinners such as the Voblex or smaller sizes of Mepps are taken greedily. Any kind of surface-popping, spinning, jigging, splashing artificial lure is worth trying.

Although working a baited spinner is one of the most popular methods across the Atlantic, I must admit that until visiting the Zambesi River in Zimbabwe in 1991 to do battle with the legendary tiger fish for my 'Go Fishing' television series, I had no idea of its devastating effect on predatory fish.

North Americans add all manner of things to the hooks of spoons and spinners – pork rind, fish gut, rubber and plastic worms in an unbelievable range of fluorescent colours, plus crayfish tails, salamanders and so on. And as I was to experience with tiger fish and other tropical river oddities, especially the predatory bream and perch, swapping the treble hook for a large single and loading it with a bunch of worms instantly doubled the chances of a hit compared with an unbaited spinner. Fish strip worked effectively too.

And so it has proved since for me with predatory fish in British freshwater. The addition of worms, for instance a bunch of brandlings, especially to a small spinner, drives chub and perch so wild, they lunge at it with real venom. Every so often you need to top up the bunch of worms as one flies off during casting, but this can be remedied to some extent by casting gently, and by sleeving the point of the single (fine wire) hook through and along the body of each worm, rather than once only through its middle.

Chub and perch also love what the Americans call spinning jigs, which have a vibratory blade on top and below, and a lead-headed single hook onto which a synthetic work or grubtail is threaded. Of course, there is nothing to stop you threading on a real worm, and a big juicy lobworm does the job admirably. A 6 lb test line coupled to a light-actioned spinning rod of 7–9 ft is perfect for working these small artificials, allowing you the maximum enjoyment from chub and perch, yet with enough in reserve should a good pike happen along, and they usually do, just when you don't expect them. To be safe rather than sorry, use a short, 10 lb wire trace.

FLYFISHING

Setting out to catch coarse species on a fly-fishing outfit opens up a whole new and exciting world of technique and challenge. Fly fishing even allows you to approach and subsequently catch species like grayling and roach living in ridiculously shallow or overgrown streams for instance, where no other method could possibly be employed.

Although not an accepted method (or yet), I have in recent years enjoyed hooking and landing on a super-light fly outfit numerous carp running into double figures after spectacular fights – fish that I could perhaps have more easily hooked on a simple floating controller rig. I reasoned that as they were rising so freely to small floating biscuits, and sucking in all manner of items floating on the surface, why not offer them a mayfly. Like all the cyprinids, carp consume a quantity of emerging aquatic insects, so why not present them with artificial imitations.

I also pursue pike with the fly rod by offering large, gaudy streamer flies and jigs presented on 4 in of 10 lb test alasticum (otherwise bite-offs are inevitable) tied to a 6 ft, 10 lb leader. Double-taper fly lines are useless when casting heavy flies and lures. I even cut down the front end of a weight-forward line by 3 or 4 ft so the thickest, heaviest part is as close as possible to the artificial. If you can obtain one, an American bass-bug taper floating line greatly improves casting accuracy and distance.

With perch in mind, I revert to standard tackle using a weight-forward line for easy casting, because perch go absolutely mad over the jigging action of lead-headed lures

With an imitation sedge pupa stuck in its lower lip, this grayling has every right to look sorry for itself.

such as the dog nobbler. By reducing leader length to just 4 or 5 ft, and by casting carefully, the very tiniest of spinners or fly spoons may be worked close into the bank around pilings, beneath bridges and beside wooden stagings.

In European freshwater rivers and lakes the coarse species most likely to provide enjoyment with the fly rod on a regular basis throughout the warmer months are dace, grayling, chub, roach and rudd.

DACE

Dace are forever willing to suck in artificials, and because they rise to the dry fly so quickly, they are actually more difficult to catch than trout. This provides a wonderful challenge on a lightweight dry-fly outfit (see Tackle, p. 84–5), requiring a leader point of no more than 2 lb. In fact, when presenting tiny size 18 dry flies, I taper the leader down to a 1½ lb point.

The splashy surface movements of dace are easily seen at the tail end of shallow runs and pools, where several fish might all hit the surface together during a prolific hatch.

You can match the hatch of natural insects or present any small patterns and expect to see some action, so long as the fly is gently put down just upstream of the shoal on a snaky line so it does not drag. Remember to grease the cast well, and make use of any available bankside cover to creep into a casting position a little downstream of the rising shoal. You cannot wait a second or two, as you must with trout, for the fish to get its head well down. Dace rise to and eject that fly like greased lightning. So you must strike and pull into them with equal speed.

DACE AND GRAYLING

Presentation of the dry fly is a super way of tempting really big dace and grayling inhabiting clear, shallow streamy runs where they repeatedly refuse baits on float tackle

because presentation is difficult due to the extreme shallowness of the water. And this is the real beauty of using the fly rod to catch coarse species because they can be

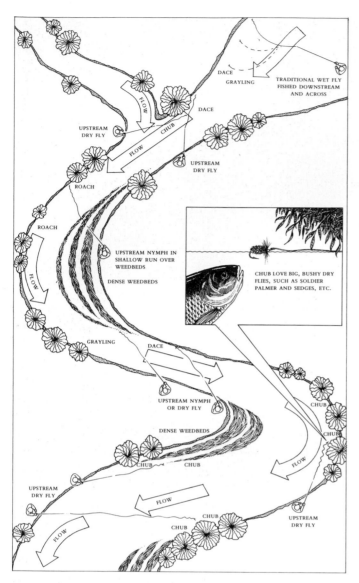

FIGURE 5.93 *Fly fishing in rivers during summer for roach, dace, grayling and chub*

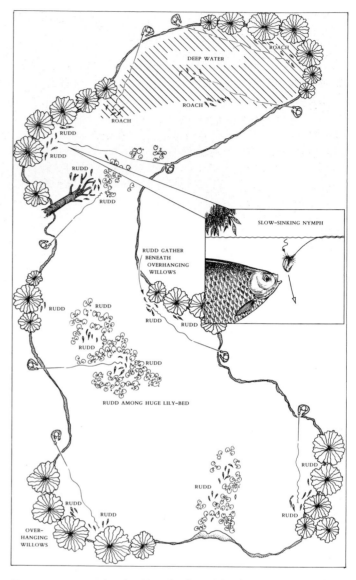

FIGURE 5.94 *Roach and rudd on dry fly and the slow-sinking nymph in a summer lake*

extracted from spots where no other method will work (fig. 5.93).

Wherever dace and grayling are not interested in accepting the dry fly on the surface, try them on a slowly sinking nymph. Grease all but the last 2 or 3 ft of the cast and offer a size 16 leaded shrimp or pheasant tail. Cast it upstream to the head of the run, watching the ungreased line sink as the flow brings the nymph downstream

towards you. Any sudden twitch, jerk or obvious slow pull should be instantly met with a firm pull on the line with your left hand (assuming you hold the rod in your right) and a lift of the rod. Both dace and grayling also take the wet fly when it is presented in the traditional manner downstream and across on a sunk line, but they are far more sporting and challenging to catch on a dry-line outfit.

CHUB

The chub may well be treated by some as the poor man's trout but in many small rivers and streams, the fly rod adds another string to your bow. The saying, there's more than one way of skinning a cat, could not be more true of chub.

On the dry fly, big sedges, mayflies, craneflies (daddy long legs), the chub offers wonderful sport particularly at dusk and even during the heat of a summer's day when numbers of them forage between long flowing beds of

A light fly-fishing outfit provides you with an effective way of tempting several freshwater species in addition to trout. Pike, perch, chub, rudd, roach, dace, grayling and even carp can all be tempted with artificial flies.

weed in search of tit bits brought down by the current. When shoaled up in reasonable numbers they are not so selective as a lone brown trout, so provided your casting is accurate and the fly is cast from a downstream position so it alights gently at the head of the run it won't be there long (fig. 5.93). Chub also respond to buoyant patterns like deer hair sedges, and muddler minnows skated deliberately across the surface as the light is failing and at dawn.

In really streamy, broken water where heavy beds of rock or gravel are almost completely clear of weeds the traditional wet fly cast downstream and allowed to swing across the current will take chub. Use flies with silver bodies imitative of tiny fish fry such as the butcher or dunkeld in sizes 12, 10 and 8 on a 3 lb cast.

For extra fun try a large heavily weighted nymph such as a Montana stone or the mayfly patterns, cast well upstream and twitched slowly along the bottom as it is brought back down by the current. As long as your approach is stealthy, chub will gobble up almost any large, weighted nymph pattern presented in the clearest water. I particularly like to tempt chub that are lying beneath floating canopies with lead-headed lures like the dog nobbler.

ROACH

Roach lack the agility of the dace and grayling but are wily. They are also most partial to a slowly sinking nymph. Grease the cast to within 2 or 3 ft of a slightly weighted nymph if fishing a shallow river (4 to 6 ft for stillwaters), and watch like a hawk as the tip of the cast descends, striking at any unnatural movement.

Where possible, try to identify what is actually being taken and match it with something from your box. Alternatively, where roach are known to inhabit a certain spot but are not actually moving up to intercept pupas prior to hatching, offer a small leaded shrimp or pheasant tail nymph, sizes 14 and 16, to stimulate their interest.

In deep, steady pools a much larger artificial, such as a heavily leaded mayfly nymph, will attract roach. Size 12 and 10 are not too large, and remember to use a leader point of no less than 2½ lb.

RUDD

During those really warm, sultry days of summer, rudd are readily fooled at the surface with small dry flies. And as the artificial could be floating for some time in stillwaters, I prefer the extra buoyancy of winged patterns like the coachman, alder and small red sedge, on size 14 and 16 hooks tied to a 2 lb point, well rubbed in mucilin.

Where rudd exist in numbers, the disturbance they cause at the surface, swirling after hatching aquatic flies, can be relied upon as the sun starts to set. And this, incidentally, is when specimen rudd move close in to the margins in large lakes and pits.

Rudd might also rise at any time of the day, even in bright sunshine, whenever there is a hatch, but they are more likely to be located basking around the trailing branches of overhanging willows and beneath large lily patches (fig. 5.94). A dry fly delicately presented close by is rarely refused, but even more deadly is a slowly sinking nymph. As rudd obtain most of their natural food during the summer months from the upper water layers, a pheasant tail, shrimp, sedge pupa or corixa plopped deliberately beside a lily-pad or overhanging branches, and allowed to sink slowly, promotes really positive takes. The cast shoots dramatically across the surface as a rudd inhales the artificial and darts immediately away lest other shoal members attempt to get in on the act.

A favourite oddball method that I favour and practise regularly in the summer, when rudd and roach are visible through the clear water of estate lakes, pits and weedy, slow-moving rivers, but are not rising, is to put the shoal into a feeding mood by creating my own hatch and regularly catapulting out maggots. Once fish are freely accepting each maggot as it descends (you can, with practice, even work the shoal into a feeding frenzy on the surface), I tie a size 16 or 14 hook to the end of the cast and nick on firmly a couple of maggots. Provided that the casting is not fierce, only occasionally does one come off (hence the reason for putting two on), you have the option of watching the maggot slowly sink or the cast for indications of a take – or both. Give it a try; it is also a fun technique incidentally for chub, dace and even grayling.

INDEX